D0400411

The Best American
Sports Writing
2016

GUEST EDITORS OF
THE BEST AMERICAN SPORTS WRITING

1991 DAVID HALBERSTAM
1992 THOMAS MCGUANE
1993 FRANK DEFORD
1994 TOM BOSWELL
1995 DAN JENKINS
1996 JOHN FEINSTEIN
1997 GEORGE PLIMPTON
1998 BILL LITTLEFIELD
1999 RICHARD FORD
2000 DICK SCHAAP
2001 BUD COLLINS
2002 RICK REILLY
2003 BUZZ BISSINGER
2004 RICHARD BEN CRAMER
2005 MIKE LUPICA
2006 MICHAEL LEWIS
2007 DAVID MARANISS
2008 WILLIAM NACK
2009 LEIGH MONTVILLE
2010 PETER GAMMONS
2011 JANE LEAVY
2012 MICHAEL WILBON
2013 J. R. MOEHRINGER
2014 CHRISTOPHER MCDOUGALL
2015 WRIGHT THOMPSON
2016 RICK TELANDER

The Best AMERICAN SPORTS WRITING™ 2016

Edited and with an Introduction
by Rick Telander

Glenn Stout, *Series Editor*

A Mariner Original

HOUGHTON MIFFLIN HARCOURT

BOSTON • NEW YORK 2016

The Bay School Library
35 Keyes Avenue
San Francisco, CA 94129

Copyright © 2016 by Houghton Mifflin Harcourt Publishing Company
Introduction copyright © 2016 by Rick Telander

ALL RIGHTS RESERVED

The Best American Series® is a registered trademark of Houghton Mifflin Harcourt Publishing Company. *The Best American Sports Writing*™ is a trademark of Houghton Mifflin Harcourt Publishing Company.

No part of this work may be reproduced or transmitted in any form or by any means, electronic or mechanical, including photocopying and recording, or by any information storage or retrieval system without the prior written permission of the copyright owner unless such copying is expressly permitted by federal copyright law. With the exception of nonprofit transcription in Braille, Houghton Mifflin Harcourt is not authorized to grant permission for further uses of copyrighted selections reprinted in this book without the permission of their owners. Permission must be obtained from the individual copyright owners identified herein. Address requests for permission to make copies of Houghton Mifflin Harcourt material to trade.permissions@hmhco.com or to Permissions, Houghton Mifflin Harcourt Publishing Company, 3 Park Avenue, 19th Floor, New York, New York 10016.

www.hmhco.com

ISSN 1056-8034
ISBN 978-0-544-61731-5

Printed in the United States of America
DOC 10 9 8 7 6 5 4 3 2 1

"Revenge of the Nerds" by Chris Ballard. First published in *Sports Illustrated,* November 24, 2015. Copyright © 2015 by *Sports Illustrated.* Reprinted by permission of *Sports Illustrated.*

"Meet Mago, Former Heavyweight" by Dan Barry. First published in the *New York Times,* May 4, 2015. Copyright © 2015 by the *New York Times.* All rights reserved. Used by permission and protected by the copyright laws of the United States. The printing, copying, redistribution, or retransmission of this content without express written permission is prohibited.

"He's the Last Boxer to Beat Floyd Mayweather Jr., and He So Regrets It" by Sam Borden. First published in the *New York Times,* April 4, 2015. Copyright © 2015 by the *New York Times.* All rights reserved. Used by permission and protected by the copyright laws of the United States. The printing, copying, redistribution, or retransmission of this content without express written permission is prohibited.

"Hold On, Boys" by John Branch. First published in the *New York Times,* March 15, 2015. Copyright © 2015 by the *New York Times.* All rights reserved. Used by permission and protected by the copyright laws of the United States. The printing, copying, redistribution, or retransmission of this content without express written permission is prohibited.

"Zilong Wang and the Tale of the White Dragon Horse and the Karmic Moonbeams of Destiny That Restored All Faith in Humanity" by John Brant. First published in *Bicycling*, October 28, 2015. Copyright © 2015 by John Brant. Reprinted by permission of John Brant.

"A Long Walk's End" by William Browning. First published in *SB Nation Longform*. Copyright © 2015 by William Browning. Reprinted by permission of William Browning.

"It's Only a Few Words, But It's Motivation from Lynch" by Matt Calkins. First published in the *Seattle Times*, December 6, 2015. Copyright © 2015 by the Seattle Times Company. Used with permission.

"The King of Tides" by Kim Cross. First published in *Southwest Magazine*, July 2015. Copyright © 2015 by Kim Cross. Reprinted by permission of Kim Cross.

"Rotten Ice" by Gretel Ehrlich. First published in *Harper's Magazine*, April 2015. Copyright © 2015 by *Harper's Magazine*. All Rights reserved. Reproduced from the April issue by special permission.

"Why Chris Borland Is the Most Dangerous Man in Football" by Mark Fainaru-Wada and Steve Fainaru. First published in *ESPN the Magazine*, August 20, 2015. Copyright © 2015 by ESPN, Inc. Reprinted by permission of ESPN.

"Spun" by Steve Friedman. First published in *Bicycling*, June 2015. Copyright © 2015 by Steve Friedman. Reprinted by permission of Steve Friedman.

"There's Somebody Ruthless on the Way" by Chris Jones. First published in *Esquire*, May 2015. Copyright © 2015 by Chris Jones. Reprinted by permission of Chris Jones.

"Follow the White Ball" by Sam Knight. First published in *The New Yorker*, March 30, 2015. Copyright © 2015 by Sam Knight. Reprinted by permission of Sam Knight.

"Learn to Dunk" by Michael McKnight. First published in *Sports Illustrated*, June 3, 2015. Copyright © 2015 by *Sports Illustrated*. Reprinted by permission of *Sports Illustrated*.

"The High Life and Fast Times of Jim Dent" by Michael Mooney. First published in *D Magazine*, August 2015. Copyright © 2015 by D Magazine Partners. Reprinted by permission of D Magazine Partners.

"Her Decision, Their Life" by Eric Moskowitz. First published in the *Boston Globe*, January 25, 2015. Copyright © 2015 by Boston Globe Media Partners, LLC. Reprinted by permission of Boston Globe Media Partners, LLC.

"About Winning" by Henley O'Brien. First published in the *Sun*, December 2015. Copyright © 2015 by Henley O'Brien. Reprinted by permission of the author.

"Stopping the Fight" by Brett Popplewell. First published in *Sportsnet Magazine*. Copyright © 2015 by *Sportsnet Magazine*. Reprinted by permission of Rogers Media.

"A Woman Fell from a Stadium" by Michael Rosenberg. First published in *Sports Illustrated*, February 10, 2015. Copyright © 2015 by *Sports Illustrated*. Reprinted by permission of *Sports Illustrated*.

"Ruck and Roll" by Steve Rushin. First published in *Sports Illustrated*, November 2, 2015. Copyright © 2015 by *Sports Illustrated*. Reprinted by permission of *Sports Illustrated*.

"Why Him, Why Me?" by Eli Saslow. First published in *ESPN the Magazine*, November 17, 2015. Copyright © 2015 by ESPN, Inc. Reprinted by permission of ESPN.

"American Hustle" by Alexandra Starr. First published in *Harper's Magazine*, April 2015. Copyright © 2015 by *Harper's Magazine*. All rights reserved. Reproduced from the April issue by special permission.

"The Greatest Hitter Still Lives On" by Wright Thompson. First published in *ESPN the Magazine*, May 5, 2015. Copyright © 2015 by ESPN, Inc. Reprinted by permission of ESPN.

"Going Home" by Chris Van Leuven. First published in *Alpinist*, August 14, 2015. Copyright © 2015 by Chris Van Leuven. Reprinted by permission of Chris Van Leuven.

"The Patriot Way" by Don Van Natta and Seth Wickersham. First published in *ESPN the Magazine*, September 7, 2015 (Original title: "Spygate to Deflategate: Inside What Split the NFL and Patriots Apart"). Copyright © 2015 by ESPN, Inc. Reprinted by permission of ESPN.

"Smack Epidemic" by L. Jon Wertheim and Ken Rodriguez. First published in *Sports Illustrated*, June 22, 2015. Copyright © 2015 by *Sports Illustrated*. Reprinted by permission of *Sports Illustrated*.

"Board in the Florida Suburbs" by Chris Wiewiora. First published in the *Atticus Review*, October 13, 2015. Copyright © 2015 by Chris Wiewiora. Reprinted by permission of Chris Wiewiora.

Contents

Contents

Foreword

ALL WRITERS HAVE their own creation myth—or, as one of
my nonfiction friends prefers, an "origination story," the turning
point where it all began, where the past became the past and the
writing life took over, present tense, never to leave again.

Mine begins sometime in 1975. I had just turned 16 and was still
in high school in a small town in central Ohio. Nearly every weekend I would borrow the Dodge Dart, and with maybe $10 in my
pocket saved from what I earned cleaning bathrooms after school,
I would travel from the cornrow-straight country road where I
lived toward Columbus, a half-hour trip through the wealthier suburbs. The drive would take me by the Scioto Country Club, site of
the 1926 U.S. Open, and past Nicklaus Drugs, where I wondered
if Jack's dad still filled prescriptions or if the Golden Bear himself
sometimes dropped in for some Ben-Gay. As I neared High Street,
the major north–south thoroughfare that skirted the campus of
the Ohio State University, I would see, on the horizon, Ohio Stadium, OSU's Horseshoe, once the largest poured-concrete structure in the world, brutal and cloudy gray as if covered with all the
dust churned up from those three-yard plunges into the line. My
mother worked at another nearby drugstore and had once waited
on coach Woody Hayes and his wife. (She told me that he was impatient and not very nice, and that when he spoke he sounded like
my grandmother.)

I'd turn right onto High Street, and then onto a side street.
There, I'd find a place to park in front of one of the slowly decay-

ing houses in that neighborhood, populated mostly by students basking in the last fading afterglow of the 1960s.

Whenever I got out of the car and walked up to High Street, along the few blocks of Columbus that ever so vaguely and briefly resembled what I imagined Haight-Ashbury to be, I was transformed. Wrapped in my jean jacket, wearing an army shirt and tattered jeans, with strands of hair getting longer leaking out beneath my cap, I was no longer just some kid who couldn't wait for high school to be over and to leave home. For a few short hours I could be who and what I wanted.

And what I wanted to be was a writer. Little kid dreams of playing in the big leagues were fraying as quickly as my fastball and rotator cuff. A few years before, I had decided that I wanted to write, seizing on that most unlikely life raft because there were no others. In a few years I had ferreted out all the books that interested me at our tiny local town library and moved on to the larger and far better stocked library of that wealthy suburb. However, the kind of stuff I was interested in then—the Beats, the proletariat poetry of the 1930s, more recent experimental fiction, and the like —was in short supply. For a time it seemed as if every book on the shelf was either Erich Segal's *Love Story* or *The Little Prince,* budget paperbacks that hung on every slot of the wire display stands near the circulation desk.

Most bookstores were little better. The chain store at the local mall featured perhaps two shelves of poetry, mostly either Rod McKuen, the blessedly almost-forgotten poet laureate of the obvious and vapid, or, as inexplicable now as it was then, copy after copy of *Touch Me* by Suzanne Somers, the blowsy blond actor not yet famous for appearing in the sitcom *Three's Company.* Her work, impossible as it sounds, was far more treacly than McKuen's and simultaneously almost blindingly, obliviously, and unintentionally surreal. Illustrated with gauzy portraiture, *Touch Me* featured Suzanne pondering a head of lettuce artfully placed before her chest, or wandering barefoot through fields, her skirt salaciously askew.

Although I enjoyed the pictures, I couldn't really imagine that what I wanted to be had anything to do with these books. In fact, they sort of made me want to die.

Fortunately, there was another place. Up on High Street, tucked away in what had once been a residential building that also housed Bernie's Bagels and Deli—which counted as ethnic food in Columbus back then—was a different kind of bookstore.

It was called My Back Pages, named after the Bob Dylan song. I had not heard much Dylan yet (although I titled my column in our high school newspaper "Idiot Wind") but was already deep into a (still-active) Neil Young phase, and the sign outside—handmade and hand-painted, featuring the pages of an open book—was welcoming. And there were bagels.

Inside were some creaky wooden steps, a hallway plastered with political and psychedelic posters, piles of the *Columbus Free Press* stacked in a corner, and then a door wide open into what at some point must have been the living room of an apartment, or perhaps two rooms; I seem to recall a half wall somehow dividing the space, or maybe it was just the shelving. But I do know this: there were shelves and shelves and shelves of books.

They were mostly used books, interspersed with a few of what I would later learn were "small press" titles—chapbooks and self-published titles run off at some copy store, bound in construction paper, and numbered in an obscure corner ("6 of 25").

The poetry section was huge, at least to me. Maybe six or eight shelves, a whole section of shelving or more, old textbooks and anthologies and books whose spines bore the names of poets I'd heard of but whose work I'd never read—or maybe I'd read one of their poems but now here was an entire book, or two or three or four, by that poet. There were university press titles and collections published by New Directions, Grove Press, and City Lights. There were more shelves marked for Eastern religion, nature and ecology, politics, revolution, and fiction, and more names of writers I knew but whose books I'd never found—John Dos Passos, Henry Miller, and Jack Kerouac, not just *On the Road,* which I already had, but the other titles, long out of print, tattered, and hard to find: *Tristessa, Big Sur, Vanity of Duluoz.* In this bookstore there was no *Love Story,* no McKuen, no Somers. The combined impact was that of an egg cracking open to reveal another world.

But that was not the best part. I had been in a few such stores before, all of them bigger and messier and somehow intimidating. This bookstore was different.

Two guys, both hippies, worked behind the counter—I assumed

they were co-owners. One was lithe and slender, with a wispy mustache and fine thin hair, while the other was larger, darker, fully bearded. I'm sure they noticed me right away. I was younger than most visitors, but this seemed not to matter.

I'd roam the small store for an hour, two hours, sometimes even three, picking up book after book, reading, then putting them back down, wondering how best to spend the $5 or so I had set aside for books, balancing volume (one or two or three thick titles) versus quantity (a half-dozen or so slimmer volumes).

Unlike the chain bookstores I sometimes visited, no one ever stalked me to make sure I wasn't stealing or interrupted me with a chirpy "Can I help you?" that served the same purpose. Here, they left me mostly alone and only offered help in the gentlest, most unobtrusive way possible.

So for a few hours my fantasy was fueled. I felt like a writer there in the bookstore with my own kin. And when I finally went to the counter and counted out my change to buy what I'd decided on, the fantasy would be fulfilled. The two guys would comment on my purchases, ask me who else I liked and whether I'd ever read X, or what I thought of Y. Most exciting of all, they once asked, "Are you a writer?" Not if I wanted to be one, but if I *was*.

This might be the most important question a writer is ever asked—it certainly elicits the most important answer. To say yes is to know, to stake that claim and all the responsibility it entails.

The slender man with the wispy mustache was a poet, and the store featured several slender volumes of his self-published work. He was the first writer I ever met in the flesh, and *look!*—he wasn't all that different from me. I imagined that he too grew up in some small town, or maybe in a tough part of a city, and had gravitated toward words just as I had, following an impulse buried deep in our ancestry, like salmon swimming upstream toward inevitable death, no matter what. One day as I was leaving he slipped his thin pamphlet—which probably sold for 50 cents—onto my stack, gratis, one writer to another.

I cannot recall a more important gift.

Armed with a bag of writing bona fides, and with the clock ticking toward 2:00 p.m., the time when I usually had to have the Dart back home, I'd go across the hall to the bagel shop, which would be quiet now after the morning rush. I'd take the rest of my money

and order a toasted plain with cream cheese, slathered in strawberry jam—no lox yet for me—and then, lowering my voice, I'd
order a beer. I was never carded, but also knew better than to order more than one. I imagined my restraint showed my sophistica-
tion.

I would nurse the beer for the next hour, till it was nearly flat,
while I ate and skimmed and read and scratched out words in
my notebook, imagining I was elsewhere—New York, San Francisco, hell, even Cleveland—as I completed the weekly pilgrimage
by confirming with each word either read or written that *I* was a
writer . . . *I was* a writer . . . *I was a writer.*

Then, buzzing slightly from the beer, or maybe only from the
sound of that phrase, I'd drive back, past the golf course and gated
homes with their neat stone fences, across the narrow metal bridge
over the river, then down the twisting road that led toward the
straight road home—a small ranch house, surrounded by corn
and soybeans and barbed-wire fences, where the lawn was newly
mown, clothes hung on the line, and Curt Gowdy and Tony Kubek
(who worked on his delivery in the off-season by reading poetry
aloud) were welcoming viewers to the Game of the Week, just coming on. For the next week, despite all evidence that said otherwise
as I negotiated the emotional bloodbath of high school, I knew
exactly who I was. The next Saturday I would do it all again. I repeated this pattern, more or less, for years, in other places and in
other ways, until finally one day it was true—I was a writer.

I think now of those two men at the bookstore and of what they
meant to my younger self—to be seen and recognized and heard
for what I imagined I was. When a young person contacts me today
and thanks me for listening or paying attention, or says that *The
Best American Sports Writing* has helped foster their love of words, I
think of those long Saturdays at My Back Pages, now long gone but
as real as ever, and of what really matters. I write back, or call, and
I say, "Well, then, now you know the rule. And one day, when you
have the chance, you'll know just what to do."

Each year I read every issue of hundreds of general interest and
sports magazines in search of writing that might merit inclusion in
The Best American Sports Writing. I also contact the editors of many
newspapers and magazines and request submissions, and I make

periodic open requests through Twitter and Facebook. I search for writing all over the Internet and make regular stops at online sources such as Gangrey, Longreads, Longform, TheSportsDesk, NiemanStoryboard, and other sites where notable sports writing is highlighted or discussed. And since this book belongs to the reader, I encourage everyone who cares—friends and family, readers and writers, editors and the edited—to send me stories they believe should appear in this series. Writers, in particular, are encouraged to do so—it's okay to send your own work or the work of those you admire.

All submissions to the upcoming edition must be made according to the following criteria. Each story

- must be column-length or longer.
- must have been published in 2016.
- must not be a reprint or a book excerpt.
- must have been published in the United States or Canada.
- must be received by February 1, 2017.

All submissions from either print or online publications must be made in hard copy and should include the name of the author, the date of publication, and the name and address of the publication. Photocopies, tear sheets, or clean copies are fine. Readable reductions to 8½-by-11 are preferred. Newspaper stories should be submitted as a hard copy or a copy of the same as originally published—not a printout of the web version.

I ask all individuals and publications to please use common sense when submitting multiple stories. Owing to the volume of material I receive, no submissions can be returned or acknowledged, and it is inappropriate for me to comment on or critique any submission. Magazines that want to be absolutely certain their contributions are considered are advised to provide a complimentary subscription to the address listed below. Those that already do so should extend the subscription for another year.

All submissions must be made by U.S. mail—even in the midst of global warming, midwinter weather conditions at BASW headquarters often prevent me from easily receiving UPS or FedEx submissions. Electronic submissions by any means—email, Twitter, URLs, PDFs, or electronic documents of any kind—are not acceptable; please submit only some form of hard copy. The February 1 deadline is real, and work received after that date cannot be considered. Please address all submissions to

> Glenn Stout
> PO Box 549
> Alburgh, VT 05440

Previous editions of this book can be ordered through most bookstores or online book dealers. An index of stories that have appeared in this series can be found at glennstout.net, as can full instructions on how to submit a story. Those with questions or comments may contact me at basweditor@yahoo.com. For updated information, readers and writers are also encouraged to join the Best American Sports Writing group on Facebook or to follow me on Twitter @GlennStout.

I played a role as editor of one selection this year, yet like all others, it was put forward to the guest editor blindly, not identified by source or author, and like all submissions in every edition of this series, it was chosen entirely on merit. My gratitude goes to guest editor Rick Telander, who took extraordinary care in making selections and who himself has long served as an example and mentor to other writers. I also thank all those at Houghton Mifflin Harcourt who have helped with the production of this series, Siobhan and Saorla for putting up with the burdens that sometimes come with the words, and those writers who always seem to know what to do.

GLENN STOUT
Alburgh, Vermont

Introduction

WHEN I THINK about writing, I become almost hallucinatory. My thoughts shoot off in every direction like shrapnel from an exploding cherry bomb. (I had a lot of those as a kid, BTW — Silver Salutes, and M-80s too. I got them on summer trips to southern Georgia, where my grandparents lived on Jekyll Island, about 30 miles north of the Florida border, a crossing to which my sweet grandmother, Nonnie, would take me in her big black Cadillac, smoking unfiltered Pall Malls all the way, when I begged her to take me and my parents were off somewhere else, and I'd walk alone into a place called Krazy Ken's or Daffy Dick's or something like that and offer up several weeks of allowance and lawn-mowing money to a disinterested, criminal-looking clerk behind the counter for the treasured cube-shaped boxes of firecrackers — each holding a gross of what was essentially weapons-grade near-dynamite.)

But when I collect myself I realize it's all too true: I am wedded to the printed word the way a turtle (had a lot of those as a kid too) is to its shell. My life, basically, has been dedicated to the printed word, to the reading and writing of it, for better or for worse.

I don't think I amount to much without writing, whether the doing of it or the thinking about it. Or at least, my life has little meaning — to me, at this point — without writing at its core. Sometimes I wonder what I would have been if not a writer — a sportswriter, to be precise. I really don't know. Maybe a carpenter, a builder of some kind. (I like the smell of cut wood and the sound of hammers on nails.) An architect? (My mom always says she thought that's what I'd be, because I drew stuff all the time with rulers and compasses and built balsa wood cages for my pet crickets and toads and the like.) Maybe a lawyer? Don't think so. A businessman? Possibly. No. A coach? No. A teacher? Of what? I'm guessing other writers have asked themselves the same question and come up with the same clueless responses.

The printed word sings to me the way a palette of paints sings to an artist, numbers to a mathematician, notes in harmony to a musician. My middle daughter, Cary, had a school friend who practiced the cello for hours each day, not out of duty or obedience —though she was a virtuoso and needed to practice to maintain her virtuosity—but because the vibrating strings and their tonal resonance within the curved walls of the precision-built wooden instrument soothed her in a way that was primitive, fundamental, and nearly obsessional.

I'm not a person who can't wait to sit down at the laptop, who claps his hands together as he looks at that hinged slab of techno crap every morning, come hell or high water, and says, "Whoopee, here we go, baby! I'm a-writin'!" I've met those kinds of people and I don't understand them. Or they don't understand themselves. Or they don't understand me. Or something.

Writing isn't *fun.* (And that should be said to oneself the way Tom Hanks, in *A League of Their Own,* says, after looking incredulously at his star pitcher: "There's no *crying* in baseball.") But for those of us who see words as our way of release and expression and freedom, writing is necessary. You always scratch where it itches, and the itch never goes away. What is it? I don't know. It's there, though. The itch to communicate through symbols of thought, perhaps.

Let me note that unfocused blabbering and venting in print can be *fun,* the same way pounding on a guitar and screaming stuff into a microphone can be fun. (I do that sometimes too, with my band of 45 years, the Del-Crustaceans.) But writing words that state precisely what you want them to state, something that is meaningful, intelligent, well conceived, and important, in a clear, true, and entertaining style, *writing something that people will want to read*—that is hard. And since when is hard fun? Hard is the opposite of easy. And easy lives next door to lazy. And lazy is not worth talking about. But hard, when done right, leads to something beyond worthwhile, beyond fun—it leads to fulfillment.

Writing well is far more about restraint and self-editing and viciously searching for the exact word and rhythm to say what you want to say skillfully and artistically than it is about having a whomping good time. In fact, it's not about joy at all. It's about necessity (yours as a writer) and craft and the internal reward from having done it well. If those two things can come together and create beauty, then wonderful! The fun is entwined in the outcome. You created art. And art is primal, and it sustains us.

The guidelines that hold for great writing of any type hold for the writing in this book, sports be damned. Sports are only the subject, not the essence. Here, as elsewhere, we're dealing with people and written symbols (marks that form letters that are made into words that can be turned into sentences, paragraphs, stories, books) that must be honored no matter what they are about, because writing—and therefore reading—is hardwired into us somewhere not far from the need to eat and sleep and procreate and send our genetic information into the future.

These building block symbols—these words—are processed by an intricate system in our brain that begins organizing things the moment we are born and sounds and other stimuli are perceived and the need to communicate to stay alive begins. The ability to create printed words and read them, and to have the process reflect the world as we perceive it, is a mystery and miracle of our species.

These days I sometimes fear for the printed word. My own business of newspaper and magazine and book writing has been diminished as steadily as the bark that sheds from an old tree. Newspapers—printed stories written on what has come to be called "hard copy"—are in rapid decline. I stayed at two hotels in the last few months that did not even sell newspapers in the gift shop. This is nobody's fault. This is progress. This is technology and what it wants, since machines have a goal (paperlessness being one) that is imparted to them by us, the inventors. "Our genes have co-evolved with our inventions," writes former *Wired* editor Kevin Kelly in his forward-thinking book *What Technology Wants*. "As fast as we remake our tools, we remake ourselves . . . If all technology —every last spear and knife—were removed from this planet, our species would not last more than a few months. We are now symbiotic with technology."

Obviously, fighting whatever new means of communicating comes along—from smart phone emoticons (do any of those little things remind you of the wall drawings in the Chauvet Cave in France from 30,000 years ago?) to virtual reality to artificial intelligence—is foolish, if not impossible. Technology has an idea of what it wants to do, and where it will go, and we set that goal into motion long before we wedded ourselves to the printed word. The ultimate goal of all technological advancement, most scientists agree, is sentience—the ability to feel, to sense, to be conscious.

The human brain's abilities seem to come down to electrical matter and circuitry and algorithms and mechanical interplay, all someday knowable as a map, no matter how complex. That "thinking" is possible by machines has already been proven many times over, most recently and amusingly by the Google computer that beat a grandmaster in the astoundingly complicated ancient Eastern game of Go. The notion that the soul was created by divine touch and exists as a penumbra shimmering six inches above the head is pretty much as gone as medieval paintings of saints with glowing halos and cherubs fluttering around them like bats.

"We are all machines that think," writes Caltech theoretical physicist and cosmologist Sean Carroll in an essay in the book *What to Think About Machines That Think,* "and the distinction between different types of machines is eroding." MIT physicist Max Tegmark adds, "The advent of machines that truly think will be the most important event in human history." Well, I would guess so. But here's the kicker: "Whether it will be the best or worst thing ever to happen to humankind depends on how we prepare for it, and the time to start preparing is now."

Short of digging bunkers and filling them with anti-robot laser guns and locker-sized nuclear devices, I'm not sure what we normal people can do. One possibility is simply to think about the way our world is changing, so rapidly, faster than we probably want, and to ponder anew our role in it. We can think about the printed word, about how it now is so often electronic and accompanied by music or photos or even a talking head reading aloud the words we could read ourselves if we cared to. Is a virtual reality tour through a western rodeo better than a written story about that same rodeo? Is an edited (on your own device) film about a man flying in a squirrel suit off a mountainside better than a well-worded story about the same?

These things matter because this book honors the craft of writing about sports, not the craft of symbolizing sports stories in some other way. What we're dealing with is the part of your brain that is stimulated—that learns—when you *read* something rather than when you get the information in another fashion. Because there is a difference. And I feel, deeply, that something big is lost when the printed word is bypassed in favor of something technologically "advanced."

So if you've made it this far—if you even picked up this book—you probably believe in the printed word as something of unique value, symbolizing much. As I've said, I certainly do. If you read series editor Glenn Stout's foreword, you know that he believes wildly in the printed word, that he was as giddy as can be when he realized he might actually be called in life a "writer." Glenn and I have talked often about the business of writing, one memorable time being on St. Patrick's Day a few years ago at a bar in Burlington, Vermont, the town where my son was going to college and where Glenn was playing bodhran in an Irish band. Glenn knows how thrilled I was to be chosen to pick the stories in this year's edition. He knows that I am in love with writing too.

It wasn't easy, making the final selections, trust me. The volumes of submitted stories had been winnowed to the many by Glenn, before he sent them off to me in Chicago, and I picked the few, my favorites. Writing—communicating—is not an absolute, and I'm sure some other judge could have picked an entirely different set of stories. But as I told my students when I was a lecturer at Northwestern for a few quarters back in the 1980s, "What I say about your work is just my opinion, based on my knowledge and preferences and quirks, and don't take my word as gospel because I could be completely wrong and what I say utter nonsense. But I doubt it."

The stories came to me anonymously, in generic print, except for a couple that were in magazine type, with their magazine labels at the bottom, because they couldn't be downloaded from the Internet and had to be photocopied from real "hard copies." Those pieces also had the authors' names removed, and it didn't matter an iota to me where the stories had appeared. I read each piece at least once, some more than twice. I sorted them into three stacks

—no, yes, maybe—and when I'd finished I took stock. I needed none of the maybes, good as they were, since my yeses held up after further scrutiny. I cataloged what I had: five football stories, three basketball, two bicycling, three boxing, and one each from baseball, running, hiking, hockey, rugby, rowing, rodeo, snooker, wingsuit flying, fishing, drug abuse, skateboarding, and nature, as well as—by God—one about a sportswriter himself, run amok.

My choices of sports were not conscious. I went into each piece looking for a good tale, coherence, sweet word usage, wit, intelligence, knowledge of the topic, and descriptive sentences that painted a vivid picture in my mind's eye (without using pictures!).

Special points were given for effort by the writer—effort in making the piece smooth, fluent, and provocative without giving the *appearance* of effort. After all, good writing, like good acting or platform diving, is artifice, making the difficult look graceful and simple. And points were given for physical effort, for those writers who pounded the pavement, worked the phones, interviewed, delved into difficult situations, perhaps even journeyed by boat, snowmobile, dogsled, and snowshoe, at deep personal risk, to the remotest parts of Greenland (thank you, Gretel Ehrlich for "Rotten Ice"!) to report on the way the only world we have is changing for sportsmen—and all humans—for all time.

Another of those effort pieces comes from *ESPN: The Magazine*'s Don Van Natta and Seth Wickersham, who, in "The Patriot Way," take on the monolith that is the NFL, this season's version of Big Tobacco. Similarly, brothers and co-writers Mark Fainaru-Wada and Steve Fainaru nail the NFL and its concussion myopia by detailing the retirement of San Francisco 49ers linebacker Chris Borland after a single season because of his concerns over potential brain damage.

Three more of those dig-in-and-do-it stories are Alexandra Starr's piece, "American Hustle," Jon Wertheim and Ken Rodriguez's "Smack Epidemic," and John Branch's epic "Hold On, Boys," a story that won me over as it wove together rodeo, family, and the essential freedom that Americans cherish and will fight not to lose.

I found myself thinking long and hard after reading William Browning's detailed piece "A Long Walk's End," about a multimillion-dollar embezzler who eluded capture for years by courteously hiking the Appalachian Trail with other outdoorsmen; and Eric

Moskowitz's emotion-packed "Her Decision, Their Life," about a victim of the Boston Marathon bombing having to choose, after months of rehabilitation, whether to have her remaining but crippled leg amputated or not. It's hard to forget a line like this, describing the medical pain chart that goes from zero to 10: "Ten was the worst you could imagine, pain she never knew until she got blown up."

Not every selection is grim (and even the grim tales are told with beauty). I laughed out loud and nodded with understanding at Matt Calkins's tale about the impact on one man of the Seattle Seahawks nearly mute Marshawn Lynch, and Chris Ballard, a *Sports Illustrated* treasure, had me chortling and spewing with his tale about the nerd Caltech hoopsters' rise to success (for them).

Michael McKnight's yearlong quest to dunk, "Learn to Dunk," is both funny and crazily earnest. Me, I love obsessive nuts like McKnight. As with many of these stories, there's a brief Internet video accompanying it. It's downright ridiculous, time-lapsing his quest over 363 days. But read the piece—it's better.

I don't have the space to praise every contributor. I wish I did. Brilliant writers Chris Jones, Wright Thompson, and Michael Rosenberg you'll find within. And veteran Steve Rushin does his crazy thing, this time having a ball at the 2015 Rugby World Cup in England, where he "saw English knights dropping chain-mail trousers, Tonga supporters parting grass skirts, and kilted Scotsmen fartin' through tartan."

I'm sorry, I have a thing for silliness too. But above all, what I wanted here was entertainment, value for your effort as a reader with all those techno distractions all around. You deserve to be entertained. A reader makes a pact with a writer, and that bond must be honored and respected.

Note, too, that it's hard for any account of a big sports event or a much-watched game to make it into these pages. Those uber-stories, viewed and dissected firsthand by audiences everywhere, have been told and retold in too many places to be original anymore. I mean, is there one more thing you want to read about the great Tom Brady? Last year's World Series? Lance Armstrong's demise?

I prefer John Brant's lovely, zesty tale about the curious Chinese student Zilong Wang, who rode a bike across our country and found America in the process. I prefer, too, Chris Wiewiora's magic piece "Board in the Florida Suburbs," about how his own

teen slacker skateboard ways led him to college and pending adult-
hood. And the story "About Winning," by college champion female rower Henley O'Brien (a pseudonym, but don't worry, she's
real) — please just read it and you will know more than seems possible in so few words about the overbearing, damaged, needy men
who so often coach us and our children.

The power of words. The splendor of words. The transcendence
of words. The grip of words. All here.

High tech, see ya later.

RICK TELANDER

The Best American
Sports Writing
2016

MATT CALKINS

It's Only a Few Words,
but It's Motivation from Lynch

FROM THE SEATTLE TIMES

IN ABOUT 1,100 words, Marshawn Lynch will be quoted for the first time all season, but that's not even close to the best part of this story. Not when Jake McCluskey is involved. Not when a guy who couldn't run 100 feet is getting set to run 100 miles.

Twenty months ago, you see, McCluskey was a 380-pound sloth. He lived next door to the bottle shop he worked at in San Jose, and spent his free time gulping down beer and snacking on sweets.

For years, friends and family tried to get him to exercise, but he wouldn't respond. As much as McCluskey wanted to slim down, the task was too overwhelming for him to conjure the motivation.

But on April 12, 2014, Jake came across a video on YouTube that changed his life forever; a clip he found so powerful that he watched it 30 times in a row.

It was an interview that originally took place five days before the Seahawks' Super Bowl win. An interview between Deion Sanders —and Marshawn Lynch.

"I had been thinking that it had been time to make a change for a while, and after I watched that interview, I immediately went out for my first run," said McCluskey, 42. "It wasn't anything I was seeking out, but somehow it came to my attention at a time that I needed it most."

Lynch, as you know, may be the most reluctant interviewee in professional sports. His back-and-forth with Deion lasted just two

minutes, but included a six-word response that would become Mc-
Cluskey's mantra.

When Sanders noted how Lynch didn't like to talk, the running
back replied, "I'm just 'bout that action, boss." And that's how it
began—McCluskey's transformation from Obese Mode to Beast
Mode.

At three o'clock that morning, Jake ran about a tenth of a mile,
walked another four-tenths, and said he felt like he was going to
die. The next day, he watched the interview another 30 times and
did the same thing.

A couple weeks later, he could jog the full half-mile without
stopping. A couple months after that, he completed a five-mile
race.

McCluskey didn't mention his training to friends, because as
Lynch told Sanders in that interview, "I ain't never seen no talkin'
win me nothin'." But it wasn't long before most of the neighborhood had taken notice of Jake's morning jogs.

In early October, McCluskey finished the San Jose Rock N' Roll
Half Marathon in two hours, 47 minutes. His first thought upon
crossing the finish line?

"That I wanted to run a full marathon."

Keep in mind that Jake still watches that interview about 50
times per week. Also keep in mind that this guy is not a quack.

A Massachusetts native with a college degree, McCluskey moved
to San Jose at the turn of the century to take a stab at the tech
world. He decided he liked the craft beer world a whole lot better.

Now, he is an assistant brewer at Santa Clara Valley Brewing and
still drinks beer every day. He said allowing himself a cold one or
two keeps his regimen maintainable.

But he also hasn't missed a day of training since that very first
run.

"I can't," said McCluskey, who dropped more than 140 pounds
in those first 12 months. "Because if I skipped one day, it would be
easy for me to skip two."

As a tribute to Lynch and his hometown, McCluskey chose the
Oakland Marathon for his first 26.2-mile endeavor. And despite
rigorous training for the early-March event, he said he hit the wall
at mile 18.

For Jake, the last third of that race was hell. But when he crossed
the finish line in 5:19, he immediately set his sights on 50 miles.

If you think McCluskey's ambition is just plain stupid, he won't disagree with you. He knows the human body isn't designed for such punishment, but this undertaking has gotten bigger than just him.

Locals see Jake running and join him like he's Forrest Gump. Jack Tse, one of McCluskey's former customers at a bottle shop, directly credits Jake as the reason he lost 20 pounds.

And last June, McCluskey—who grew up without a father—raised over $18,000 for the Silicon Valley Children's Fund, an organization that helps send children in foster care to college.

How did he do it? By running from San Francisco to San Jose.

This wasn't a sanctioned event, by the way. This was McCluskey celebrating his 42nd birthday by jogging from one brewery to another one 50 miles away. His training included a 72-hour stretch in which he ran a marathon on three consecutive days.

Might not have been enough, though. McCluskey collapsed at the 48th mile.

Because there was no sodium in his system, Jake's muscles couldn't retain any water. Luckily, one of the friends trailing him on a bike recognized the problem and gave him some salt water to drink.

Still, while that helped, it wasn't enough to get McCluskey off the ground. Then, another one of Jake's friends whipped out his phone and played the Lynch interview.

McCluskey sprang to his feet and conquered the last two miles.

"He's Beast Mode," said the aforementioned Tse, who said McCluskey has gone from "Big Jake" to "Sexy Jake." "Any time he walks in the bar, that's what we call him. He's amazing."

Last week, McCluskey announced that he plans to run 100 miles on April 9, 2016—which is just shy of the two-year anniversary of that initial jog. Down to 205 pounds, he continues to watch the Lynch interview every day, although he says his favorite team is the Oakland Raiders.

Oh, and in case you're wondering, Jake has no aspirations of meeting Lynch in person. Doesn't want an autograph or a picture or anything like that. All he really wants to do is pass on a message.

"Marshawn gets such a bad rap in regards to media relations, but I just want him to know that he saved my life," said McCluskey, whose racing bib has the words THAT ACTION underneath his number. "It's important to me that he knows that."

Well, here goes nothing.

A couple weeks ago, while most of the media was in the auditorium with Earl Thomas, I walked into the Seahawks locker room and spotted Lynch. Aside from asking Valerie Masterani to homecoming, I've never been so nervous approaching anyone.

"Marshawn, I want to show you this guy from the Bay Area," I said, pointing to my phone.

He looked up and asked why my hand was shaking.

"I don't know," I said, reaching into my bag of clever responses. I kept going.

I showed him a picture of McCluskey at 380 pounds and another one of him at 210. I read him the email Jake sent me about how Lynch's interview with Deion motivated McCluskey to change. I told Lynch how, because of his message, McCluskey had gone from 0.5 miles to 50 miles.

That's when Lynch, clearly impressed, offered the highest of compliments.

"That's gangsta," he said.

"Yeah," I replied. "What do you think of all that?"

Lynch paused.

"I just told you," he said. And then he walked away.

Hey, Marshawn Lynch has never been one for talking. But Jake McCluskey will tell you that his words can go a long way.

How long? We'll see.

Maybe 100 miles.

SAM KNIGHT

Follow the White Ball

FROM THE NEW YORKER

EARLY ON A TUESDAY MORNING last fall, Ronnie O'Sullivan was running through the woods near his home, in Chigwell, Essex, northeast of London. It was damp and muddy, England in November. O'Sullivan, who is 39, loves the anonymity of running. About ten years ago, he discovered that it was one thing that truly takes him out of himself—more than the drink and the drugs and the antidepressants—and suspends the otherwise unavoidable fact that he is the most talented snooker player of all time. At the age of 11, O'Sullivan was making good money in the sport, and in the past three decades he has won five World Championships and set a number of records while enduring a bewildering odyssey of breakdowns, addictions, and redemptions, largely precipitated by the imprisonment of his father, whom he loves, for murder. O'Sullivan is frequently described as a genius. But he does not see how this can be so. Most days, he feels like a fraud. His game comes only in fits and starts. He wins because the others lose. He has wondered for a long time whether he would be happier doing something else. He has moved nine times in the past ten years. "I'm fucking, you know, searching," he told me recently. "I kind of know who I am but I don't like who I am, do you know what I mean? I wish I was a bit more fucking stable."

O'Sullivan tries to run six or seven miles a day. That morning, he was with his best friend from school, George Palacaros. (O'Sullivan grew up a short distance from Chigwell, in the town of Ilford.) It was a final run before the U.K. Championship, snooker's second-biggest tournament, in York, 200 miles to the north.

O'Sullivan's first-round match, against an amateur named Daniel Wells, was two days away. About five miles into the run, Palacaros called out to O'Sullivan to check the heart-rate monitor that he wears on his wrist. As O'Sullivan turned to reply, he slipped and fell, breaking his left ankle.

He tried to carry on. "I thought, I ain't going to waddle back," he said. He jogged another mile, but whenever he looked down he saw his ankle swelling up. By the time O'Sullivan reached the changing room at his running club, he couldn't put any weight on his leg.

At the hospital, O'Sullivan was told that he had a simple fracture. His ankle wouldn't need surgery, but it would take 12 weeks to heal and he would have to wear a protective brace. He called his psychiatrist. In the afternoon, O'Sullivan posted a picture of his ankle, bulging alarmingly, on Twitter, with the message "Might be one legged Snooker at the #UKChampionship on Thursday." He found a pair of soft blue boots in his closet that fit over the brace. The next day, a friend drove him to York so that he could keep his foot elevated on the way.

Snooker, like its poor relation pool, is a cue sport. Unlike pool, snooker has 22 balls: 15 red, six of other colors, and one white. (Pool and its variants involve 16 balls or fewer.) Players take turns attempting to clear the table and earn as many points as possible, using the white cue ball to "pot" a red, then a colored ball (which is returned to the table), then a red, and so on. When all the reds are gone, the players dispatch the colors in order of their value, from the yellow, which is worth two points, up to the black, which is worth seven. If a player fails to pot a ball at any point, he must yield the table to his opponent. Matches are divided into frames, each won by whichever player scores the most points. In the professional game, frames tend to unfold with vivid, unsettling ease —the balls slide into the pockets as if there were nowhere else for them to go—or with staggering, metaphysical difficulty, as the players foil one another by arranging the balls in illogical patterns, a type of play known as "safety," and everyone's nerves go to hell.

Snooker's civilized appearance belies its vicious and enervating nature. A snooker table is three times larger than a pool table and its pockets are an inch smaller. Even the most basic shot is a concatenation of foresight, friction, and various Newtonian laws.

Players seek to control where at least two balls are going: the red or colored "object" ball, preferably toward a pocket; and the white ball, its rate of braking and spin carefully calibrated, either to stop near another object ball, so the process can begin again, or to continue toward some hostile district of the table, from where the opponent will be unlikely to score. The best players string together 30 shots in a row, in a hushed environment of thick carpet and dinner suits. (Snooker's dress code recalls, more or less, that of a 1930s music hall.) Players compete to pot the same balls, so every shot has a psychological echo: What is good for me is bad for you. The longer I am at the table, the longer you must watch and fret. Players avoid eye contact. No one speaks.

At the U.K. Championship, all matches except the final were the best of 11 frames. O'Sullivan was reluctant to put weight on his ankle. "I feel like a baby that's trying to learn to walk," he told reporters. He limped through his first match but won, 6–2. Three days later, in the second round, he faced Peter Lines, a 44-year-old journeyman pro. I traveled north to watch him play. I reached the Barbican Theatre in York, just outside the city's medieval walls, early in the evening.

O'Sullivan had been debating whether to pull out of the tournament. His balance wasn't right. There was no sign of him by the practice table, where the other players, dressed in bow ties and waistcoats, waited, leaning on their cues. Referees pulled on white gloves. Nevertheless, at 7:00 p.m., O'Sullivan appeared, walking out under the lights in answer to the snookering nickname that he has had since he was a teenager, "Ronnie (the Rocket) O'Sullivan!" In a dinner suit and his blue boots, his sideburns shot with gray, he looked like a croupier on his way home from work.

"You don't feel comfortable when Ronnie's playing," Barry Hearn told me. Hearn has been snooker's dominant impresario since the 1980s. He controls the commercial rights to the sport and has managed O'Sullivan three times, on and off, throughout his turbulent career. (O'Sullivan fired two managers during the reporting of this article.) "You're almost watching an accident waiting to happen," Hearn said. Against Lines, O'Sullivan was obviously out of sorts. Most snooker players, obsessed with repetition, seek to become robotic versions of themselves. But O'Sullivan in full flow is always in motion, checking this, squinting at that, buzzing backward and forward around the table, grimacing at the balls, fussing at chalk marks on the baize. His ankle made that impossible. Every movement was an effort.

Still, it was too much for Lines. Ranked 61st in the world, he seemed unnerved by the television cameras and missed a number of easy shots. Many lower-ranked players find it hard to concentrate when they play O'Sullivan. The crowd is against them, and they wonder what he thinks of their game. The match was untidy. In the fifth frame, with the score at 3–1, O'Sullivan potted a fluky red and the balls suddenly opened. In the course of 29 strokes, he scored 106 points—a "century"—and it seemed as if he might race away. But Lines came back. O'Sullivan was distracted; he picked his teeth and watched the game under way at a nearby table. "Come on, Ronnie, our son," a Yorkshire voice called out from the crowd. By the time the game finished—6–3, to O'Sullivan—it was 10:30. O'Sullivan was exhausted. I caught up with him in the corridor as he hobbled back to his dressing room. In person, he can be disarming—trouble, but you want him to like you. I congratulated him on the match and said I enjoyed it. "Fucking hell," he said. "I didn't."

People who grew up in Britain in the 1980s, as I did, found themselves steeped in snooker whether they liked it or not. The game was invented in 1875, by British military officers in colonial India, but for the next 100 years it was confined mostly to gentlemen's clubs and dubious billiards halls. (In the 1950s, Charlie, Ronnie, and Reggie Kray—London's best-known gangsters—got their start running a snooker hall in East London.) In 1978, however, the BBC broadcast the sport's 13-day World Championship, at the Crucible Theatre, in Sheffield, for the first time. Television transformed snooker: the game's slow, hypnotic quality; the trapped, pacing players; even the acidic colors of the balls seemed made for the small screen. Tobacco companies poured money into events. In 1985, almost 20 million people stayed up past midnight to watch the World Championship final, in which the top player of the era, Steve (the Nugget) Davis, was beaten by Dennis Taylor, an underdog with specially adapted eyeglasses to help him see down the table.

In the sport's heyday, two snookering archetypes seemed to be at war, and television dramatized the duality. There were the champions, clean-cut automatons who ruled the game for years at a time before abruptly burning out: Ray Reardon, a former policeman, in the 1970s; Davis, in the 1980s; Stephen Hendry, a baby-faced Scot who won a record seven world titles, in the 1990s. And there were the broken and the beautiful, who produced exquisite passages of play but couldn't keep their heads together: Kirk Stevens, a Canadian cocaine addict who played in a white suit; Alex (the Hurricane) Higgins, who died, furious and alcoholic, of throat cancer, in 2010; and Jimmy (the Whirlwind) White, who reached six world finals and lost them all.

Ronald Antonio O'Sullivan was born in 1975. His parents, Ron and Maria, had met a couple of years earlier, as teenagers, working at a vacation camp. They moved to London and cleaned cars to make ends meet. When their son hit the professional snooker scene, in the early 1990s, he was younger, more gifted, and ruder than anyone else. He won his first major title at 17. In 1996, O'Sullivan was accused by a Canadian opponent, Alain Robidoux, of disrespecting him by playing left-handed. O'Sullivan arranged to be certified as good enough to play professional snooker with either hand. That same year, he was suspended for head-butting an official. He drank too much and saw too many first-round exits. He talked openly about his loathing for the game, and for himself. In 2000, O'Sullivan went to rehab, to seek treatment for an addiction to marijuana. By the time he turned 30, the age at which other great players, such as Davis and Hendry, were beginning their decline, O'Sullivan had won two world titles, the same number as Alex Higgins—respectable, but well short of his potential. Between late 2009 and early 2012, O'Sullivan failed to win a single ranking tournament.

"My arsehole had gone," he told me. "My fight. I had nothing in me." But the following year, at the age of 36, and long after he had given up on the possibility, O'Sullivan began to win again, rediscovering a consistency and a freedom of play he had not experienced since he was 16. Since 2012, he has reached three successive World Championship finals, winning two of them. At this year's tournament, which starts on April 18, in Sheffield, O'Sullivan will be expected to reach his fourth final in as many years. This late, unexpected flowering has altered his standing in the game. "Ronnie is the genius that sort of sits over everyone," Hearn said. "He is not a normal bloke." Earlier this year, O'Sullivan overtook Stephen

Hendry's record of 775 century breaks. Many wonder whether
O'Sullivan can equal Hendry's record of seven world titles and officially become, in his forties, the greatest player the game has ever
known.

He remains fragile, though, and amazed by the turn of events.
Damien Hirst, the artist, is fascinated by snooker: the promise of
its seemingly straight lines, "the grid over the landscape," as he
calls it, and the struggle of the players caught up in its geometry.
Hirst is close friends with O'Sullivan and often accompanies him to
tournaments. When we met, I asked Hirst if he thought O'Sullivan
was afraid of the future and of what would happen when his talent
eventually faded. "I think he's scared of everything," Hirst said.
"That's his beauty—that he is absolutely shitting himself. Do you
know what I mean? He doesn't know what the fuck is going on."

The evening after O'Sullivan defeated Lines, he had dinner at
Toto's, an Italian restaurant in York, with Gary Smith, his manager,
and Chic Gourlay, a friend from Glasgow. O'Sullivan was in good
spirits. He flirted with the waitress and ordered a steak. His ankle
was feeling stronger, and he had found a pair of black sneakers,
which looked better with his suit. "I feel all right now," he said. "I
feel like a snooker player again."

At the next table, Ken Doherty, a crafty Irish player who won the
world title in 1997, was eating with friends. Doherty and O'Sullivan
have known each other since Doherty, at the age of 18, became
the club pro at the Ilford Snooker Centre. O'Sullivan, six years
younger, would take the bus there to play after school. It was the
late 1980s—peak snooker—and O'Sullivan was the game's prodigy.
He won his first tournament at the age of nine and made his first
century break at age ten; his chubby face was all over the snooker
magazines. He stuck out at the club in Ilford: prepubescent, foul-
mouthed, his afternoons at the table bankrolled by a seemingly
limitless supply of five-pound notes from his father, Big Ron, who
had become wealthy running a chain of sex shops in London's
West End.

"He would just smile at you sometimes when you were playing,"
Fin Ruane, another young Irishman who hung around the club,
told me. O'Sullivan's father would drop by: good-looking, thick-
set, ready with jokes. "Ron's the name, porn's the game," he used

to say. "He would come in, and if there was 20 people in the room he would have to buy 20 teas," Doherty recalled. "No one put their hand in their pocket. It would have been an insult." People liked Big Ron, but they didn't cross him. He told everyone that his boy was going to be world champion. His uncles had been boxers, and he taught his son to think like one: "Take his head off." "Don't get beat." "Fuck 'em, son." Ruane said, "I remember his dad, he would be playing cards and someone would say, 'Ron, it's your deal.' But he would just be looking over at his kid playing. He just loved him, loved watching him."

The young O'Sullivan worshiped Steve Davis, the champion at the time. He wore the same waistcoat, without a cinch. When he was nine, O'Sullivan heard Bill King, the father of a rival junior player, say that Davis was "never a foot away" in snooker, and it struck him as a profound truth. Unlike the other players, who relied on forms of backspin ("stun" and "screw") to position the white ball for their next shot, Davis played with topspin and used the cushions to play longer and more inventive strokes that flowed around the table. It was riskier and more technically challenging, and often got the white only a few inches closer to the object ball, but it was worth it. When O'Sullivan finally beat Doherty at a local tournament, he decided to become a professional. "That was the day," he told me. "I'd done everything. I used the cushions. I beat Ken. I played to a level where, fucking hell, I fancied it."

At Toto's that night, the two men swapped stories about Goffs, in County Kildare, a sporting resort where the Irish Masters tournament used to be held. In 1998, O'Sullivan beat Doherty in the final but was stripped of his title a few weeks later; he had eaten a hash cake, and failed a drug test. It was a beautiful place to play. "Everyone used to go, take their wives," O'Sullivan said, shaking his head. "Lovely."

The next day, in his third-round match, O'Sullivan found that he could move more easily. He won, 6–2, against Ben Woollaston, a player ranked 27th in the world. Woollaston took the lead in the third frame but lost his nerve. "It was embarrassing to be out there," he said afterward. In O'Sullivan's fourth-round match, a 29-year-old named Matthew Selt disintegrated completely. Once O'Sullivan was ahead 4–0, he started looking for a maximum. A maximum in snooker is the perfect break: 15 reds, 15 blacks, and

the rest of the colors—147 points in a single spell at the table.
It is the sport's equivalent of a hole in one or a pitcher's perfect
game. Joe Davis, snooker's undefeated world champion from
1927 to 1946, made the first official 147, in 1955, at the age of 53.
O'Sullivan made his first maximum when he was 15. Against Selt,
he recorded the 13th of his career—two more than Hendry, the
nearest player. "Nothing special," O'Sullivan told me later. "If he
had made it hard, I could never have got there."

O'Sullivan trains in a first-floor office in an industrial park in Romford, a few miles from his house. The surrounding blocks are occupied by accountants, insurance brokers, and gas-meter retailers.
The office belongs to one of his former managers, Django Fung,
who allows him to practice there as much as he wants. Fung, who
is from Hong Kong, represents several Chinese players, but they
are often out of the country. When I arrived to watch O'Sullivan
train one day in January, there was no one else in the building.
The blinds were down. Five snooker tables sat under fluorescent
lights, on a spartan floor of blue carpet tiles. O'Sullivan was looking in the fridge for milk, to add to a cup of tea. Often, he craves
company. Since 2011, he has worked without a coach, hitting balls
in myriad patterns for three or four hours a day.

When discussing O'Sullivan's game, commentators and rivals
often talk about his unusual sequencing—the way he links shots
together around the table. Phil Yates, who was the snooker correspondent for the *Times* of London for 20 years, compares
O'Sullivan to a savant, able to perceive mathematical solutions
without knowing how or why. "I don't think he can break down
why he is as good as he is," Yates said. "He just is." According to
Hirst, O'Sullivan often comes off the table in a fugue state: "I go,
'What about that pink you potted?' And he'll go, 'What pink?'
He's blank. He's totally startled. It's like van Gogh. I go, 'You did
brilliantly there.' And he goes, 'Did I?'"

O'Sullivan spends a lot of time thinking about the white ball.
He has come to believe that the quality of the initial contact between his chalked, pressed-leather cue tip and the phenolic-resin
sphere—the momentary grip, the transfer of energy and intent
—is what decides everything else. If the white responds, he will not
lose. "You're using force," he said, after making his tea. "You're using your hands. You're creating. You're making that white dance."

When the connection isn't there, O'Sullivan feels it right away. "It's invisible, but it's night and day to me," he said. During the good days and the good months, he senses it in every stroke. When he is cueing well, he leaves fat chalk streaks on the surface of the table, like a golfer's divots, and the white ball topspins extravagantly, slowing down across the nap and then accelerating again, as if late for an appointment. There is a particular echo as balls hit the middle of the pocket. He disregards the score. "I know I'm playing a different game from what they're playing," he said. And, because of the duel-like intimacy of snooker, O'Sullivan is able to observe the mesmerizing effect that his skill has on his opponents: "You're thinking, 'You've got that on a string, mate. That cue ball. It's just . . .' And you just sit there. And that is what beats you."

In 1992, when he was 16 and had just turned professional, O'Sullivan went to snooker's "qualifying school"—a three-month marathon of knockout matches, in Blackpool, during which fringe players competed to enter the tournaments of the season ahead. Matches were played on 24 snooker tables in the Norbreck Castle Hotel, a colossal sand-colored structure on the city's seafront. O'Sullivan was one of the youngest competitors. "Up against the world," Hearn, his manager at the time, recalled. "Everything was new."

The previous summer, O'Sullivan's father had been arrested after a fight in a nightclub, during which a man had died. (O'Sullivan found out while playing in a junior tournament in Thailand.) The dead man, Bruce Bryan, had worked as a driver for Charlie Kray, the gangster. He was stabbed after what Big Ron later claimed was an argument over the bill. While O'Sullivan was in Blackpool, his father was out on bail, charged with murder. He came up to stay with his son. Each day, the seats around O'Sullivan's snooker table filled a little faster. "All the old soaks and all the old dyed-in-the-wool players would go and watch him play," Yates, who was covering the event, said. "Because they couldn't believe what they were seeing."

In Blackpool, O'Sullivan won his first 38 matches as a professional snooker player—a record for consecutive victories that still stands. He won 36 of the next 38 as well, losing just two games at the qualifying school. People who saw him there like to argue about whether he has ever played as well since. "It was a bit like Tiger Woods or Mike Tyson, when they came along," O'Sullivan told me. "That is how my life should have been, if my dad didn't go away." O'Sullivan played his last match in Blackpool on September 20, 1992. The next day, his father was found guilty of murder. In his summation, the judge referred to "racial overtones" in the case —Bryan was black—and sentenced Big Ron to 18 years in prison. The story made all the newspapers. O'Sullivan said, "From that moment onward, everything was shit, to be fair."

Three years later, O'Sullivan's mother, Maria, was also sent to prison. She had taken over the management of the sex shops and was found guilty of tax evasion. She served seven months. During her absence, O'Sullivan's younger sister, Danielle, who was 12, went to live with family friends. O'Sullivan, who was 19, went off the rails. He partied in his parents' house, got stoned, and put on weight. When he turned up at tournaments, he would look at the other players and envy the small, stable groups they traveled with: parents, managers, drivers. "They had this wall built around them," he said. "I had no wall." For several years, O'Sullivan was accompanied on tour by a man known as the Yunzi, a friend of one of his father's friends in prison. He thought about his father constantly and sought to win on his behalf. "It was me and Dad, fighting the fucking world," he said. But he also held his father responsible for the chaos that had enveloped his life. The table became complicated, loaded with meaning. His game went haywire.

The white ball could dance, or not, at any time. In the first round of the World Championship in 1997, O'Sullivan made a maximum in five minutes and 20 seconds, surpassing the previous record by almost two minutes. He was knocked out in the next round. The British press called him "the Two Ronnies," after a comic duo who were big in the 1970s. During the 2001 World Championship, in Sheffield, where he won the title for the first time, at the age of 25, O'Sullivan called the Samaritans, a suicide hotline, and started taking Prozac. The unpredictability was exhausting. He was desperate for a thought system that would make sense of his life. He saw shrinks and gurus. He tried Christianity, Buddhism, and Islam. After recovering from his addiction to marijuana, O'Sullivan tried all of the Anonymouses, out of a sense of completism. He went to sex-addiction meetings even though he was not addicted to sex.

Nothing helped. During the 2008 season, by any measure one of his most successful, O'Sullivan would get drunk every weekend. His long-term relationship with Jo Langley, the mother of two of his three children, whom he met in rehab, was falling apart. (O'Sullivan has an 18-year-old daughter, Taylor, from an earlier relationship.) "I was cueing well, but I had no family, no home," he said. Between tournaments, he stayed on a friend's sofa, reading *How I Play Snooker,* Joe Davis's classic manual from 1949.

O'Sullivan's father was allowed out of prison on day release for the first time in early 2009. In the latter stages of his sentence, he had been held at a low-security facility in Sudbury, in the Midlands. O'Sullivan went to meet him at the gates. He was shocked by his father's appearance. "He looked like a burglar," he said. They spent the day at a hotel. When Big Ron called O'Sullivan's mother, his hands shook. In the evening, O'Sullivan dropped his father off in the prison parking lot and watched him troop inside with the other inmates; he seemed happy to be back. "I just thought, Where do we go from here? I've been waiting twenty years," O'Sullivan said. Since his father's final release, his parents have lived apart. After one or two experiments, Big Ron decided to stay away from O'Sullivan's snooker matches as well. (He declined to speak with me for this article.)

When O'Sullivan took a break at the training facility in Romford, he invited me to share his lunch—salmon with ginger, which he had cooked and brought from home. "This game can fuck your head up like no other game," he said. Another player had come in to practice, and in the background there was the quiet, irregular sound of colliding balls. "I have told my son he ain't fucking playing snooker, because I love him too much." His son, Ronnie, is seven years old. "I love him too much to see him coming in here. Because, you know what, there should be no money in this game. There should be no fame in this game. They should take TV away from this game. They should take it away. This is like a fucking . . ." O'Sullivan hesitated, grasping for a word of sufficient violence. "An *eccentric* sport."

By 2009, O'Sullivan was 34, old for a snooker champion, and playing poorly. He came to believe that his decline was permanent. His breakup with Langley dragged through the courts. They fought over money and the custody of Ronnie and his older sister, Lily. O'Sullivan lived on a barge. He lost in the first round of four consecutive major tournaments. His income from snooker fell from around 750,000 pounds a year ($1.1 million) to 150,000

($220,000). He pulled out of risky shots. He lost the conviction necessary for topspin. "I was stuck inside," he said. "I couldn't really deliver the cue."

His manager persuaded him to see Steve Peters, a professor of psychiatry at Sheffield University. Peters used to be a doctor at Rampton Hospital, one of England's three maximum-security psychiatric facilities, but in the past 10 years he has enjoyed a second, high-profile career working with elite athletes, including the British Olympic cycling team, to improve their mental performance. Peters, who is 61, lives in a gloomy villa in the Peak District, a region of gaunt beauty in northern England. O'Sullivan arrived in the spring of 2011. "He was in a really bad place," Peters said. "It was quite disturbing to see."

Many of the surfaces in the psychiatrist's house are filled with plastic, china, or knitted figures of chimpanzees. In the 1990s, Peters came up with what he calls the "chimp paradox" to explain to first-year medical students how the mind functions. According to his analogy, there is a contest within the brain between its more rational, "human" parts and its anciently evolved "chimp" regions. The chimp fulfills essential functions, but it is also powerful and prone to panic. "A chimpanzee is five times stronger than us," Peters told me. "If you have this animal sharing your life with you, you have to treat it with respect." Peters does not call himself a doctor when he is dealing with athletes. He thinks of himself as a coach, teaching them how to manage their chimps.

O'Sullivan immediately related to the idea: "I was, like, 'That's how I've been living my life for 17 years.'" Since his father's imprisonment and the subsequent fracturing of his snooker and his life, O'Sullivan had alternated between searching for inner peace and trying to stop thinking altogether. Peters encouraged him to write down his negative thoughts—O'Sullivan's chimp worries a lot about his right arm—and then rebut them with proven facts about his ability and his achievements. Peters calls this inner dialogue "boxing the chimp." For O'Sullivan, it was revelatory. "I didn't know I could behave like this," he said. "I didn't know I had the ability to hold it down."

At first, seeing Peters had no effect on his snooker. At the U.K. Championship in 2011, O'Sullivan suffered a particularly dispiriting defeat to a player named Judd Trump. Trump, who was 22 at the time, has a flamboyant potting style, which he calls "naughty snooker," and he is often described as the closest thing to O'Sullivan's heir. He plays in spiked Christian Louboutin loafers and has black stars sewn into the collar of his shirt. In York that year, O'Sullivan lost to Trump even though his mind felt clear and he thought he had played well. "I didn't think that was possible," he said.

The following spring, the white ball came back. In the quarter-finals of the China Open, in Beijing, O'Sullivan was clearing the table and on his way to victory in the game's deciding frame. He faced a routine backspin stroke to position the white for the final red. "I remember thinking, Well, I know that is the right shot to play," he said. "Ten times out of ten, it will go in." Instead, O'Sullivan went for a subtle, almost impossibly difficult topspin shot—entirely needless under the circumstances. The ball loped across the table, touched the cushion, and rolled a few inches too far. It cost O'Sullivan the match, but he was elated. No one else plays like that. "That shot still sticks in my mind, because it was the wrong shot to play but I didn't care," he said.

He won his next tournament, the 2012 World Championship, and put his cue away. He fully intended to retire. He went running, and spent time with his children. Away from the table, O'Sullivan's life is modest. He goes to the gym, and buys bagels in Chigwell. He likes finding new Chinese restaurants. He hardly played for the rest of that year. In the winter, he volunteered to work on a local farm. He dug ditches and fed the pigs. He was somewhat afraid of the goats. People didn't ask him questions or seem to know who he was. He enjoyed the quiet solidarity of the farm and of his running clubs, spending time with ordinary people, with ordinary lives and families. But life without snooker was boring, and frightening too. "It's scary," he said. "I thought I could look at it, and then I looked at it and I didn't like it."

O'Sullivan became anxious about money. He fell behind on his children's school fees and realized he hadn't planned adequately for the future. "I was quite happy not playing," he said. "But then it hit me—'Fuck, I've got another 40 years to get through, here.'" He announced that he would defend his title in Sheffield. The book-makers made him one of the favorites. O'Sullivan practiced for six weeks. Even if he lost in the first round, he reasoned, he would still make 12,000 pounds, enough for a semester of school fees. In the end, he won his fifth World Championship and 250,000 pounds,

becoming the first player since Stephen Hendry to win in successive years. "This is my last farewell," he told reporters during the
tournament. "I can't keep putting myself through being unhappy."
A month later, O'Sullivan decided to rejoin the tour.

Since his return, in 2013, O'Sullivan has thought more about
what comes after snooker. He has his own TV program, *The Ronnie
O'Sullivan Show,* on Eurosport, and wants to do more broadcast-
ing. But preparing for the rest of his life is distracting. This past
winter, he was worried about his form. He felt vulnerable and wondered if he was sufficiently focused on his game. In early February, he began to prepare for this year's World Championship. But
on any given day, he said, his mind throbs with what he should
or shouldn't be doing: "Should I be playing more? Am I taking
on too much other stuff? Am I becoming a jack-of-all-trades and
master of none? Am I now becoming this person, a commercial
animal?"

In tournaments, he remains a bully, a greedy old king. In December, at the U.K. Championship, the injured O'Sullivan was,
by turns, kindly and vicious toward opponents. After he beat Anthony McGill, a young Scottish player whom he admires, he spent
ten minutes advising him on his technique. (McGill stayed up all
night replaying the game and texted O'Sullivan to thank him.)
In the semifinal, O'Sullivan found himself 4–1 down and on the
brink of losing to Stuart Bingham, the ninth-ranked player in the
world. "That was a match where I just thought, I'm not going to
be pushed around by someone like Stuart," O'Sullivan told me
afterward. "I'm not ready to accept that role yet. I fucking hated
that match." He won, 6–5.

The final was against Judd Trump. Their rivalry is now snooker's
main attraction. The match spanned 19 frames; the winner would
be the first to 10. It started at lunchtime on a Sunday, 12 days after
O'Sullivan had broken his ankle. Outside, it was a sunny winter
afternoon. Inside the Barbican, it was the perpetual midnight of
snooker. A thousand people were there. Trump walked out first.
"The ace in the pack," the emcee hollered, "with his own brand of
naughty snooker!" Tall and thin, Trump retained the disconcert-
ing legginess of a teenager who's grown too fast.

In the early frames, Trump drew frequent gasps for the skill of
his potting. When he arranges himself for a shot, it is like watching

a heron preparing to catch a fish. But he found himself in dead ends. He would pot five or six balls and then have to cede the table to O'Sullivan. Most of the match was played in silence. Spectators at snooker matches often wear earpieces, to listen to commentary on the subtler points of the game. Through a trick of acoustics, this commentary sometimes drifted into the hall, and the players heard themselves being described. In the fourth frame, O'Sullivan lifted his injured ankle up on the table behind him to sink an awkward brown. "He makes shots look so easy," a voice said. At the end of the afternoon session, O'Sullivan was ahead, 5–3.

In the evening, he took control. Every time Trump faltered, O'Sullivan rose to clear the table. He won four of the next five frames. In the 12th, he made a break of 133, zigzagging the balls home around the black. Two red balls hugged each other in the middle of the table, seemingly inseparable, until O'Sullivan broke them apart with a ricochet that bordered on the abstract, like a thought. "It's beautiful, isn't it?" a man behind me murmured.

When O'Sullivan got to 9–4, a frame from victory, his friend Chic Gourlay emerged from the dressing room to watch. Then Trump woke up. With nothing to lose, he began to hit balls even harder than before, and now they flew in. Trump reclaimed a frame, and then three. In the space of 26 minutes, he scored 333 points. O'Sullivan, more or less stuck to his chair, scored eight. "O'Sullivanesque," the wandering voice of the commentator said, describing Trump. The score moved to 9–9.

How does it end? O'Sullivan's untrustworthy mind leaves him fearing that he will not recognize the signs. "I could lose it for the next two years, and then come back for another two years," he said. "That's the worrying thing, in some ways. How do you get closure on something like that?"

The players came out for the final frame. They shook hands. A spectator near the front wore a T-shirt that said, KEEP CALM AND PLAY SNOOKER. Trump broke. O'Sullivan potted an early red. Suddenly, it seemed dangerous to go first. With 16 points on the board, O'Sullivan missed and gave up the table. But Trump couldn't take advantage. The men exchanged safety shots: long flicks of the white ball, down the table, to catch the edge of a red, hit a cushion, and then retreat up behind a barrier of colored balls. They did this until Trump snagged a red and brought it back up the table as well. "All the fancy fucking footwork, the con-

trol that he has had for maybe 20, 30 shots," O'Sullivan told me
once about the art of safety. "Bang, I'm going to pounce on him."
He blocked the white ball behind the green. Trump missed his
shot, and O'Sullivan had the freedom of the table. He opened his
mouth slightly and padded faster in his sneakers. The match clock
showed four hours, 53 minutes, and six seconds.

There was a moment, only a moment, after that when O'Sullivan
was in trouble. He got too close to the blue and had to sneak
around it. But for the rest of the match the balls were where he
wanted them to be. Red followed by pink, red followed by yellow.
The white stayed with him. He got to the end. Later, after the con-
fetti and the prize, I found him backstage. Workmen were disman-
tling snooker tables, to transport them to the next tournament. "It
came back," O'Sullivan said. He looked relieved and haunted at
the same time. "Sometimes you know it will."

CHRIS BALLARD

Revenge of the Nerds

FROM SPORTS ILLUSTRATED

PICTURE A SOLITARY FIGURE, shooting baskets and muttering. The man is pale and skinny, with round glasses and wispy brown hair. Looks fortyish, like he should be teaching calculus. But instead he's here in an otherwise deserted gym, in Pasadena, on a warm fall morning and he's—well, it's not clear exactly what he's doing. But whatever it is, he's taking it very seriously. He shoots, mutters, shoots again.

Get closer and you can hear him. "Fourteen for 22," he says. The man is a coach, and he is conducting an experiment. He has rewatched every shot his team took last season—because this is the type of thing he does—and noticed something peculiar about home games. On one basket in this gym, his players made shots. On the other, not so much. Was that a fluke? Are the windows of the fitness center distracting? Are his players simply tired when they go that direction in the second half? He needs to know, because he needs every edge he can get.

So now he shoots, and he counts, and he instructs his assistants to do the same three times a week. All because the coach believes he's on to something, a philosophy of academia and athletics that will enable him to accomplish a feat few thought possible: turn around the most un-turn-around-able program in the history of college basketball.

If, that is, he can just get his players to stop studying so much.

*

Perhaps you are familiar with the California Institute of Technology, a school of 1,000 in Pasadena, and, if so, perhaps you are also familiar with its contrasting reputations.

Academically, Caltech has few peers. It's regularly ranked as the top research university in the world, and faculty and alumni have won 35 Nobel Prizes. Albert Einstein once mulled his theory of relativity on campus, not far from where Richard Feynman hit upon the concept of nanotechnology. Students who survive the grueling course load make an average starting salary of $82,000 upon graduation. Most have paid off the bulk of their debt by then anyway, working summers at places like Google, Microsoft, or Uber, bringing in up to $30,000 in three months. When the entertainment industry needs to depict really smart people, it often puts them at Caltech, from *Real Genius* to *Num3rs* to *The Big Bang Theory* to *Modern Family*.

Athletically, Caltech has few peers too, though for different reasons. The baseball team hasn't won a conference game this millennium. The football program was euthanized in 1993. But the hoops team's struggles are the most infamous. The Beavers once went a quarter-century without winning a game in the Southern California Intercollegiate Athletic Conference (SCIAC). They regularly lost by scores that, if they occurred in youth sports, would be considered cruel. Occasionally, players did homework on the bench during games, because at least that way they were being productive. When a filmmaker followed the team in 2006, in the midst of a historic, ongoing losing streak, the resulting documentary, *Quantum Hoops*, was optioned by Ben Stiller. As a comedy.

Indeed, it's been easy to treat the team as a joke, as Rick Reilly did in *Sports Illustrated* nine years ago. (Sample line: "Wouldn't you think just once a ball would bounce off a pocket protector and in for a win?") Context is important, though. Unlike the Ivies or its Division III opponents, Caltech makes no allowance when admitting athletes. Only a handful of students have the grades (3.8 GPA) and median SAT scores (2230 to 2340) to get in, and only a handful of those happen to be good at basketball.

Then there's the matter of time, or the lack of it. Students regularly study eight to 10 hours a day, slogging until the gray light of morning. Five times last December alone, starting guard Andrew Hogue arrived at practice having gone sleepless for more than 30 hours. At one point, after he slumped into the campus's lone minimart to purchase yet another bottle of 5-hour Energy, the caffeine-laced elixir of truckers and ravers the world over, the cashier threatened to cut him off. "Dude," Hogue remembers the man saying. "You really can't keep doing this to your body."

Hogue's classmates couldn't figure him out. Here he was, a computer engineering major who'd spent his summer working at NASA's Jet Propulsion Laboratory. Why not just skip basketball practice? Why play basketball at all?

And it raises a valid question: why would anyone sacrifice, and work so hard, when all he is going to do is lose?

Two hundred and sixty-nine.

Oliver Eslinger sat on the worn couch in his apartment in Somerville, Massachusetts, in the summer of 2008, staring at his laptop. He pondered the odds of a college team losing that many conference games in a row.

"Are you sure you want to do this?" his fiancée, Austin, asked.

After six years as an assistant at MIT, Eslinger had been hired as the new head coach at Caltech. The job only paid 10 months a year. He'd have to teach PE. And move across the country.

Still, Eslinger was an optimist by nature, fond of saying, "Well, if you look at it as an *advantage*," when confronted with a problem. The dirt around his childhood backyard hoop in Broken Arrow, Oklahoma? An *advantage;* it forced him to keep his dribble low. The lack of competition in the burbs when his family moved outside Albany, New York? An *advantage;* it forced him to venture to Washington Park, where his real basketball education occurred. When his father, a petrochemical geologist, lost his job? Well that sucked, for Eslinger idolizes his father, carries his handwritten advice notes in his wallet. And yet, still, an *advantage;* the family learned about resilience.

At D-III Clark University in Worcester, Massachusetts, where he played guard for two seasons, Eslinger was shorter (6'1"), skinnier (160), and less springy (as in, not-at-all springy) than his teammates. His solution: work harder and be smarter. Just as a small animal puffs itself up to look bigger, he decided to use illusion to his advantage in sports. He took three giant strides off the line during suicides to create "competitive separation." After one par-

ticularly brutal set of ladder sprints during his senior year, a teammate stood nearby, panting. "You actually like this s—, don't you?"
he said. To Eslinger, it was the greatest of compliments.

Around the same time, Eslinger fell in love with sports psychology and later titled his dissertation at Boston University, "Mental
Imagery Ability in High and Low Performance Collegiate Basketball Players." His conclusion, after studying 172 players of both
genders across all NCAA divisions: envision your performance and
you can enhance it.

Now, after beating out 120 candidates for the job, Eslinger had
big dreams for Caltech: To win the SCIAC. To make the NCAA
tournament.

And then he met his team.

They were smart, and nice and one—center Ryan Elmquist, a
computer science major who is now a software engineer at Google
—was even tall (6'5") and bouncy. Still, there was no depth or ball-
handling. The roster contained more valedictorians than high
school basketball players (a long tradition at Caltech). Eslinger
was pretty sure they would have lost to his high school squad. During the second practice, he told them to do the weave, a sixth-
grade-level basketball drill. The team couldn't make it down and
back. He never tried it again.

Even so, Eslinger's preseason entries in his journal, a black
Moleskine notebook he filled with small, neat script, were infused
with hope. He wrote of "shocking the world." Then the Beavers
—so named because they are "nature's engineers"—engineered a
whopping 38 turnovers in one of their first games. "I'm at a loss
right now," Eslinger wrote three weeks in. "How do you get students to play basketball confidently if they've never played? Is it
impossible? . . . I miss home." In mid-January, the team lost 90–25
to SCIAC opponent La Verne. "Stumped. Helpless. No direction,"
Eslinger wrote. "[Our guys] fold like a poker player who has never
seen a good hand, not even a LUCKY hand that he can win with."

Meanwhile, he acclimated to Caltech culture. Austin was still
back East, finishing grad school at Tufts, so he lived in Caltech
housing. Without a car, he walked everywhere until the son of an
alum brought him a used mountain bike. Often, he bummed rides
from his assistant coach, Jamayne Potts, a gregarious man who
Eslinger hired partly because he was willing to work for next to
nothing.

Once upon a time, Eslinger learned, Caltech was something of an athletic powerhouse. In the '30s and '40s, the football team regularly beat UCLA. Basketball won its lone SCIAC title in 1954. Occasional bouts of hope followed. In 1980, the Beavers beat Pomona, then helmed by a first-year coach named Gregg Popovich. In 1985 they defeated La Verne. And then . . . nothing. The team went 0 for the 1990s. Had Huck Seed stuck around it might have been different. Six-foot-seven and springy, he left Caltech after one year to use his brain for more lucrative pursuits. In 1996, he won the World Series of Poker.

By Eslinger's arrival, in 2008, losing had become a badge of honor at Caltech; being bad at sports only proved how smart the students were. Two years earlier, the Provost's office had even explored the idea of eliminating the school's NCAA program entirely. "There were some dark years," says Robert Grubbs, a Nobel-winning chemistry professor and one of the few hoops boosters on the faculty. "The first time I took my older son to a basketball game here, by halftime he was cheering for the other team."

To change the culture, Eslinger knew he needed allies. He contacted former players. Spent long lunches at the campus cafeteria and befriended the head of the dining center, the custodians, and the sports equipment manager. Since there was no Sports Information Director, he launched a PR makeover that included regular e-newsletters (The "THROOP Times"), a redesigned website (the existing version appeared cached from the early Netscape era), and tri-fold recruiting brochures ("Become the Evolution").

None of it muted the pain of losing. Caltech finished the season 1-22, 0-12 in conference. The players ran hard but played soft. They led the nation in the only category you don't want to lead the nation: turnovers.

"What else can I do?" Eslinger asked Amherst coach David Hixon, after losing by 50.

Hixon was stumped. Finally he said, "Get some players."

In the spring of 2009, Jeff Bowker, the coach at Colony High, outside of Wasilla, Alaska, received an email from a college coach in California who was interested in one of his players, Collin Murphy. Bowker was shocked. Murphy was a terrific kid, tough as they came, but, as he wrote to Eslinger, "He is not a very skilled basketball player." Though a 5'11" shooting guard, Murphy neither shot (two three-point attempts all season), scored (six points per game), or handled the ball (Bowker forbade Murphy from bringing it upcourt).

Still, Eslinger persisted, asking for film. So Bowker scraped together "highlights" of a short-ish, wild-haired blond kid setting screens, sprinting on the break, and throwing his butt into people on rebounds. For reasons Bowker couldn't fathom, Eslinger remained enthused. He wanted Murphy's home number. Bowker warned him that the family had dial-up Internet and the Murphy kids often tied up the phone's line all night. Eslinger didn't care. He knew he couldn't change Caltech's culture by himself.

The summer before his freshman year of college, Murphy tossed a bag in the family's beat-up Expedition and, three hours by car and three by boat later, arrived with his father at Main Bay, in the Prince William Sound. They had three months to catch enough salmon to support the family for the year.

As they'd done since Collin was a boy, they set to work each morning at 5:00 a.m., when they shuffled out of their eight-by-twelve shack, the one with a tarp for a roof and walls jammed with newspaper insulation. On busy days, when the six-pound sockeyes were slamming into the 100-fathom nets, they ate only once. By midnight, when Collin crawled into a sleeping bag, his forearms burned from hauling, lifting, and cleaning the nets and his cheeks were raw from salt and the jellyfish.

His friends wondered why he still did it. Many of them dropped out of school at 15, as soon as they could find work driving oil rigs on the tundra. But Murphy was different. He scored 1860 on a practice SAT as a 12-year-old. By high school he was choosing between the Ivies, Rice, and Stanford. Dartmouth and Cornell recruited him to play football. And then Eslinger called. And called again. And again. The guy was so persistent, and optimistic. *This is my first recruiting class and I want to make it special,* he told Murphy. *You have a chance to make history.* All the coach could offer was a vision, and playing time.

Eslinger saw Murphy as the foundation of the program he intended to build: tough, resilient, unlikely to be intimidated by an eight-hour problem set. Who cared if the kid wasn't good at basketball? Neither were the rest of his players.

By the fourth game, Murphy was bringing the ball up, for lack of a better option. On defense, he guarded 6'5" forwards and quick point guards, outworking, out-thinking, and out-cheating them all. Murphy stepped on shoes, locked down off-arms, grabbed jerseys. "He was," says Eslinger with awe, "exceptionally dirty."

Sarcastic and goofy, he wore shirts that read I'M NO ROCKET SURGEON and yelled "Shooter in the corner" whenever he spotted up in scrimmages. On the website, he listed his career aspiration as "professional fantasy football player." He spent his free time in the basketball office, watching film. From the start, Eslinger knew he wanted Murphy as an assistant one day.

And yet, loss followed dispiriting loss. Against Claremont McKenna, the Beavers fell prey, as Murphy calls it, to "an 87–21 run." They finished the season 0-25, extending the conference streak to 297 games. "It was," Murphy says, "straight awful."

At least the 2010–11 season began auspiciously. Some nonconference wins. A few close SCIAC losses: in overtime, by a point, by two points. Eslinger's plan was working: the recruiting, the scheming, the positive reinforcement. "Does anyone else believe?" he wrote in his journal. "It's my job, a coach's manifest, to make others believe . . . Confidence will conquer."

Still, by the eve of the season finale, at home against Occidental, Caltech's losing streak had reached 310 games. That week, Murphy sat in a dorm room with Elmquist, now a senior, downing vodka. "I can't believe," Elmquist finally said, "that I'm going to go four years and not win one f— game."

Sometimes inspiration comes from unlikely places. Like, say, the trunk of a friend's car.

The weekend before the Occidental game, Eslinger played pickup ball with Doug Eberhardt, a coach from Vancouver in town for the NBA All-Star game who had recently embedded for a week with the Knicks. Eslinger peppered him with questions until, finally, Eberhardt said, "Why don't I just give you D'Antoni's playbook," he said. "I've got it out in my car."

That night, Eslinger stayed up late studying the diagrams in the two-bedroom house he now shared with Austin, now his wife and seven months pregnant with their son Julian. (They now also have a daughter.) Occidental's switching defense had hurt the Beavers the first time they played. What if, he now wondered, he just ran never-ending pick-and-rolls between the 6'5" Elmquist and freshman point guard Todd Cramer, a legitimate ball-handler whose arrival had moved Murphy to two guard?

And so, the following Saturday, in front of a relative throng of 400 on senior night in Braun Athletic Center, the Beavers came out in an unorthodox scheme: two shooters in the corners, one on the wing, and Elmquist and Cramer in the roles of Steve Nash and Amar'e Stoudemire.

For one glorious half, it worked. But then, inevitably, Occidental pulled away. With four minutes left, the score was 45–37. For years, Eslinger had peddled the silver lining. He tried to empower the at-times disinterested Elmquist. In disastrous three-on-two drills he chose to praise the defense. He focused on two-minute sequences hidden in 50-point losses. It was time for the hard truth. "If we let them score again," he said now. "We lose."

And, amazingly, it worked. Occidental didn't score again. With eight seconds left, Caltech had the ball in a tie game. On the right wing, Murphy spread to his slot, sure he was about to take the last shot. After all, he was a sophomore averaging 1.3 points per game. Sure, they were using two players to box him out on some possessions, but he had yet to attempt a field goal. If he were coaching Oxy, he says, there's a 100 percent chance he'd have made the Murphy kid shoot it.

Instead, inexplicably, Occidental didn't run a hard double. Elmquist slipped the screen, Cramer lobbed it high, and, as Elmquist went up, the whistle blew. Two free throws. Three seconds left. Silence. Elmquist stepped to the line and . . . time-out, Occidental.

As the team walked to the sideline, Eslinger racked his brain for what to say. And then it came to him. "This is *perfect*," he said to Elmquist, a 67 percent free throw shooter. "I read a study about field goal kickers. It proved that icing doesn't work!"

For the first time in a life of constant inquiry—of nearly acing the ACT, of spending a summer working with the autonomous navigation of mobile robot teams at the University of Minnesota, of subjecting everything to a decision matrix—Elmquist felt his mind go blank. He heard nothing, remembers nothing.

Swish.

The second free throw missed. Oxy's desperation heave went wide. And then: nerd bedlam. Students stormed the floor. Nobel winners celebrated. On the baseline, television cameras rolled. No one wanted to leave the court.

The next day, for undoubtedly the first time in school history, Caltech basketball players missed class for a press conference. The news of the win even briefly led the Caltech website, just above coverage of the lab's development of a new Mars Rover. And in the heady days to come, in between appearing on ESPN and in the *New York Times* and receiving a deluge of ecstatic alumni emails and an invitation to coach the Washington Generals against the Harlem Globetrotters, Eslinger remembers a sneaking feeling. Everyone was celebrating one win. But few noticed that Caltech made only 12 field goals and shot 24.5 percent. Or that Occidental's best player was injured. Or that Elmquist was graduating.

After all, the goal wasn't to win one game. It was to turn around the program.

Looking back now, it sounds comical: NCAA violations at Caltech? But integrity matters, even for losers. When Betsy Mitchell was hired as the new athletic director in August of 2011, she did what all good administrators do: familiarized herself with protocol. Tall and solid, with a booming voice and ready smile, Mitchell set the world record in the 200-meter backstroke in 1986 and won a gold and two silver Olympic medals. After retiring, she climbed Mount Kilimanjaro, competed in the world sculling championships, and got a master's from Harvard. As the AD at Allegheny College (Pennsylvania), she oversaw a national champion football team. Her whole life had been about winning. And now she was at Caltech.

The week she was hired, she called the registrar to inquire about eligibility. "Well of course they're eligible," the woman said. To which Mitchell thought: *Oh crap.*

Under the NCAA's byzantine logic, being a good student didn't necessarily equate to eligibility. And, since Caltech allows students to "sample" classes for three weeks before officially registering, Mitchell found 30 instances over four years when athletes were briefly ineligible. There was only one thing to do: self-report. "We teach through our sports," Mitchell explained, "and we're teaching through this."

Caltech punished itself with a $5,000 fine, vacated ineligible wins, banned off-campus recruiting for a year, and instituted a postseason ban on 12 sports. And that, everyone assumed, would be that.

But then the NCAA, clearly with nothing better to do as scandals raged at USC and Miami, weighed in. Rather than commending Caltech for being a model of integrity, it piled on, adding public censure and a three-year probation. Wrote Bill Plaschke of the *Los Angeles Times*, "[Caltech] has chosen to vacate wins it doesn't have, shut down the recruiting it doesn't do and be ineligible for championships it never wins."

But that wasn't true. The basketball team had won—and, to everyone's relief, that Occidental victory stood. And Eslinger *did* recruit. Now he was stuck on campus, on the phone, explaining bizarre NCAA sanctions. Meanwhile, two of his assistants were gone, with his blessing. Worse, in January of the following season, Cramer transferred to MIT with no warning and, shortly after, stopped playing college basketball.

It was a crushing sequence. Instead of building on the Occidental win, Caltech again finished winless in the SCIAC.

The Streak was dead; a new streak was born.

In the spring of 2012, a 22-year-old named Dave Briski saw an online job posting at Caltech. The son of a construction worker, Briski had never been to California but, after four years as the student manager for the University of New Hampshire, he was desperate to get into coaching. Reading Eslinger's bio on the school website, he was impressed: school records, historic accomplishments. "I was like, 'Wow, this team must have gone like 26–3 last season,'" Briski remembers. "Then I got further into my research and I read about the streak. And I was like, 'These guys are jacked up after winning one game!?'"

Still, Briski couldn't be choosy. He applied, got the job, and called a cousin in Glendale, who let him crash in his unfinished basement. His salary for the year was $1,000. To make ends meet, he worked part-time as a lifeguard, arriving at 5:30 a.m. To hide his age, he grew a beard and kept his hair short, the better to highlight his encroaching widow's peak.

Briski proved a welcome contrast to the analytical Eslinger, forever trying to exude professorial calm. Briski drank life out of 24-ounce steins, a scruffy, enthusiastic bulldog of a man. When he jotted down recruiting notes at elite academic camps, his assessments included technical terminology like "Plays his f— a— off";

"STUD, Big, great hooks with both hands"; and "Fast as f—, lefty, tremendous passer."

At first, Briski tried to connect to players by talking academics. Then Kc Emezie, a polite, talented freshman, set him straight. *I don't want to talk to you about computer science,* Emezie said. *I want to talk to you about basketball.* Thank god, thought Briski.

It made sense. The students spent the rest of their lives geeking out. School pranks were legendary. During the '90s students soldered networks of copper tubing, reconfiguring old refrigeration units and priming them with Freon so they could turn a dorm hallway into a sheet of ice for skating. Another time, students hacked into an electronic Coke machine on campus using an old Compaq with an 8MHZ processor and 640 kB RRAM, creating prepaid accounts, a ledger system, and, eventually, rigging it to serve Miller Genuine Draft. Most famously, in 1984 a group of Techies snuck in and rewired the scoreboard during the Rose Bowl so that it read CALTECH 38 and MIT 9.

Still, even the smartest kids in the world sometimes wonder if they're smart enough. Elmquist compares Caltech to a treadmill forever speeding up. "You have to make a serious calculation," he says. "Is this hour lecture worth my time when I can spend my time doing homework?" Junior guard Ricky Galliani's low point came freshman year while sitting in the library at 6:15 a.m., realizing he'd been there eight hours and his paper was due in six. Says Arjun Chandar, a reserve guard, "Anyone who tells you they didn't think of transferring at least once is lying to you." Murphy, who worked at the campus coffee shop, regularly had to cut off jittery students trying to blaze through the night. "They'd come up, hands shaking, and try to order another triple espresso," says Murphy. "I was like, 'No way, man. I don't want to be responsible for your heart attack.'" There's a reason the marriage rate is one of the highest in the country, despite the three-to-one male-to-female ratio. Nothing bonds humans like surviving a crisis.

For many, basketball became an escape from schoolwork or, as Chandar says, "a coping strategy." Elmquist liked that during practice he could "turn my brain off." But of course that wasn't truly possible. Not with these kids. Eslinger struggled at times to reach them. Some players didn't look up when he spoke; eventually he realized they were just processing the information. Others wanted to engage, just not about basketball. Wilson Ho, a 5'6" chemistry major, once described to Eslinger how you could theoretically stop time, scrawling equations on scrap paper.

The previous Caltech coach, Roy Dow, was an old-school yeller. Eslinger's college coach was too, once challenging the whole team to a fight. Now, Eslinger tried a different approach. He understood basketball came second. So if players were burnt from all-nighters, he held them out. Later in the season, when the cumulative sleep deficit grew, he reduced team conditioning. He learned to explain the purpose of drills, lest students raise their hands to debate the rationale. After all, they were trained to challenge professors, to think outside the box. Or, as school president Tom Rosenbaum puts it, "to try to solve unsolvable problems." To expect blind, militaristic submission was silly. Instead, Eslinger read about relative value systems, trying to see the world through his students' eyes. In the end, says Murphy, "I actually felt like he was a little nicer to us during the losing than we deserved."

The defeats continued. In 2012–13, the Beavers again finished winless in the SCIAC. Murphy soldiered on. "I'm from Alaska," he explains. "The darkness never bothered me." Still, he finished his career with one conference win. He's more proud of the fact that he never missed a game, even when he fractured his elbow. His career averages were pedestrian; his impact was not. "The best leader I've ever seen," says Eslinger.

By this point, Eslinger's confidence was wavering. Self-analytical by nature, he began to question his grand plan. He changed the offense from game to game. In his lower moments, he couldn't help but wonder if that Oxy win had been a mirage. If maybe it wasn't possible to build a real program at Caltech. If sometimes a problem wasn't an advantage; it was just a problem.

There is, Eslinger believes, a life lesson to be gleaned from what happened next: if you think you've looked under every rock for what you seek, your problem may simply be that you need to find more rocks.

By the spring of 2013, Eslinger had changed the culture. Alumni were engaged, returning for fund-raisers and attending games. He'd initiated Midnight Madness events. *Hit a half-court shot and win a ball signed by five Nobel winners!* He'd logged more than a dozen nonconference wins. Early recruit Mike Edwards, a deadeye shooter, broke the school scoring record. The team now understood defense, passing, and teamwork. The only thing lacking was the same thing as ever: talent. And then one day Eslinger picked up the right rock. Under it was a kid named Nasser Al-Rayes.

Once upon a time, Nasser's parents, a normal-sized man and a normal-sized woman, met at the University of Denver. During the Gulf War they eloped to Qatar and had Nasser. To their surprise, he grew to be more than normal-sized: 6'10". And, after four years at the American School of Doha, he boasted both a prodigious GPA and an abundance of athletic potential.

Eslinger first heard about the 6'10" Al-Rayes from John Alexander, the head of an international basketball academy and the brother of former NBA player Joe Alexander. Eventually MIT, Wesleyan, and Williams also called, among others. Al-Rayes made a flow chart, weighing his interest in going to a winning program against the strangely persistent Caltech coach's assurance that his program was *about* to win. When he finally committed, he came with a bonus: a friend from Alexander's team named Lawrence Lee, a 6'6" post player from Hong Kong.

And thus, Eslinger welcomed his first, honest-to-goodness big man recruit. That fall brought a good omen: the school broke another drought, seven years without a Nobel laureate, when Martin Karplus won for the development of multiscale models for complex chemical systems.

Al-Rayes's first season was rocky—which is to say, winless in SCIAC as usual. But by last fall, Al-Rayes had matured. Hogue, now a senior point guard, rebounded like a forward. Emezie, an athletic 6'6" wing, only had one move—drive right and finish right —but it was a hell of a move. And, to Eslinger's delight, Murphy had returned as an assistant coach, while also working at a start-up. (Naturally, it's a pickup hoops app.)

The 2014–15 season started well enough. Then conference play began. The Beavers lost by 25 to Claremont, 19 to Redlands, 21 to Cal-Lutheran. They hung in against La Verne, only to fall in double overtime. As January turned to February, the losing streak stood at 55 games. Hogue realized he was about to "go donut" for his career.

It was time, Eslinger decided, to change it up. He'd long since embraced analytics with a gusto rare for D-III, tracking usage rates and true shooting percentage and a host of other stats. At one point, he logged the outcomes of practice drills, hoping to determine why some players always win, but the data was too noisy. He videotaped and rewatched practices. He consulted with former Caltech player Dean Oliver, considered by many the father of basketball analytics. He and Briski uploaded game film to a service called Krossover, a do-it-yourself version of Synergy that quantified the footage. His journals, once filled with musings and occasional poetry or the odd Billy Joel quote, now contained pages and pages of scribbled plays with names like Pitch, Gimme, Fade, Flare Bang Bang, and Black Deal. And now, while watching scouting film of Redlands, he and Briski noticed something.

Against Redlands on February 3, Caltech started with a normal alignment. But as the game went on, it became clear that Al-Rayes was rarely venturing further than 10 feet from the basket on defense. It was akin to what Golden State Warriors center Andrew Bogut would do months later in the NBA playoffs: lay off the non-shooter and pack the paint. Flustered, Redlands made just four of 15 threes while Al-Rayes clogged the lane, swatting shots. At 8:06 p.m., Josh Sonola, a onetime walk-on and one of the team's biggest fans, madly tapped out an email to the entire campus. "Basketballs winning vs Redlands, 22–13," it read. "Come to the damn game."

Some even did, leaving their studies. Meanwhile, at the half, Caltech led by eight. Slowly, inevitably, the lead dwindled. And yet, with 17 seconds left, the Beavers were still up three, and Emezie, the team's best free throw shooter, was at the line. But this was Caltech, so naturally things went awry. Emezie missed. Redlands raced down and sank a three. Tie game. On the sideline, Briski felt a familiar pit excavating his stomach. "Now," he remembers, "the mountain feels tall."

Study game theory and you're familiar with the concept of the gambler's fallacy. Just because a quarter comes up heads 40 times in a row doesn't mean it is more likely to come up tails. Each moment is independent of the last. Or at least this is what Eslinger wanted to believe as he drew up a play in the huddle. It's what Hogue wanted to believe as he charged downcourt and, seeing the middle cut off, dished it to Emezie at the top of the key, who did what he always did: drove right. His best move. His only move. Only he took off too deep on the baseline. In retrospect, teammates swear he couldn't even see the hoop.

The ball hit the glass at a crazy angle. And, against the longest of odds, historically and technically, it spun in.

Joy. Players hugging and jumping. Murphy joining them, now part of a second SCIAC win in five years. Eslinger, jubilant, looking for his dad, who stood in the back of the crowd, smiling.

The final stat line was bizarre. Al-Rayes went scoreless but finished with six blocks. The scheme had worked; Redlands shot a dismal 25 percent for the game. Caltech had simply out-thought its opponent. For Eslinger, it was validation. This time, the opponent's best player wasn't injured. This time, Caltech hit 40 percent of its threes. Hogue didn't care how it happened, just that it had. He dashed off a campus-wide email: "Yo, we're studying after our win. Come by." By the time they were done that night, the ceiling of their group house was stained with champagne.

And if that were the end of the story, it would be fine. Another streak broken. But it's what happened five days later that changed everything. All season, Murphy told the other coaches that if they could ever win a conference game with at least one more to play —just one—watch out.

The opponent was Whittier, which beat Caltech by 14 a month earlier and was notorious for rubbing it in. Hogue remembers his freshman year, when the Poets were up 57 late in the game but still playing their starters. And pressing. While their fans chanted, "Win by 60!"

From the opening tip, Whittier pressed. Caltech, as it reliably had for decades, succumbed, falling behind early. But then, an unlikely surge. Flying layups. Deep threes. Dunks. By half, the Beavers were up nine. And that's when, to the players' surprise, a torrent of students entered the gym, many in formal wear. It was Wine and Candlelight dinner—the Caltech version of Valentine's Day—and word had gotten out about the lead. In a testament to the culture Eslinger, Murphy, and the rest had created, the students actually left a rare social opportunity and walked 10 minutes to watch a basketball game. Now 200 of them stood, a couple of glasses of chardonnay deep, jumping and chanting "I believe that we will win!"

Meanwhile, the players were transformed. Call it confidence, or perhaps straight-up swagger. Three players slapping the floor on defense simultaneously. Al-Rayes throwing down a thunderous follow dunk off a free throw. Three-pointers raining down. On the sideline, Murphy fretted that the team was bound to go cold, or that Whittier would adjust. But neither happened. Caltech extended the lead. "Guys," Eslinger shouted as he walked the length of the bench, eyes afire. "*We're for real!*"

And they were. This wasn't a squeak-it-out, low-scoring, ugly Caltech win. This wasn't a fluke. This was an old-fashioned, high-scoring 92–77 butt-kicking. Al-Rayes finished with a fantasy basketball line: 22 points, 12 rebounds, six assists, and six blocks. "For the first time," says Hogue, "we had no regard for the other team."

Now, as the clock wound down, the crowd stood and sang: "Na na na na, na na na na, hey hey hey, good-bye." The starters sat on the bench—no longer even needed in the game—arms around each other, grinning in disbelief. The buzzer sounded and a wave of students in loosened neckties and black strapless dresses crashed onto the court, whooping and hugging the players. The Whittier players trudged by, dejected, but no one paid any mind. Meanwhile, Eslinger kept his composure, at least for the moment. Later, when he and Briski and alumni bar-crawled through Pasadena, they drank away years of frustration one frothy pint at a time.

Then, the icing: 10 days later, in its next home game, Caltech beat La Verne 70–69. In three weeks the team had equaled the number of conference wins from the previous 43 years.

For Eslinger, the future had finally arrived.

"Go, go, go!"

It's 7:30 on a recent October morning and the Caltech players are charging through suicides and then the weave, the drill that once flummoxed their predecessors. One pass leads crisply to the next until 6'4" freshman Brent Cahill catches it and, with shocking nonchalance, hammers down a two-hand dunk. Cahill, it turns out, declined a walk-on spot at UCLA. He's a basketball unicorn: a crazy smart kid who can shoot and, if he really tries, come close to grazing his head on the rim. And he chose Caltech.

Al-Rayes is next. He yanks the rim hard, so hard you fear for its mooring. Rather than working for NASA, Al-Rayes spent last summer at IMG in Bradenton, Florida, training with Trail Blazers forward Moe Harkless and others. He still intends to go to grad school, and become an engineer—once he's done playing professionally overseas.

The team is stacked by Caltech standards. There's Emezie, second-team All-SCIAC last year; Galliani, who can stroke it; and Lee, a gregarious big man who dropped 38 in a game last year and is nicknamed "Larry Love" on account of his big heart. (When feeling down he says he'll go to the theater alone and see a movie like *Frozen*.)

Still, because it's Caltech, nothing is easy. Ty Ochse, an athletic guard and elite math student, is sitting out the season as he endeavors to simultaneously earn a master's in math in four years. Nick Buoniconti, the grandson of the Dolphins linebacker and a key 6'7" post defender, also opted not to play to focus on academics. Meanwhile, Murphy finally left to work full-time on his startup, replaced by Jordan Mast, a former walk-on at Gonzaga. But this is the new Caltech. No longer is the program about one or two players. No one talks about winning "a" game anymore.

Today's players reject the stereotypes of the past. Lee says he gets "weird, judgmental looks" when he admits that he "only" studies four to five hours a night because basketball is his priority. Galliani says, "I might be learning more from the basketball part of my education than the actual part of my education." It's a fascinating transformation. For decades, Caltech acted as the counterbalance to the bloating of corporate college sports, an exemplar for those trying to put athletics in perspective. But perhaps it went too far. "In the past, being a jock was almost a negative," says Grubbs, the Nobel winner. "At least now it's not a negative." He laughs. "That's sort of progress."

Last year, women's tennis posted its first winning season since 1997. Cross-country sent a runner to the NCAAs for the first time in forever. And, despite the crushing academic load, the GPA of athletes at Caltech is just as high as that of non-athletes. "We hear from the recruiting wars that people are being told to choose," says Mitchell. "Do you want to be an engineer or do you want to play sports?" But isn't that why D-III sports exist? An Ernst & Young study found that 52 percent of women at the C-suite level played college sports, and one imagines the number is similar for men. "Some of those will be Stanford and the like," says Mitchell. "But by definition, a lot of that will be a D-III thing."

At Caltech, basketball didn't get the players into the school and it won't lead anywhere afterward. "I don't want to go to some C league in Iceland," says Galliani. Cahill chose Caltech over UCLA because, "Why would I want to practice four hours a day if I'm not going to the NBA?" Others say they would have transferred if not for hoops. "No one at Google cares what grades I got," says Elmquist. "They cared that I learned stuff and can do things." And guess what he usually ends up talking about over drinks? He laughs. "That time I helped Caltech break the streak."

The man who spearheaded this change sits in the cramped office he shares with Briski, squinting at a computer screen. On the wall above his desk, in neat cursive script, is a congratulatory note on Spurs letterhead from Popovich, one of the last SCIAC coaches to lose to Caltech prior to 2011. It came attached to a case of pinot noir. Nearby, overstuffed shelves are lined with Phil Jackson books as well as titles like, *Help the Helper: Building a Culture of Extreme Teamwork.*

On this morning, Eslinger and Briski are going over potential recruits. The pickings remain slim. Anyone with a GPA under 3.8 gets discarded. Anyone not good enough to play gets bumped. How many does that leave?

"In the whole country?" Briski asks.

He does some math, consults his Front Rush recruiting software, then says, "About 250."

The vast majority of those, he explains, will choose a place like Harvard or Columbia or, if cowed by Caltech's academic load, a less-stressful D-III school. Others won't get in. One of last year's top recruits had to settle for his safety school, MIT.

For now, Eslinger can't worry about that. He is fixated on the final step in the program's evolution: shooting. Last season, the Beavers hit 29 percent of their threes. Upon analyzing the data, Eslinger noticed something: "When we hopped into a shot, we hit 40 percent of our threes," he says. "That was 20 percent better than when they one-two stepped into it."

He heads downstairs to the gym, eager to demonstrate: hop and you're already squared up; step and you're out of balance. He is pumped. "I'm going to blow their minds when I show them the video and data!" Eslinger still regularly plays pickup ball and recently completed Tim Grover's "Jump Attack" workout, hoping to glean tidbits for his team. Players like Al-Rayes notice; if their coach is working that hard, then they should be too.

Now, as Eslinger shoots, a bald man with a bushy gray beard peeks into the gym. He is wearing a Hawaiian shirt, old jeans, and sandals. His shirt pocket bristles with pens. He is, naturally, a Nobel Prize winner, the theoretical physicist David Politzer. He ambles over. At this point, the season is still a few weeks away. Eslinger has yet to determine the truth about the discrepancy between the two baskets—in the end he will conclude the 12 percent gap is an anomaly, though he will still stage shooting drills on the better hoop, in case it boosts confidence. Likewise, he has yet to institute his dream of a nearly position-less team, with Al-Rayes launching threes. And he has yet to break down film from the Beavers' emphatic 86–77 preseason road win at Occidental a month later—the first road win against a conference opponent since 1980—searching for insight that he hopes will allow Caltech to chase its first conference crown in a half-century.

No, for now he is just a skinny guy in glasses who looks an awful lot like an older version of the kids he coaches, gleefully shooting jumpers while a Nobel laureate watches, all the while working toward the same goal as every Caltech student: trying to solve the unsolvable problem.

Spun

FROM BICYCLING

THE WRENCH ADORED the junkie's calves. A tragedy launched by innocence and good intentions. He had heard about her calves, about her, but still. They were magnificent. The wrench had never seen such noble calves.

"You must be the triathlete," the wrench said.

Men had always liked her. Good guys, not-so-good guys. Some no-question-about-it awful guys. She had never been so great at telling them apart. Still, she tried. This guy? Soft eyes. Wolfish smile. A deep voice that made something in her chest hurt. Shit.

"You must be Dominic," she said.

Women had always liked him. Nearly every one of the wrench's girlfriends (he was seldom without one) had blossomed into a fiancée not too long before she shriveled into an ex. A former bodybuilder, former break-dancer, and soon-to-be former bartender who, as a child, had dreamed of becoming a hairdresser, his most consuming passions now were raising pit bulls ("If you've got a really game pit bull, there are only three ways you're going to get it to let go of another dog. One, you're going to shoot it . . .") and dreaming of a comeback in a nearly forgotten sport.

Chronically restless, reckless, a once and future heavy drinker, a recovering crackhead, the wrench calmed himself by watching Sylvester Stallone movies and the filmic Batman oeuvre, particularly "when he's old and he's out of his prime. He's slower. He isn't capable of what he used to be." The wrench was 34 years old and he lived with his mother.

The junkie had left high school early, dropped out of college, been hospitalized, released, hospitalized again, arrested twice, lasted at a corporate job for seven years where she never felt like she quite fit in. The FUCK OFF tattoo on her right ankle didn't help. To take her mind off past mistakes and worries about the future, and to avoid another trip to the hospital—to calm herself —she had recently taken up endurance sports. She was estranged from her wealthy father, caring for two large Dobermans, wondering what she was going to do with her life, and dating four guys a week, not loving any of them. She was 37 years old and had sunk her life savings into a brick, one-story, two-bedroom house for herself and her dogs. She paid $64,000. It squatted at the end of a cul-de-sac in a sketchy neighborhood that she was betting would get better. Soon the house would be worth $19,000.

After he met the junkie, the wrench called his best friend. "I just met the female version of myself," he said.

"Well, that's scary," his friend replied.

While he was lifting her bike onto the rack on top of her car, a friend of the junkie's telephoned.

"What are you doing?" the friend asked.

"Watching this hot guy put my bike on my car rack," she said.

"Oh, god," the friend replied.

It was August 21, 2007, and Judi Rothenberg and Dominic LoPresti were both too old and too damaged to believe that love conquered all. Each had known love, and it had brought them debt, dead friends, hungry dogs, addiction, dreams that seemed to curdle and recede every day. Might this time be different? Probably not. The best predictor of the future, as no shortage of lip-pursing therapists, exfoliated authors, and grouchy relationship coaches murmur and scold, is the past. And these two had some pretty gnarly pasts. Their story set to music would be a melancholy hymn, played in a decidedly minor key. The wrench and the junkie were doomed.

The Junkie

This is what loss looks like: a woman sitting in a window. Long platinum hair with black roots. A black T-shirt, sleeves cut off, with a band's name that is difficult to make out. Black stretch jeans. In her lap, in her hands, held tenderly, as one might cradle a baby, a 40-ounce bottle of beer. Near her right shoulder, a skull impaled

STEVE FRIEDMAN

42

by a knife, and on her forearm a slithering snake thrusting its
forked tongue.

Wide eyes, lifted brows, and a half frown that says, "Get away!"
and "Help me." She is 20 and has been in San Francisco for three
years. It's 1990 and a photographer has asked to snap her picture.
He is working on a book about street kids.

How does a nice Jewish girl from the Cincinnati suburbs end
up in a book called *Raised by Wolves*? Why would a teenager leave
school, leave her life, and spend her days shooting heroin? Why
does any kid leave comfort, in search of peace?

Audrey Martin (then Rothenberg) was 33 when Judi was born,
with a 10-year-old son who would be diagnosed with schizophrenia, and two daughters, eight and five.

Judi's father, a wealthy real estate executive, left the family when
Judi was one, remarried, moved into a house of vast lawns and dig-
nified driveways. Audrey and her kids stayed where they were, in
an area that at its peak was the worst part of a nice neighborhood
but that now seemed to decay by the week.

Audrey took a typist job at the University of Cincinnati. When
she left for work, the baby stayed at home with sitters, or was
dropped off at a day care center, or if it wasn't a school day and
Audrey had to work, handed to her big sisters. Judi would have
missed her mom—she can't remember—but she doesn't blame
her. "My mom busted her ass to take care of us. He screwed my
mom."

When she got a little older, she would see her dad sometimes,
at the Jewish Community Center swimming pool, but he was always
with his new wife and their new son, just a year younger than Judi,
and she didn't know what to say, what to do, and it was weird. But
she didn't complain. She studied ballet, and her teachers whacked
her legs, told her she was too fat. She didn't complain. She remembers "a great childhood. It wasn't bad. I had everything I wanted
and more." She didn't complain about anything. But she worried.
About her mother. Her father. Her ballet teacher. Homework. Every day on the way to school, she threw up into a plastic bag she
carried with her for just that purpose.

She grew from an anxious, puking 12-year-old into a sulky bal-
lerina at the Cincinnati School for the Creative and Performing
Arts, a teenager who snuck out of the house, and who drank. A

bunch of her friends—"scummy gutter punks"—were headed to San Francisco. Why not?

Her first day, she crouched over a table at a McDonald's at the top of Haight Street, snorting crystal meth through a dollar bill. It was her first time. After that, there wasn't so much to worry about. She didn't need to eat. She didn't need to sleep. She could walk around the city for hours and hours and it was great. Then she met a guy and that was great too. They hitchhiked to New York, camped out in the Connecticut woods, cadged meals, snorted cocaine, and when it got cold, she returned to Cincinnati, got an apartment, got a bicycle, got a job at Planned Parenthood, and courtesy of the free tuition possible from her mother's job, signed up for college courses at the University of Cincinnati. Six months later, she was back in San Francisco. She was 18.

She hated heroin at first. Then she liked it. Then she needed it.

She worked as a bicycle messenger, gathered with her colleagues every lunch hour at a deli on Howard and Fourth, where the owner gave them sandwiches on credit, ran tabs, and after he took his cut on payday, cashed their checks. Often Judi didn't eat, but pedaled three miles to her dealer's apartment on Valencia and 14th, shot up, then floated out the door and onto her mountain bike with the handlebar chopped so she could slide and swerve between cars and buses. Work was painless. Life was painless. No worries.

Okay apartments turned to crappy apartments turned to crappier apartments turned to beds in homeless shelters, then when she didn't check in early enough, to chairs in homeless shelters, then to sheets of cardboard on the street.

There were various boyfriends, some good, none great, some terrible. She doesn't blame the boyfriends. "All the relationships I had back then were shitty. We treated each other like shit. 'What was gonna benefit me from hanging out with you?' That's all we worried about."

On one of Judi's periodic trips to visit her mother, Audrey took her to an addiction specialist at the University of Cincinnati, who asked to see Judi's arms, and asked how she felt. "Get off me!" Judi screamed. On another visit, she showed up at Audrey's house dressed in the only clothes she owned—an Abercrombie sweatshirt, black sweatpants, and a pair of gym shoes from Payless—and after a meal and a shower, headed downtown to score some drugs. She was arrested, thrown in jail, released after vowing to show up in court. Instead, she headed for New York the next day with a friend who had a van, but no license plates. Cops found black tar heroin already mixed up in syringes. At sentencing they weighed not just the drugs, but the syringes as well. Judi thought that was unfair. It still pisses her off a little.

Audrey spent a lot of time those years wondering if she'd get a call from a hospital. In 1993 (or '94, Audrey can't remember), she got it. Ten o'clock on a winter Friday morning. Her daughter was in a coma, and Audrey had better hurry. Audrey was at the airport by 1:30, shoving her way through people and onto a plane that waited for her because the flight attendants had been told the situation.

At the hospital, nurses told Audrey that no, she couldn't see her daughter.

"Is she dead?" Audrey asked.

The Wrench

He lived with the woman he loved and his 50-pound pit bull, Bruno, in a third-floor apartment with good light and slanted ceilings. He made good money as a bartender at a swank restaurant, installed flooring by day, wrenched here and there for extra cash, dreamed of opening a bicycle shop, and of making a triumphant comeback at the age of 28 in the sport where he'd once been a reigning, charismatic prince. Every night, and every morning, he could feel those dreams, and his life, slipping away.

He had always been a hard worker. But he wasn't saving any money. He definitely wasn't getting anywhere with what he had thought would be his livelihood and his passion, BMX freestyle. He had devoted much of his childhood and adolescence to making his body and bicycle move in ways that demanded strength and balance and agility and stillness. "Like ballet on a bicycle," he says. "Like break dancing on a bicycle." But just when he was about to break through—he was a semipro getting paid to ride places, receiving free product—BMX riders discovered big-air jumping. No one paid a lot of attention to ballet on bicycles after that.

He had planned to be famous, to do what he loved. He was

a flabby bartender who installed flooring. What had seemed like the good life was revealing itself to be pathetic. He wanted more. But he didn't know how to get it. He had tried to cut down the drinking, with limited success. To calm himself, to help forget the dreams that he was starting to realize were stillborn, he snorted cocaine. Then he started smoking crack every morning, every lunch hour. His girlfriend wondered why he was so distant at night. When he was 29, she told him he had to leave.

He took his clothes, his flooring tools, his bicycle tools, and Bruno. Man and dog moved in with Dominic's mother, Peggy Sinclair. She was disappointed, but not entirely surprised.

He had been such an odd child. Other kids pleaded with their parents to buy them polo shirts and penny loafers. Dominic dyed his hair blue. Other children daydreamed. Dominic chattered. Other children read comics. Dominic crocheted. Others dreamed of being firemen and doctors. Dominic thought hairdressing sounded interesting. Other children came home with grass stains and breathless tales of home runs and leaping catches. Dominic showed up for dinner soaked in blood, with head wounds and torn clothes. When he was seven, when the LoPrestis were living in Cambridge, Ohio, he nearly bit his tongue in half. The wound was so deep that the doctors at the hospital stitched it. Doctors almost never stitch tongues. "The only good thing about that," Peggy says, "is that Dominic stopped talking for a while."

He fell in love with BMX racing when he was 10, then saw his first freestyle show, and never wanted to race again. At 15, he was ranked one of the best freestylers in the country. He dropped out of high school his senior year. When he was 18, his parents divorced. When he was 19, he moved to his own place. He managed a Subway sandwich store. He wrenched. He learned to install flooring. Mostly, though, he practiced pirouettes, held handstands, spun and danced with his bicycle in empty parking lots.

The X Games phased freestyling out. Years spent on a career that would never be. He was drinking more, and more. More cocaine. Then jail. "Sheer stupidity, for being violent, for assault charges."

He cut back, then started again, cut back, then started again. "I realized I couldn't stop. I went from, 'I love the nightlife,' to 'Oh, my God, I'm a flipping drug addict.' I turned 30 and it was like, 'Man, I'm going to die.'"

He tried to manage. To limit himself. After he left his bartending shift one night, on his way to his mother's house, he decided he wanted a drink. He deserved a drink. Just one drink. He pulled in to a bar. He doesn't remember the rest of the evening.

When Peggy saw her son, prone and unmoving in the backyard, she called Dominic's father, Tom LoPresti. He arrived as she was getting ready to call the hospital, but he told her to stop. He had worked in pharmaceuticals and he knew how doctors and nurses in emergency rooms often felt about heavy drinkers and drug users. "They might let him die," he said. Instead, he got the hose and sprayed Dominic till his eyes fluttered, then walked him around and fed him ipecac syrup and then Pedialyte, and for nine hours his son took his medicine and passed out and woke up and vomited and repeated the cycle until Tom and Peggy knew he would survive. At least for the day.

"They didn't know how to make me better," Dominic says. "I didn't know how to make me better."

The Junkie: Searching

After her arrest in 1996, Judi was sent to a drug rehabilitation unit (in lieu of jail) for six months, and then to a halfway house. She attended three 12-step meetings a day, borrowed a bike from her best childhood friend, and on weekends when the residents were let out, she rode to the nearest liquor store and drank till midnight Saturday so she could pass the urine test on Monday. When she was released ("I told them everything they wanted to hear"), she rented an apartment, got a job waiting tables, then went back to heroin and stayed on it for two years. On October 8, 1999, she locked herself in her apartment for seven days. She ate grilled cheese sandwiches brought by her "really shitty boyfriend, God, I hated him, but he helped me." She sweated and trembled and vomited. And that was it. She never used heroin again. "It was just like I couldn't do it anymore. I said, 'I'm done.'"

She enrolled in Cincinnati's Tri-State Travel School, learned "how to be around other people and pretend like I was a normal person," was hired to arrange travel for executives at a large corporation. It was steady, and she saved money, and once every six weeks for the next four years she woke early, drove 45 minutes to

Dayton where a doctor removed a spider, a spiderweb, a skull and crossbones, a skull on a stand, an eyeball, and the FUCK OFF tattoo. Then she drove to work.

She was clean, but something was missing. She wasn't supposed to worry about the past or obsess about the future—that's what they told her in the recovery groups—but couldn't she at least feel some peace? Couldn't she find love? Couldn't she find a non-shitty boyfriend? Couldn't she put her undeniable business skills —those had been a surprise, who knew all these years she had an affinity for numbers—to more profitable and enjoyable use than booking trips to Las Vegas for executive vice presidents and putting through their expense reports? (A few days after reviewing a $10,000 report for a luxury cruise, she received a 25 cents an hour raise; that burned.)

Maybe exercise would help. She enrolled in step classes at Bally Total Fitness and "it took about seven years for anyone to speak to me." She ran two laps around a high school track. Two became four and four became eight and after a while, four became Cincinnati's Flying Pig Marathon in 2007.

She had always excelled at bold moves. It was the details that had tripped her up. She entered an Olympic-distance triathlon. She swam the first leg in a wetsuit designed for scuba diving. It was like wearing clothes. She rode the second leg on a mountain bike she had bought on Craigslist for $60, an old, steel "big hunkin'" hog of a thing the race director had assured her would be just fine. When she stumbled across the finish line after the 10K run, so far behind everyone else that workers were dismantling the stands, she was gasping, sobbing, quivering with fury. She managed to summon the energy to loudly curse the race director, who probably regretted sticking around.

She entered another Olympic-distance triathlon in July. This time she wore just a swimsuit and used a road bike. She finished last again, but an hour faster than her first time.

She was going to fewer meetings, spending more time training. She hadn't found love, hadn't found a job where she could utilize her talents. She didn't talk much with her older sisters, who had moved away and had lives of their own. One had a PhD in theoretical accounting, the other had a PhD in statistical mathematics. Her older brother lived with their mother, and it fell to Audrey to help him manage his schizophrenia. Judi hadn't found any kind

of happy, peaceful relationship with her father. He was a multimil-
lionaire, a real estate king, while "my mom is on a pension from
UC as a secretary."

She wasn't puking into a plastic bag every day, or sticking needles into her arms, but she wanted more. She wanted to feel better.

She decided for her third race, she would use clipless pedals.
First, though, she had to learn how to use them. A woman named
Wanda who had worked on Judi's road bike told her about a
wrench who could help her. He knew bicycles. He used to be a big-
shot BMX rider, the old-fashioned kind, the break-dancing kind.
He was older now, about Judi's age. Wanda thought they might get
along.

The Wrench: Searching

His days as a reigning prince were over. He attended recovery
meetings and listened to people jabber about slow and steady and
easy does it and a day at a time, but Dominic had never been a slow
and steady easy does it one day at a time kind of guy. He wanted
to feel better *now*.

No one cared about flatlanders anymore. The moves were too
subtle, the movements too small, the discipline—intense, demanding—too difficult for any but the true BMX cognoscenti to appreciate. Everyone wanted to watch skinny kids catching big air. There
were exactly two flatlanders in Cincinnati, four in Cleveland, one
in Columbus. "I was like the Forgotten Samurai," he says.

He bought a mountain bike, and after three months he was still
bloated, not drinking or using, but not feeling much better either.
He might be lost, and fat, and living with his mother, but once a
flatlander, always a flatlander. He wheeled one of his BMX bikes
to the Walgreens parking lot nearby. Some kids watched him, gog-
gle-eyed, told him he should check out this mom-and-pop bicycle
store they knew about, the owners were big into BMX. If he was
going to lose weight, though, he needed a road bike. The Forgotten Samurai walked into the store and announced, "Dudes, I need
to get a bike. But I don't ride freaking factory bikes. I was like, 'I've
got to build something. You've got to let me build it.'"

Dom and the bike shop owners hit it off. He started hanging
out at the shop, talking about BMX, musing about his lost tribe,

a lost era. Sometimes while they worked, he would lend a hand. "And they're like, 'Oh, you can wrench?' I'm like, 'I'll build you anything.'"

When he wasn't wrenching or bartending, Dominic rode his new bike. He rode up to 400 miles a week. He lost 50 pounds in two months. So what if he was living at his mother's and he still got that restless, sad, why-can't-I-feel-more-peaceful ache every so often? He worked and he rode and he worked and he rode. "If I wasn't working, I was riding. I would just keep my whole system pounded to where I was too tired to even go out and do something even if I wanted to."

He got involved with some women, nothing serious. He stopped recovery meetings. He was sober, so what was the point? The husband-and-wife bike-shop owners worried about him. The wife, whose name was Wanda, told him about this woman she knew, an athlete. Wanda told Dom that the athlete was coming by the store, and that he was going to teach her to use clipless pedals. Oh, yeah, and Dom wouldn't believe her calves.

The Wrench and the Junkie: Still Searching

"I used to be a crackhead," the wrench said to the woman with the calves.

"I used to be a heroin addict," she replied.

A parking lot. Tuesday afternoon on a late August, Ohio afternoon.

"But I don't do it anymore," Judi said.

"Neither do I," Dominic said.

"I still smoke a little weed here and there," Judi said.

"Me too!" Dominic said.

They exchanged high fives. They laughed.

He called her two days later and wished her luck in the tri and when she asked what he was up to, he said he was planning to go for a 35-mile ride on Monday, and she said she wanted to go too. He reminded her that she was competing in an Olympic-distance triathlon the day before, and she would probably want—and need —to rest.

Really? She—who had swam in a scuba wetsuit and pushed her big hunkin' hog of a machine the distance in her first tri, who had

puked every day on her way to middle school, who had kicked
heroin with a week's worth of grilled cheese sandwiches—she
wouldn't be able to handle a leisurely cruise on a road bike? She
would need to take it easy? The wrench thought he knew what was
best for *her*?

Judi told Dominic what she wanted and would need. Maybe
she cursed a little. That's when it occurred to Dominic, who had
bossed around most of his many fiancées-turned-exes, that he was
not going to spend a lot of time bossing around the woman with
the calves.

He didn't call for a week, and by then Judi had decided he was
the man she wanted to spend her life with, so she was annoyed.
When Dom came to his senses, he introduced her to Bruno and
Judi bought Bruno a new collar and took him running and Dom
watched and learned that not only was she strong, she was "an awesome dog handler." Judi introduced Dominic and Bruno to her
two Dobermans, Ari and Lucy.

In August, Dom (everyone calls him Dom, except Judi, who
calls him Dominic) moved in with Judi. A few months later, after
Bruno had learned to coexist with Ari and Lucy, he moved in too.

They dreamed of maybe one day opening a bike shop. Dom
would make it in his image, high energy and down to earth, a haven for BMXers and kids, maybe a big plasma screen that would
show kung fu movies for the customers (and Dom) to watch. Judi
would use her business skills for something other than expensing
$10,000 cruises for other people. They would be partners. But they
had only $500 between them. Unless a big sack of money fell from
the leaden Ohio sky one day, booking travel and bartending would
have to do.

Dom cooked, Judi ran the dogs. They both stayed away from
recovery meetings—Judi because, "I was addicted to races." She
was doing criteriums by then. "I thought this was how I could avoid
doing AA. I could just go out and train." Dom stayed away because
he was Dom.

Judi left the corporate world and took a job as a barista. Dom
started drinking, and stopped, and started, and stopped, and
stayed sober. Bruno died, of cancer, in 2009 and a month later,
they got a replacement pit bull, Fausto. Lucy the Doberman died,
and they found another pit wandering the streets. They named
her Lola. They decided, together, to quit smoking pot.

On September 23, 2010, on the second day of the Interbike trade show in Las Vegas, they gathered a few other cyclists and friends and drove to the Fast Lane chapel, where they were married.

There was no reason to feel uneasy, or dissatisfied. They had Fausto and Lola and Ari, and their house, and income, and now they had each other. But they wanted more. But what? How? When? Would the ache ever go away?

Judi was taking the garbage out in early June 2012, when her mother called. Judi's father was dead. Audrey had told Judi days before that he was in the hospital, but Judi had been busy, and tired, and a little grouchy, and besides, she'd never been that close to him, there had never been much happiness between them. He'd been hospitalized before and survived. And her mother had always been dramatic.

Judi let go of the garbage bag. She lay down on her back, in her yard, still holding on to her cell phone. She looked at the sky.

A month later, Audrey called again. Judi's father had left some money for her. A minuscule fraction of his estate—much, much, much less than he left to his child by his second wife, not an amount Judi cares to discuss.

Still. A big bag of money from the leaden Ohio sky.

Judi hung up the phone, and she looked at Dominic and told him the news.

"A fucking dream come true," she said.

"And he goes, 'We're buying a house, I'm getting a new car!'

"And I said, 'No, we're opening a bike shop.'"

Judi & Dom

Judi stares at a computer screen, at skinny wraiths with wrecked, luminous eyes. One of them, a boy in jeans and a T-shirt, appears, then disappears. "He's dead now," Judi says. Another lost child, grinning with rage. "Him, I don't know." A girl. "I think something bad happened with her." And another boy. "He's dead too."

One image slides onto the computer screen and stays. The woman with a skull on her shoulder, platinum hair, holding a 40-ounce bottle like it's the most precious thing in the world, like it might save her. Judi doesn't say anything.

On the wall opposite Judi, a young man flies over concrete can-yons, shoots down rails, catches gaudy, dangerous-looking amounts of air. Dom installed the 64-inch plasma screen when the store opened in February 2013, and when Dom is working, the screen is always on, filled with reigning BMX princes (there aren't a lot of princesses) or kung fu movies.

Judi and Dom named their store Spun because when you're on a mountain bike and you're in trouble on a trail, you are "spun out," and because when tweakers take too much crystal meth, they become "spun." And, Judi says, "spun rhymes with fun and that's our thing. We're here and we're keeping the fun in cycling. You ride it, we'll dig it, that's our motto."

They knew there was a heroin trade in the neighborhood, Cin-cinnati's Northside, and crime, but tough neighborhoods didn't scare them and they were learning that one of the things that could fill that nameless emptiness they shared, that could ease that nagging ache, was helping others. The dogs taught them that. Other addicts and drunks taught them that. To calm themselves, they could be useful. "The neighborhood needed a bike shop," Judi says.

They knew that many of the merchants carried guns, and 18 months after they opened, a man was shot and killed in the middle of the street, just a few doors down. His daughter had been one of their regular customers, "always mad, just a little butch," Judi remembers. "We started calling her The Girl Who Wouldn't Smile. And that was before the shooting."

Kids often get free repairs at Spun. Customers who buy new bikes get free tune-ups for a year. Dom offers free courses on how to fix a flat and keep bikes clean. Judi runs a Ladies' Night, where she springs for pizza, and any woman who walks through the door gets a slice or three, along with lessons on how to do a basic tune-up. Judi also works with a nonprofit group, Wordplay, to deliver books by bicycle to low-income children around the city for an organization called Ride for Reading.

Bicycle commuters without cars who need repairs get bumped to the front of the line. The work is done immediately, usually the same day, even if it involves Dom working late, which it usually does, "because that's how they get to work every day." Everyone else comes next. Spun doesn't specialize in high-end merchandise. You can't find a bike for more than $1,000 there. But you can find a lot of other things. "I give them options," Dom says. "I tell them, 'If you spend this money, this money, or this money, here's what you get, here's why you get it, and here's what makes things better than other things.' I spell things out for them.

"I want a blue-collar bike shop, the working man's bike shop. Those people deserve to have one-on-one attention with people that are knowledgeable too. They might not have all the money to buy a $4,000 bike, but it's a market that's screaming to be helped."

The market seems to have gotten the message. The BMXers came, naturally. The young ones because word got out about the free wrenching, and because every BMXer in Cincinnati worth his grind wax knew or had heard of the Forgotten Samurai. Many had watched him shred (he still had it) at Delhi Park, a place Judi considered slightly sketchy, or indoors at Ollie's Skatepark.

At Ollie's, Judi would sit with the mothers. One day, one of the mothers' mothers—a grandmother—asked Judi, "Which one is yours?"

"That one there," Judi said. "That 40-year-old bald guy. That's my boy."

Kids love him. Adults too. Sometimes it seems that the lonelier they are, the less they fit in, the more people love Dom. A young man with severe ADHD, who talks even more than Dom, visits the shop several times a week, asking questions, studying parts, chewing the fat with the Forgotten Samurai. A mentally disabled man in his thirties rides a city bus to visit Dom and Judi twice a month, and his father, who lives out of state, emails Judi when his son needs parts for his bike. An 11-year-old girl visits the shop regularly. Once tough and always angry, now she's just tough. She jokes with Dom. Judi sends her Instagrams, and teases her when she's in the shop. The Girl Who Wouldn't Smile smiles now. Every so often, she giggles.

They sell BMX bicycles and affordable commuter models and mountain bikes, and the rare custom job, like one Dom built for a doctor, "a murdered-out flat black with all-anodized red cabling. It weighed sub 17. Hand-laced Belgian wheels I did for him, red spoke nipples, black rims. A beautiful, beautiful bike. Worth about five grand. I cut him a deal, about four grand. I still made my money, he was very freaking happy." (That's how Dom speaks, in paragraphs filled with action, adjectives, and great enthusiasm.)

From its first year to its second, Spun's sales jumped 41 percent.

"Forty-freaking-one percent," Judi says. (That's how Judi speaks, with precision, economy, and great enthusiasm.)

In 2014, the National Bicycle Dealers Association named Judi and Dom's business one of the 297 best bike shops in the United States, out of 4,000 independent shops in the country.

"It was like, 'Oh, shit, we're legit,'" Judi says.

It's January, only midafternoon and already almost twilight. The couple is in the shop, on the bench opposite the 64-inch plasma screen, holding hands. The wrench and the junkie are too old and too damaged to believe that love conquers all, or even that it conquers most. Judi's house, which is now their house, still hasn't regained even a third of its value. The BMX ramp that Dom built takes up the entire garage. Dom needs to cut down on caffeine, not only because he's plenty jacked up without it, but because drug use has left him with some kidney issues. (The doctors also told him to stop drinking Monster Energy and Red Bull.) There's still too much crime in the neighborhood. Lola the pit attacked another dog earlier this year and Dom and Judi held Lola as she was put down. Dom stayed up all night. Judi stayed up too. She was worried he might drink.

That was a bad night. There are others.

They know that getting high will only make things worse. Staying healthy helps, but good intentions aren't enough to make everything right. They were never enough.

So they will feed and run the dogs and Judi will do her best to make the tough little girl not so tough and Dom will do favors for kids and commuters and even a few adults and just to make sure that Dom's kindness doesn't kill them both, Judi, when she's in the back office, "I have to come out and say, 'Okay, there's too many discounts here, how much are you charging for this? What's labor going to be on this?'"

A wintry Wednesday afternoon. Dom and Judi holding hands on the bench, murmuring things to each other, and every so often Dom glances at the kid on the plasma screen catching air the Forgotten Samurai never caught, never will catch, and Dom looks okay with that. Judi will telephone her mom tomorrow morning, as she does most mornings. Dom will work on bikes, a few for free. Judi will turn 45 on July 30, and six days later, Dom will turn 42. They'll celebrate with their families. Next week, Dom will hang out at Delhi Park where he'll tell kids to always wear helmets, to not do stupid things like he did. He'll call each one of the boys "little man." It's quiet at Spun this day, which is rare. If you're the type of person who inclines toward anxiety, who tends toward rumination and angst, who in the past has done terrible, awful things to yourself just to find a little peace, but can't do those things anymore, then this would be a good time to ruminate. To engage in silent battle with phantom demons. But there are dogs to feed, numbers to crunch. There is inventory to order. There are bikes and broken lives to mend. Demons will have to wait.

The couple that met at Ron and Wanda's never would have worked out. The wrench and the junkie were doomed. But these two holding hands, whispering to each other, that's another matter. Their song is a honeyed ballad. The story of Judi and Dom might have a happy ending.

KIM CROSS

The King of Tides

FROM SOUTHWEST: THE MAGAZINE

MY FATHER AND I leaned into the current, waiting for the salmon. We were up to our hips in the Kasilof River, a milky-blue ribbon of glacial melt that snakes through southern Alaska. It was nearly midnight, and the stars winked faintly through a pewter sky. Beneath the brim of his fishing hat, my father, a month shy of 73, smiled into the sweeping twilight.

We had traveled more than 3,000 miles to catch an Alaskan king salmon. Formally called the Chinook, it is a bucket-list fish, the largest of all salmon and notoriously elusive. Landing one is an angler's version of sinking a hole in one. Our whole family—my husband, parents, uncle, and three boy-cousins—had traveled from Alabama and Florida to pursue this singular goal.

It was the last big family fishing trip before life would change forever. My husband and I had just seen our baby's heartbeat, a flickering light on an ultrasound screen, a glimmer of our future. I wasn't showing yet, so it still felt theoretical that this tiny tadpole swimming inside me would grow into a man. I imagined my father teaching this future person how to fish.

On this Friday night, the river bend was buzzing with locals and a smattering of tourists. Two Texas boys in their twenties wobbled over the rocky shore in skinny jeans and cowboy boots. "We been fishing for three days," one said, "and not a single bite!"

Within minutes, a brawny local hooked a fish and handed him the rod. "Boy, you said you wanted to catch a king," he said. "Here you go."

The skinny Texan tottered down the bank, fighting to keep his rod tip up as it bent with the weight of a keeper. The locals hollered from the sidelines: "Keep some pressure on him!" "Don't let up!"

The Texan wrangled the monster onto shore, where he bent, panting, over the thrashing fish, not knowing what to do. Someone sauntered over with a river rock and bashed it in the head. The fish went still. I felt a twinge of envy. Then I felt my rod tip nod. As we entered the ancient paso doble of angler and fish, I recalled the words of my favorite guide, who taught me how to land a whopper on a pencil-thin rod. *Let him run when he needs to run, then gently bring him back. Not too much pressure, or you'll snap the line. Be patient and tough. You'll tire him out.*

Slowly, deliberately, I let him run and brought him back, the whine of the spinning reel sinking lower each time. When I saw the arc of his back break the water, my king took away what little breath I had left. He was big. He was strong. And then he was gone.

Dad smirked and deadpanned his favorite line: "There's a reason they call it fishing, not catching."

I was not a natural-born angler. Just an only child who tried too hard to be the son her father never had. He was a man who worked long hours and closed each day by wetting a line on the dock behind our North Florida home. As the bay turned silver in the dying light, he would reel in a trout, a black drum, or a redfish. He would clean it with an ancient blade and toss the scraps to the gathering fish. Mom would cook it, and after dinner we'd scrape our plates off the dock.

My father never taught me how to swing a bat or throw a ball. But he taught me how to throw a cast net, bait a live shrimp, and remove a swallowed hook without turning the fish inside out. And he coached me through landing my first real lunker: a 40-inch jack crevalle.

It was the spring I turned 13. We were staying at my uncle's house on the inland waterway near Destin, Florida, where a billboard welcomes tourists to THE WORLD'S GREATEST FISHING VILLAGE. My uncle first sounded the battle cry: "Jacks!"

A distant relative of the tuna, the fork-tailed jack is a fighter, aggressive and powerful, built like a bullet of muscle. Reeling one in is like breaking a mustang, or so I had heard over tables piled high with boiled shrimp.

Dad and I sprinted, barefoot, to the dock, where we spotted a fountain of baitfish leaping, the sign of predators attacking from below. Dad unmoored the Boston Whaler and put me at the helm, rigging the rods with steady hands while I motored toward the bait spray.

I killed the engine 100 yards away and coasted toward the ripples. Dad sailed his lure hundreds of feet, the silver cigar minnow arcing through the air in an elegant parabola. Flustered, I botched my own first cast, releasing the line with my thumb a little late, and my lure splashed awkwardly close to the boat. Embarrassed, I reeled in for another try. And then the line came alive in my hands.

We fought for an hour, the jack and me, forked tail versus teenage biceps. Dad talked me through from the sidelines. "Let him run," he said. "Keep tension on the line."

I did as I was told, and the jack ran again and again, exhausting the both of us. He dragged the boat 300 feet before he lost his fight. When he surfaced in a flash of silver, I gasped. I had never seen anything so big, or so lovely.

Dad gaffed him in a single swipe and heaved him into the boat. That fish weighed roughly a third of me. My heart still races, remembering.

Our first day of fishing in Alaska was not what we expected. We stood shoulder to shoulder with hundreds of fishermen lining Ship Creek in the heart of Anchorage. The stream is only 10 or 15 feet wide, yet it holds king salmon that weigh up to 40 pounds. Their shiny backs protrude from the shallows as they slide their bellies over the rocks, through a hallway of anglers casting close enough to catch each other (and they do). They call it "combat fishing." The poor fish seem to have no chance, until you consider that spawning salmon do not eat. They have, in this final stage of life, a single-minded mission: get home, procreate, and die.

Like all salmon, kings spend their lives in a round-trip journey between river and sea. After hatching and feeding on insects, the year-old fish make their way to the ocean, riding the current downstream for hundreds or even thousands of miles. They spend the next few years in salt water as eating machines, packing on fat for the journey home. And then, at some genetically preprogrammed point in time, each one yields to the ancient call of the stream where it was born.

Salmon imprint the smells of all the places they have traveled and remember the Earth's magnetic fields where they entered the sea. The homecoming fish transform from silver "brights," darkening into deep olive and red. They stop eating, fueled by their body fat for the unrelenting fight upstream. Their homing devices bring them remarkably close to the spot where they hatched, sometimes within yards. There, they find a mate, leave a fertilized clutch, and yield to immutable death. Their bodies are absorbed by the stream, adding nutrients to the water, feeding generations of insects that will one day nourish their young.

The only thing my father loved more than fishing was taking others fishing. No guest was spared a 5:00 a.m. wake-up call and an eight-hour trip on the Boston Whaler to fish the Gulf of Mexico. He would stay up late the night before, rigging tackle. He never overslept. I wonder if he slept at all.

When I came home from college, he'd shake me gently awake with a weathered hand already cold from the bait well. I would stagger downstairs, rubbing my eyes, and fumble over the coffee. By now Dad would have been up for an hour, readying the boat. My only job was to drag the cooler of snacks—beef jerky, powdered doughnuts, and potato chips—to the boat, where I'd promptly make myself a pallet of towels and fall back asleep on the bow.

Those fishing trips were a way to connect with my dad, who struggled with small talk but delivered eloquent fatherly lectures on the end of the dock. The Boston Whaler was our sacred place. For boyfriends, it was a test.

In college I brought a boyfriend home, a nice guy, but not much of a fisherman. My father took him out and treated him kindly, but had to bait his hook. The guy stuck around for six years, but he wasn't a keeper.

One year after college, I came home from California with an Eagle Scout who caught trout on dry flies in mountain streams and cooked them on a one-match fire. This one knew a blood knot from an improved clinch and actually owned a rod. The day before Thanksgiving, we motored into the predawn. I was allowed, by now, to drive the boat, but no matter how many times I had navigated the shallow pass through the bay, Dad made me use the GPS.

The swells were fairly big that day, and as we trolled the Gulf for king mackerel, the boat rolled, pitched, and yawed. The Eagle Scout had good sea legs, but he had worn running shoes, which gave little purchase on the sea-slick deck.

"Fish on!" I yelled. Dad brought the boat to an idle. Mom danced around the console, trying to stay out of the way. The Eagle Scout, not one to be outdone, soon had a fish on too. Mine came in first, a good-size king, about 20 pounds. Dad gaffed it and hauled him in, still flapping. As he knelt over my fish, removing the hook, a rogue swell pitched the boat. The Eagle Scout lost his balance. His foot flew up behind him.

And kicked my father squarely in the face.

My father looked up, more in shock than pain, with a look I had never seen. His glasses were askew. One eye was bruised. Blood gushed from a cut beneath it. My mother and I rushed to his side and fussed.

The Eagle Scout kept fishing. He knew that if he lost that fish, his first trip on the boat might also be his last. He landed the mackerel and then apologized. My father accepted with a smirk. He stashed this away as material for a wedding toast.

On the fishing trips that followed, the Eagle Scout knew he had been forgiven when Dad let him drive the boat. One day he made the trip to Florida alone, to ask for my father's blessing. On the boat, he chickened out. That night, on the dock, he mustered the courage. "Fish on!" my father said. He made the Eagle Scout wait until the fish was in his hands.

Five years later, on that dock, we handed my parents a picture of an ultrasound.

On our third day in Alaska, we stood on the edge of a manmade fishing hole called, inventively, The Fishing Hole. Stocked for tourists and boatless anglers, it was a gravel pit circled with lawn chairs. It required a new rig: two piggybacked hooks with hunks of herring dangling from a red-and-white bobber. I scowled at that sad plastic bobber.

"Just think of it as a strike indicator," the Eagle Scout said.

He was right. It was no better or worse than the sprig of yarn that served the same purpose on fly-fishing trips. But the aesthete in me took umbrage. "Why don't we just throw out a trotline?" I snarled.

I introduced my father to fly-fishing on a private stream in Georgia. I had learned how to lay a midge on top of a pool, dimpling the surface. I loved the dance of sunlight on water, the music of the stream, the sigh of the line monogramming the air with elegant cursive loops. *If you are going to fish and not-catch,* I thought, *this is the way to do it.*

But we caught. Big fish. Fish-tale fish, the kind you recount to eye-rolling grandkids. I wanted my father to catch one and fall in love with fly-fishing too.

Gear helps, so I gave him a fishing hat with a handsome, sweeping brim. He loved that hat. But he did not love fly-fishing. With failing eyesight, he struggled to thread the microscopic eyes of dry-fly hooks that vanished in his saltwater hands. His sea legs were useless on slick river rocks, and once I saw him hand the guide his tangled line, too fine to unravel by feel. He would never do that on his boat. I should have realized, then, that my father belongs to the sea.

Instead, I took him on a float trip. I rented a charming riverside fish camp and hired a guide with a boat. It was a perfect spring day, with golden light and trees shooting out their first buds. The river was freckled with rising fish, and our guide knew their favorite shoals. We caught a few rainbows and threw them back. My father smiled a lot and thanked me.

Later, Mom and I ran out for a bit. We returned to a sink filled with trout. Dad smiled and held up a spinning reel. "I'm a member of the catch-and-fillet club," he said.

Day four in Alaska, and still no salmon. Desperate to avoid getting skunked, we chartered a deep-sea boat. The vessel could not hold all of us, so the men motored out to sea. Some say a woman on a boat brings bad luck. Mom and I didn't want to chance it.

They came back with sunburned smiles in a boat riding low in the water, fish wells brimming with 50-pound halibut. "It's like pulling a car hood up off the bottom," my father said. But it wasn't king salmon.

On day five, the Anchor River opened at midnight. We arrived at 11:30 p.m. to find the best spots on the river occupied. At precisely midnight, the rods began ticking like metronomes. Cloud cover blocked the northern lights, but even in the dark I could feel the salmon darting all around me. The water thrashed as they leaped upstream, fighting the current, finding their way.

I snagged the bottom again and again, snapping my line and tying on lure after lure, until my jaw grew sore from biting off line. I caught bushes behind me, logs in the river, and trees on the opposite bank, where countless lures dangled like ornaments.

Just before we left, a king salmon swam right into me, colliding with my wading boot with such downstream force that it nearly knocked my feet out from under me. Dad laughed at me—fishing, not catching. We flew home without a king.

Two months after the trip, on our four-year anniversary, my husband and I learned our baby's sex. My father would have a grandson.

That same evening, we learned the news about Dad: small-cell carcinoma. Stage 4. Inoperable. Prognosis: one to two years.

A month later, in September, he took one final fishing trip to Alaska with his buddies. This time, he got a king salmon. He did not catch it in a stream. He caught it in the sea.

Two days after Christmas, he was there when his grandson found his way into the world, and he held the boy—seven pounds, seven ounces—a keeper. On Dad's good days, we stuffed his fishing vest pockets with diapers and toys. On the bad days, he fought an upstream battle with a single-minded goal: live to see his grandson's first birthday.

He died 17 days too soon. But those 348 days their lives overlapped were a journey I would not change. He got to stare at his sleeping grandson's face, feel tiny fingers paw his nose. I like to believe there is healing in that.

We held his service on the dock, a wake in a no-wake zone. The pastor wore a fishing shirt. The Eagle Scout rigged the boat for a trip but left it in the slip. We set Dad's rod on the end of the dock so friends could wet a line and say good-bye.

Six months later, on what would have been his 75th birthday, we drove his boat into the Gulf. Crying quietly, eyes stinging with sunscreen and salt, we gave him back to the sea. I watched my father's ashes disappear into the endless blue. Then we rigged a solitary rod and trolled the lonely waters without him.

My son was five years old when I dug out the last Alaskan fillets. They were freezer-burned beyond edible, but I had never been able to bring myself to throw them away. I decided it was time. I held them in my hands, then let them slip from my fingers into the trash, exhaling as I turned away, pretending it did not matter.

Within seconds, I came apart. I dug through the garbage, heaped our sad catch on the counter, and sobbed over it, tasting the salt of tears before they froze on the icy fillets. I gathered the fish in my arms and gently placed them back in the freezer.

When it came time to sell the Florida house, I took my son and the freezer-burned fish to the dock where my father had raised me. I unwrapped each piece, and with Dad's old knife I cut each one into chunks small enough for my son to hold in his hand. And there, beneath seagulls wheeling above, we fed the gathering fish.

ELI SASLOW

"Why Him, Why Me?"

FROM ESPN: THE MAGAZINE

FOR THE FIRST few seconds after the collision, the game continues as if nothing has gone wrong. The crowd cheers in approval. A
coach screams: "Great block!" Cody Seward, 17, who delivered the
hit, stands and chases the play a few yards downfield. Only after
the punt return ends does Cody turn back and notice Tyrell Cameron, 16, still lying there behind him. "Come on. Get up," Cody
says, but Tyrell doesn't respond, and he doesn't move.

Soon a trainer sprints toward the players, followed by a few
coaches, Tyrell's aunt, and a chaplain, who huddles the group together in prayer. "Please, Lord, let this boy wake up," the pastor
says. An ambulance races onto the field, its wheels digging ruts
into the grass, and one paramedic cuts off Tyrell's jersey while another administers CPR. "Go, go, go!" a paramedic shouts. They
strap Tyrell to a gurney and speed to the hospital. Cody walks back
to the visitors' sideline with nine minutes and 11 seconds left in a
Louisiana high school football game he no longer wants to play.

"How bad is it?" Cody asks his coach, Jason Thompson. "Does
he have a concussion? Could he be paralyzed?"

"We just don't know yet," Thompson says.

"But it can't be that bad, right?" Cody asks, because nothing
about the play was particularly violent or memorable. It had been
a routine block made away from the ball on a punt return. Cody is
only 5'5" and 145 pounds, a diminutive linebacker who had never
intentionally hurt anyone: he had spent most of his childhood acting in community plays and musicals before arriving at Sterlington High School, which to his disappointment didn't offer a the-

ater program. What it did offer was a 4,000-seat stadium with new artificial turf, a state-of-the-art weight room, and a football team that serves as the cultural heart of a rural community in northern Louisiana. So Cody went out for the team, set a state record in an off-season weightlifting competition, and earned his way into the defensive rotation. "All heart and hustle," the coaches say of him, and now on the sideline of the field at Franklin Parish High, Cody wonders whether maybe his hustle had been the problem. Why hadn't he let Tyrell stumble by him? Couldn't he have relaxed on an inconsequential block in a meaningless fourth quarter? Why had he leaned into the hit with his shoulder?

The stadium remains eerily quiet for the rest of the game. Tyrell's relatives leave to follow the ambulance to the hospital, and one of them calls Tyrell's mother, who starts racing home from a family funeral in Texas. When the clock runs out, the stands are almost empty. Thompson gathers his Sterlington players onto the field. On this early-September evening, they've beaten Franklin Parish, a bigger school, 14–0. "I'm so proud of you for this win," he says, launching into a standard postgame speech, but then someone whispers into his ear. The person has just received word from one of the medics. Tyrell had broken his neck—and never regained consciousness. Thompson turns back to face his team. "I don't know how to tell you guys this, but he didn't make it," he says. "He's dead."

Cody, kneeling at the edge of the team's postgame circle, stands, screams, and starts to run. He throws off his helmet. His hands rip at his jersey. "I killed him. I killed him," he shouts. The team pastor chases him down and wraps him in a hug. An assistant coach forces him back onto his knees. "This isn't your fault," the pastor says, but Cody covers his ears and shouts into the turf. "I killed him," he repeats again and again, until his teammates finally lead him off the field and into the parking lot. The rest of the players climb onto the school bus, but Cody gets into the front seat of his mother's car. "What can I say to make this okay?" she asks him, and he tells her not to say anything. They ride 65 miles in the darkness, their silence interrupted only by the beeping of Cody's cell phone.

"It wasn't your fault," the opposing team's quarterback texts.

"We will get you help, some therapy, some counseling," a mentor messages.

"Psalm 56-4: When I am afraid, I will put my trust in you," his youth pastor writes.

Cody turns off his phone, retreats into his house, and takes melatonin to help him sleep. He lies on the couch until 3:00 a.m., replaying the collision in his mind, then finally drifts off until well after noon. A parade of visitors comes by, each one offering help in his or her own way. Cody's mother takes him to church. His friends take him out for barbecue. Thompson, one of the best defensive coaches in the state, comes over and says he has watched the videotape and studied the collision from every angle. Cody had delivered a textbook hit as his team set up a wedge block for a punt return. Tyrell had been stumbling. He had seen Cody only at the last moment. He had dipped his head at impact. "There's no reason," Thompson says. "It was just a fluke thing."

"Please," Cody tells his coach. "I just don't want to talk about it."

He stays home from practice Saturday, skips it again Sunday, and by Monday, Thompson's concern for Cody has turned to fear. On social media, there are unsubstantiated rumors that Cody is depressed, even suicidal. Thompson calls a meeting with the team's unofficial pastor, Chad Merrell, to seek advice.

"Doesn't Cody need to talk to somebody about all of this?" Thompson asks. "I don't want to pretend to know what he's feeling right now, because I don't."

"There's probably one person in the world who really understands," Merrell says, remembering another football collision, from a college game 26 years before. That hit also resulted in a catastrophic neck injury. It also left one player dead and another despondent—blaming football, blaming himself.

"I think I know who can help," Merrell says.

Brad Gaines receives a call Tuesday morning on his cell phone, which has as its screen saver a picture from that football game long ago. Every time Gaines's phone rings, every time he checks his email, there it is staring back at him—an iconic image from the worst moment of his life, 26 years ago. In the picture, Chucky Mullins's neck compresses awkwardly against Gaines's back. Mullins's arms begin to sag and his head starts to droop. The memory of that hit always lurks in Gaines's mind, sneaking up on him a dozen times each day. "You can't ever run from it," he explains, so it feels easier to look down at his cell phone and be confronted by a picture of it.

"Hello," Gaines says now, and on the other end of the line, Jason Thompson introduces himself. Gaines has gotten several calls and emails over the past decades from strangers in times of trauma, and the frequency has increased in recent years. Seven high school players have died as a direct result of injuries in 2015 alone, and now Thompson tells Gaines about one of those: another fluke, another dead player, and another survivor who seems lost.

"I know it's a lot to ask, but I thought maybe you could call Cody," Thompson says.

Gaines thinks it over for a few seconds. His schedule is already packed. He is in the middle of moving into a new home. He has a health care business, a wife, and four children in Nashville.

"Why don't I just come down there?" Gaines says.

A few days later, he leaves in the evening to drive 460 miles and meet a 17-year-old stranger in Sterlington, Louisiana. He has always liked driving at night, when the roads are quiet and he can hear himself think. "My therapy time," he calls it, and he finds himself returning to the same memories. "It's like I'm always trying to fit the pieces of a puzzle together in my head. Why him? Why me? Why couldn't we both walk away? Why were we chosen?"

He drives through fields of white cotton and rolling hills dotted with poplars and elms until he comes into Oxford, Mississippi, its hulking white football stadium so familiar to him from that October Saturday in 1989. It had been homecoming in Oxford, and Gaines and his Vanderbilt teammates emerged out of the locker room to a frenzied pregame crowd that dumped cups of Coke over the opposing players' heads. "Let's shove it down their throats," the Vanderbilt coach had instructed, and Gaines and his teammates marched down the field on the first drive. Gaines, a wingback, went out on a short passing route on a third-and-goal and made the catch near the end zone just in front of Mullins. The defensive back leaped into the air and dipped his head, planting his helmet in the middle of Gaines's back and making the tackle. Mullins collapsed to the ground, arms and legs flailing in all directions. He couldn't feel his hands or fingers. Four of his vertebrae were broken. He was airlifted to a hospital in Memphis while

Gaines went back to his own sideline, so nauseated he thought he might throw up.

Two hundred and forty miles away from Sterlington now. Gaines continues out of Oxford and drives into Clarksdale, birthplace of the blues, with its faded brick juke joints. "Some places get stuck in time," he says, tucking a pinch of chewing tobacco into his mouth.

He had gone to visit Mullins in the hospital a few weeks after the collision, even though Gaines's coach warned him it was a bad idea. "I have to know what he thinks of me," Gaines told his coach then, so he drove to Memphis on his Christmas break and took the elevator to the intensive care unit on the fourth floor. He was wearing his Vanderbilt letter jacket, and the hallway was filled with Ole Miss fans who had come to Memphis for a bowl game. "Why wouldn't they blame me for being the reason he's in here?" Gaines wondered. "Couldn't I have run a different route? Couldn't I have ducked when he hit me?" He walked into the hospital room and saw Mullins lying flat on his back, his body withered to 125 pounds and his head bolted in place so all he could see was the ceiling. Gaines considered backing out of the room before Mullins saw him but instead stepped up to the bed. "I'm so sorry for all of it," he said, introducing himself. Mullins motioned for Gaines to lean toward him. A surgery had taken away Mullins's voice. "It's not your fault," he whispered.

They became friends in the months after that, talking on the phone every few days and often discussing football. Mullins asked Ole Miss to set up a special phone line that would broadcast live sounds from the team's practice field. That way he could dial in each afternoon and hear the familiar soundtrack of his life: whistles, shouts, and collisions. He missed the game in the same way he missed the person he had been.

Gaines, meanwhile, had started skipping his practices, avoiding the sport that had defined so much of his worldview. His dad had played in college. His uncle had won a Super Bowl with the Steelers. Two of his older brothers had already made it to the NFL, and that's what Gaines seemed destined for too. He finished out the season after Mullins's injury with "no fire for the game, no passion, just faking it," he said, yet still managed to lead the SEC in receptions. Then, early the next year, he left the team. Every play felt to him like a potential catastrophe. Every defender reminded him of Mullins. He stopped attending any games and rarely spoke to his family about the hit. "When I thought about football, all I could think about was what was happening with Chucky," Gaines says. The screws in his head. Those ghostly arms. The get-well bouquets wilting away in his hospital room. The smell of antiseptic. And then, in spring 1991, the call Gaines received from Mullins's guardian. "It was a blood clot. He's on life support. Come fast."

One hundred miles left to Sterlington, and Gaines presses down against the accelerator on an empty two-lane road, trees blurring into the horizon, picking up speed.

He'd driven to the hospital to stand vigil for Mullins during those last three days, after doctors could find no evidence of brain activity. He had stayed up with him into the night, then slept in his old Buick in the hospital parking lot. On the last day, he had watched as the nurses removed the tubes, screws, heart monitors, and breathing machines and then propped Mullins into a reclined position, placing a football in the nook of his limp arm so he could take his final breaths. Gaines had stayed in the room until the official pronouncement, then sprinted down the hallway, out of the hospital, off to a distant helipad, down into the woods, and out onto a country road. He needed air; he needed space. And 24 years later, he was searching for it still.

Sixty miles away now, well after midnight, and his car is alone on the road. He had made so many lonely drives like this, including dozens to Russellville, Alabama, to visit Mullins's grave three times each year. He always goes on Christmas Day, on the anniversary of the hit, and on the anniversary of Mullins's death to weed the ground and polish the gravestone. It began as a ritual of obligation, or even guilt, but for the past few years he has gone for his own reasons. His wife can't quite understand it. His children never make the trip with him. "It's almost a relief to be there," Gaines says, because he thinks about Mullins at least 20 times each day. "I'm carrying this around all the time, and finally I'm not alone with it. I'm in a place where the gravity is totally understood."

He arrives in Sterlington a few minutes before 2:00 a.m., checks into a roadside motel, and sends a text to Cody.

"Hey bud, see you in the morning. I might get more out of this than you do."

They meet at the Sterlington football field and go out for lunch. "Thanks for coming, sir," Cody says. He seems nervous, and now

Gaines feels anxious too. If he had spent 26 years trying to understand his own collision, how could he help Cody make sense of his
in a few short hours? Rather than offer advice, he decides to listen.
They talk about the fried chicken. They discuss Eminem. Cody
brings up his girlfriend, whom he met at a local haunted house
after a football game.

"Girls and football," Gaines says, and they both laugh.

It has been a little more than a week since the collision, and
Cody has tentatively returned to the Sterlington football team, unsure what else to do. "I have to at least try it," he says. His friends
are connected to the team, and so is his routine and his identity,
and all of that just seems like more to lose if he quits playing. He
had spent his first practice back in the coach's office, sitting on a
couch and watching video of the hit. What everyone had told him
seemed true: it was a clean block, unremarkable, a fluke. "I know
I didn't do anything wrong," he says, and so he has gone back to
being a linebacker and back to his place on the punt return team,
even though the new anxiousness he feels sometimes manifests in
chills and sweats. He can still deliver a hit. He can still make his
reads on defense. "The old Cody," coaches have begun saying of
him, but the game feels different.

He has been taught at Sterlington to play football with joy and
controlled adrenaline but also with solemnity. He and his teammates lift weights in the off-season under the picture of a gigantic
panther, its blue eyes staring down at them: "The eyes of the past,
present and future are upon you," it reads. They walk into a field
house where trainers have posted a motivational quote on the wall:
"The measure of a man is the will to fight, and fight and then fight
some more, because surrender is death, and death is for the weak."
They stand together to listen to pregame prayers over the stadium
loudspeaker: "Lord, protect these athletes and make them strong
for their battle." And Cody has believed all of those things — has
hit the weights harder than any of his teammates, cranked music
into his ears before the games, bit down into his mouth guard at
the first whistle, and then lost himself in the delusion of the game,
as the best players always do.

And yet: "Now it's kind of like I'm playing but not feeling all the
things I used to feel," Cody tells Gaines. "It's still good. It's okay.
But it isn't the same."

"I get that," Gaines says, because after he left the team at Vanderbilt he avoided even watching football for seven or eight years.

"I always feel like I'm going to wake up feeling better and not think about it, but it's kind of always there," Cody says.

"It takes time," Gaines says.

"When does it start to go back to feeling normal?" Cody asks.

"I don't know," Gaines says, even though he does in fact know. There is no going back. He has come to think about his life in two chapters, a before and after, and the dividing line is the hit. Mullins's former teammates became some of Gaines's closest friends. He chose health care for his career and named his first business after Mullins's jersey number, 38; he still hopes to open a medical center for athletes with head and neck trauma. His own son, 11, begged to play football, and Gaines spent months debating the conflicting influences in his life before allowing it. "You have to understand the rewards and the risks," Gaines told his son, and to prove he did, his boy chose to wear number 38.

But why should Cody know any of those things now, at 17? He still drives a truck his father had given to him, and it smells like his girlfriend's perfume. He calls his teachers "sir" and "ma'am." He is a junior who has barely begun to think about where he wants to go to college, or what he might study. In the months before the collision, his only medical concern came every few weeks when he visited the team trainer to ask for extra Tylenol after his braces were tightened.

"This might be something you think about for a long time," Gaines says, simply. "You have great support and a lot of people who care about you. There's no one right way to go through this. You can decide what you need. You can decide how to carry this."

What Shamikka Cameron needs in the days after her son's death is to speak with Cody. "I'd like to talk to the one who made the hit," she writes, in a message to the Sterlington football team's Facebook page, but at first Cody tells his coaches he isn't ready for that conversation. He doesn't know what to tell her. He has no idea what she might say to him.

"Whenever he's ready to talk, Mikka's ready," Shamikka says in another message, then she waits for Cody to call.

Tyrell had been the oldest of her three children, with big eyes,

a goofy smile, and an infectious love of football. "Show me something!" he had yelled at his teammates on the sideline, so often
that Franklin Parish had turned that phrase into its motto. Tyrell
had been playing since he was 10, at linebacker and receiver, and
had hopes of making it at Alabama or Ohio State, the two teams
he loved to watch each weekend. "All he knew about his future was
that it was going to include a lot of football," Shamikka says, and
Tyrell had told friends to expect a breakout sophomore year. A
week before the season started, he ordered a pair of cleats online
with his mother's credit card for $143, the most expensive shoes
he'd ever bought. "Boy, that's a crazy price!" Shamikka said, so
Tyrell had promised to wear the cleats for at least two years.

On the day of the season opener against Sterlington, Shamikka
and her family had traveled to a cousin's funeral in Texas. Tyrell
stayed behind in Louisiana to play, and he inked his cousin's name
next to the letters "R.I.P." on his new shoes in the moments before
kickoff. Then, a few hours later, Shamikka was eating fast food
when she received a series of frantic messages from her sister, who
was at the game. "He's hurt," she said. And then, a few minutes
later: "It's bad, real bad." By the time Shamikka drove four hours
back home, the hospital had collected her son's uniform and cleats
in a duct-taped box labeled "personal effects." She went straight to
the funeral parlor, arriving in the middle of the night, and asked
to see Tyrell.

"He was just laying there, looking pretty much how he always
did, and that just destroyed me," she says. "I hated myself for not
being there when it happened."

Coaches from both teams wondered whom Shamikka might
blame: Herself for letting Tyrell play? His teammates for failing to
protect him? Paramedics for being unable to save his life? Cody for
delivering the hit? Football itself?

Instead Shamikka went back to the cab of her truck and sobbed,
drove home, prayed, and then posted a message on her Facebook
page: "Let go and forgive. He died playing a game that he loved."

Coaches gave her a DVD of the game, but Shamikka didn't want
to watch it. The medical examiner released the autopsy report—
broken neck, internal bleeding—but she had her own explanation. "It's a God thing, not a football thing," she says. "There's no
logic. It just happened. Now it's all about how we respond."

Days later, when three of Tyrell's teammates considered quitting football, she called and told them Tyrell would have wanted them to play. When the Franklin Parish coach asked how he could help Shamikka's kids, her 12-year-old said he wanted a jersey with his brother's number and a guaranteed spot on the team. And when Franklin Parish couldn't decide whether to postpone its next game, scheduled for the week after Tyrell's death, Shamikka insisted that the team play.

"Those kids need to be together, doing what they always did," she says. She knows football is a dangerous sport; she had once watched Tyrell collapse on the field and sprinted out to check on him, fearing the worst, even though it was only a cramp. "It's a serious game," she says. But she also believes that football had given her son close friends, self-confidence, and joy. "Getting back to football is the only way these kids are going to get through this," she says.

So on a Thursday night six days after Tyrell's death, she forces herself back into the stands to watch Franklin Parish play again. It will be a month more before she can talk about Tyrell without crying and two months before she feels well enough to return to work, but there she is sitting in the stands. "All these people coming up to me, and inside I just want to scream," she says. She watches as Franklin Parish players walk onto the field standing arm in arm with 50 players from Sterlington, who have come to support them. And then the next night, a Friday, Cody and his Sterlington teammates take the field for their game surrounded by Franklin Parish players, who have come directly from Tyrell's wake.

Tyrell's funeral is on a Saturday, and more than 200 people from Sterlington want to attend. The church is already expecting an overflow crowd, and Thompson, the Sterlington coach, doesn't want to take up seats. He asks Shamikka whether she and her family would greet the Sterlington group for 10 minutes before the funeral. They meet her in a large room at the River of Life Church in Winnsboro, Louisiana, where Tyrell's custom-made casket lies, imprinted with his jersey number. The Sterlington team gives Shamikka a donation check in Tyrell's memory. Then the players come up to her, one by one, to pay their respects.

Somewhere in the back of that line is Cody, nervous, still not quite sure what to say. He introduces himself. He starts to fumble for the right words, telling her how sorry he is, how much he'd been thinking of her, how . . .

"Come here," she says, interrupting him, pulling him into a hug. Cody feels surprised, then grateful, then relieved. "It's okay," she says, and that is all she wants to tell him.

Nearly a month later, Cody and his Sterlington teammates host one of their biggest rivals, Ouachita Christian, and Gaines decides he wants to be there. He has been texting Cody and talking with him on the phone, and now he sets out again from Nashville. Another 460 miles, another quiet road, and this time when he reaches Sterlington he sees lines of traffic stretching from the stadium, a mile in every direction. The school parking lot fills with cars, and so does an adjacent field. "Is everybody in Louisiana going to this?" he wonders. He parks at a barbecue restaurant down the block and follows the crowd.

By the time he climbs into the stands, they are already filled with more than 3,500 people. The band plays the national anthem. The student section starts the wave. Sterlington players run out from the field house, rub a panther statue for luck, then sprint through an inflatable tunnel. "Ladies and gentlemen, your undefeated team, the boys in your hearts, the pride of Sterlington, here come your Panthers!" says a voice over the loudspeaker, and the metal bleachers begin to tremble and shake.

Cody runs out in his number 44 jersey, coincidentally Gaines's old number, and for the next two hours the man traces the boy's path across the field. Gaines spent nearly a decade avoiding football, but eventually the game pulled him back in. "If Chucky didn't resent it, why should I?" he has recently decided, especially since the game had shaped some of the most significant relationships in his life. His family now has season tickets at Vanderbilt, and sometimes he goes with his brothers. They make for a "battered crew," he says. There's Chris, 50, his ankle disfigured from a dozen football-related surgeries; Greg, 57, already receiving permanent disability payments from the NFL after 40 surgeries on his back, knee, and shoulders that resulted in an addiction to prescription pain drugs; and then Brad, the youngest brother, with scars of his own. But they still sit together in the stands. They still cheer and lose themselves in the game.

In Sterlington, Gaines is on his feet to watch Cody in a tight second half, banging the bleachers in excitement after a late home-team score and then biting his lip when the win escapes the Panthers on a last-minute interception. "So close," he says. He walks onto the field to see Cody.

"Unbelievable game," Gaines tells him. "I really got caught up in it."

"Yeah, heartbreaker," Cody says, and then his family members and some of his teammates come over too, and for a few minutes they rehash it all.

Once the crowd thins, Gaines asks, "You doing okay with everything?"

"It gets better and better, and then it just kind of stays there," Cody says.

"Yeah, it does," Gaines says.

They hug and make plans to meet the next morning for breakfast, then Cody heads back to the locker room. The stands empty out. The coaches leave the field. But Gaines is still standing on the turf, and nearby two 10-year-old boys start playing catch. "Here, I'll be quarterback," Gaines says, calling for the ball, and he begins throwing passes, huddling the boys together to draw up plays on his hand. The janitorial staff starts cleaning the field. The opposing team boards its bus. "I should really go," Gaines says, and there are so many reasons to walk away: seven high school players dead in the year, Tyrell Cameron among them. Chucky Mullins long before that.

But right now it is just a football and an empty field, and he is throwing 40-yard strikes and his arm feels good. His mind is clear. The game seems simple. The boys run fly patterns into the end zone, and each time they return, Gaines tells them the same thing.

"Let's do another."

ERIC MOSKOWITZ

Her Decision, Their Life

FROM THE BOSTON GLOBE

HALFWAY BETWEEN THE Calphalon pans and the electric toothbrushes, Jessica Kensky's right leg began to throb. She made it 20 minutes at Bed Bath & Beyond before the pain forced her to abandon the errand in search of a place to sit.

She found relief on a barstool in clearance, but her leg ached the moment she stood to rejoin her husband, Patrick Downes. He examined one trash can for their kitchen and then another, considering their merits like a person without pain. "Just *pick* one!" Jess wanted to scream.

Sweat beaded on her forehead; she bent her knee to take pressure off her foot. It was too much to stand, so she limped to the car to wait it out.

Nearly two years had passed since the Boston Marathon bombing stole the left legs of both Jessica and Patrick below the knee, and Patrick was becoming himself again, like most of the survivors they knew. But Jess remained a full-time patient at 33, trapped by a damaged right leg that refused to heal.

For so long, she had wrestled with what to do, but alone in the parking lot she now knew. I can't live like this, she thought, ready to amputate.

And then the next morning in the shower, she dropped the soap. Sitting on the tile bench, she reached down and picked it up. It was that easy because she still had a right leg to plant, however imperfect. In her mind, she saw herself as a double-amputee, two partial legs dangling over the edge, no way to reach the soap. Like Humpty Dumpty, she thought, and she filled with doubt.

It had become her life. Pain and doubt, doubt and pain.

Back when they had been clinging to life in separate hospitals, a photo of them—their engagement shot, Jess leading Patrick by the hand in a vivid dress—had gone viral, a captivating image of the newlyweds who lost their left legs. They managed to preserve their privacy through that first year of healing, but they felt compelled at the anniversary to come forward with other survivors as ambassadors of the city's recovery.

Last April, Jess sat with her service dog, a black Lab named Rescue, and watched Patrick rise before a packed Hynes Convention Center at the televised tribute service and speak of the "individual snapshots of grace" that had buoyed them all after so much pain. They gave their first interview as a couple, honest about their challenges, grateful for so much generosity—the tailor who altered Patrick's wedding suit to fit over his prosthetic, the employees at the hospital where she worked who donated enough vacation time to keep her on the payroll and preserve her health insurance for years to come. On Marathon Monday, they pumped hand-cycles from Hopkinton to Boston, crossing the finish line together while holding hands; a photo of the moment beamed around the world, a symbol of triumph and hope.

Things had seemed so bleak after the bombing. Jess could barely stomach the sight of her amputated leg, burying it under blankets, refusing when doctors wanted to remove her right leg too. "They'll have to kill me first," she told her father in the hospital that first week.

But it was like her even then to set a timeline. A driven oncology nurse who had run two marathons, she vowed that they would be through all this in a year. By the second summer, she told herself, Patrick would resume his training as a clinical psychologist and she would return to MGH. If she could no longer handle the physical demands of long shifts on the chemo and bone-marrow transplant unit, she would study for a nursing doctorate and another job at the hospital.

And from afar, it looked like they were turning the corner. But when the tributes and cameras receded after the first anniversary, Jess felt hopelessly behind. The bomb had destroyed her right Achilles' tendon and shattered her ankle and heel, and a year after reconstructive surgery she could still barely walk on it, even with a high-tech brace designed for the military.

She consulted experts in Boston, Baltimore, and Seattle, in Philadelphia, Orlando, and Houston. Each surgeon offered a different idea to make her leg more stable, less painful—harvesting bone from her hip or her thigh to construct a new heel; weaving this or that tendon to build a new Achilles; fusing the bones in her ankle to lock her foot into place.

Each time, she and Patrick would get their hopes up. Then doubt would creep in or another specialist would dash the plan. Even as a nurse, with a radiologist father, she found it impossible to navigate. And the more her leg ached, the more she felt stranded, lagging her own timeline and everyone else—ready now for some doctor to declare they were wasting time and should just amputate. But none did, not yet.

Then there was the money. The year before, she had left $1 million on the table by insisting on saving her leg. The two survivors who lost both legs had gotten $2.2 million apiece from the One Fund, while the 14 of them who initially lost one leg got $1.2 million each.

She was grateful for that sum and appreciated how many people lost limbs to illness or accident and got nothing. She knew the expenses this money would help cover—an adaptable home, an SUV big enough for two wheelchairs, special prosthetics for running or sports, not covered by insurance. But how could she not dwell on the other million, especially if she missed it only for the sake of an excruciating year followed by a lifetime as a double-amputee? With a summer deadline looming for a supplemental award, she thought about cutting off her leg for the money.

But she feared aging, having seen so many older patients who still had both legs struggle, scared how she and Patrick would ever care for each other if he had one leg and she had none. And the thought of losing her toes—the pleasure of a pedicure, of sinking them into the sand, of warming them against Patrick in bed —made her despair.

She didn't want to amputate, and she didn't want to keep her leg like this either. What she wanted was her old life—still caring for patients at Massachusetts General Hospital, running along the river or walking through Harvard Square with Patrick, cooking dinners together and bringing meals to friends. She wanted to go back to a time when she could envision needing a wheelchair only to leave a hospital with a baby in her arms, Patrick pulling the car around.

What she needed was to figure out the better of two bad options and restart her life.

So she agreed when an MGH orthopedist recommended more imaging last June. A scan showed a misaligned ankle, a mysterious chunk of floating bone, and a fibula (calf bone) that had never properly healed, all potential causes of her dysfunction and pain. A follow-up scope showed something even worse: her ankle was so out of whack that mere movement made cartilage and bone shear off.

In the OR, the surgeon removed the debris but said the grinding would continue unless she underwent major surgery to fuse her ankle and lock her foot at a right angle. Except that could change her stride and put more pressure on her compromised heel—relieving pain in one place but worsening it in another.

While they were trying to sort this out, a painful knot of bone grew at the end of Jess's amputated left leg, making it impossible to wear her prosthetic—heterotopic ossification, a haywire response to blast trauma that has also afflicted many Iraq and Afghanistan war amputees. On top of that, her vision was fading, another delayed symptom of the blast.

So there she was in her wheelchair, feeling desperate and trapped, when her sister called early last summer. She said Jess needed to talk to a soldier named Ferris Butler.

Sarah Kensky, six and a half years younger, had dropped everything after the bombing to move from California and become their live-in caretaker. Now she was a BU public health student with an internship at Walter Reed National Military Medical Center, working on a study of resilience in wounded soldiers. That was how she met Butler, a double-amputee.

Jess sat on his number for a few days. She had talked to so many amputees that first year, when everyone who knew anyone missing a limb had offered a phone number or an email address, well-meaning if not always helpful. Some of them she could not relate to; some made her feel worse. "All these one-legged, no-legged people," she thought. "What's one more going to do?"

Then she thought of how good Sarah had been to them and

decided to text Butler for her sake, setting up a time to Skype. On the surface, they had little in common besides amputation. He was a ninth-generation soldier—a Butler had served in every conflict since the American Revolution—who loved to fish and trapshoot and lived on Maryland's rural Eastern Shore.

She opened her MacBook, and Butler appeared on screen, ruddy-faced and friendly. He told her his story: He was a newly promoted first lieutenant leading an infantry platoon in Iraq when a hidden explosive launched his armored vehicle into the air in December 2006. The blast shattered his legs but left them attached, and after medics saved his life, surgeons tried to save his legs.

Jess had wondered whether soldiers were better equipped to handle trauma like this, braced for it in some way that a Boylston Street bystander could never be, but so much of what Butler said matched her experience.

He recoiled at the thought of becoming a double-amputee. He struggled with depression, and when he watched soldiers who had arrived after him at Walter Reed—new amputees—walk and then run on artificial limbs, he was angry at how his real legs kept him stuck in a wheelchair. "You feel like your life is on pause, that you're wasting time," he said, and she knew just what he meant.

After 52 surgeries and more than a year trying to save his legs, Butler and his team decided to amputate below the knee, first the left side, then the right. And he had come through it to the other side, getting married, earning an MBA, serving on nonprofit boards, starting a business, leading a full life. He was where he wanted to be at 36, even if the "middle got a little mixed up."

They talked for three hours. Butler could see how badly she needed help—the kind of expert advice they could provide at Walter Reed, which had treated hundreds of blast amputees from the Iraq and Afghanistan wars. He had an idea.

"I don't even know if this is possible," he told her, speaking quickly now. "I don't even know if they're allowed to see you. But if I reached out to the doctor I'm thinking of, would you be willing to come down?"

Jess hesitated. The thought of navigating airports with Patrick —two prosthetics, a wheelchair, a service dog, and one healthy leg between them—made her shudder.

But Butler's adrenaline was going. He called his old surgeon and asked whether he could bring Jess in for a tour and some advice. He reached out to Veterans Airlift Command, a network of private pilots who transport wounded soldiers and their families. All he had to say was "Boston Marathon," and both immediately wanted to help. So did a car service and a Sheraton near Walter Reed, where Butler lined up an accessible guest room with a roll-in shower.

He called with the good news and promised to meet Jess and Patrick after they landed. But when they got to Hanscom Field to board the plane—a low-bellied turboprop chosen for ease of entry from a wheelchair—he surprised them at the airfield.

Butler felt like he was on a mission—never forgetting the way people had taken care of him, wanting to pay it forward—and tried to think of everything for the two-day trip. They landed in Gaithersburg, where Butler and his wife had prepared Jess and Patrick's room with a welcome kit—Maryland craft beers, Old Bay seasoning, even a crab chew-toy for Rescue—and took them to dinner.

The next day, he drove them through the checkpoint at the front gates of the base known as Naval Support Activity Bethesda —243 acres of green lawns and glimmering buildings anchored by the new Walter Reed, born from the merger of Washington's old Walter Reed Army Hospital and the National Naval Medical Center—and guided them to the America Building, a 515,000-square-foot outpatient recovery center.

They stared in disbelief at the technology—labs with infrared cameras and interactive screens surrounding special treadmills—and the presence of an on-site prosthetics lab, where amputees could drop in for adjustments or new limbs altogether. In the civilian world, you needed a prescription and appointment to see your prosthetist, whose office might be miles from your home, let alone your doctor, physical therapist, and occupational therapist. Here, you rolled out of bed and saw them all at once, your care team working together.

Most of all, they were awed by the gym at the heart of the America Building's Military Advanced Training Center, known as the MATC (pronounced "mat-see"). Back home, rehabilitation meant elderly people learning to walk after breaking hips. Here, they saw young men sweating in Under Armour gear—double- and even triple-amputees hoisting heavy medicine balls or charging around the track in a harness hooked to the ceiling.

Then they got a workup from Dr. Benjamin "Kyle" Potter, chief orthopedic surgeon for Walter Reed's amputee program, and Dr. Paul Pasquina, director of physical medicine and rehabilitation. Jess's case presented nothing new to them, and they gave her what she craved, a clear message: it's premature to give up on your leg, and here's what we propose to try to save it.

They recommended fusing her ankle while resetting her lower-leg bones, smoothing down the remnant of her heel, and manipulating the tissue underneath for more cushioning. They said her left leg should be shortened to better fit a prosthetic, in addition to the need to excise her painful bone growth and remove more shrapnel. And they suggested doing it all at once, one long operating session and concentrated recovery, instead of the endless surgery-recovery, surgery-recovery cycle proposed by her civilian doctors.

But it was just advice. Jess wasn't their patient. The day was dwindling, the turboprop waiting to carry them back to Boston. She could see everything she needed was right here—the expertise, the facilities, the peer support. She joked about chaining herself in place. And then, gravely, asked whether she could stay.

"This is way above my pay grade," thought Potter, a lieutenant colonel in the Army Medical Corps. He had treated occasional civilians at Walter Reed, but they were all government contractors with high-risk jobs or allied foreign nationals wounded overseas —never someone hurt at home on a city street.

But they could try. Pasquina, a retired colonel, offered to draft a memo to the Pentagon seeking what they called "Secretarial Designee" status for the two of them. Patrick's case was less complex, a "paper cut" in Walter Reed terms, but they could push him to a higher level and keep the couple together. Even for Jess's dire case, though, it was just a shot.

Getting status was mysterious, not like filling out an application for grad school. Jess tried not to think about it too much, knowing she would be more devastated if it fell through. Patrick was invigorated, though, seizing the opportunity to do more than comfort her while she suffered.

He made a list of everyone who might help and contacted them all. People like U.S. Representatives Doris Matsui and Jim McGovern, for whom they once worked as new college grads trying out life on Capitol Hill; former Boston mayor Tom Menino, who had taken them under his wing after the bombing, ailing himself, and was close with the vice president; and Senator Elizabeth Warren, whom Jess had regaled in the hospital that first week with a story about sprinting home from work to vote for her before the polls closed.

They all said the same: we'd love to help, but what do we do? None had gotten this request before.

For weeks, people called and wrote on their behalf, while Jess and Patrick girded for life without Walter Reed. "No news," they wrote August 20, on a recovery blog for family and friends. Jess booked two dates at MGH in September, one to meet again with surgeons, one to schedule the OR—maybe for fusion, maybe amputation.

And then, August 22, Jess woke to a text from Dr. Potter: You're in!

They cheered from the bed. Potter was heading into surgery but would call again soon. Her phone rang while they were in their apartment-complex gym. Potter read a letter from the Pentagon. For a full year, Jess could receive care from Walter Reed's doctors, prosthetists, and therapists—billed to her insurance. It was Friday. If she could be there by Monday, he could get her in the OR by the end of the week.

There was no word on Patrick's status, meaning he could come only to support Jess, not to receive care himself. Monday would be their second wedding anniversary. And he was preparing to start a new fellowship soon at BU. But there was no doubt in his mind that he would put his career on hold, that they would both go, leaving immediately. They hung up and started packing.

Recovering Among Fellow Fighters

On the drive down, anxiety set in, like they were heading off for freshman year of college. They worried about fitting in on a military base, two Cambridge residents who could count the soldiers they knew on one hand. And they felt pangs of guilt about Jess receiving the highest care an amputee could imagine—care meant for people wounded serving the country—when so much generosity had already come their way. "How much do you get in a lifetime?" she wondered.

Thursday she went into the operating room with Potter and Dr. Scott Shawen, an orthopedic foot-and-ankle specialist and Army colonel, for extensive surgery on both legs, nearly eight hours on the table.

If all went well, by mid-fall her left leg would be healed enough to be fitted for a new prosthetic, and by Thanksgiving she could try putting weight on her right leg too. The three to six months after that would serve as a "stress test," revealing whether to keep going or amputate.

She spent a week in the hospital, where her Walter Reed nurses impressed her with their kindness and skill managing her wound pain and phantom pain, which returned with surgery on her left leg. Her pulse was so rapid that doctors feared an embolism, but Jess knew it was from anxiety and being out of shape, cooped up so long in her wheelchair. She urged them to let Rescue crawl into bed with her, his soothing powers outweighing the infection risk. He had been trained to fetch objects and brace her in a fall, but now he brought her heart rate back to earth.

She was still an inpatient when her physical therapist, Kelly Mc-Gaughey, appeared, getting her arms moving and giving her a ball to squeeze between her bandaged legs. No time for self-pity here; they had to keep the hip muscles she would need for walking from getting any weaker.

Jess hoped to move from there into "wounded warrior" housing, a dorm with 153 two-bedroom, two-bath apartments for soldiers doing full-time rehab and their spouses or caregivers, but that would take some work. They moved instead into Fisher House —like the Ronald McDonald House, but for families of patients at military hospitals—getting a hotel-style room with two twin beds. "Return to the '50s," she posted online.

She started rehab in the MATC, five days a week; Patrick came along for support, doing his own workouts on the side. She saw her physical and occupational therapists, McGaughey and Annemarie Orr, as she had seen herself, young women in the health care field who were skilled and demanding and compassionate, fast friends who soon felt like family. And the doctors, they were like brilliant camp counselors, CVs a mile long even as they traded jokes and worked out beside patients, in gym shorts and with lanyards around their necks.

On weekdays, the base hummed with 15,000 people moving among 70 buildings, some rolling by on Segways or in wheelchairs, others running, a mash-up of street clothes, uniforms, and scrubs. Turn a corner and you might find a Marine in workout gear with a gym bag and extra leg over his shoulder, or a visiting Brad Pitt, or a pile of cards from schoolchildren thanking soldiers for their service.

That Jess and Patrick had not served made them self-conscious at first. But the soldiers took what happened in Boston personally and embraced them. They made friends in the gym and the cafeteria line, people inviting them to come shopping at the Navy Exchange or sit by the fireplace at the ski-lodge-style USO. They stood at attention when "Reveille" echoed across campus, and they learned to recognize the distinct camouflage patterns of each service branch.

On weekends, quiet set in, and they relished it or left to spend time with Patrick's brother or Jess's aunt and uncle nearby. Ferris Butler invited them for a visit to the Eastern Shore, and Jess studied all he could do on two prosthetics, an energetic host fixing breakfast and moving around with ease. That lifted some of her fear.

But outings in Washington were bittersweet, the city where Jess and Patrick met, layered with memories of being young and dating. Now they stuck to restaurants that were ADA-compliant, but still there were places like the Bethesda brewpub where she had to ride a boxy lift down the steps from the entrance to the dining room, the noise making everyone turn and stare. Patrick climbed in with her, hugging her and kissing her forehead.

The Walter Reed campus still felt surreal, but she found a comfort there she hadn't known since before the bombing. They could move about with prosthetics, in a wheelchair, no limbs on, whatever, and nobody would blink. These are my people, Jess thought.

Medication stabilized her vision, and by the second week of October, her left leg had healed enough to don a new prosthetic. Jess stood, with assistance, for the first time since spring.

"Vertical again!" she posted online, beaming next to Patrick while propped on a set of parallel bars. She was still not allowed to put weight on her right foot, but she practiced walking on crutches, supported by a harness hooked to the gym ceiling.

Around Halloween, Patrick got Pentagon approval for his treatment too. They celebrated with friends and took a tour of the Naval Academy in Annapolis, dressing up Rescue in a midshipman's costume. Jess received a protective "walking boot" for her right foot and permission to stand long enough to brush her teeth, with the hope that she would be well enough to try walking in a few weeks.

Her right leg healed ahead of schedule. The doctors studied her imaging and said the fusion looked just how they hoped it would, her bones lined up, no more grinding and scraping. Though her ankle would be sore, it should get better with time. And while there was no substitute for the fibrous fat of the body's natural heel pad, they hoped the cushion they had manipulated there would help her pain underfoot too. On November 12, the day after Veterans Day, they gave her the green light to walk.

Finally. She had not been allowed to walk since June. Now she stood and put one foot in front of the other and walked—real walking, no parallel bars, no crutches, no harness hooked up overhead—and everyone around her beamed. Ferris Butler was there, and when they walked down the hall to get coffee in the lobby, he had a hard time holding back tears. None of them had ever seen Jess up and about like this.

But as satisfying as it should have been—she envied people who could walk and talk and get coffee, no big deal—her heart sank. The pain was worse than she had anticipated, radiating from her ankle, heel, and foot all at once.

The doctors asked for patience. She had been living with this for more than a year and a half; they had been with her only a few months. One day became two days. Two days turned into two weeks. When the pain did not improve, they tried steroids and collagen injections, gave her anesthesia, and deployed the OssaTron, a shockwave device to deaden nerves and stimulate blood flow, deafening as a firing range. They were trying so hard it scared her a little, made her want to get better for them as well as for her. But still her leg ached.

She thought about nursing school at Johns Hopkins, when they talked about understanding pain as the "fifth vital sign." Pain was subjective, they said. Pain was whatever the patient said it was, rated from zero to 10. Zero meant no pain, 5 was distracting, 10 was the worst you could imagine, pain she never knew until she got blown up.

This wasn't that awful, but it was close, an 8 or a 9 if she spent more than a few minutes on her foot. She knew what it felt like to run through pain in a marathon, and this was different, this was worse.

As November rolled into December, her doctors could propose only one other surgery that might help, fusing her subtalar joint — the lower joint that allows the foot to tilt inside or out — the way they had fused the ankle. But it was no guarantee.

She wasn't interested, not with more wheelchair time before she could test it again, not with her Pentagon status running out in the summer and her own clock ticking, all those months when she could be practicing on two prosthetics instead.

Her care team knew how hard she was working, how much she had tried, how bad the pain remained. There would be no six-month "stress test." If she wanted to amputate, they were ready.

Projecting Confidence Despite Pain

Hearing them say it out loud brought relief, but also fear. Suddenly, this was real. She tried to tamp down her nerves. She wanted to schedule surgery as soon as possible, cut down the wait. She had one last box to check before the OR: the psychological evaluation.

Everyone knew what it meant, giving her a wide berth as she left the MATC for the corridors linking the America Building to the Eagle Zone hospital, home to psychology on the seventh floor. She tried to project confidence as she walked, passing a hall of flags and a statue of a medic hauling a wounded Marine, and she wondered what questions they might ask that she hadn't been turning over in her mind for months. She knew what it was like to lose one leg and had tried everything reasonable to save the other.

Two and a half hours later, she emerged in a daze. A psychiatrist and a psychologist had asked so many questions, drilling down to her childhood and back. It was December 9. They advised her to take more time. They wanted to meet again, not just with Jess but with Patrick and the team around her, her doctors, her physical and occupational therapists, her prosthetist and case manager and social worker. It would be tough to get them all together before the holidays, and better for her not to be recovering from surgery during Christmas and New Year's, they said—better to go home and be with family. Keep thinking, they said.

The last thing she wanted was more time on hold. She considered advice Butler had given her, and a Vietnam veteran had given him: "Whatever you do, you can't spend the rest of your life playing the what-if game." Now she doubted herself. What if she *had* rushed into it?

Head swimming, she retreated to the grass beside the America Building to toss the ball with Rescue, her favorite escape. Watching people run and jump could make her feel jealous, but watching Rescue do it made her feel free. This time, though, she could not clear her mind. She kept thinking of her leg—the one she was standing on this very minute—and her five remaining toes, the ones she had sunk into the sand on their honeymoon in Aruba just two years before. She wanted that old life back. Was getting rid of this leg the best way to do it?

Because she had told herself the psych eval would be a formality, she had scheduled an appointment afterward to get fitted for a better wheelchair. She canceled that now and went back to the MATC to find Kelly McGaughey and Annemarie Orr. They knew she could get overwhelmed when the pain was at its worst, and they talked with her about trying to find a way to compartmentalize it—to tap her nursing instincts and monitor her leg on the trip home without letting it spoil the holidays.

She left the base with Patrick, driving to a coffee shop to be alone together. She didn't feel like calling her family or updating her blog, not yet. Back at the Fisher House, she napped until evening. When she woke up, she felt lighter, glad now that the psych eval had slowed her down.

In the morning, the two of them called for the usual shuttle to take them across campus to the MATC, sitting close together in the van, knees touching. They climbed out at the America Building, walking past a piano player in the lobby, heading for the gym. From a therapy bed in the middle, McGaughey called out to Jess.

"Wait till you see your book!" the physical therapist said.

Over in OT, Orr waited at a butcher-block table with a three-ring binder they had prepared for Jess to track her leg over the holidays. The therapists decorated it with a cartoon of Jess, Patrick, and Rescue and musical notes, titling it "Track Yourself a Merry Little Christmas."

Jess laughed. "You guys are so cute," she said.

"We're such dorks," Orr said. They joked about how the male soldiers might respond to the same festively decorated book. But Jess knew it was what she needed, a way to be her own nurse, monitor herself, make something like an evidence-driven decision.

They talked about the coming trip home: When Jess and Patrick had left suddenly in August, they were poised to move into a Cambridgeport condo renovated for accessibility. Now they could finish outfitting it, and Jess could try life again in a neighborhood designed for walking and riding the T, venturing out on her own for errands or appointments.

"Do you normally just take the T to do that?" Orr asked.

"In my *normal* life," Jess said. "Not since this happened."

They talked about distance, stamina, and pain, about how standing could be as hard as walking, about what might happen if she got all the way to the T but found it too crowded to get a seat. "Don't overdo it in the morning," Orr suggested. Think about "energy conservation"—sit to brush your teeth or cook, save standing for when you need it. But really test what it would be like to live with that right leg.

"Max it out," she said. "If you have doctor's appointments, just be like, 'Patrick, I'm gonna see you later,' and go do it. You have his phone number if you need it."

In a month, when she came back, they would go over the notebook. In the meantime, Orr said, she could call or text about anything. "That's what I'm here for."

"Make sure you have fun," she added, but "don't limit what you're doing. And push it."

"I promise," Jess said.

One Last Effort Before a Change of Course

Six hundred days had passed since the bombing. Jess wanted to try something different each day home, something she had not done since back then. On the third day, they drove to Bed Bath

& Beyond to buy odds and ends for the condo. On the Friday after Christmas, she would try walking to the grocery store. She conserved her energy all day, venturing no further than the dog park beside their building, sitting on a bench while Rescue rolled in the mud.

At 4:00 p.m., it was time. Patrick grabbed some reusable bags, and Jess picked up the vest that tells strangers Rescue is working. "Let's get dressed," she said to the dog.

They started down the sidewalk holding hands, laughing and smiling. When they reached the turn, Patrick pointed to construction down the block—on the supermarket side—and suggested they not cross yet, to avoid extra steps.

They had been walking five minutes when Jess—wincing now, her breathing labored—tugged Patrick's hand toward a bench on the left. "I'm gonna sit for a minute," she said. "I don't even know how far it is, but I'm a 7 or 8 out of 10 right now."

They had gone fewer than 800 feet, halfway from their condo to Star Market. Pitiful, Jess thought. Rescue crawled under the bench.

The pain receded once she sat down, as it almost always did. She exhaled. "Let's go," she said.

They walked silently to the store, where leaning on a grocery cart helped. Jess's smile returned, and she read items they needed from a list on her phone while Rescue sniffed under the dairy case. By the time they turned for the second aisle, she was walking gingerly again. She waited with the cart, bending her knee to take weight off her foot, while Patrick grabbed what they needed.

They loaded up ingredients to host a weekend chili party, a reunion for Boston-area bombing amputees. In produce, Patrick's phone rang, Marc Fucarile calling, one of the survivors from Stoneham.

"Heather's coming, Roseann's coming," Patrick said, continuing to fill the cart. "Come at six . . . We're making chili."

At the register, Jess bit her lip in silence while Patrick chatted with the cashier, ran back for more butter, and swiped the credit card, looking, in his jeans, like any other able-bodied shopper. On the way home, Jess clutched a bag in each hand, rocking as she walked, too determined to talk. In the kitchen, she sank onto a cushioned stool, letting Patrick put the groceries away.

Before dinner, she went upstairs to take Tylenol for the pain from a baggie in the master bath filled with orange prescription bottles, skipping the narcotics. A Boston Strong bracelet rested under her toothbrush on the vanity.

A lift had been installed in the condo, but she took the stairs, clutching the railings, one careful step at a time. When she returned, Patrick had started chopping vegetables for dinner, and Jess grinned.

For 20 minutes, they worked the way they used to in the kitchen, side by side, Jess joking about Patrick's music selection ("You going for the dance club tonight?" she teased him, as Usher streamed from his phone), the only difference from the old days being her stool. When she stood, though, the pain returned.

Once dinner was in the oven, she brought out her notebook. "Star Market," she wrote under that day's activities, marking the pain as a range from 5 to 9. Under activities avoided, she put, "Unload groceries (Patrick does)."

She flipped back through their 12 days home. On December 19, she walked to the T and met a friend at Crema Cafe, their favorite coffee shop. On December 23, she took herself to the dentist and Rescue for a real walk, all in one afternoon. On Christmas Eve, they hosted a party, Jess circling the room to freshen glasses and collect plates.

But some days she had done nothing. No day involved as much walking as a single day back at work or school. The pain was consistent—so many 7s and 8s, code for sweating and lip-biting, desperate to sit. After the Christmas Eve party, both legs throbbed for hours even after she lay down.

"I wish someone else could crawl into my body," she said, "and confirm that *that* is too much pain."

She dropped the pen. She put her head in her hands and exhaled. Patrick leaned in and touched her cheek. In their hearts, they both knew.

That night Jess looked through photos on her laptop: Standing in the sand on their honeymoon, sipping cocktails, arms entwined. Reading on a beach chair in a bikini, toes painted. Sitting on the floor in Cambridge, Patrick's parents' Bichon in her lap. Out in Arizona for a wedding with her family right before the bombing, hiking in shorts. All she saw were legs.

She could never look like that again. And sometimes she would ask Patrick, Do you remember what I looked like back then? He would hesitate because it was normal to forget, because he didn't want her to compare herself to the impossible. But he did remember, and she wanted him to.

After New Year's, she called Walter Reed to plan their return. They had been approved for "wounded warrior" housing, which would make recovering from surgery easier. She booked a second psych eval and a date to amputate the following week.

Part of her still felt like she could wrestle forever with what to do, waiting for the invention of some miracle brace, fearful of being a double-amputee in old age, but she would not. She needed life to get better now. She needed less pain. She had tried hard to save her leg, and now she would try something else.

Their family helped them pack, and two weeks ago, they climbed into the car, leaving the condo they had known for a month. Pulling out on a misty evening, they turned right and then right again, heading for the highway, back to Walter Reed.

On the day before her surgery, they made another trip: out to the beach in winter, so Jess could feel the sand between her toes one more time.

CHRIS WIEWIORA

Board in the Florida Suburbs

FROM THE ATTICUS REVIEW

I KEPT MY RIGHT foot planted on our driveway as I rolled the skateboard back and forth, feeling and hearing the slow rotation of steel ball bearings turning inside the wheels. Specks in the black sandpaper-like griptape reflected the sunlight and the grit scraped my sneaker. I heaved in the thick, humid air that kept my sweat from evaporating.

I was psyching myself. I couldn't determine if I was psyching up or out. I was delaying gravity. I looked like I was supposed to ride, but I wasn't riding.

It wasn't even my board. My buddy Dylan had loaned me his board. I had biked home with it on my handlebars and then hid it in my closet. I'd been practicing rolling down the driveway since I came home from my new bus stop.

I didn't yet know the meaning of the words *shape, flow,* and *pop.* I would come to know those words as the feel of a board; the motion of arcing in crisscross lines on the ground like a surfer riding up and then looping—cutting back—on a wave's crest; and the pound of the tail and then lift of the nose into an ollie that raised the board magically above the ground.

I was still at the top of our driveway—Mom was out on errands and Dad had hours left at work—in the lull of the suburb's afternoon. I was considering riding into the street.

I took my right foot off the ground and placed it on the board's tail, careful not to set my weight on it and seesaw backwards. For a second, I stood still. Then, the board began to roll.

I was headed down to the street, but first the gutter. I'd jumped off or run out and away from the board the other times I rode toward it. This time, I stayed on. I bent my knees. I led with my shoulder.

The front wheels dipped into the gutter. I tipped forward, the board's nose dove, and then I was pitched off. My knee shredded along the asphalt.

Blood leaked down my leg. I wouldn't be able to hide the blood that would ooze through pants. I was marked and I would have to show my parents what happened and then tell them how I wanted to do that forever.

On a sheet of Mom's stationery I wrote:

I want to skateboard.

Then I added a comma and what I meant:

I want to skateboard, and you can't stop me.

I tore the sheet from the pad. The sheet underneath had a ghost of my sentence above. I tore that second sheet off the pad too. I crumpled it together with the first sheet. I threw them both away in my bedroom's trash can.

I had taken the stationery from Mom's drawer by the telephone. I only used my desk in my room to work on freshman geometry homework. I didn't have any small pieces of paper to write important notes on.

I set the board on my lap and the stationery pad on top. I tapped a pen on the image of a panda printed on the bottom of the board. The panda looked like the logo from one of Mom's World Wildlife Fund posters. Except this panda's eyes drooped. Also instead of WWF the skateboard company's name "enjoi" was written next to a turd behind the panda.

I needed to tell Mom about skateboarding. She would be the first one home. I didn't want to wear pants and cover up my scraped knee. I didn't want to practice rolling down the driveway when my parents were gone. I didn't want to keep hiding the skateboard in my closet.

I tried again, explaining what would happen and why:

I am going to buy a skateboard. I want to ride. I like it.

I tore the sheet off the pad. I set the board against my bedroom's wall. I thought I might as well let it be seen.

I walked down the hallway from my side of the split-plan house to my parents' bedroom by the garage. On the way, I replaced the stationery pad by the phone. Then, I placed the note on Mom's pillow. I went back to my room to wait.

Soon, Mom came home and said, "Hello," to the house. I scrambled for my math book so it looked like I was working on equations. Mom appeared around the corner of my bedroom's door.

"I want you to wear a helmet," she said.

I looked up from my desk. It wasn't the argument I expected. I wanted to skate the way I wanted to skate.

"No," I said.

Mom stared at me. I glanced back at the geometric combinations of angles and sides like they were important. I felt Mom fill the door frame.

"Think about it," Mom said.

I shook my head.

"I'll buy one for you," Mom said.

"I won't wear it," I said.

I felt Mom leave.

The next day at our family computer I printed out a list of reports on head injuries for boys playing high school sports. Football topped the list. Skateboarding was a footnote.

The last time I skated over to Dylan's, his mom pointed me to his room. I found him holed up. I noticed the enjoi board that I had returned sticking out of his closet, while he was studying for engineering exams at his desk.

I was always skating by myself. I downloaded skate videos from the Internet. Issues of *Transworld, Slap,* and *Thrasher* filled the mailbox. I brought skateboarding to me.

I started buying skate gear for cheap off the other quitters. I didn't go back to Dylan's house for boards, because I hoped one day he might roll again. Instead, I paid this one kid Francesco, who lived at the front of the neighborhood, 20 bucks for his scuffed-up Toy Machine board with a graphic featuring an orange Cyclops's unblinking red eye.

At home, I waved a hair dryer over the worn griptape and then fit a razor blade between it and the board's wood. I stripped off the griptape in pieces. Underneath, I discovered the wood was dyed green and a graphic printed on top of the board too. I left a gap in

the new tape near the tail to show a cartoon drawn yellow-horned
devil with a black, spiky mohawk who said out of a word bubble,
"Grip it and Rip it!"

I had scoped out several houses with pool filter machines churning on the side of garages. I found crabgrass-clogged lawns and
gnats that swirled out of the weedy shoots sprouting up higher
than the deed restrictions' limit; junk mail that crammed boxes;
and fliers stacked on doormats. I ding-dong ditched those places
and noted where nobody answered the doorbell.

I had narrowed it down to two houses with their backyards ending at a lake-size retention pond: one with an unlocked chain-link
fence and the other a shoulder-high wooden fence. Both were on
the corners of intersecting roads. I would have several directions
to scatter if someone called the cops.

The chain-link house had a kidney pool with a nice curved shallow end that sloped into a bowled deep end. I imagined pushing
off in the shallow end by the stairs and swooping up in an arc over
the light in the deep end to clack my wheels on the tiles. Maybe
I could push myself to grind over the deathbox where the water
filtered out to get cleaned in the pool system.

I walked around the back porch. Through the sliding glass door
I noticed a yellow light. I curled my fingers around the door clasp
like grabbing the edge of my board during an air. I pulled and the
door slid along its track.

Just inside, a single bulb shone from a lamp without a shade.
The thermostat was set at 79 degrees, probably to cut the humidity,
but speckled black dots of mold covered the carpet. A stale smell
hung in the air. I went back outside to breathe.

The wooden-fenced house had a square pool with a plungingly
deep deep end. I would have to deal with skating several feet of
vertical cement after draining the entire thing. If I rode up its
walls, then I would be parallel, and a dozen feet, to the flat bottom.

When I climbed into the backyard, I felt a presence like someone squatted there. The dried scrub grass was short. I wasn't sure
if it had been cut. By the pool, several dusty, unbroken beer bottles
sat next to a sagging deck chair. Under the porch, ashes swirled
when I lifted the lid of a grill.

I chose to drain the kidney pool because it felt safer. One night,

I rode over there in the dark. I unraveled a coil of garden hose. I plunked one end in the pool's murky water and then spooled the hose's length over the deck, across the lawn, threaded it through the chain-link, and put the other end to my mouth. I sucked in through my mouth and breathed out through my nose. I pulled the water out of the pool through the hose. I could taste the empty rubber. I hacked when a mouthful of water siphoned out. I aimed the hose out to the retention pond. I camouflaged the hose's copper end with brush so it just looked like a swampy spot.

My wheels held to the ground bumping over the pebbles and crushed seashells mixed in with the asphalt. I stomped my back foot down as I flicked the board by pushing out with my front foot out at the same time. The board clicked against the ground, spun a half-rotation clockwise below me. I pulled up my legs and then caught the board with my feet. I loved doing pop shuv-its with the crack, swirl, catch that quickly traded the nose from the front with tail in the back of the board.

I carved around the corner, away from our street, off to check on the kidney pool. On the small stretch I did a 180 and then quick shuv-it, no pop, just to set my board back up. I was riding fakie so I 180-ed again to ride in my regular stance onto the main street.

I heard the clink of metal on metal and then the slap and clip of urethane landing. Whoops came from a lanky kid with exaggerated long legs that sloppily careened with his board while his arms swung. I couldn't figure if he was grasping the air for balance or pumping his arms in joy. His smile got me stoked.

I saw a sheet of particleboard, not even plywood, hauled up on top of a plastic green recycling bin set next to a rail in a house's driveway. This kid had been rolling up, grinding across, and then hopping off. The metal on metal sound must have been from a 50-50 grind.

It was janky do-it-yourself-itude. I knew exactly how that felt. To make something happen with what you have, like finding a backyard pool to skate.

I figured the pool would still be there as I showed off to this kid skateboarding in my neighborhood. I started stretching my foot as far forward on the ground as possible and then pulled my board along and pushed fast, faster. I set my foot on my tail and tilted back, lifting my front truck off the road and balancing a manual in front of the kid's driveway with my back to him.

I set the front wheels back on the ground and pushed off again. I wanted to snap and grab my board on the wedge-like driveway a few houses down. As I pushed to pick up speed again, I figured if I made the trick I would introduce myself, but if I bailed then I'd pick up my board and skate off to the draining pool.

I rode up the driveway and popped an ollie. Up, up. My trailing hand grabbed the side of the board in front of me between my legs. My thumb caught the griptape and my fingers curled underneath on the board's laminated bottom. I floated and turned in an arc.

I released the board. My wheels landed. So, I rolled across the street to the kid.

He introduced himself as Adam and said, "That was rad, man."

"Thanks." I nodded my head. "This is kinda cool too." I pointed to his ramp-to-rail setup.

"Wanna try?" Adam asked.

We tried each other's tricks: grinds and airs. It was like a demo: showing off and having fun just sessioning. I skated with Adam until the streetlights flickered on.

A few weeks later when I remembered to check, the kidney-house's chain-link was padlocked, the hose gone, and the pool refilled. I thought about going back at night with bolt cutters and renting a diesel pump, but I was skating every afternoon with Adam. I could already boardslide—that perpendicular *shush* sound as the middle of the board's wood skimmed across the metal railing was thrilling—and Adam could launch up and tap his fingers to his board in a quick grab.

Dad squeegeed the condensation off his car's windshield. He wore clip-on shades over his glasses even though the sun's orange ball of fire barely lifted over the horizon at the end of the street. I walked down our driveway. My cargo shorts swished above my Vans. When I opened the passenger door, jazz on the radio hummed with a double bass and swishes from the brush-sticks on drum skins with occasional tinkerings on cymbals. We always listened to public radio on the way to my high school, because we rarely talked.

Dad shook his wrist and droplets of water flicked from the squeegee. He set his squeegee underneath his seat and sat down. Dad started the car, but left it in park.

"You know," Dad said, "you need to write your application essay?"

I pinched the bridge of my nose and nodded.

Dad drove me half an hour to school every day before driving back south another 20 minutes to his work. The bus stop was only one mile away. I walked home every afternoon. I never asked Dad to drive me to school, he just did every morning.

As we started to roll down the road, I stared out the window at spots I skated on our street: The bricked driveway my wheels clicked over. The border of hedges I carved as I imagined their green semicircle to be a wave. The manhole cover I ollied. The curb I scraped with my trucks as I took the corner against traffic.

Dad drove out of the neighborhood. At the bus stop for another high school for kids zoned in our neighborhood, I lifted my chin to Adam. He waved.

The land opened wide to fenced-in pastures. I imagined crooked grinding from one railing over the post and then sliding and rolling to the next along the entire row parallel Dad's car. I stared out my window framing the landscape and put myself on it, riding it, like playing *Tony Hawk Pro Skater* and finding impossibly connected lines.

I projected myself skating onto a strip mall: powerslide down the parking lot, slappy the curb, and then roll up the wheelchair-accessible ramp to launch into a wallride on the side of the building. My eyes connected the line and my feet on the floor of the car twitched.

A fart-like honk of a saxophone from the radio pulled me back into my body. I wished I had that bag of tricks and that release from physics to float all over the constructed world. I glanced ahead on the road filmed with rainbow slicks of oil dripped from cars like ours following a track to school and then jobs. I turned back to look out my window.

My wheels clacked over the spaces between the orange-stained sidewalk blocks. I pushed along the zigzag next to the curving road. I listened for Adam's wheels echoing behind me.

As I picked up speed I bent down and reached out my hand to brush the spongy Saint Augustine grass. Sprinklers clicked in yards and misty well water stunk.

We had skated almost two miles out of the neighborhood. We passed the red-sided, silver-roofed, open-aired elementary school. We skated where a few years before there had been only cattle that chomped on scrub brush and slept under the shadow of an occasional oak draped with the curly seaweed-green of Spanish moss. This new neighborhood was called The Preserve. An egret with its golden eye staring out was stamped on an emblem of both sides of the front gate.

A cluster of pines bordered a retention pond. When I spotted a low, gray rectangle of thin wall supported with arm-thick steel pipes rising out of its edge, I stepped off and scooped up my board. I walked through a mound of bark mulch piled around squat palms. The landscape sunk toward the pond and the gray walls.

Two brownish wedges faced each other with a straight flat bottom between them. Trails of parallel lines curved and arced and traced on the surface. I made the marks with my skateboard's wheels when I first discovered the drainage ditches.

I dropped my board at the top of the bank and shoved off. My wheels dipped over the angled transition to flat bottom. I pushed one, two, three quick times. I set my foot on the tail and carved up to the lip of the bank, which jutted out and where the sandy soil had washed out an edge. I locked my back truck and Smith grinded. Metal crushed rock. Speckles of aluminum flaked off.

I shifted my weight off my back truck and unhooked from the lip, turning back into the bank. I skated to the other side. I stepped off my front foot, my back foot snapping the board's tail to the ground, and then I lifted up and turned doing a no-comply. I looked like a stereotypical plastic flamingo in a retiree's lawn, except that I spun and then stomped back onto my board and continued my line.

I crossed the middle of the flat bottom. I leaned forward with my weight to pump the board, to keep momentum. My wheels etched a figure eight onto the concrete. I rode up the angle, bent down to grab the edge of my board, took my front foot off the board, and pushed off the ground and pulled up into a boneless.

My right foot rose and my left foot lifted. I floated. My left foot returned to my board. Then, I landed with my wheels spinning and I rode up the other side to Adam. He gave me a high five as I heaved in the dusty air.

My sweaty T-shirt felt shellacked to my back. After skating, I grabbed the bottom and tugged up. The shirt made a wet smack when it landed at the bottom of the plastic laundry bin in my room.

I noticed a piece of paper on my desk. Dad must have printed the University of Central Florida's application essay questions. Question four was circled: *What qualities or unique characteristics do you possess that will allow you to contribute to the UCF community?*

I knew I needed to write an essay for my college application there. Everything else was done. I sat at my desk and took out a pencil.

I set my middle finger on the tip and my pointer finger on the middle of the pencil. I used the tip as a tail. I popped a mini-ollie up and onto the edge of my A/P American History book and slid the pencil along the hardcover's edge. I flicked the pencil off, spinning it around, and then caught it with my fingers to land on the desk.

I looked at the question again. I only had to fill one page. That wasn't too much. The only thing I had honed for years had been skateboarding. It hadn't just been a physical activity. It was natural history: surfers evolved out of the waves and carved up onto the asphalt and over the concrete landscape. It was physics: establishing and breaking rules. It was law: freedom and happiness by trespassing and destruction of property. It was life: I woke up staring at the Popsicle shape of my board leaning against my wall and I thought about riding through each class period where I used my pencil for fingerskating just like at my desk. At home, I skated until dinner and sometimes went back out again in the evening. At night, my legs shifted under the sheets with dreams of landing tricks.

I remembered a video I watched sometimes before I sessioned called *Modus Operandi*. One skater, Marc Johnson, had an interview at the beginning of his part. Over the clip of him grinding on a desk dumped in an alley, he said something about the process. How he did it.

I grabbed the question sheet and took it to the family computer. I booted up the PC. I put on a fresh shirt. I knew I'd want to skate afterward.

I opened up the video I had downloaded. I clicked forward and found Marc's part. His head was shaved bald and he spoke with a coastal vibe:

"The craziest thing about skateboarding is you say, 'What if I could do this? You know? I think I could probably do this.' And you can do it. You can take something that was pure thought and you can make it reality."

I leaned back in the chair. I scribbled about how I could bring creativity to UCF. Then I clicked back on the video. I wrote Marc's final sentence down about making a thought a reality, like wanting to go to school and then going to school. I had filled up the entire page.

I knew that what Marc said applied to more than my college essay, it also applied to how I had been trying to land a full-Cab. On the street, I would roll backwards and wind up to turn, but then make a 180 and maybe my wheels would screech a bit more of a turn on the ground. I would be facing perpendicular to where I had been going. I couldn't get myself to fully rotate and return back in the same position.

I watched a full-Cab video online in slow-mo. I noted how the skater's shoulders directed him. If I could turn my shoulder, then my body, legs, and board would follow. I grabbed my board and headed outside.

I rolled down the driveway, hopped the gutter, and then started pushing backwards. I set my foot on the nose. I crouched down ready to spring. I snapped an ollie and turned 180, but then kept my shoulders twisting and my board followed around full circle. I landed and continued to roll.

MICHAEL MCKNIGHT

Learn to Dunk

FROM SPORTS ILLUSTRATED

WHEN JOE FORTENBERRY, a farm boy from Happy, Texas, threw one down at the West Side YMCA in New York City on March 9, 1936, he may not have been the first man to dunk a basketball, but he was the first to do it in an aesthetically stirring way, and in front of the right people.

Cameras of that era were too crude to capture the split second when the rules of both Newton and Naismith were bent, so it was fortuitous that *New York Times* writer Arthur J. Daley was at the Y that day covering the tournament that would decide which Americans sailed to Berlin for the Olympic debut of the 45-year-old sport. This new "version of a layup shot," Daley wrote, "left observers simply flabbergasted. Joe Fortenberry, 6-foot-8-inch center . . . left the floor, reached up and pitched the ball downward into the hoop, much like a cafeteria customer dunking a roll in coffee."

Seventy-nine years later, the feat that Daley unwittingly named "the dunk" still flabbergasts. But how it felt to Fortenberry, a pioneering barnstormer whose name we've forgotten despite the gold medal he and his teammates won in 1936, remains a mystery. "He never talked about being the first person to dunk and all that," says 65-year-old Oliver Fortenberry, the only son of Big Joe, who died in '93. Indeed, the famous dunkers throughout history have been either reticent on the subject or unable to adequately express how it felt to show Dr. Naismith that he'd nailed his peach baskets too low. After more than a year of rigorous research on the subject, I've concluded that the inadequacies of modern language —not the ineloquence of the dunk's practitioners—are at fault. In the eight decades since Fortenberry rocked the rim, words have repeatedly fallen short in describing the only method of scoring, in any sport, that both ignores one of its game's earliest tenets and, in its very execution, carries a defiant anger.

Which is why, on April 1, 2014, I dedicated myself to dunking a basketball for the first time. So that I could live it, breathe it, perhaps take a crack at it with my pen. I had tossed this idea around for years, realizing with each passing birthday that my chances of success were dimming. However, on that April Fool's Day (a coincidence) I spent three hours on the court and at the gym, with a promise to myself to return several times each week until I threw one down like Gerald Green. Or at least like Litterial Green, who played in 148 NBA games between 1992 and '99, and who, like me, was born in the early '70s, stands 6'1", 185 pounds, and is at no risk of having dunker carved into his epitaph.

I gave myself six months to dunk because that was the low end of the "six to eight months" prescribed on the website of Brandon Todd, a 5'5" former D-III star who set the same goal for himself in 2005, and then, at age 22, accomplished it. When I first contacted him, Todd perfectly expressed the more shallow reason behind my goal: "When you can dunk, it means you're a good athlete. Period. It takes away any subjectiveness." I also chose six months because, as would be proved repeatedly during this mission, I am prone to tragic spells of overconfidence.

The things I had going for me: an understanding spouse; a modicum of foot speed and leaping ability, flashed during the occasional Motrin-supported pickup game; proximity to one of the best training centers in the world; and, again, an understanding spouse. The forces working against me made for a longer list and included (but were far from limited to) my average hand size and arm length, a lower-back injury that I suffered while playing semi-pro football in 2009, and my age. I was 42.

My wife of 11 years, who isn't a sports fan, knit her brow in confusion and nodded when I raised this idea for the first time. She wanted to care but could not muster the attention span, for she had given birth just three weeks earlier to our third daughter. I would be needed at home in the coming weeks—a reasonable expectation. Although I look back today with pride at how I balanced that responsibility with the time-consuming and far less important dedication to dunking, I knew at the time that I would miss a lot of family dinners, bath times, and diaper changes so that I could ride my bike to the gym or to local playgrounds, with no guarantee that I would reach my goal, or even come close.

Justifying these selfish, skewed priorities in my head as I stuffed a basketball into my backpack and pedaled away from our home would turn out to be one of the most formidable obstacles in my path. I must have whispered, *What the f— am I doing?* as many times as I leaped toward one of the rusty rims scattered around the south Los Angeles beach community where we live. That latter number tallied somewhere around 5,000, according to my journal and 24-plus hours of video. Many of these jumps were attempted while wearing a weighted vest that pulled me downward, the same way that home pulled me sideways.

I thought I needed a rim. But what I found I really needed was a constellation of them. Having choices would prove useful because of the daytime obstacles, like elementary school PE students and our own kids' after-school activities; and nighttime obstacles, like chain-link and padlocks, that I encountered. My training windows were narrow, so I learned to employ these outdoor rims strategically, the way the skateboarders in *Dogtown and Z-Boys* timed their secret sessions at drained swimming pools. The six or seven courts nearest our house featured rims that measured anywhere between nine feet and 10'2", a variance that allowed for different kinds of practice. The blisters and flayed calluses that soon bloodied my hands instructed me in the value of breakaway rims—the less rust the better. Because a Snap Back wasn't always available, local residents may have spotted a sweaty fortysomething man rubbing Vaseline on his hands in the corner of their child's favorite playground last year. Sometimes he wore a weight vest that made him look like a jihadist. What I'm saying is, Thanks for not calling the cops.

My early efforts were clumsy. Jumping willy-nilly as high as I could, with no regard for technique, I occasionally felt my finger graze the underside of the rim. Most times I did not. What I did feel early on was a firm self-awareness that I was a two-foot jumper (like Spud Webb, Dominique Wilkins, Vince Carter, and myriad NBA Slam Dunk champions with whom I have nothing else in common athletically) as opposed to a one-foot jumper (see: Julius Erving, Clyde Drexler, Michael Jordan). This meant that my best

shot at dunking would be to elevate like an outside hitter in volleyball—that is, by stepping forward with one foot, quickly planting
my trailing foot next to it, and then propelling myself upward off
both.

Less helpful was my early realization that I was a two-*hand*
dunker, in light of my inability to palm a basketball on the move.
It's common knowledge among dunkers that throwing down with
two hands is typically harder than with one; the former requires a
higher vertical leap. So as I flailed haplessly at the rim last spring
with one hand, I felt not just discouragement but also fear. Fear
that I would miss big chunks of my kids' ninth, sixth, and first
years on earth just so I could come up embarrassingly short on a
senseless goal that my wife and I would later estimate consumed
15 to 20 hours a week, on top of my normal work hours. And fear
that I had shared this idea with my editors way too soon.

Four times a week, from April through October, I embarked on
90-minute explosive weightlifting sessions based on the years I'd
spent working as a strength coach to club, college, and professional volleyball players. Squats, squat jumps, deadlifts, lunges, box
jumps, cleans, sprints . . . Three or four days a week I visited one
of my local blacktops, where I tried to dunk tennis balls on 10-foot
rims or throw down basketballs and volleyballs on lower ones. By
May 3—one month in—I could dunk a tennis ball on a 9'10" rim.
I considered this a better-than-good start, not realizing that compared to dunking a basketball, this tennis-ball jam was akin to a
child scrawling the diagonal line that begins a capital A on his first
day of learning the alphabet.

About 100 yards away from this 9'10" breakaway rim (which
came to sound, each time I grabbed and released it, like someone
closing the metal baby gate at the top of our stairs) was a brown,
oxidized, immobile 9'1" version, a hand-ruining iron maiden
where, in front of the occasional puzzled onlooker, I practiced
(and practiced) the timing and the hand and wrist work required
to dunk. I knew early on that my regulation dunk, if it ever came
to pass, would have to come from a lob of some sort—a bounce
to myself, either off the blacktop or underhanded off the backboard—after which I would hypothetically control the ball with
one hand just long enough to flush it. Mastering the placement
and the delicate timing of such lobs would prove to be a quixotic

pursuit in and of itself. But it was necessary, not just because of my hand size (7¾ inches) but also because I needed to keep my arms free so I could swing them at takeoff, adding much-needed lift to my leap.

A two-foot Dominiquean jump, a perfect lob (and I mean *per-fect*), and a quick flush with my right hand—that was my only shot, my only window. My odds, I sensed, were extraordinarily s————.

If anything came to surprise me about this journey, it was the sheer volume of physical pain involved. I had taken on impressive physical feats before. I had run a sub-3:30 marathon back in 2003 (my first and only attempt) after putting in the hundreds of training miles required. I'd done some of the most grueling weight training on offer, most of it either on the beach or at The Yard, a nearby temple of athletic performance where Maria Sharapova, Kobe Bryant, and Tom Brady, among many others, have kneeled with exhaustion. But the physical toll of trying to dunk made the marathon and the semipro football and the parenting and everything else I'd ever attempted seem like mere rubber band snaps to the wrist. The lifting didn't hurt as much as the jumping, the banging of my quadragenarian appendages into the ground, taking off and landing 50 to 200 times a day. My legs never got used to this bludgeoning, never got better at recovering from it, despite my daily foam-rolling, stretching, icing, and hydrating. Even on my off days, a quick game of tag with my kids or a bike ride to the park meant daggers in my thighs and a gait like Fred Sanford's.

I wondered: Does jumping hurt this badly when 38-year-old Vince Carter does it? Did Carter's legs ache like this when he was 13, on the outdoor courts at Ormond Beach (Florida) Elementary, trying and failing hundreds of times to get his first dunk?

"There aren't many people in the world who can [dunk], that's why it has this allure, I guess," Carter told me last fall, during his first training camp with the Grizzlies. "As far as trying to do it, there are so many ways people can go about it. The approach you're taking is the right approach. When I was younger, that's how I started. Tennis ball, to the point that it became easy. Then a volleyball. Then a girls' ball. Finally I took—it was like a dodgeball. I dunked that and said, 'You know what, I'm gonna try it.' Next thing you know . . ." He shrugged and smiled, the gray whiskers on his jaw sinking into a dimple.

"How old were you?"

"It was seventh grade. No, it was sixth grade. I was, what, 12 or 13?"

Joe Fortenberry was 18 or 19 when he first dunked. "He was 6'7" back then too," said his son, Oliver. "He and his friends would practice on a barrel ring or a wagon-wheel ring nailed to a barn."

"What was he like in his early forties?" I asked. "Was he the kind of dad, the kind of husband, who would take on something this impulsive and inconsequential and time-consuming? The kind who would make himself scarce for a few months so he could, I don't know, restore an old car or try to hit a hole in one?"

"No, not Dad," Oliver said in the brick tract home where he grew up. "He was an older dad, like you, and his family was the focus of his life. The only time he wasn't home with us kids was when he went out on the road for Phillips Petroleum, buying and selling leases in western Kansas and Oklahoma. When he got back he'd say, 'All I wanted to do was come home.'"

James Naismith, I learned, was a bit different. "I was only three when he passed away [in 1939]," said his grandson, James Naismith, 78, of Corpus Christi, Texas. "He was known as a tender-hearted man, but he also had"—the doctor's namesake pauses—"the polite term is 'firmness of mind.' It's kind of a family trait. He devoted his life to improving the lives of others through physical activity, through games. That took time.

"A lot of people don't know this," he continued, "but Granddad patrolled northern Mexico when Pancho Villa and his troops were down there. [Naismith served as an infantryman and chaplain with the Kansas National Guard.] He spent time in France during [World War I]. He had five kids at home."

That I had abandoned my wife and children for something far less significant than world war was still bothering me. Brent Barry, who is not only a 43-year-old dad and a neighbor but also the 1996 NBA Slam Dunk champion, nodded knowingly when I brought this up over coffee last fall.

"There's something about dunking a basketball that lures us in," he said, reflecting on his first jam, during lunch period his sophomore year at De La Salle High in Concord, California, back when his driver's license read 5'11", 112 pounds. "It stokes the imagination. It's something you always dream of doing. I have a friend whose father, at age 50, is trying to dunk."

Barry, who retired from the NBA in 2009, recalled that a few days before our sit-down he "drove out to the Clippers' practice facility, wearing sneakers and board shorts, just to get my basketball fix in. Between games I pick up a ball and start shooting. In the back of my mind I'm thinking, *You're 42, man; can you still?* So I get a rebound, do a little power dribble in the paint, and, sure enough, throw it down. I put the ball down and walked out. I can still do that. That's good."

Unfortunately, I'm not the 6'7" son of a Hall of Famer, so I had to resort to desperate devices—like Hennessy, an infamous and inexpensive cognac that, according to one of the two NBA players who recommended it to me, "will give you that *Yah!* That bounce. That little bit of meanness you need." The little minibar-sized bottle that I downed 30 minutes into an intense session of dunk attempts on a sweltering day last summer had no effect other than scorching my esophagus, giving me a headache, and releasing from my pores an aura that, as my six-year-old put it that evening, "smells like medicine."

After four months of failing to pull off anything even resembling a real dunk, the planets aligned on August 9: after at least 19 failed attempts that afternoon, I dunked a soccer ball on a middle school court whose rim measured 9'11". (The original basketball, incidentally, *was* a soccer ball, property of Dr. Naismith's employer, Springfield College.) Video from that afternoon shows me standing there, looking confused, in the moment afterward. *Did that just happen?* Failing had become so routine that even this small success felt foreign.

The soccer ball dunk was fool's gold, of course. I knew I could never swing my arms that pendulously, that fast, while palming a basketball. The good news, as I was about to learn: I had reached that height despite jumping, as Brandon Todd described it, "wrong."

I sent a video of my soccer ball dunk to Todd, the #fivefive-dunker, who informed me that I was leading with the wrong leg. I'd been taking my last big step with my left foot, which, as a righty, was like swinging a bat cross-handed. A few days later I encountered a blogger and 43-year-old dunker named Andy Nicholson who showed me, among many other things, that I wasn't the only one with blood on my hands. Nicholson was one of dozens of You-Tubers, young and old (mostly young), who were documenting online their attempts to dunk. "Yes!" he yelled over the phone when I told him about the open sores on my fingers. "Those are badges of honor!"

Like Todd and me, Nicholson was a two-foot jumper, and he echoed what Todd had told me was another flaw in my technique: "Your next-to-last step has to be a lot bigger. That big leap forward with your right foot—your penultimate step—that's what allows you to explode off the ground." To demonstrate, Nicholson sent me a video of Carter's performance at the 2000 NBA Dunk Contest, which was a bit like showing a Monet to a finger-painting kindergartner and saying, "No, like *this*."

The way Arthur J. Daley and the other spectators at the Y felt when Fortenberry dunked—that's how fans at the Oakland Arena felt on February 12, 2000, when Vince Carter shoved his forearm into the rim and swung there by his elbow. What only the initiated noticed about Carter's dunk was that if you froze him during his approach, he looked like Bob Beamon. Carter long-jumped some 12 feet, right foot leading the way, before landing for a nanosecond and blasting off into his two-footed ascent.

"That big step before the explosion," Carter explained to me, "is for the sole purpose of getting height above the rim. Ever since I was a kid trying to dunk, I never aimed for the rim. I tried to jump toward the top of the backboard. Aim for the moon and get the stars, right?"

"What single piece of advice," I asked Carter, "would you give a teenage kid—or a 43-year-old man [as I had turned two weeks earlier]—who is trying to dunk?"

"Put in the work. It's muscle memory, first and foremost. Training-wise, people say, 'You gotta do this, you gotta do that.' I didn't believe in that. I never worked on my legs in high school or middle school. I would just go through this routine over and over and over, visualizing that day when you dunk on the court. And then you live in that moment."

Three weeks after I received that counsel, on a rare afternoon when I felt fully rested, I dunked a volleyball on a 9'11" rim. Again, I knew I could never swing my arms while palming a basketball the way I'd swung them while palming that volleyball, but I'd be lying if I said it didn't feel badass. Thirteen failed attempts later, I did it again. Then two more times, each one an unexpected thunderclap. All of the explosive Olympic lifting I'd been doing was paying off, but my problem wasn't going anywhere: How could I get my hand *and a basketball* over the cylinder? A lob to myself off the backboard? A big bounce off the blacktop?

Imperfect as my two options were, I had to choose one and commit. I didn't have time to play around. I had kids to raise, other projects to work on, an impending hip replacement to schedule.

What if someone lobbed it *for me,* though? This would violate my criterion that I do this all by myself—but no one has ever claimed that those Clippers who throw home Chris Paul's lobs aren't dunking. I didn't decide on this third option; not yet. But it was on the table. My main task was still finding a way to jump higher.

The days and jumps and deadlifts and calf raises rolled on, rep by rep, protein shake by protein shake. Six months became seven, then eight. To protect my right hand, I began wearing a canvas gardening glove with the fingers cut off. It soon became stained with blood—the equivalent of Curt Schilling's bloody sock, but with one-millionth the significance. The rims where I toiled belonged to me now, such that I barely noticed the toddlers wobbling nearby, the skateboarders swirling around me as day turned to dusk, the elderly couple ambling arm in arm, looking for all the world like my wife helping me to the shower on the morning after a double day.

I grew so desperate that I fell victim to a hoax in the form of a fake tweet from @NASA promising that on January 4 earthlings would experience a short period of weightlessness. If you think I was above circling the date and scouring the Internet to find my precise window of zero gravity, you are mistaken.

Early in my mission, my editor had given me a book, *Jump Attack,* by Tim Grover, personal trainer to Jordan, Dwyane Wade, and myriad other NBA stars. I'd ignored it at first; I figured I knew plenty about how to jump higher. When I finally opened it last December, I was further dissuaded. The exercises Grover prescribed to increase one's vertical leap looked either nonsensical (hold a deep lunge for 90 excruciating seconds, without moving) or sadistic (the series of rapid-fire bursts and landings that he'd named "attack depth jumps"). These self-immolations, Grover wrote, would last for three months.

When I phoned Grover and explained what I was up to, he dug right in. Helping people do the physically impossible is his stock-in-trade. "Everybody these days, they want it quick and easy," he said in his round-voweled Chicago accent. "Everybody wants quick results. They want gratification right now."

Grover had not built his empire by misleading clients or blowing smoke between their glutes. So I took it to heart, and felt a burst of hope, when he said, "I'd be shocked if you do everything in this book and you're not dunking." Which was all I needed to hear.

I followed the *Jump Attack* program to the letter, and my training in December, January, and February looked and felt nothing like what had preceded it. I spent a month doing those nonsensical lunge holds (and squat holds, push-up holds, chin-up holds). I trusted those holds, and the tendon-testing leg workouts that lasted two and a half hours and left me tasting my own broken-down muscle in my mouth. I trusted all of it because I was living in that moment, as Carter put it, when the hammering of Carter's "muscle memory" into my body finally would bear fruit and I'd pitch the ball downward into a 10-foot hoop like a cafeteria customer dunking a roll in coffee.

After a one-week recovery period in January following Phase 1 of *Jump Attack*, Phase 2 brought an increase in intensity and time investment. This was the last stop before Phase 3, the wilderness where those attack depth jumps lived. (Attack depth jumps: Rest on your knees in front of a box; explode to your feet without using your hands; immediately jump onto the box; immediately jump as high as you can off the box, landing on the balls of your feet. Repeat. Many times. No blacking out allowed.) Phase 3 brought dramatic increases in both explosiveness and hip flexibility, two critical ingredients that I started to feel working in tandem. I emerged both confident and in dire need of another one-week recovery period, which I spent playing with our kids, watching dunk videos, and mouthing the syllable *Ow*. Once healed, in early March, I returned to the rims with a friend whom I'd asked to toss lobs to me. There would be no more lifting. (After *Jump Attack*, what else could there possibly be?) From here on, I just jumped and recovered, jumped and recovered, attacking this tiny window of three or four weeks before my time away from the gym began to sap my strength. It would be over at that point, all over, whether I wanted it to be or not.

I was still doing 200 calf raises every night, only now I did them with a 50-pound sandbag on my shoulders. Soon I began doing them one leg at a time, creating the sensation of twin blowtorches charring my posterior lower leg.

The calf raises weren't what caused the Achilles pain that had sprung up in February. That sting, combined with pain deep in my left knee, turned my quest into a race against the clock. What would I reach first: my goal or the nearest urgent care center? Which would survive intact: my corny belief in hard work and sacrifice or my patellar tendon?

When a scheduling conflict arose with my usual lobber, another friend, Jeff West, a 45-year-old neighbor whose daughters are the same ages as mine, offered to jump aboard my journey to irrelevance. He also ended up injecting a crucial element that I hadn't realized was missing.

Fun.

I had allowed what began as an adventure to turn into hard labor, an eternal grind. I realize now that one of the reasons I had trained and jumped in solitude for so long—wanting to do everything by myself—was embarrassment, fear that passersby would see what I was doing and judge me for embarking on this vain vision quest.

I had worked alone in this vacuum for so long that when Jeff, in our first session together, began responding to my near misses with stuff like, "You are *right there!* You got this, bro! You just have to visualize it!" it hit me as if Jordan himself were saying it.

Dunking became a game again. After my closest misses I'd hop around and swear like a golfer whose playoff putt had lipped out. These outbursts were no longer harsh self-admonitions but celebrations of my progress, acknowledgments that I was getting tantalizingly close. I could feel my legs gaining in bounciness. I could feel my hips, quads, and calves learning to fire simultaneously. My original lobber returned to the scene and suggested I try dunking in the morning instead of the evening, when the batteries in our old bodies are as low as the ones in our phones. I added this sage advice to the long list of microdetails "that help you steal inches," as Todd had phrased it months earlier. "A quarter-inch here, a half-inch there."

March 27 was yet another in a long string of days, each feeling as if it would be *the day*. Fully rested and caffeinated, I arrived with Jeff at a court, recommended by Brent Barry, whose rim heights fluctuated but which I'd recently measured at 10 feet. The rims at New York City's famed Rucker Park, incidentally, both measured under 9'9" on a recent visit, which raises all sorts of questions about what a dunk is and what it isn't. The famed outdoor rims along Venice Beach, if lined up next to each other, would look like a graphic equalizer during a Ray Manzarek keyboard solo: 9'9", 9'11", 9'8".

After warming up, I proceeded to slam Jeff's best lobs off the back rim at least 10 times, watching these missed dunks rebound high over the lane and land somewhere near the three-point line. It's tough to express how difficult it was to pack up and walk away from the court on such days, to listen to my body when it told me it had reached the point of diminishing returns. To come up with yet another way to tell the wife: No, not today, Sugar. But I came *reeeally* close.

My warm-up on March 29, following a day of recovery, left me feeling hoppier than I'd expected, and not nearly as achy. After 10 devastating near misses, and several others that weren't as close, Jeff lofted the best lob I would see during this journey. I leaped, controlled it with one hand, and— *boodaloomp*—in and out. I could have wept. "You got this!" Jeff implored. "You know you got this!"

Maximum force into the ground, I whispered to myself, a key reminder I'd picked up at The Yard.

Big step.

Jump through the backboard.

Forty-five seconds later, when Jeff's next lob drifted into place, I reminded myself to mentally record what happened in the next half second so I could replay it whenever I wanted. Sure, I could always watch the video, but the lens in my mind provided a clearer view, a closer angle of the ball leaving my hand, shooting downward, denting the net.

The first sound I heard was Jeff's single clap of celebration. I erupted, sprinting to the iPhone that had captured the moment and thanking my friend, my wife, The Yard. It had taken 363 days.

Among the hundreds of lessons I learned during my youngest child's first year of life was this: If you earnestly pursue dunking after your athletic peak years of 18 to 30, give or take, it can be done. You can enjoy what it feels like to dunk. You can even feel it more purely than I did, maybe without needing a lob from a friend, and hopefully without all the hand damage. But you should expect a long, frustrating, demeaning war of attrition that pits mind, body, spirit against the most oppressive, unrelenting opponent of them all: gravity. The sun rises and sets, the tides creep in and out—even taxes and death seem negotiable nowadays—but gravity remains constant, forever pounding our shoulders, stooping us shorter as we grow gray, never letting up—no matter what NASA tweets.

As planned, I delivered the March 29 footage to two judges so they could deem my dunk official. Barry's response came by text. "As Marv Albert would say: Yes! And it counts!"

When Oliver Fortenberry saw the video, he let loose a rousing, "Yes, sir!" that reminded me of a story he had told during our first talk:

"My dad tried dunking when he was in his mid-fifties. Got a wild hair one day and went out in the driveway with a ball. We all followed him. He was wearing slacks and hard-soled shoes, and when he went up, his pipe and his tobacco flew out of his shirt pocket. He lost his balance and almost fell over when he landed. But he did it."

Joe would die some 30 years later, at age 82, but what he said that day as he stood in a puddle of dry tobacco—his clothes disheveled, the other Fortenberrys yelping a chorus of excited *Yessirs* —spoke to me in a way that can only be understood by those who blindly take on missions that exact a greater toll than was envisioned. "Well," he said with a grin, "that's the last time I'll ever do that."

CHRIS VAN LEUVEN

Going Home

FROM ALPINIST

ONE AFTER THE OTHER, their toes compress then release from
the cliff's edge. Shoulders hunch forward, chins are tucked in.
Toes are pointed. Legs are spread apart, holding their wingsuits
open. Streaked granite surrounds them: El Capitan, the 3,000-foot
wall they've climbed for years, its golden polish framed by pon-
derosa pines. Rushing air fills their ears. They thread a channel
that opens toward the Cathedral Spires across the Valley floor. The
orange sky feels thick, heavy.

Because their activity is illegal in Yosemite, they often flew during
first and last light, when the atmosphere's static blues mixed with
gray, shrouding them from sight. The last time I saw Dean jump, I
watched his figure, wrapped in black, leap from the rim of El Cap,
then fall as if endlessly, his charcoal chute popping open against
the sky. He landed, gently, in the meadow by us. And then he disappeared.

On May 17, 2015, I heard the news that Dean and Graham had
died the night before, during a wingsuit flight in Yosemite—a
year, two months, and three days after Stanley crashed in Zion.
Although I hadn't met Graham, I knew Stanley and Dean. We were
part of the same community, one that extended from the far end
of the Valley floor in Curry Village to Yosemite West, Foresta, and
El Portal. Memories flickered in my mind: black, gold, and white
granite walls; mist rising from El Cap Meadow; the silhouettes of

friends. The way I mistook the BASE jumpers for swifts, their shadows flitting past me while I climbed.

I've never flown in a wingsuit, but I've tried to understand the lure. During my late teens and early twenties, I often free soloed flowing slabs and flared cracks. With practice, I found I could approach my limit, summoning my will to live. Once high on El Cap —roped up, but dangerously runout and exhausted—I knew I had to stop clenching the shallow piton scars; letting go of my fight was the only option left. Instead of falling, I began to climb from a different place. It was as if I barely needed to touch the stone, as though my body transformed into something almost weightless. I believed that wingsuit flyers found such moments along Yosemite's vast walls, when the choice to hold on to anything vanishes. I wasn't willing to join them, because I was afraid to die.

"It's incredibly beautiful—the walls and big waterfalls, and the Valley itself. Then you jump off . . . and you have a moment of quiet peacefulness," a wingsuit flyer, JT Holmes, told me. "You're going really, really fast, and you're boom, back at the car. It's like a magic porthole."

Yosemite is a place of overwhelming beauty. It's also a place of death. Over 600 pages, *Off the Wall: Death in Yosemite* tells stories of the lost: drownings, falls on rock, parachute failures. Days after Dean and Graham's accident, I take a plane from Vermont to California. Under the moonlight, I drive from Fresno toward the Valley. And as the farmland rolls into steep, winding roads with dark oaks and rippling grass, I only know that I need to be back in my community.

For more than a decade, this was my home.

Stanley

The next afternoon, I sit with an old friend, Julia Reardin, by the Merced River. Damp greenery surrounds us. A smooth rock digs into my ribs. Julia and her roommate let me sleep on their body-width cabin floor for many seasons over the years. Once again, I'm staying with her, this time at her rental in El Portal.

Earlier in the day, we followed the narrow passage of Incline Road, along repurposed railroad grade, to Stanley's place. The slackline was still set up in his yard. A blue crash pad perched against the trailer. I peered through the windows: carabiners spilled from the lid of a haulbag. Aside from the river, all was quiet. Julia leaned against me, her tears absorbed into my shirt.

Below us, now, the water funnels ceaselessly around river stones. I think about the gear inside that haulbag, collected for adventures that he'll never have. What death leaves behind.

Stanley took his nickname from the hardware-store claw hammer he carried on his first El Cap nail-up, Zodiac. He lived in an orange-brown trailer with peeling paint. He loved the location, but the trailer felt confining so he sometimes slept in a tent in the yard. Eventually, he and his wife, Annamieka, bought a yurt. It stayed folded up until his death, when his friends erected it in his memory.

Originally from Pine Grove, California, Stanley guided for the Yosemite Mountaineering School in the late 1990s. Later, he rigged vertical camera systems and orchestrated stunts for film and TV. In 2003, on a trip to Mexico, he found a mutt with her neck slit, covered with flies in a garbage heap. He nursed the dog back to life, named her Nexpa, and brought her home.

We sometimes bouldered together in Camp 4, rolling from tall, blank slabs to sharp arêtes. Lanky, he moved softly over the rock, stepping high and slapping his hands on single-pad edges, jeans gripping his knees as he rocked over his feet. When we climbed the North Face of the Rostrum, he chimneyed, jammed, and crimped for 800 feet in near-perpetual motion.

One day, Stanley and I sat with a group of friends outside Degnan's Deli. Lost Arrow Spire poked out of the Yosemite Falls Wall like a candle high above. Stanley began talking about Roberta Nunes, a Brazilian climber he'd met in the Valley. They'd fallen in love. As they drove to Moab to visit the house they planned to buy together, Stanley noticed their truck drifting across the center line. Nunes, who was driving, overcorrected and went off the road. Stanley spoke in circles, blaming himself for her death.

BASE jumping forced him to choose between living and dying, between pulling his chute or crashing to earth. He pulled his chute. In 2008 he started dating his future wife, Annamieka, then a medical student from Oregon. "There was an intensity to everything [Stanley] did," she recalls, "whether it be climbing, making coffee, or growing tomatoes in our garden. The sense of adventure and passion he brought to each day was truly inspirational."

His sense of urgency intensified in his final years, as if he wanted to live every moment as fully as possible, his friends tell me. Stanley broke the Nose speed record with Dean in 2010, clocking in at 2:36. For the Asgard Project, Stanley and Leo Houlding jumped out of a plane over Baffin Island wearing parachutes. As soon as they touched down, they ran to each other laughing.

Friends say Stanley was hard to keep up with. He tried to cram so much into a day that sometimes he ended up jumping in the dark, instead of at twilight.

He dreamed up increasingly technical flights, gliding close to cliffs, darting over ridges, and shooting through waterfalls. His last jump was by moonlight in Zion. Before he hiked to the rim, he called Jeff Shapiro, a falconer and mountain-flying partner. "The wind was blowing a bit," Jeff told me. "I could hear it in the phone."

Stanley aimed toward a notch that led out of the park so he could land legally. Narrow gullies often have higher gusts than vast clearings. He might have been lower than usual—during a previous flight from this exit, he'd cleared the notch by 100 feet or more. But there are downdrafts at night. And darkness makes it hard to navigate. He struck the cliff edge. Dean, who joined the search party, sat with his body before the helicopter arrived.

Soon after Stanley's death, I hung a photo from his wedding on my wall. He was dressed in a dark-gray suit, his hair trimmed. His broad smile pushed his cheeks back toward his ears. I felt as though I was back below the boulders with him, standing on red piles of soft bark.

A few months later, Annamieka gave birth to their son, Finn. "I imagined growing old with him," she says of Stanley. "I'm a single mom now." Finn squints his eyes when he smiles, just as his father did. "It's like he's still with us. It's the greatest gift I could ask for. It's too bad he can't share it with us," Annamieka says.

The loss rippled through our community with an empty darkness. Patti Haskins, an old friend, adopted Nexpa. His partner Leo Houlding gave up BASE jumping. Dean hung up his wingsuit for some time, but the pull of his dreams brought him back. Graham spent three weeks at Jeff's house in Missoula. During the evenings, they sat on the porch. "We talked about life and love," Jeff recalls, "and how we would live our lives in [Stanley's] memory."

Late afternoon on my fifth day back in Yosemite, I wander uphill to the Wine Boulder area. I slip my shoes on and climb a shallow corner with palm-sized holds, a line I frequented since my teens. The summer heat makes the rock feel greasy. This time, I don't trust my balance, and I sway between reaches. Midway, I pause, questioning my path.

On top, I stand above a sea of rolling evergreens. Camp 4 is hidden by branches. I miss the simple entrancement of moving over stone. I miss those times when the feeling of being dangerously high above the ground, but in control, brought out a sense of focus instead of grief.

Graham

You find the Yosemite lifers in old El Portal, downriver and several thousand feet lower than the west entrance of the park. Broken pavement snakes past old miners' sheds, upgraded with added rooms or extended porches. Retired climbing hardware hangs from one entryway, bong pitons clipped to Forrest Tetons, aluminum blocks shrouded in cobwebs. A general store, grade school, post office, and community center make up the middle of town.

A few miles west, I visit another friend, Alison Tudor, who lives with her fiancé uphill from one of Graham's old places, a shanty above the Merced River. Alison tells me how Graham loved death metal and the band Tool. How he would bring her tea when she was sick. She cries.

For a few months, Graham stayed in Stanley's trailer with his girlfriend, Rebecca Haynie. Just weeks before Graham and Rebecca met, her cousin had been diagnosed with cancer for the second time. Life seemed more fleeting than ever. In December 2014, Rebecca drove out from Moab alone to climb and skydive in California. She stopped at Lodi to make a tandem jump from a plane. There, she learned that Tommy Caldwell and Kevin Jorgeson had almost finished the first free ascent of the Dawn Wall. She hopped in a car with some people headed to El Cap Meadow to watch them top out.

Soon after, she arrived in Camp 4, and her friends introduced her to Graham. When he told her his name, she giggled shyly. "That's my name too," she said, referring to her middle name. He laughed, but he was gazing at her so intently he didn't hear what she said.

That night, they walked to Mirror Lake. Four winged figures stepped off the top of Half Dome. Graham and Rebecca watched their chutes gradually sway until they disappeared behind the trees.

The next day, Graham led her up Serenity Crack and Sons of Yesterday, across the Valley from the shimmering fan of Glacier Point Apron. "I was afraid of his intensity," Rebecca tells me. "He knew exactly what he wanted. Making myself vulnerable was always hard for me, but he chipped away at it."

Rebecca soon became his ground crew, rising before dawn and communicating by radio near the landing zones. Sometimes Graham jumped with Dean, sometimes alone. She came to know Graham's gentle arcs, impeccable timing, and focused grace. Within months, they were talking about building a home together.

Graham had first come to the Valley in 2007, two years after I left. He followed a new climbing partner, Sean Jones, to El Portal. The two friends meandered up climbs with Sean's young son, M'so, taking him up the East Buttress of El Cap when he was only eight. To earn money, Graham worked as a carpenter, occasionally donating his labor to the community. He started BASE jumping under Stanley's mentorship.

Once, Graham leapt in street clothes from the Porcelain Wall, a sweeping, almost crackless wave that glows deep orange during last light. Because he overestimated how long he could track without a suit, he ended up too low. He pulled the chute close to the base of Half Dome, and touched down unintentionally on the Death Slabs. Without a headlamp, he navigated by a slender crescent moon, sliding through a gravelly maze.

I've been lost there before, and I spent hours following dead ends, tiptoeing across narrow ledges, all the while hovering near 100-foot drop-offs. Many climbers have. At night, it's even more disorienting: hollow, rotten slabs with black veils of organic matter intersect sandy terraces that lead in all directions. I imagine that he looked for patterns in the rock, the same way he followed currents in the air.

With Dean, Stanley, and Jeff, Graham pioneered new launch points. They planned their flights carefully, using Google Earth to calculate the distance of the glide and dropping rocks to determine the time to impact. Sometimes they measured the rise and run with a range finder and then generated the hypotenuse —their flight path—according to the Pythagorean theorem.

In recent years, Dean and Graham made flights that required minute precision and favorable conditions to complete, clearing gaps that others rarely, if ever, attempted. They traveled to the Alps to establish the highest exit point on the Monch. From the Mittellegi Ridge on the Eiger, they flew for nearly five miles, extending the descent over 9,000 feet, passing swaths of gray, blocky limestone above shining green meadows.

In one video, I watched Dean's red and purple suit contrast against smooth ridgelines. Clouds rose on either side of the rock. He took off and soared from high on the mountain, leaving it behind in a flight that didn't seem to end. "As soon as you step off and in the air, you're so utterly committed, you don't feel the fear or that rush people refer to . . . All the emotion comes at you after you land," Jeff says.

Three weeks before he died, Graham completed the first-ever wingsuit flight off Castleton Tower, near Moab. He flew like an airshow plane, aggressively nose-diving, fueling himself with wind, then almost hovering like a plane in stall. During the first wingsuit descent from the Dragon's Nest, he buzzed past the 900-foot Titan at more than 100 miles per hour, its red-orange walls transforming into a blur of flame. Combined, the two men practiced their final jump nearly 10 times. After dropping hundreds of feet from Taft Point before their wingsuits caught lift, they planned to take a straight line to a narrow opening at the end of a U-shaped bowl atop a scrappy formation called Lost Brother. From there, they would cut over the Valley and pull their chutes.

Dean went first. Graham followed closely behind. "It's a 20-second flight. Twelve seconds into it you're committed," Jeff says. Midway to the notch, Graham overtook Dean near their commitment point. Something went wrong. Graham leaned left, Jeff tells me, potentially looking to exit the bowl, and veered back right. Sixty feet above the bottom of the notch, he made contact with a small tree and struck the wall. Dean cleared the notch by several feet, but he wasn't high enough to stay above the terrain on the other side.

In the days after, I viewed images on social media of two people leaping from the white granite of Half Dome's Visor. One man was in a front flip, while the other's arms were upright. Piercing orange light flared into the corner of the image. They looked as though they had superpowers.

Dean

Spring in Yosemite, 1996. Moisture hung in the air. I was barely 19, cleaning rooms at the Ahwahnee Hotel. One afternoon, I took the tourist bus from Curry Village to Yosemite Lodge and tucked into the boulders. I tinkered around on a shaded line with rails of smooth stone until my fingers pried open and I fell onto a creaky-springed Curry Company mattress someone had stashed.

A tall man approached the boulder, his dark hair sheared short. At first, he was just another unfamiliar figure in the forest. He reached up a tall arête that cleaved the white and black rock, grunting as he spanned gritty holds with enormous limbs. He had more strength and boldness than anyone I'd met.

After we introduced ourselves, Dean Potter mentioned that he wanted to free solo the Steck-Salathe on Sentinel Rock, the 1,500-foot dark face that loomed above. I asked him if he thought about Derek Hersey's death on the same route a few years prior. Dean said it wouldn't happen to him—he wouldn't slip. And then he was gone.

From time to time, Dean reappeared, suddenly, like a ghost. Once on a break from work, I was standing on the back dock of the Ahwahnee. Air from large vents blew past the dumpsters, over a grease layer. I was smoking rolled cigarettes. Dean scolded me, pointing out the obvious: tobacco hinders performance. Again, he vanished amid the trees.

I admired Dean from afar, but for years I was too shy to leave the security of Curry Village and venture to Camp 4 where he and Stanley hung out. I imagined they felt a connection to the vertical world that I only hoped for. I believed they climbed with less fear than I did, continuing beyond the point where I stopped.

In *Alpinist* 27, Dean described his earliest memory:

I dreamed of feathers sprouting on my arms, fields rolling far below in waves of cloud-streaked green, distorting into burnt wastelands of faint sand dunes and dust storms . . . Underneath me a blurred tunnel formed. I began plummeting, out of control. A dead tree spiked up, its branches like the hand of a corpse . . . All my life I wanted to make the first part of this dream real, but find a way to decipher the ending.

At age five, he'd fallen trying to climb the stone wall outside his family's house in Israel, where his father, a military man, was stationed. After Dean recovered, he seemed to find a new ease in the heights. When they moved to New Hampshire, he scrambled alone on nearby granite outcrops, reveling in the sun and the wind.

By his early teens, he'd set up a training schedule for himself, lifting weights and running, developing immense force. "He could break an oar," says Valley regular Stu Kuperstock. "He could've been an Olympic oarsman, and rumors are that he once did a 100-mile run. When he wasn't being active, he'd just lie around like a dog." I imagined a Great Dane flopped in the dirt.

Soon after we met, Dean damaged his finger and wrapped it with a thick wad of athletic tape. He channeled his drive into a hybrid of soloing, speed climbing, and aid on El Cap and Half Dome, linking the tallest formations ever more rapidly.

"I wish I could find that heightened awareness without risking my life," he said in a documentary. "Right now that's the only way I know how to find it." Again and again, he seemed to see his existence unfold according to the patterns of his childhood dream. As he explored near and distant ranges, he merged different forms of what he called "aerialism"—soloing, highlining, BASE jumping —hoping to turn the fear of falling into the sensation of flying. He looked for signs everywhere: the wing-shaped camber of a drop of water, the spreading branches of a leafless tree.

In 2008 he climbed Deep Blue Sea, a 1,000-foot route on the Eiger Nordwand, in a style he named "FreeBASE," free soloing with a parachute on his back. During a month and a half of preparation, he sometimes slept in a high cave, listening to the rain fall. Before his father died of a heart attack, he'd written a last letter to Dean, and the words still swirled in his mind . . . *the landing problem can be solved.* As the ripples of smooth, burnished stone flowed beneath his fingers, he wondered whether his father had some secret to share with him, "how to follow your passion completely, without losing your loved ones or your life," Dean later wrote.

A year later, at Taft Point, near the place where he took his last jump, Dean walked a slackline 3,000 feet off the ground. After rehearsing for a week, he dropped his red swami-belt tether and crossed the span unprotected. In the photo, his arms curve like the wings of a bird as he seeks his balance. The thin, pale strand of webbing gleams electric above the void.

For a long time, he'd hoped, one day, to land in his wingsuit on a snow slope without ever deploying his chute. By subtle adjustments to his tracking, he thought, he could slow the fall of his body just enough. "Innovation or insanity, blue sky or buoyant liquid, infinitesimal changes in the curve turn impossible to reality," he wrote. After Stanley fell, he gave up his vision of parachuteless flight.

Somewhere in the quest to find the farthest boundaries of potential, there lies a threshold. Beyond it, everything ends.

Just a few weeks before his death, Dean scrambled up Half Dome from Mirror Lake in 2:17:52 round-trip, cutting nearly six minutes off the record. He carried no food or water, and he wore only shorts, socks, and sticky approach shoes. He planned to run the loop weekly, to break the two-hour mark. Edges and small holds became mere details rushed past in frantic paddling. Holds became insignificant, replaced by momentum and power.

He and his girlfriend, Jen Rapp, had recently bought 31 acres of land in Yosemite West where they planned to build a home. He liked to sit in El Cap Meadows for hours, listening to frogs and insects, feeling the light warm his skin or watching the snow fall on stone. "I too have been trancing out on the landscapes," he'd written to *Alpinist* editor Katie Ives in 2009. "Mostly, though, I am too focused on seeing through to the other side that I forget what really matters, what's right around us." At times, when he concentrated on his writing, he could reach those heightened states through the breathlike rhythms of meditation and words.

Leo Houlding tells me Dean planned each of his feats obsessively, trying to make them as safe as possible. Leo lists the names of the fallen from his group of friends. "I hate to think of it as past tense," he says. "We're going extinct."

"It's like if El Cap were gone," Heather Sullivan says. As she pours me four shots of espresso at her house in El Portal, her black stocking cap is pulled down over her hair. She hides her eyes. She'd once been Dean's roommate in Foresta. Pictures of

Dean and Graham lie scattered on her tables. In some, Graham snuggles with a puppy. In another, Dean holds his dog, Whisper, like a baby.

Heather says that two ravens have been visiting her lately. Ravens were a symbol of protection to Dean. He asked an artist to paint one on the helmet he wore on an expedition to Patagonia: the bird spreads its wings against an orange sun.

At the far end of her property, the ravens dive behind a tree. Their dark feathers morph into shadows.

In a strange way, my acquaintance with Dean intersected with my choice to leave Yosemite a decade ago. It began when a friend, Ivo Ninov, dozed at the wheel while we were driving through Nevada before dawn. The feeling of brush beating against the undercarriage brought us out of sleep. He swerved to get us back on the road. The small white car became airborne.

As we tumbled down the highway, I realized I wasn't in control of my life anymore.

Ivo and I crawled from the wreckage, battered but intact. We smoked and walked through scraps of metal and cubes of shattered glass. An 18-wheeler pulled to a stop 50 yards away, but no one got out. Sunlight broke through the dusty air.

We called Dean from the wrecking yard to pick us up. I stared out the window of his station wagon while they talked about Dean's plans to free the triple—El Cap, Half Dome, and Mount Watkins—with Leo in a day. I don't remember what Dean and Ivo said, only the feeling of leaving the deathlike emptiness of the desert behind. As we headed back to the Valley, I started to piece together plans to move to a new place, where I might escape my compulsion to stray so close to the edge.

On my final evening in El Portal, I meet up with friends of Dean, Graham, and Stanley in a wooden backyard structure. Plastic candles surround us. Their small bulbs flicker above the glowing bases. Children's fingerpaint streaks the walls.

I think about something Jeff said: "Everything in life requires balance, and losing balance in this—the highest-risk of dangerous activities—is catastrophic. We go into the mountains to be in touch with living in the present, and flying forces this balance. The magic is in the action, and it changes you as a person." His words remind me of moments when I felt invincible. Of times when friends and I giggled, soloing in unison on routes we hadn't climbed before. And then of other, later days, when I chased that feeling until a crippling fear set in, like a hand pulling me earthward. I thought of how Dean, Graham, and Stanley had leapt, so often, through that twilight, finding that brief balance as they emerged somewhere past their uncertainties, traveling through the sky under the power of the wind.

"You found your path, and now you're questioning it?" I ask one of Dean's and Stanley's jumping partners.

"Yeah," she says in a soft, childlike voice. She pauses as if she's deep in the process of answering this and many other questions in her head. "Every time someone dies, that becomes part of you. One after another."

Then she tells me about jumping off El Cap in the moonlight with Dean and Stanley: "It feels better than anything I've ever felt as a human." Human. She pronounces it as if we're just another animal in the kingdom. A sedan crawls along the dirt road behind a fence, briefly interrupting the stillness. Its headlights blink through the slats. Red taillights leave tracers in our peripheral vision. The sky emanates a dark blue, the stars blurred by yellow lights from El Portal.

"Every time you stand on the edge of a cliff and then step off," she says, "you know that if you don't pull your chute you will die. Right before that is when the fear hits. The second you hit the air, it's just smooth. You know what needs to happen. It's like going home."

JOHN BRANT

Zilong Wang and the Cosmic Tale of the White Dragon Horse and the Karmic Moonbeams of Destiny That Restored All Faith in Humanity

FROM BICYCLING

THE COSMIC TALE of the White Dragon Horse neither begins nor really ends when, after arriving in San Francisco at the conclusion of a 3,400-mile bike ride across America that was part bildungsroman, part research project, and part spiritual journey, Zilong Wang parks the bicycle he calls the White Dragon Horse —a Surly Long Haul Trucker—outside a Mexican grocery in the Mission District and goes inside to buy an orange. But this is, perhaps, the pivotal moment of the Cosmic Tale, or at least the most outrageous, so we'll start there.

"It was a warm day," Zilong says, "and an orange seemed like just the thing." It would be only a three-minute errand, so he didn't worry about the White Dragon Horse. He hadn't worried about it in Chicago or Salt Lake City or Omaha or in any of the scores of small towns and farm hamlets where he'd stopped during his cross-country trek, so why fret now? He draped a soft-cable lock around a parking meter, went into the store, and bought his orange.

When he came out to the sidewalk, the White Dragon Horse was gone.

At that point, you or I would have barked an expletive. Indeed, Zilong admits that "my first reaction—I wanted to punch the guy in the face."

Alone and powerless in an unfamiliar city, as he was, we next probably would have made a sputtering call to the police, relying on official, faceless channels to deliver justice. When those channels failed to deliver, we would've turned resigned and ultimately cynical, putting on a fresh layer of anger, mistrust, and fear to shield us—and separate us—from the world.

However, says Ken Rosenthal, founder of Hampshire College in Amherst, Massachusetts, Zilong's alma mater, "Zilong is . . . well, I've never met anyone quite like him."

Strictly speaking, the Cosmic Tale of the White Dragon Horse begins without the White Dragon Horse. In the spring of 2005, in Shanghai, a high school classmate offered for purchase a bicycle that Zilong knew, but didn't want to believe, was stolen. But the bike was such a beauty, a Giant hybrid, sleek and gleaming, unlike the mass-produced clunkers Zilong and most other citizens used to get around the thronged streets of Shanghai.

In the first years of the new century, China was maturing into the economic miracle that had begun in the last years of the old one. Zilong's mother was a physician, a radiologist who mostly stayed home after Zilong, the family's only child, was born in 1991. His father served as a manager of an enterprise that manufactured shipping containers.

"We had a comfortable apartment and I attended some of the best schools in Shanghai," Zilong says. "Education was paramount; everything was based on my getting ahead in life. During vacations we would take road trips around the country, which aroused my appetite for travel."

Zilong's parents sent him off to boarding school at the age of seven, "because they wanted me to learn to be independent and to think for myself," and brought him home at age 13, in order to more closely supervise his adolescence. It was at about this time that the classmate approached Zilong, tempting him with the suspect bicycle.

"The bike had all the signs of being stolen," Zilong says. "It was

basically brand-new, and my friend was offering it at a bargain
price. But I really wanted that bicycle, so I tried to pretend I didn't
know where it came from. I made my friend sign a contract saying
it wasn't stolen."

Zilong bought the bicycle. One summer afternoon he rode it
to a public swimming pool. He locked the bike in a rack and went
for a swim. When he came back out, the bike was gone. "Karma,"
Zilong says.

To avoid the notorious cramming and rote memorization of col-
lege-prep studies in China, Zilong's parents encouraged him to go
abroad for his senior year of high school. The boy located a for-
eign-study program in Germany. "Every student in China is crawling over the next one to get to the U.S.," Zilong says. "There isn't
much competition for Germany."

Moreover, the teenaged Zilong was already following an alterna-
tive, individualistic path. He began each morning by hand-copying
a page of a classic Chinese literary or philosophical text (a practice he continues today; when the books are completed he gives
them away to friends) and finished each evening by recording his
thoughts in a diary. Still, for even the most adventurous, indepen-
dent-minded kid from Shanghai, spending a year in a small city in
eastern Germany was tantamount to a moonwalk.

In Germany, Zilong started the personal blog he still maintains.
The earliest entries are in Mandarin, but quickly shift to German.
("Not so hard a language to learn," Zilong insists.) Finished with
his year in Europe, Zilong entered Hampshire College, a private
liberal arts college that eschews grades in favor of interdisciplinary,
experience-based learning. He wanted to study the great books,
explore the big ideas, and become a well-rounded individual. On
one of his first days on campus he met Earl Alderson, an instructor
in the college's outdoor-education program.

"Zilong showed up at the pool to try kayaking," Alderson recalls. "He ended up going on many whitewater, rock-climbing, and
backpacking trips with us. At first glance, Zilong may not come
across as a physically gifted athlete, but he's open to challenges
and approaches them analytically. Rolling a kayak, for instance.
Most students get freaked out and freeze up while they're learning, but not Zilong. He was patient and stayed relaxed. I don't
think he ever ended up in the water."

Says Jonathan Lash, the president of Hampshire College who also supervised Zilong's senior research project, "Every class he took, Zilong stood out. It might sound hackneyed, but he's one of those rare individuals with an honest, innate, unquenchable hunger to learn."

He used a bike to get around campus, but wasn't a dedicated cyclist. "I never got into cycling for its own sake," Zilong says. "I think the longest ride I ever took in college was around 20 miles." But, as graduation approached in the spring of 2013, Zilong dealt with a quiet but intense sort of intellectual crisis. After years of study, he'd grown obsessed by the scientific method and worldview. He wrote in his blog: *It's as if a parasite of rationality has taken over my brain, siphoning off the vital energy and humanity.* "I was having trouble sleeping. I needed a break from logic. I needed to explore the spiritual, artistic dimensions. I also needed a physical challenge and release. That's when I hit on the idea of the bike trip."

Not just any trip: Zilong resolved to ride all the way from Amherst to San Francisco, where an internship with an environmental consulting firm would begin in August. Alderson remembers that, "from a cycling perspective, Zilong wasn't near ready. But he was meticulous about his research. He read all he could about bike touring and reached out to people with experience."

Preparing for this journey makes me feel like a homo sapiens again, Zilong wrote in his blog. *I need to worry about clean water, proper nutrition, where to sleep, how to stay dry in the rain, etc. How refreshing, how humbling, how necessary!*

At some point, he determined that a solitary transcontinental bicycle journey wasn't challenge enough; he decided to shelter with strangers, knocking on doors and pitching his tent in backyards. And he resolved that, on the road, he would listen to recordings of seminal religious and literary texts: the Bible, the Koran, the Book of Mormon, and, on the recommendation of President Lash, *Moby Dick*.

Alderson helped Zilong choose his bicycle (which was paid for by an alumni supporter) and assembled it. Graduation day finally arrived. Zilong delivered the student address at commencement, giving a heartfelt, humorous talk that aroused a standing ovation. Then he turned to his journey.

During his final stage of preparation, Zilong moved out of his dorm and pitched a tent in Alderson's backyard. "Three days went by and he was still sleeping in our yard," Alderson says. "I told him, 'Z, you're never going to feel like you're completely ready. Time to get it on, bud. Don't think about riding all the way to California. Just think about each day's distance, the mile you're covering now.'"

An attorney and elder in the Mormon Church who befriended Zilong when he reached Salt Lake City, Gary Anderson, says he can understand the young man's hesitancy. "Zilong wasn't just traveling," Anderson points out. "He was on a mission, or perhaps a pilgrimage."

On his first night out, Zilong wavered on his resolution to seek shelter with strangers, pitching his tent in a vacant Boy Scout camp. He fought off clouds of mosquitoes, and when he turned on a water spigot a flood of ants poured out. "That was the worst night of the entire trip," he says. "I determined that from then on, no matter what, I'd knock on doors."

The second night, after a few refusals, a man let Zilong sleep in his horse barn. "After that it got easier," Zilong says. "Knock on enough doors, meet enough strangers, and you know how people are going to respond. You know the questions they're going to ask. But people are so sincere and curious, you never get tired of answering them."

Chris Henschen lives in Bowling Green, Ohio, and one July evening he looked out his front window just as a violent thunderstorm struck. Through a sheet of blinding rain a spectral figure appeared at the foot of the driveway: Zilong, wobbling to a stop. Henschen offered shelter on his porch, and Zilong ended up staying the night. He asked searching questions about the family's evangelical faith. He explained to Henschen, his wife, and their five children that, even though organized religion was restricted in China, people there hungered for spiritual meaning. The government, he added, permitted only one or two babies per household.

"Riding a bike across America is probably the last thing on earth I'd want to do," Henschen says. "But at the same time, I sort of admired Zilong. He was like a guy on a lawn mower. You know when you're mowing your lawn, isolated with your thoughts, you get into that speculative state of mind?"

About a week after leaving Bowling Green, Zilong pedaled into the life of Todd Sieben, a retired corn and soybean farmer and

Republican state representative in Geneseo, Illinois. "The night before, Zilong had stayed with my cousin near Chicago," Sieben says. "That morning my cousin called, raving about Zilong, saying we had to put this young man up for the night. I said sure, we have plenty of room." Late in the afternoon, Zilong sent a text message. "He was behind schedule due to strong headwind," Sieben says. "He said he might not make it to us until the next day."

Sieben decided to go out and find the traveler. "I start driving east on Highway 92, and within 30 minutes there he is, this guy on a bike, riding west. I flag him down. We load his bike into the van and then he climbs in." Sieben, who has completed RAGBRAI (the annual mass ride across Iowa) three times, speculates that a more hard-core cyclist might have declined getting a lift. "But Zilong wasn't like that," he says. "He didn't have a rigid idea about what he was doing. If he needed to ride in a van for 20 miles out of 3,000-plus, what was the big deal?"

That night, Sieben and his wife hosted a barbecue at their house. "We were all much older than Zilong, and a lot more conservative," Sieben says. "But, still, none of us who were there that evening will ever forget him. Not that Zilong tried to dominate the conversation. He was as polite and respectful as could be. He had this unique take on America. He was amazed at all the stuff we accumulate. The concept of yard sales just fascinated him. He couldn't believe all the time and energy and resources Americans pour into mowing their lawns. Zilong had us laughing, but he also made us think."

The figure of the lone existential traveler looms large in the American imagination. The Easy Rider or Man with No Name shows up one day to disrupt routine, challenge assumptions, fight off the rustlers, and charm the farmer's daughter. Zilong combined that role with the one from the 1970s TV show *Kung Fu:* the wandering Chinese monk whose spirituality stands in appealing contrast to American materialism. He learned that people are sometimes more likely to confess their deepest longings to a stranger passing through than to a life partner or other loved one.

In a blog post dated July 17, 1,500 miles into his journey, Zilong reflects on this phenomenon: *So far, people have been most welcoming and generous. Every evening, someone lets me camp in their yard. Over half of the time, they let me sleep inside, often on a comfortable couch or*

even a bed. About a third of the time, they feed me, and send me on my way
with snacks. Always, they most generously share their life stories, dreams,
beliefs, and take great interest to hear my story.

With striking perspicacity, Zilong speculates on why he was
"uniquely positioned" to receive such hospitality: *Just imagine: If I*
were black, I would be a good target for some paranoid neighborhood watch.
If I were Hispanic, people might wonder if I am in the country legally. If I
were Middle Eastern, I might look like a terrorist to some. If I were a white
American, I wouldn't be as interesting as someone from China. If I were
bigger and more muscular, I would be just a little threatening. If I were not
a college graduate, with a job waiting for me, I would be less trustworthy.
If I were riding a motorcycle or driving a car across the country, my requests
to camp in people's backyard would not be legitimate at all. If I were a girl,
I wouldn't feel comfortable staying in a stranger's home.

So, all the stars are aligned: I am a college-educated, employment-wor-
thy, well-spoken, nonthreatening young man from Inner Mongolia, travel-
ing across the U.S. with an American flag on my bike.

One night he stayed with a woman whose husband had recently
died suddenly of a heart attack; on another night, with a man
who'd made a bad business decision and lost his family fortune.
Zilong stayed with small organic farmers, and at large commercial
farms that use pesticides.

"Some evenings I had just ridden 70 or 80 miles in 100-degree
heat, and all I wanted to do was wash up, put some food in my
belly, and lie down," Zilong says. "But then people started telling
their stories. That always refreshed me."

The cycling itself proved harder than he expected. During the
first few days, crossing the Berkshire Mountains in Massachusetts,
he often had to dismount and push his rig uphill. Zilong kept
plugging. He got used to the bike and eventually learned to love
the White Dragon Horse. His muscles hardened. If he felt strong,
he cranked. If he felt especially sore he would slow down or take a
day off. He discovered that the trailer was unnecessary and got rid
of it in Chicago. He decided he didn't need to carry a heavy lock,
and mailed it back to Alderson in Amherst.

Zilong pushed west, his mind wheeling on three levels. He paid
attention to the wind, weather, dip and rise of the road, and passing traffic. But he also reflected on his experiences, and he listened to the words streaming through his earbuds.

The Bible took him through the Eastern states, the Koran

through the Midwest, and *Moby Dick* through the Great Plains and into the Rocky Mountains, the Book of Mormon through Utah and Nevada. Some passages he followed word for word. For others, the music of the sentences formed a soundtrack. At times he couldn't tell where the book ended and the road began: *Listening to the story of the ocean, of whales and whaling, in the midst of huge mountains . . . The fisherman's life stories were projected onto the screen of the Rockies. Sometimes I can even see the backbone of a sperm whale emerging from the landscape of the mountains. I almost confuse where I am on this planet.*

On August 21, 2013, after 74 days on the road and 73 nights spent with families and individuals who spontaneously opened their homes to him, Zilong Wang left Davis, California, and rode 65 miles west to the Bay Area city of Vallejo, where he boarded a ferry that delivered him to the terminal at the foot of Market Street in San Francisco.

"I pedaled the final mile up Market Street in wonder and bewilderment, yet calm," Zilong says. "I couldn't believe I had actually ridden all the way across America. Of course I was exhausted, but I never felt more alive."

Had the Cosmic Tale of the White Dragon Horse ended at this point, it would have made an unforgettable, inspirational bedtime fable about openness and curiosity and kindness for Zilong and, perhaps, his many hosts, to someday tell their grandchildren. But less than a week later, the White Dragon Horse disappeared.

Outside the bodega, a frantic Zilong pulls out his cell phone and reports the crime to the SFPD.

"It just happened!" he tells the police. "You still might be able to catch the guy!"

The voice on the phone tells Zilong to wait where he is, that an officer will be there shortly. Ninety minutes later, Zilong is still waiting. Devastated, he walks home and tells the story to his host family.

The next day, Zilong returns to the scene of the crime. He feels puzzled and troubled. He knows this is one of the busiest blocks in San Francisco, and that, as he says, "scores of people must have seen my bike get lifted, and apparently no one did anything to stop it." Such callousness and passivity run counter to Zilong's deepest instincts, to the character of his just-completed bicycle trip. He enters the bodega and asks to see the store's surveillance video. He studies the video, and there it is—the guy lifting the lock off the White Dragon Horse, three or four people watching. Zilong thanks the grocer and walks to the BART station at 24th and Mission, a neighborhood nexus for street people.

He approaches a man and says, "Excuse me, sir. I'm in the market for a bicycle. Might you know where I can get a deal?"

Within two hours he has talked to a dozen sources, and his investigation has taken him two miles north to the Civic Center. He is eventually introduced to a man named Cory, who says he can hook Zilong up with whatever he wants. Zilong describes a touring bike, one much like his, they exchange phone numbers, and Cory tells him to return tomorrow.

Zilong relays the phone number, along with the other intelligence he'd gathered, to the police department, but by the responses and feedback he receives he accepts that there is almost no chance of recovering the White Dragon Horse.

The loss is greater than the bike. If, as he's always believed, the stolen bicycle he'd bought back in Shanghai was taken from him as some sort of cosmic retribution, what does it mean that he's now also lost the White Dragon Horse—the honestly acquired engine of his transformation and his great understanding and appreciation of so much of life, knowledge, and America? Is this really, he thinks, how the Cosmic Tale of the White Dragon Horse was supposed to end? And, if so, what to make of it? What is the lesson?

On the evening a thief lifted the soft-cable lock off the White Dragon Horse, Vanessa Christie was finishing up a day at the office about a mile away. Christie, 31, works as a marketing manager for Timbuk2, the bike-messenger–bag maker, at the company's headquarters in San Francisco's Mission District. She climbed aboard her commuting bike and rode off to meet some friends for a drink. She noticed a man riding a bicycle on the sidewalk, moving against traffic.

"Something looked wrong about the picture," she says. "Everything looked wrong about it."

The man was dressed raggedly, not like a touring cyclist the bike was obviously suited for, and the frame was much too big for him. In fact, he was sitting on the tube instead of the saddle. "It was a full-on touring bike with big-ass racks and a soft-lock chain wrapped around it," Christie says. "But if I hadn't known bikes, I probably wouldn't have noticed."

Fortunately, Christie did know bikes—she commutes, tours, races cyclocross, and helps manage a website connecting bike travelers with places to stay in the Bay Area—and since moving to San Francisco two of her own bicycles had been stolen. "I realized that right about now, and somewhere pretty close, the bike's rightful owner would be panicking."

She decided to trail the man at a distance for a block or two. Soon, he pulled into an alcove of an apartment building. Surprising herself, Christie confronted him.

"My heart was booming," she says. "I had no proof that the bike was stolen. I couldn't flat-out accuse the guy. But I could make him think."

Excuse me, sir. That's a very cool bike. Where did you get it?

"To be honest, if he'd been bigger, I would have played it differently," Christie says. "But if it came down to it, I thought I could hold my own against him."

She took out her cell phone and told the man she was going to call the police. He made a move to bolt, but Christie jammed the front wheel of her bike against the doorway. "Dude—that's not your bike!"

They briefly locked eyes. Out of nowhere, a name came to Christie's mind, and she said, "That's Paul's bike!"

"Who was Paul?" Christie asks, laughing. "I have no idea. But somehow, that broke the spell."

He let go of the bike and vanished into the street. "It took me a minute to calm down," Christie says. "My heart was rocketing. I can't tell you how out of character that whole episode was for me. I'm not an especially brave person. Also, I'm not into moonbeam stuff, but that whole time, I felt like something outside of me was in control."

She rolled the stolen bike back to her office, locked it inside, then rode on to meet her friends.

The next morning, Christie's boss at Timbuk2 posted a photo of the White Dragon Horse, along with a summary of how it landed at his office, on the company's Facebook page. The posting was tweeted and retweeted among the San Francisco bicycling community, eventually reaching the screen of Officer Matt Friedman, who'd established an anti-bike-theft website and Twitter account for the SFPD. Friedman matched the photo with the detailed crime report Zilong had filed the day before. That afternoon, Friedman emailed a link to the Facebook posting to Zilong.

Less than 48 hours after the White Dragon Horse had been stolen, Zilong arrived at the police station to retrieve it. He told Christie, "You've restored my faith in humanity."

In the annals of long bicycle treks, by any objective measure, Zilong Wang's journey would fall pretty far down the list. He didn't set a speed record, didn't blaze a new trail, and didn't meet his own true love; Zilong didn't even decide to write a screenplay or a book proposal about his adventures. That's probably for the best. For all the magic of his crossing, for all the cosmic connections that were forged, there was little conventional drama—no fights, no violence, no steamy love scenes. Just a young man pedaling a bicycle all day and talking quietly to people in the evening. The single act of heroism occurred offstage, after the main action, performed by a supporting character. And yet, because of his modesty, not in spite of it, Zilong Wang's journey seems more fable than narrative. With little previous experience on a bike, he pedaled into cycling's heart. Raised on no religion, he somehow found America's soul.

One day in the midst of his journey, as he crossed the high table-land of eastern Colorado, the White Dragon Horse lifted abruptly off the asphalt. A moment later, Zilong came to consciousness, lying in a roadside ditch. Had he been hit by a rogue gust of wind, by Queequeg's harpoon, or by the hand of Yahweh? Would he ever find the answer to these questions?

Zilong rose, righted his bicycle, and continued pedaling west.

WILLIAM BROWNING

A Long Walk's End

FROM SB NATION LONGFORM

ON A SATURDAY MORNING in May 2015, a group of law enforcement agents, the FBI among them, knocked on the front door of the Montgomery Homestead Inn in Damascus, Virginia. The proprietor, a retired kindergarten teacher who lives across East Laurel Avenue from the inn, happened to be there at the time. She does not know for sure how many agents were on the inn's porch. She guesses three or four, though her husband told her later another man was positioned at the back door.

"There were just a lot of men out there," Susie Montgomery said.

Damascus (population 800) is in a valley in the Blue Ridge Mountains, along the Appalachian Trail. Downtown consists of about five blocks, "but in those blocks there are five churches," Montgomery said. A visitor crosses one bridge coming in, another heading out. Idyllic is the word. The Montgomery Homestead Inn is only an old, two-story brick home with four bedrooms travelers can rent. On the morning those FBI agents came knocking, it was the weekend of the annual Appalachian Trail Days Festival, when something like 20,000 hikers descend on the town for fellowship and revelry, and the inn's four rooms had been booked for weeks. Montgomery did not know what business the men crowding the porch could have there.

When she opened the front door, one of the agents held up a photograph of a man and asked if she knew him. She looked at it and said, "Yes. That's Bismarck."

Bismarck was the trail name of an Appalachian Trail hiker who had checked in the previous day. He had been staying at Montgomery's inn periodically since 2010. She considered him an "easy guest." He usually stayed for three days, paid in cash (like everyone else), and each time he left, the bed would be made and the room was clean.

The agents asked if Bismarck was inside. Montgomery said she was not sure, and what was this about, anyway? The men identified themselves as law enforcement agents and said they needed to talk with Bismarck about a case of fraud. Montgomery asked for identification, which they provided, and she took them to the room where Bismarck was staying.

She knocked on the door and a man answered. She said there were some people who wanted to talk to him and the door opened from the inside. The agents stepped in.

"At that point, I got back out of the way," Montgomery said.

Montgomery could not make out what words were spoken, but the tone, she said, was calm. No guns were drawn, no voices raised. After a brief chat, the agents put Bismarck in handcuffs, walked him out of the room, and took him away.

"There was nothing mean about it," Montgomery said recently, cooking dinner as she spoke. "But apparently he was who they were looking for."

Two days later, on Monday, May 18, the FBI announced the search for a 53-year-old accountant accused of embezzling $8.7 million from an Ohio-based Pepsi distributor had come to an end. His name: James T. Hammes. His story had been featured on two fugitive TV shows, *America's Most Wanted* and CNBC's *American Greed*. Authorities say Hammes, over the course of 11 years, took the funds through a series of banking transfers while working as a controller for the distributor. Then he vanished.

The amount of money he is accused of taking could unleash a man from most things that hold him in place. The world bows to that amount of money. You could pay the toll on any of life's roads. You could step through any of life's doors. What would you do with that freedom?

Sip cool drinks in the shade on a beach in Mexico and feel small before the Pacific Ocean? Pay a plastic surgeon to change your appearance, plant a young and willing blonde on your elbow, and drive a Bugatti across Europe? Or find a quiet spot and live an unassuming and comfortable life off the stash?

James T. Hammes, aka Bismarck, apparently did none of those things.

James T. Hammes went hiking.

On the Appalachian Trail.

For six years.

Several weeks after being handcuffed beside a queen bed at the Montgomery Homestead Inn, Hammes appeared inside the Potter Stewart U.S. Courthouse in downtown Cincinnati, Ohio. Federal Magistrate Karen L. Litkovitz denied bond. The order stated Hammes "poses a substantial risk of flight given he has no current residence and no identifiable place to live . . . and no contact with family or employment since 2009."

Today, the man who spent six years eating gorp, sleeping beneath stars and in hostels, and swatting mosquitoes while walking through wilderness and washing his clothes in laundromats is inside a jail cell in Butler County, Ohio. He has pleaded not guilty. A September trial is scheduled. Zenaida Lockard, his attorney, did not respond to messages. Late last week, however, she filed a motion stating that "plea negotiations are ongoing and more time is needed to see if a non-trial disposition can be reached in this matter." Hammes faces up to 1,130 years in a federal prison if convicted.

There are people who cannot believe he was in the United States all this time. But apparently, he was.

And there are people who cannot believe the man they knew as Bismarck could possibly have done any of these things.

Appalachian Trail thru-hikers, those who walk the entire 2,100-mile trail in a single season, beginning in Georgia in spring, knew Bismarck as a smiling Catholic with a Jerry Garcia beard, baker's belly, and fondness for hammocks. They liked him. There is something hikers call "trail magic" that the Appalachian Trail Conservancy defines as "an unexpected act of kindness." In nearly every story about Bismarck on the Appalachian Trail, or AT as it is commonly called, trail magic appears. He took to people. People took to him. Up and down the length of the trail, he was well known for his gentle, good nature. Beginning in 2010 the name Bismarck began appearing regularly on blogs written by hikers recounting their trips. His picture pops up in their snapshots.

Millions of people step somewhere onto the AT each year. That anyone stands out to the degree he did is astonishing. Yet

Bismarck did. Veteran hikers, encountering newbies, sometimes asked, "Have you met Bismarck?" It was a way of gauging just how experienced a hiker was, how long they had been on the trail, and how well they fit in with others. If you knew Bismarck, your boots had many worthy miles already worn on their soles. A man who hiked with him last September said the general consensus along the AT was that he was "on his way to becoming a trail legend" —someone whose story hikers share amongst themselves, one with inspirational overtones. Like that of the late Earl Shaffer, who in 1948 became the first person to hike the entire AT in a single season. Like Matt Kirk, who two years ago hiked the trail in 58 days. Such was Bismarck's reputation that this past spring, David Miller, the author of *AWOL on the Appalachian Trail,* a popular book about hiking the AT, was on his phone talking with the owner of a North Carolina hostel along the state's western edge, near Nantahala Lake. In an offhand way, the proprietor mentioned Bismarck was there, similar to the way Grateful Dead followers once mentioned an encounter with Jerry, a measure of his own familiarity of trail culture, a touchstone showing he, too, knew the ways of the wandering tribe.

When the other hikers learned that Bismarck had been taken into custody at Trail Days, shock bloomed through the AT community. Word spread along every step of the trail—hushed tones spoken at campfires from Georgia to Maine—in a matter of days.

"So many people liked him," Susan Montgomery said. "I feel sorry for him, if he did what they say he did, because he loved the outdoors. He really did. He loved the outdoors so much."

Karl Humbarger, who works at a hostel in Maine where Bismarck stayed the last few winters, said, "At least in my book, if he faces what he's accused of, pays whatever debt he has coming, then he is welcomed back here always."

What Montgomery and Humbarger and other Bismarck acquaintances likely did not know is that some believe he did more than allegedly take $8.7 million that was not his.

They believe James T. Hammes had committed a crime and walked away once before.

They believe he may have played a part in his first wife's death.

During the summer of 2003, Joy Hammes was in her bedroom in Lexington, Kentucky, sleeping alone, when her home caught fire.

She was 40 years old and had been married to James T. Hammes, her college sweetheart, for nearly two decades.

Things seemed to be going well. She had taken a job at a food pantry she had been volunteering at for years. Her daughter, Amanda, a smart, successful high school student with medical school in her future, was out on a date that night. Joy Hammes went to bed early. Her husband, James, did not.

Then the fire started.

Joy Hammes survived the flames, but never regained consciousness. Investigators would eventually rule that the fire was accidental. No criminal charges have ever been filed in connection to it.

There are those, though, who believe James T. Hammes could have orchestrated the fire.

On the night of the fire, he was not at the house on Turkey Foot Drive. He had been there earlier, but by the time the flames grew and sirens of fire trucks and ambulances began bleeding into the neighborhood air, he was nowhere to be found.

He had gone on a walk.

American Greed is a true crime series that claims to "examine the dark side of the American Dream." The episode featuring James T. Hammes aired in 2012, and it included a narrative about the fatal fire, raising the question that he may have been involved. Recently, a relative of James Hammes described their family as "boring." But he also said that when he watched the segment of *American Greed* on Hammes, called "Deceitful Dad and the Missing Millions," the hairs on the back of his neck stood up.

"We learned a lot of things," Jeff Sadler, one of Hammes's cousins, said.

Joy Hammes had no life insurance policy. But the life James Hammes was living at the time of his wife's death feels like one on the verge of crumbling: solid on the outside, rotting on the inside. He had at least one girlfriend. He also had a daughter no one knew of. And if the FBI is right, he was embezzling from the company he worked for. Joy Hammes, until getting the job at a food pantry, had mostly been a mother and a wife and a community volunteer. Her husband earned a good salary, but she had become suspicious. She had started asking her husband, who handled the finances, how he could afford to take week-long scuba diving trips to the Caribbean, alone, while she stayed at home with their teenage daughter.

"Maybe he got tired of her asking questions," Jane Ryan, the sister of Joy Hammes, said.

Two days before Bismarck was arrested in Damascus, he ate dinner with a group of hikers he had met on the AT over the years. Thru-hikers tend to move together in a loose pack that stretches along the trail. It is not uncommon for them to encounter each other over and over again as everyone travels at their own pace, resting and moving according to whim and the weather. Friendships are made and often hikers keep up with one another after leaving the wilderness. Hiking the trail is both a physical and spiritual challenge and each day spent walking alongside another hiker links you together in personal, emotional ways to one another. Bismarck made plenty of bonds and had many friends.

One of the hikers he dined with that Thursday night was Patrick Bredlau, a retiree who lives near Chicago. They also ate lunch together Friday. They had met on the northern end of the AT in 2014, at Speck Pond Shelter in Maine, on the last stretch of the trail before it reaches its end on Mount Katahdin, and kept in contact over winter.

Bismarck had told his fellow hikers many, many times through the years that he would stay on the AT as long as he could.

"He wanted to live out his days in the woods," Bredlau said. "He loved the simplicity of living in the woods."

Bismarck told Bredlau his plan was to slip back out onto the AT on Saturday morning, when dew still laid across the ground.

"The FBI just barely caught him," Bredlau said. "According to his plan, he wasn't hanging around."

What Bismarck did not know is that one night in March someone who had thru-hiked the AT in 2014 was at home in Mississippi, sitting in front of a TV, when a rerun of the 2012 episode of *American Greed* came on. As the story unfolded, and images of Hammes spread across the screen, the hiker recognized him as Bismarck, who he had spent a short amount of time hiking with the previous year. The hiker then emailed Joy Hammes's family and the FBI. Working off that tip, agents learned Bismarck typically attended the Trail Days celebration in Damascus. They began coordinating with the Washington County, Virginia, Sheriff's Office, the Damascus Police Department, and the Virginia State Police, and circled in.

James Hammes's last walk was about to end.

At the Ohio jail where U.S. marshals are keeping Hammes to-day, inmates cannot accept phone calls. I wrote him a letter in June. I addressed him not as "Bismarck" but as "Jim," which is what people who knew him before 2009 call him. I asked him about himself and his past; about his time on the AT; about where he stayed in deep winter, when the trail grows too cold to camp along-side; and about what he might want people to know about him.

In the package I sent I included some paper, an envelope, and some Janis Joplin stamps, and I asked him to drop me a note. Or call me collect.

As of this writing, he has not responded.

I found the answers to most of my questions without his help.

But others remain unanswered. Like the one about the money's whereabouts.

"That's the $8.7 million question, isn't it?" Jane Ryan said.

Authorities are not talking.

"At this point, we are not going to discuss the money that was allegedly embezzled," Todd Lindgren, a public affairs specialist with the FBI in Cincinnati, said. "That is something that may be discussed at trial."

Federal court documents indicate that of the millions Hammes is accused of embezzling, only $698,956 has been seized.

The other unanswered question, the one that will likely stir backcountry rumors and campfire theories for decades, is of all the places James T. Hammes could go, *Why the Appalachian Trail?*

"That's the biggest mystery," said Jeff Sadler, Hammes's cousin. "And it's one only he can answer. We may never know."

The Appalachian Trail stretches nearly 2,200 miles from Springer Mountain, Georgia, to Mount Katahdin, Maine. The idea was born less than a century ago. The Appalachian Trail Conservancy describes on its website how in 1921 a Harvard-educated conservationist named Benton MacKaye proposed "a series of work, study and farming camps along the ridges of the Appalachian Mountains." MacKaye envisioned a refuge from industrialized urban settings. "Hiking was an incidental focus," the Conservancy states. The AT was completed in 1937.

Its popularity has exploded since the 1970s, mainly because of magazine articles and books that suggest to readers the ways that walking the trail can help travelers find themselves. Even in the digital age, the romance of the trail continues to resonate. Author

Bill Bryson's classic memoir, *A Walk in the Woods,* which came out in 1998, will appear as a movie this September, starring Robert Redford. Ben Montgomery's current best-seller, *Grandma Gatewood's Walk,* tells the inspiring story of the first woman to walk the trail from top to bottom. At this moment, people are eagerly following ultra-runner Scott Jurek on social media, in the midst of his quest to run the entire length of the AT in record time.

With the swell of the Internet in the past 20 years, which provides ready resources for hikers and hundreds of personal memoirs about the AT, the number of people who take to the trail has more than doubled. The Appalachian Trail Conservancy says two to three million people step foot somewhere onto the trail each year, some hiking for an afternoon or a day, others for weeks or even months at a time. Larry Luxenberg, the author of *Walking the Appalachian Trail,* said that is a conservative estimate. He noted a poll taken not long ago at Newfound Gap, a well-known mountain pass on the AT along the border between Tennessee and North Carolina in the Great Smoky Mountains National Park, indicated nine million people passed through the area.

When considering the high number of travelers, petty crime on the trail is rare; violent crime is more rare. There have been a handful of murders—tales of shootings, stabbings, and strangulations circulate—but they are mainly isolated incidents committed by criminals who happened to be crossing trail areas, not living or hiking there, and they are conveyed like ghost stories between hikers. Tales of fugitives are exceptionally rare. Kori Feener, a filmmaker who released a documentary about the AT in 2013, said that taken as a whole, there have been fewer killings on the AT "than there were murders in my hometown of Boston last year." Fifty-two people were murdered in Boston in 2014, but since the trail first opened, only a dozen or so people are known to have been killed while hiking the AT.

Hiking the AT is a personal experience. Its pull varies from person to person. But in a broad and figurative sense, it is fair to say a majority are on a search. Thru-hikers are usually in their early twenties, looking for adventure before settling down, or past 50 and seeking something else. "You sometimes have the middle-age crowd," one AT veteran said, "who hike because of a change in life. They get divorced or lose a job or quit a job." A center yet to be found is sensed, and someone finally has time to look for it and believes they will find it on that narrow pathway that runs almost the entire length of the Appalachians. One hiker called the experience an escape.

But hiking from Georgia to Maine from spring to fall is no party. It requires months of planning. Supplies must be loaded into packs with the understanding that the next town and opportunity to restock may not come for three or four days. Many hikers send supplies to themselves ahead, care of "General Delivery" at post offices along the trail.

The terrain, some of it rugged, at first tries you physically. "Over time, your body takes a beating," AT author David Miller said. "You lose a lot of weight and accumulate aches, pains and blisters." Then the mental aspect of facing thousands of miles looms. Couple those challenges with the natural introspection that happens while hiking, and the culture on the AT is an accepting one.

"The trail is a present endeavor," Feener said, "with the focus often being on the pain you are in, the beauty you saw that day, where you are going to sleep that night, and where your next water source is."

Every step puts distance between a hiker and the worries of the world. Days run together. Previous lives slip away. Hikers may delve gently into each other's pasts, but acceptance is the norm.

A hiker named Sherry Leitner said, "It's sort of a 'don't ask, don't tell' mentality. If someone wants to share something with you about their 'real life'—meaning life off the trail—then fine, but we don't probe."

In keeping with the escapist culture, trail names are common.

"A rite of passage" for thru-hikers is how Feener described the naming process, which serves to further separate long-distance travelers from their real lives, or pasts, while they are on the trail. Some choose their own names; others are given names by other hikers.

"Just one of the things most of us do to embrace the sense of escapism that goes with the adventure," said Miller, who is known on the trail as "AWOL."

Hammes's name was "Bismarck." He seems to have given it to himself.

It is an odd name for someone wandering the AT to choose. In its adoption of the name of a remote American city in the Dakotas, it brings to mind the Coen brothers' film *Fargo*, a dark tale that includes a mild-mannered protagonist who arranges for his wife to be kidnapped and eventually murdered. It also conjures up images of Otto von Bismarck, the "Iron Chancellor" of Germany who in the 19th century established the modern world's first welfare system, or the German World War II battleship that sank killing more than 2,000 crewmen. One family member of Hammes's thought it could be a reference to a crude sexual act. Or maybe a nod to a hamlet by that name in east West Virginia, where he could have laid low occasionally, or a small village in Illinois, near where he once lived.

Hammes, though, told some hikers he was born in Bismarck, North Dakota's capital, a place most have heard of but few know. ("No one is ever from Bismarck," one hiker said. "Who else on the AT is going to be from Bismarck?") He told others he had invested in a lucrative software company based there, in that cold city of 60,000. Both of these stories—one involving a personal history, the other the roots of a livelihood—served to establish along the trail things he undoubtedly needed: a past and place that were likely foreign to people he met and that explained his presence.

Neither is true.

This is what is true: James T. Hammes was born approximately 800 miles southeast of Bismarck, North Dakota, in Milwaukee on April 30, 1962. As a young man his father, a Catholic, toyed with entering the priesthood, but married and became an accountant. Three sons followed. Only James, the oldest, would follow the father's footsteps into accounting.

Everyone called him Jim. In the 1970s, the family moved to Springfield, Illinois. In the backyard of their home was a lake. Hammes attended Glenwood High School in Chatham, Illinois. He played football and wrestled at only 5'8" and someone who knew him then said there was a suggestion of the "All-American boy in him." Nothing felt amiss then. After graduating high school in 1980, he went to a mechanics' school in Iowa on a scholarship, but did not stay. Back in Springfield again, he began studying accounting at Sangamon State University (now known as University of Illinois at Springfield). There, during the spring semester of 1984, he met another accounting student named Joy Johnson, and a friendship began. She was the smart and smitten daughter of a farmer, and on their first date wore a white dress and red belt.

Joy Johnson's sister, Jane Ryan, met Hammes shortly afterward. He had a beard, long hair, and seemed nice enough, Ryan said, if a "little different." There was a suggestion of the show-off in him. Around one of his wrists, he wore a big watch. "He wanted us to like him," Ryan said. Recently, she used the word "charming" to describe him. Her tone made it sound like a sickness.

Hammes married Joy inside a Catholic church on December 22, 1984, and they moved into an apartment on Seventh Street in Springfield. He went to work for a Coca-Cola distributor and in 1986, their daughter, Amanda, was born. Then they relocated to Cincinnati, Ohio. On the surface, the move appeared to further Hammes's career. But he was also walking away from something he preferred to keep hidden.

In Springfield, Hammes had a girlfriend—an old fling named Jill from Glenwood High—and she became pregnant. Hammes's second daughter was born in 1989, a secret to his family. Years later, when the FBI was trying to track Hammes down, agents discovered that in December 2008 he had purchased her a plane ticket from New York City, where she was a student at Columbia University, to Oklahoma, where her mother lived.

The girl—her first name is Carrie, and she is a woman now—could not be reached for comment.

Joy Hammes did not know of the second daughter. She told her family her union with Hammes was stronger than ever. They moved to Lexington, Kentucky, and Hammes took a job with G&J Pepsi-Cola Bottlers and their life entered a normal pace. There were Florida vacations. They attended Christ the King Catholic Church. Hammes, who leaned conservative, seemed to take pride that his wife was a homemaker who volunteered at God's Pantry, a local food bank. He took care of all the money. When holidays came, they often went to Springfield to visit Jane Ryan and her husband. Hammes would usually make the drive from Lexington alone a few days after his wife and daughter, because, he said, of work obligations. Ryan also recalls that he liked to take long walks, alone. There were times when he spread his accounting books across the Ryans' dinner table, working and working and working. Ryan doubted at the time that any job short of president of the United States of America required that level of commitment at Christmastime. She laughed recently, and said, "Maybe he was working that hard because he was keeping two books."

That may be. What is certain is that as the years passed, the secrets kept piling up.

Federal prosecutors say Hammes began embezzling from G&J in the late 1990s. A few years earlier, he had become controller for the company's southern division, and in that position was responsible for the company's accounting and internal controls. Court documents reveal that in 1998, Hammes opened a bank account only he could control, which was tied in name only to a vendor doing business with G&J. He then moved G&J funds into the account before transferring the money into his personal accounts. Sometimes he moved as little as $9,200. Sometimes he moved as much as $200,000. Usually it was some amount in between.

Each time he did so, James T. Hammes took one more small step away from the life he was living toward something else.

For an accountant, who people expect to be quiet and reserved, Hammes was something of an anomaly, a man with a lot of personality. People who knew him say that about the time he allegedly began embezzling his temperament, never quiet to begin with, began to become more explosive. Everything he did and said began to have exclamation marks around it.

Sadler, the cousin who lives in Colorado, said Hammes was always gregarious but started to go over the top, and he had begun questioning how genuine it all was. They drifted apart. Jane Ryan said her brother-in-law liked to "one-up" people. He developed a loud persona and could be overbearing.

"When he laughed everyone in the room knew it," Ryan said. "There was nothing quiet or understated about his personality."

Hammes dressed casually (khakis, tucked-in polos) and kept less than flashy cars parked in his driveway (a purple Chrysler, a black Jeep, a Sebring convertible), but he began going on expensive scuba diving trips, sometimes leaving Joy for two-week stretches home alone with Amanda. When she kept asking about where the money for the vacations was coming from, Hammes told her he had invested in a software company and cleared an easy $100,000. He swore her to secrecy, but she told her sister. Jane Ryan said if that story were true, Hammes would have talked about it. Growing up with two brothers instilled in him a competitive nature. He was not the type to keep successes quiet.

"I think it gave him a thrill," Ryan said, "that he could steal and no one knew about it and he could live so well."

In Lexington, the Hammes family lived in a spacious, three-bedroom brick house on Turkey Foot Road. Joy liked it there. On the night of July 24, 2003, her daughter had gone on a date and she was home alone, in bed.

James T. Hammes had gone on one of his walks.

About 11:00 p.m., a friend of Amanda's, curious about her date, drove by the home, saw smoke and dialed 911. Emergency crews pulled Hammes's wife from the burning home, but the carbon monoxide had already left her unconscious.

There are two theories of how the fire began. The fire investigator concluded a chest of drawers sitting on an extension cord caused it. The insurance people said faulty wiring in a ceiling fan was the culprit. That there were two theories has always bothered Ryan. If there was a reason for the fire to begin, she said, you would think it would be a single cause.

At the hospital, an unconscious Joy Hammes was placed in a hyperbaric chamber. But a brain scan indicated no brain activity, and she was placed on life support. "There was nothing else to do," Jane Ryan said. "She was brain dead and being kept alive by a ventilator with no hope of recovery."

Ryan remembers being in the hospital room, holding one of her sister's hands while Hammes held the other. She remembers the way Joy's body smelled like smoke and walking out of that sad room just before doctors took her off life support. Hammes, there in the hospital hallway, hugged her tight and then said, "I'm sorry." She thought that was odd, that his wife was dead, "and he is apologizing to me." Today, more than two decades later, it is a cold moment in her memory.

But the image Jane Ryan cannot shake is this one: James T. Hammes, about six weeks after Joy's death, was visiting her family. She looked out her window and stretched out on the ground beneath a tree in the yard, he was on the phone, laughing.

Hammes met a woman named Deanna, who worked for the state of Kentucky, and they married in 2006. They made a home in Lexington. By now, Hammes was telling some family members about a mysterious software business he had invested in, in the Carolinas, where he would sometimes drive, alone, to check on things. The company appears to be fiction. The FBI says he was continuing to embezzle from G&J. Someone eventually caught on.

Court documents show a special agent with the FBI interviewed G&J's chief financial officer on February 17, 2009. Five days later Hammes was summoned to Cincinnati, where the company was headquartered. He did not know the purpose of the meeting. There, he was confronted about the missing funds. He said he wanted to tell his wife in Kentucky, and speak to an attorney, and he was allowed to leave. Two days later, a federal magistrate in Ohio signed an arrest warrant but it was too late. Hammes had slipped out of his life. Investigators found his wallet and cellular telephone abandoned on a road in a tough part of Cincinnati, suggesting he had met a bad end . . . or wanted people to think he had.

Roughly three months after he disappeared, the Hammes family held a scheduled family reunion in Milwaukee. Hammes did not show up. He had always promised his mother—divorced now and living out West (she declined to comment)—that he would take care of her when age caught up. At the reunion, his mother signed over power of attorney to another family member.

Jeff Sadler believes his cousin, from the day he allegedly began transferring money illegally, had a plan to disappear with the money. He remembers Hammes telling him once, "I want to retire at 50."

"In a way," Sadler said, "I guess he did."

He believes the FBI catching on panicked him, and sent him on the run prematurely, before his plan was ready.

Hammes was two months shy of 47 when he disappeared. He left his wife Deanna, who has since divorced him. And he left his daughters, Amanda and Carrie.

A little more than a year later James Hammes stopped running and Bismarck started walking the Appalachian Trail.

The FBI, soon faced with a stagnant search and few leads, eventually put a headshot of James T. Hammes on its website beneath the word "Wanted." The photograph was taken from Hammes's 2008 Kentucky driver's license, and the man in it has a professional look, clean-shaven, with short hair. It looks nothing like the man known along the AT as Bismarck.

Many thru-hikers keep online journals in public forums. They are updated sporadically, and the musings they contain typically note their progress, the most recent terrain, notes on hikers they befriend, and photographs from the journey. It appears Bismarck did not keep an online journal. But dozens of other hikers' journals contain references to him, as well as photographs of the well-known hiker. In each of them, his grin is wide and easy.

His smile, in fact, litters online journals.

"Bismarck was surprisingly engaged for a person on the run," Miller, aka AWOL, said. "He seemed not to avoid having his picture taken."

There is a snapshot of Hammes from early May 2010, only 15 months after he vanished. In it, he is reclining on a couch inside Braemar Castle Hostel in Hampton, Tennessee. He is in conversation with another hiker. His boots are off, and he already has a beard. Hair covers his ears. Comparing photographs from that time to his latest mugshot, he does not appear to have cut his hair or shaved again. That change in appearance certainly helped him evade authorities. Others say the immediacy of the trail, coupled with the culture, made it a good place to lay low. Most hikers on the trail are already more attuned to nature than current events. They do not watch a lot of television.

"The fact of the matter is, the culture of the trail almost welcomes people that are trying to hide a place to go," Feener said. "Not intentionally . . . but most people you meet are running away from, or looking for something."

But Bismarck appears to have thru-hiked the Appalachian Trail multiple times, and Luxenberg said that likely played a part in his capture. The thru-hiker community each year essentially amounts to a small town—a couple thousand people. Most start at the southern end of the trail in Georgia in early spring and head north, in something like a pack, until they reach the end. Along the way, histories are shared.

"A thru-hike is transformational for many," Miller said, "and so conversations on the trail tend to be more open and personal than in 'normal' daily life . . . you'll certainly be asked many times about your background and what inspired you to thru-hike."

Aside from making the grandiose claim one night in 2010 around a glowing campfire at Moreland Gap Shelter in Tennessee that he briefly played professional hockey, Bismarck seems to have offered a distorted version of the truth through the years.

The story: his wife had died and, stricken with grief, he told his two daughters good-bye and began wandering the trail, framing his journey as a search for peace. He missed his children, he would say, but they were both doing well in medical schools. He would occasionally bring up the Kentucky Wildcats basketball team. He could be opinionated but rarely obnoxious, and seemed to have damped down his personality a touch. Explaining how he appeared on the trail each spring, disappeared in winter, only to return when the weather broke the following March, he said that his work allowed him to take six months off each year.

Patrick Bredlau hiked with him through Maine for three weeks last year and said sometimes the story left him scratching his head. But, Bredlau said, he reminded himself of the nature of their endeavor.

"Yes, there were things that were strange," he said, "but these are people who live their lives in the woods. It's weird."

For the most part, however, Bismarck fit right in.

Other thru-hikers say he was chipper and exceedingly friendly. When he shared a car ride he always offered to split the cost. (Once, in 2013, he left a $20 bill with a friend with instructions to give it to a woman who had given him a ride because he was sure she would not accept it from him.) At Bearfence Mountain Shelter in Virginia one night a woman, spooked by a bear, decided to stay inside a shelter and he offered her a sleeping pad. Near Jo-Mary Road in Maine he once taped a bag containing ramen noodles and PowerBars to a tree along with a note explaining that the food was for an older hiker that he knew was behind him and struggling to finish the trail. When a well-known thru-hiker known as Buffalo Bobby died in 2011, Bismarck offered to carry his ashes up to Mount Katahdin. He was also eager to share his knowledge of the trail. "But not overly so," one hiker said. "Just social in the way most people on the trail tend to be."

Miller updates his guidebook to the AT each year. "There are thousands of hikers with the book," he said, "but only a few dozen write to me with updates." Over the last six years, Bismarck, from different places along the AT, was one of those who did, emailing him bits of useful information.

"David, just wanted to let you know that the Quality Inn in Waynesboro, Va., is not honoring the rate published in the guide," one reads. "In fact, the gentleman at the front desk seemed perplexed when I asked for the hiker rate."

In March, a hiker with the trail name Bingo was staying in a lodge at Nantahala Outdoor Center, near Bryson City, North Carolina. He showered and ate a lunch at River's End Restaurant, and as he was leaving, met Bismarck. They had a brief, pleasant conversation in which Bismarck said he was looking forward, after time on the trail, to a warm meal at a table.

"I remember him calling me 'brother' in that passing way male colleagues sometimes talk," Bingo said.

Later, they met again, this time at Clingman's Dome in the Great Smoky Mountains National Park. At 6,643 feet, the peak, which includes an observation tower and is accessible by a paved road, is something of a gathering place for hikers, a destination where they might pause and linger. Bismarck had been there at least once before: an online journal post from April 2010 makes mention that he took a three-hour nap in a hammock there. This time, it was cold out, and raining, and Bismarck complained that the Frogg Toggs brand of rain gear he wore tore too easily. Then he was off, catching a ride toward Gatlinburg, Tennessee, where he could resupply and get some rest in an inn.

"I don't think he was a stranger to staying at hotels in town," Bingo said.

Last year, in April, a hiker called Second B stopped for a break near Pearisburg, Virginia, and Bismarck and another hiker walked up beside him. Over the next two days they shared the trail in spots.

"I had been thinking and talking with them off and on about religion," Second B said. "I am not a religious person but I'm spiritual."

Over hand-rolled cigarettes that Second B supplied, they discussed faith. During the conversation, Bismarck spoke ill of churches that he felt focused on scare tactics and guilt, instead of love and kindness.

It is not surprising.

Bismarck, everyone agrees, had a religious streak. Like many who espouse their faith, he seemed to be a man searching for serenity, a simple life. People say he tended to wear a Christian cross around his neck, always tilted his head in prayer before each meal, and plotted his route so that each Sunday he could be near enough to a church to attend a service.

His search for religious peace seemed to be a constant.

So was the company of a woman with the trail name Hopper.

She is one of this story's mysteries.

She met Bismarck in 2010, and they seem to have been in a relationship by 2011. Some hikers described them as "boyfriend" and "girlfriend." Others say they were married. Regardless, they remained a couple until Bismarck's arrest in Damascus in May. In fact, she was there at the Montgomery Homestead Inn when he was placed in handcuffs. A law enforcement officer in the room when Hammes was apprehended claims Hopper's reaction to the arrest suggested she knew nothing of his past. Most hikers interviewed for this story showed a genuine concern for her emotional state and whereabouts in the wake of all that has happened.

In photographs of Bismarck and Hopper—behind the sign atop Mount Katahdin or having milkshakes in some cafe along the AT—they are usually side-by-side. And smiling.

A tall, attractive woman with strawberry blond hair, Hopper's real name is Teri Hanavan. She was hiking the AT at least as early as 2001, when she met a retired police officer from California known by the trail name Spike. They bonded on the trail and married in late 2002. Spike died of cancer in April 2009. The following year, Hanavan was on the trail spreading his ashes. Around that time, she met Bismarck for the first time.

Without knowing Bismarck's true past, hikers thought he and Hopper were perfect for one another. They had both lost spouses and were grieving. They were both well versed in AT etiquette and culture. They were both trail lifers. And Hopper, people say, was as religious, if not more so, than Bismarck.

In 2002, when Hopper thru-hiked the AT, she posted her name on the Appalachian Trail Conservancy "2000 Milers" list. She listed her home state then as California.

In 2014, when she posted her name again, she listed her home state as Kentucky, where Hammes had come from.

I found an email address for her and sent her a note.

She did not respond.

Bismarck did not hike year-round.

In the winter, much of the trail is covered with snow and almost impassable, and weather conditions make long treks hard. Where he lived in the off-season varied, but he spent parts of each winter in East Andover, Maine, holed up in a hostel called The Cabin operated by a couple who hikers refer to as "Honey" and "Bear."

Karl Humbarger, who works there, said Bismarck did this in 2012, 2013, and 2014. At The Cabin, travelers can exchange work for a discount on the $20 per night rate for room and board and Bismarck usually helped out to save money. Humbarger described him as always being in "good humor" and "very social." He noted that Bismarck took the work seriously, which was a welcome sight for Humbarger, who said most hikers do not. Bismarck helped build a garage at The Cabin. He helped install a heater too.

When Humbarger heard about the things people say Hammes did, he had a hard time coming to terms with that person being the same person as Bismarck.

"You would have never guessed that he was accused of what they say," Humbarger said.

Last winter, after leaving The Cabin, Bismarck lived in Apartment 234 at Parkview Studios on Harris Road in Fort Wayne, Indiana. Guests pay $158 for a week's stay; $520 for a month. "There is never a credit check, no deposit and no lease," the website states. This, of course, would appeal to a man on the run.

The apartment is a two-story building with approximately 61 rooms, each one heated and cooled with wall units. The Fort Wayne Children's Zoo and Interstate 69, which runs 635 miles from Texas to the Canadian border, are both less than a mile away. There Bismarck sat, waiting on spring to return, when he would head once again to Springer, Georgia, and begin another trek north.

One day in February, he wrote from his Gmail account—his handle was wanderingcatholic0712—to his old hiking buddy, Patrick Bredlau.

"Been working crazy hours here in Fort Wayne," he said, "but the end is in sight. So looking forward to getting out of here as I've been going at it very hard. Good for the paycheck but not the best for the soul." He described a Christmas card he had mailed Bredlau, then continued: "Hope you've had a good winter . . . springer [Georgia] fever is setting in deep here and if all goes well we'll be in Springer two weeks from Sunday."

In less than a month, the *American Greed* episode featuring Hammes would air again. When it did, a 2014 AT thru-hiker was watching in Mississippi.

Earlier this year, I sat in a coffee shop and talked across a table with Hayden Crume, the 32-year-old hiker who had met Bismarck and turned in Hammes. His trail name is Chair.

"Nicest guy ever," was how Crume described Bismarck.

Crume, a successful businessman, found himself with some free time and financial freedom last year after his business was acquired by a larger corporation. He said he wanted to "accomplish something big" and set off on the AT, hiking from Georgia to Maine.

"Going to Disney World just seemed too cliché," he said.

Not long after starting off, he met Bismarck at a shelter along the southern half of the AT. Hopper was there too. Crume, who had never hiked the trail before, was cooking oatmeal near the shelter. This is frowned upon by hikers, because food aromas attract bears. Bismarck approached and politely told him it was best to not do so there.

Altogether, Crume and Bismarck spent approximately 24 hours together on the AT. After that, their paths did not cross again.

I asked Crume what it was he noticed, while watching the *American Greed* episode, that reminded him of Bismarck. He was not sure.

"I just happened to look up at the right moment I guess," he said, "and subconsciously I immediately recognized I knew him, but [at first] couldn't quite place him."

Shocked, he later sent three emails. One went to the *American Greed* producers. One went to the FBI. And one went to Amanda Hammes, Bismarck's daughter, and it contained photographs Crume had taken of Bismarck. In one, the image was zoomed in close on the eyes, and Crume asked if the eyes looked familiar.

Amanda declined to comment for this story. But after receiving the email, she contacted her aunt, Jane Ryan, wondering if someone was playing a cruel joke.

It was no joke.

Agents kept Jane Ryan in the loop, but over the next few weeks told her to keep quiet, as locating Hammes would take some work.

"The FBI had told me before," she told an Illinois newspaper columnist earlier this summer, "that the trail is 2,000 miles long, and it may take a little while to find him. But the thing is that Jim had to be lucky every single day of his life. The FBI only had to be lucky one day."

Patrick Bredlau goes by the trail name "RW." It began as Road Warrior, but early in his trail journey he fell in with some hikers connected to the Wounded Warrior Foundation. He admires what they do for military veterans, and did not want to suggest that he was among them, so he shortened his name to RW. Along the trail, each time someone asked him what the initials stood for, he would ask them what they thought it stood for, and their answer stood until the next time he was asked.

On September 3, 2014, at Speck Pond Shelter in Maine, Bredlau met Bismarck and Hopper for the first time. Bismarck asked what RW stood for, and Bredlau told him how it worked. A heavy thunderstorm had come the previous night and Bismarck told him RW stood for "Rumble Water."

Bredlau sensed that Bismarck and Hopper—"It's like they were meant for each other," he said—were experienced hikers with a good rapport with the trail. "Taking one step at a time," he said. "Enjoying life. Moved slow." It had been a long journey for Bredlau, and he liked the couple's approach. They hiked toward Mount Katahdin together for the next three weeks, sharing their stories.

Bismarck must have liked his companion. Though he lied about his real name—he said his name was "Brian Wafford"—he offered more truths from his past to Bredlau than he typically allowed others to know. He said he was from Wisconsin (true), was 52 years old (true at the time), and a widower with a daughter (partially true). He also mentioned that he liked scuba diving (true).

When Bredlau shared his past, it must have sent a shock down Bismarck's spine.

Bredlau is a retired federal bank examiner, a former certified civil fraud examiner for the U.S. Department of the Treasury.

When asked about the fact that Bismarck sent him a Christmas card last year, Bredlau, at his home in a suburb of Chicago, laughed.

"Was it one of those situations where you keep your friends close and your enemies closer?" he said. "Or was it a game?"

Bredlau said he never suspected Bismarck's past.

"He had his story down," he said. "I took it hook, line, and sinker."

Asked where he would look for the $8.7 million, Bredlau said he would begin in the Cayman Islands. Hammes, after all, enjoyed scuba diving. And traveling alone. And the FBI confirmed that Hammes traveled to the Caribbean and Curaçao, which the U.S. Department of State listed as a "jurisdiction of primary concern" in a 2014 report on money laundering.

"I'll always want to know his motivation," Bredlau said.

So do many other people, but not Jane Ryan.

There was a time when she wanted to confront him. But not anymore. She does not want to speak to James T. Hammes ever again. Not because she has nothing to say—she still cries when talking about her sister—but because she feels it would be a waste of time.

"I have no desire to look at him," she said. "I know he would not tell me the truth. He lied about everything for so long. It came so easy to him."

Asked if she believes Hammes could have had it in him to kill her sister, Ryan said if he did the things the FBI said he did, "he's capable."

Then, of her sister's death, she said, "I don't think he cared."

Despite his obvious love of the outdoors, I struggle to understand his motivation as well, why he went to the Appalachian Trail and stayed there, so public, for so long. The thru-hiking community each season is the equivalent of a small town, and Bismarck became one of its best known, most respected citizens. It is so easy to find photographs of him, smiling among others in the community.

Then I remember something a hiker told me and I have not been able to separate his words from the image of Bismarck on the AT since.

"The outside world and its problems don't exist to you while you're walking," the hiker wrote in an email. "They might creep in at night if you're alone or away from other hikers . . . but generally it's a whole other life and it feels good. Very good.

"I dream of it still a year later."

I wonder what Hammes dreams of in that Ohio jail, and if he walks much beyond the confines of his cell. But mostly, when I think of James T. Hammes, I see Bismarck glancing over his shoulder on the sun-dappled trail, his eyes meeting others hiking toward him, halting a moment to offer a greeting, but also to gauge what they might know. Then, realizing they know nothing, he smiles, and begins walking, one step after the other, trying to leave behind the man he used to be.

MICHAEL J. MOONEY

The High Life and Fast Times of Jim Dent

FROM D MAGAZINE

HE WENT TO MEXICO planning to drink himself to death. By January 2014, Jim Dent had alienated anyone who ever loved him. He was wanted on felony warrants in at least two Texas counties —stemming from his eighth, ninth, and tenth DWI arrests. And his book was so late that the publisher canceled the contract. So he cut off his ankle monitors and made his way down to San José del Cabo, on the Sea of Cortez. He got a condo on the beach for $800 a month and started drinking big bottles of Oso Negro vodka, which he could buy for 83 pesos—a little more than five bucks. He soon decided that he liked it there, and he didn't want to die after all.

An Internet phone line allowed him to call the United States, and he started working again on what would now be an independently published ebook—the first part of a trilogy—about the hard-partying star quarterback Johnny Manziel. A friend from Dallas paid him to write a screenplay about the legendary SMU running back Doak Walker. Dent would type in the mornings, then go swimming in the warm, clear water a few hundred feet from his door. Then he'd write a little more, cut out around two or three in the afternoon, and reward himself with a drink or six. He had a girlfriend he'd see sometimes, and he made friends at a few bars in town.

By the middle of September, *Manziel Mania* was out, Dent was doing phone interviews with sports radio shows all over the country promoting it, and he had steady income. Though he was still a wanted man in Texas, he knew he wasn't a high enough priority for the federal government to get involved. He even boasted about his book's sales on his public Facebook profile.

Then Hurricane Odile hit.

Dent tells an incredible tale of survival. He says he was asleep in his condo when the storm came ashore in the middle of the night. He says he put on his ski goggles and, with his water-ski rope, tied himself to the metal railing on his porch so he could watch the hurricane.

"It was amazing," he says. "The colors and the wind and the sound. I stayed as long as I could. I ran in the side door just as my plate glass window blew out."

Then he says he got under his bed, but the water on the floor was rising too fast and he worried he'd drown. As he got up, he says, he felt the building shaking—"It was an earthquake!" He hunkered down in the closet and, though he wasn't a particularly religious man, began to pray. He says part of the roof came off in the Category 4 winds. He figured he'd be crushed. In the end, he says, his condo was completely destroyed, but he escaped mostly unscathed.

At that point, Dent says, he was planning to make his way back to Collin County and turn himself in. "I had done wrong," he says, sounding like a little boy from Arkansas. "I was gonna come back home and give myself up and hope that things were gonna go a little bit better."

He didn't come home, though. He faked a heart attack to get on a plane to Guadalajara and stayed in Mexico for another four months.

"I don't drink when I write," Dent tells me, "but I can write on a hangover. I've been known to write a 5,000-word chapter in one day."

The Collin County sergeant sitting in the small room with us smirks at the author's braggadocio. Dent is trimmer and looks healthier than he does in old photos, when he was close to 250 pounds and constantly red-faced. He says he hasn't had a drink in more than two months—since he was arrested trying to sneak back across the border in San Diego. He's wearing a green, county-issued jumpsuit, and as he talks, the echoes of metal doors opening and closing throw off his cadence.

I contacted him in the spring, as he was awaiting sentencing for his ninth and tenth DWIs, facing up to 40 years in prison. I'd never met him before, but I wanted to see for myself what had become of the man so many writers in Texas admired. From the outside it seemed like—for most of his career, anyway—Dent had the grand life a lot of writers strive for: bouncing from swanky hotel to swanky hotel in New York, Miami, L.A., drinking with people we only see on TV, getting into the kinds of Las Vegas adventures most of us only read about, all the while ferreting out the kinds of fascinating stories that command a reader's attention.

When I visit, a *Dallas Morning News* story about him has just come out, and he's bothered. He says he's considering suing. Specifically, Dent says, the paper got some of his finances wrong. He says he will still get $250,000 if his book *Twelve Mighty Orphans* is made into a movie. And he swears he never published his own obituary, though several people remember him writing one. He also estimates the *News* story's length at 9,000 words—it's actually half that—and calls it "the longest story to appear in the *DMN* since the John F. Kennedy assassination."

He's a captivating storyteller and not shy about self-promotion. Telling me the hurricane story, he imitates the loud, gushing winds of the storm, and the sergeant and I both laugh. While describing the chaos, Dent stops and points at my notebook.

"This is good shit," he says.

Of course, the fact that he's an addict makes it impossible to know whether he's telling the truth. But his résumé is indisputable. He covered the Dallas Cowboys for more than a decade, a star at both the *Dallas Times Herald* and the *Fort Worth Star-Telegram*. He was also a nationally syndicated radio host and bestselling author, responsible for some very popular sports books that either have been made into movies or will be soon. (*My All-American*, scheduled for release later this year, is based on Dent's book *Courage Beyond the Game*. The movie is directed by Angelo Pizzo, who wrote *Rudy* and *Hoosiers*.)

Dent is writing a new book in jail, he says. It's about his life as a drinker. Working title: *Last Call*. He writes it by hand, with a pen and a legal pad, and sends it to his sister in Little Rock. She types it and sends it back for him to edit. In the two and a half months he's been in jail, he's written about 100 typed pages, which he says he'll send me. He says he hopes he can publish it by Christmas.

We also talk about some of the writers and agents we both know and bars we've both patronized. Dent snaps his head a bit and sneers when I mention the name of one magazine writer, because he remembers a bad review the guy gave one of his books four years ago.

Over the course of a few weeks, I visit Dent twice in jail, and we talk on the phone a lot. We talk about how he had a happy childhood, growing up in Arkansas. Both of his grandfathers were alcoholics, he says, but his father wasn't a big drinker. Dent's father only had an eighth-grade education, but he was a successful truck salesman, and the family had season tickets to watch the Arkansas Razorbacks. That's where Dent fell in love with football. He played in high school, and except for the occasional sip of cherry vodka with his buddies, says he didn't drink much until he got to SMU.

Dent tells me he had a teacher in eighth grade who had him diagram sentences, and he liked the way they seemed to fit together like little puzzles. The same teacher introduced him to *The Grapes of Wrath*, the first book he loved.

"I felt bad for the people from Oklahoma. I wanted to fight along with them," he says. "I think that's where I got onto the underdog story."

Usually the Collin County jail is pretty strict about how long inmate visits last. We were told we would have a maximum of 20 minutes for the first meeting. But our conversation that day goes on for nearly twice that, because the sergeant in the room is so fascinated by Dent's tales.

The rules of the media golf tournament were simple: after each hole you had to drink a beer for every stroke you had over par. Dent, who was in his mid-twenties, was a pretty terrible golfer, so it didn't take long before he was wasted. The event was at Stevens Park, and a lot of the young sportswriters were there. At some point Dent was driving a golf cart down a steep hill and lost control, rolling it into some iron bars at the edge of the course. He emerged, in the words of one reporter, "pretty bashed up," but he was laughing and smiling, so everyone else laughed too. That was Dent.

By the time he was 24, he was a full-time Cowboys beat writer

—the youngest in the herd. Doug Bedell started his career with Dent in Beaumont, then worked with him at the *Dallas Times Herald* in the mid-'70s. Bedell says that back then they were "the best of friends." And it was a good time to be a reporter, with three thriving newspapers in North Texas. There was plenty of debauchery, he says, but they were always serious about the journalism. Dent got a lot of praise and attention for stories about recruiting violations and financial misappropriation and racial prejudice.

"He brought something new to sports writing," Bedell remembers. "He was chasing down rumors, doing investigative stuff that was respected for good reason."

Being a sportswriter back then also meant free alcohol everywhere. There were courtesy suites with open bars for members of the media at every horse race, every basketball game, every boxing match. After reporting on a round at a golf tournament, Dent could walk over and have a couple rounds of beers with some of his sportswriter heroes.

He says covering the Dallas Cowboys during that stretch was like being on tour with the Beatles. In every city there were fans and curious bystanders swarming the stadium and the hotel lobby. There were excited women in every direction, decadent parties, dinners at hard-to-get-into restaurants. He tells stories about getting drunk with Jimmy Johnson in Orlando and getting drunk with Randy White at White's own bar. As Dent tells it, they went back to White's ranch house in Prosper, because "he was going to show me some martial arts moves." They started "knocking the crap out of each other," before the defensive tackle sent the spry writer crashing into a wall.

For six weeks at the end of every summer, the writers all went to Thousand Oaks, in Southern California, for Cowboys training camp. After filing their daily stories, they'd gather in the hospitality suite, and the party would start. When he was back in Dallas, Dent would often close out his nights with the other young writers at Louie's or Joe Miller's.

Longtime sports columnist and radio host Randy Galloway is 10 years older than Dent and has known him for more than 40 years. He remembers Dent running down Texas Rangers quotes as an intern at the *Dallas Morning News*.

"I've always liked him," Galloway says. "Dent was as good a reporter-writer combo as you'll find. There's a lot of people who can write, but not a lot of reporters who go after it."

Working for competing papers, Galloway and Dent went on road trips together for more than a decade. One time, in 1983, they were covering a horse race in Arkansas, and after everyone else went to bed, Dent continued to drink. The next morning they were all supposed to meet for breakfast at a nearby diner, but Dent wasn't there. He called the diner and explained that he'd been pulled over for drunken driving and needed someone to get him out of jail.

A few minutes later, Galloway came striding through the front door of the police station and pointed at Dent. "Son," Galloway said in his deepest Texas drawl, "I raised you better than this!"

Both men still laugh as they recount the story. Back then, DWIs weren't as serious as they are now. Dent had to pay a small fine, and that was that. When he's talking about his list of transgressions, he sometimes forgets about this one and refers to his second DWI as his first.

"Dent wasn't any wilder or worse-behaved in the 1980s than a lot of other local sportswriters," says Bud Kennedy, who overlapped with Dent at the *Times Herald* and the *Star-Telegram*. "We all came along when sportswriters were expected to live up to this legend as the high-rolling, hard-drinking party hounds we read about in Dan Jenkins's novels. We were 25, and we all wanted to be like Dan and Bud Shrake and Gary Cartwright, or whatever we imagined they were like."

There was a Hunter S. Thompson quote Dent loved to recite on cue: "Journalism is not a profession or a trade. It is a cheap catchall for f—offs and misfits—a false doorway to the backside of life, a filthy piss-ridden little hole nailed off by the building inspector, but just deep enough for a wino to curl up from the sidewalk and masturbate like a chimp in a zoo-cage."

By the mid-'80s, recreational cocaine was all over Dallas, and Dent certainly didn't abstain. He used to tell people, "I doze but never close." Galloway remembers one night when they'd been drinking late in Thousand Oaks, and Dent got a call from Gary Busey—and proceeded to drive 45 minutes or so to Los Angeles to keep the party going.

Friends from the time noticed a change in Dent's personality.

He had a new persona and nickname in bars. As the night grew later and he was further gone, Dent would start to mumble and blow little floating spit bubbles. Eventually this became a clue that the fun for the evening was over. It's what his friends called Rocket Man, as in: "The Rocket Man came out," or "He went Rocket Man," or "The only people who could stop the Rocket Man were the people who stopped him now: law enforcement."

He says the first real troubles began when he switched from drinking mostly beer to mostly hard liquor. There were more fights, more blackouts, more problems in general. He was in the parking lot at Louie's when he first wondered if he should quit drinking. He doesn't remember the exact date—probably one of the times he was thrown out—but he was in his forties, divorced, and increasingly distant from his friends.

"I was lonely," he tells me. "Alcoholics drink because they're lonely. They may go to a bar to find friendship, but they go home to an empty house."

By then the *Dallas Times Herald* was gone, and Dent was hosting a sports radio talk show and trying to start a book career. He declared bankruptcy in an attempt to save the house he'd built in Flower Mound, and he'd gone from driving a $33,000 Volvo to driving a $2,000 Caprice. It's around then, in 1994, that he got his second DWI, this time in Denton County. He got another in Dallas County in 1997. One, he says, stemmed from a fight with his ex-wife, and the other came not too long after a girlfriend got an abortion.

One woman he dated during this stretch says their lives were fun for a while, full of glamorous parties. But the drinking was a problem, and he wouldn't stop. Like the other women I spoke to about him, she didn't want to talk much about her time with Dent and asked that I not print her name.

Jim Donovan first met Dent in 1994 through another writer. Donovan had just become a literary agent, and he was looking for authors. Dent had a solid idea: a well-sourced book about the misbehavior of Jerry Jones, from a writer who had covered the team for years. They worked on a proposal and got a deal for *King of the Cowboys*.

Book writing was harder than Dent expected, though. Structure didn't come naturally. Donovan was the first editor for each chapter. Dent was living in an apartment in Las Colinas then, and Donovan, an author himself, would go over with notes.

"He wrote short paragraphs, like a newspaper writer," Donovan says. "But he took editing well. Not all authors do."

The book came out during training camp in 1995 and sold modestly. Dent says that Jones offered him $250,000 to ditch the book before it went to print, then bought thousands of copies to keep it from the public.

He wrote a second book a few years later, this time with an umpire, called *You're Out and You're Ugly, Too.* But his first real success came in 1999 with *The Junction Boys,* the story of coach Bear Bryant's torturous Texas A&M preseason training camp. Dent says he first heard the story in a bar in 1985.

The book became a bestseller, tapping into a huge audience of fans of both A&M and Alabama, where Bryant spent most of his career. In 2002, the book was turned into an ESPN movie that aired regularly for weeks. His prose won't draw comparisons to Fitzgerald or Joyce, but his stories unfold quickly, with characters you want to root for. The subjects of his books—the Dallas Cowboys, the Chicago Bears, the football programs at UT, OU, and Notre Dame—make them great for Christmases and birthdays. And one of Dent's great skills is his ability to find the true underdog stories even in these vaunted institutions, with all their expectation and privilege.

The people who had known him for years began to see less of him. He disappeared to Las Vegas for long stretches. There are stories of tough guys in black suits and white ties showing up at his usual haunts, looking for Dent, saying he owed money. There are stories of girlfriends showing up with bruises and sore jaws.

Galloway got a call from Dent in 2002 asking if he could come on Galloway's radio show to promote his new book. They set up a time a few days later—"When it came to promoting books, Dent was always on time," Galloway says—and Dent called in. When his producer fielded the call, Galloway knew something was strange.

"Dent was in jail!" Galloway says. "He was doing the interview from the Brazos County jail."

Galloway listened in on the line before they went on the air. What he heard was Dent yelling: "Hey, you motherf—ers, I said shut the f— up! I'm doing work here!" Galloway asked if he still wanted to do the interview. "Yeah," Dent said. "They're shutting up now."

That was when Dent was serving 40 days for his fourth DWI. On the day he got out, in March of 2002, he drove up to Dallas to have breakfast with Donovan. They talked for a while about Dent's next book, his plan for research, and his goal to stay sober. Donovan gave him a little bit of money. Then Dent drove to Oklahoma, where, that night, he got his fifth DWI.

Over the years, Dent has been to Alcoholics Anonymous. He was given shots of Vivitrol, a drug that's supposed to make you sick if you drink alcohol. "The problem was I'd drink on it and not get sick," he says. At one point he wore a device on his ankle that was supposed to measure the alcohol in his perspiration every 30 minutes. Even a nearly two-year stint in prison didn't change him. He thinks of it in terms of his ability to handle his booze in public. Like he's an aging quarterback who doesn't have the arm strength he once did.

Sometimes even Dent has difficulty keeping track of his time-line. He could often go a few years without getting into much trouble. But other stretches are pure calamity, time-stamped by book publications and the arrest reports his former friends would email to each other.

When he was on the run, which was often, he'd put his belongings in storage somewhere, then hide somewhere else. Sometimes in the backwoods of Arkansas. Sometimes on the casino floors of Las Vegas. There were more arrests: a DWI in Nevada, another one in Arkansas.

By 2007, he had become a terror to the people who loved him. He was arrested or cited at least three times in Las Vegas that year. In May, he was involved in what police called a "domestic violence event," though he was gone by the time officers arrived. In September, he was cited for disturbing the peace. In October, police responded to another domestic violence call, this time arresting Dent and charging him with battery and coercion by use of deadly threats—for at least temporarily preventing a girlfriend from calling 911. There was more prison time. He says the other inmates called him "the old guy who fights" and mostly stayed away.

There were also stretches when he didn't drink. He'd go a few months here, a little more than a year there. He'd focus on writing—he published four books in four years—but then something would happen. An argument. Or bad news. Or something that just didn't seem fair. And then he'd have a drink.

"Stress is my trigger," he tells me.

There were times when Donovan, his agent, was sending checks to five different attorneys in four states. There were more court cases than he could keep track of. One time Dent asked him to take over his power of attorney. Another time Dent told a sheriff's deputy that Donovan was his brother. And it seemed like he always needed money. After 14 years as his agent, Donovan finally told him they weren't going to work together anymore.

"Life is just too short," Donovan says.

Dent stayed out of trouble for a couple more years—long enough to get off probation, at least. Then, in 2012, he got another DWI outside of Austin when he crashed into a tollbooth, abandoned his car, and was eventually found hiding in nearby bushes by a police dog. He convinced someone to post his bond there, and he moved back to North Texas, where he got two more DWIs three months apart. In one incident, he rammed his girlfriend's car into her neighbor's garage door with his F-150 pickup. The other time, police responded to reports of a reckless driver and found Dent carrying a case of beer and a bottle of wine across a Walgreens parking lot.

Feeling like his life was over, he took a plane to San Diego and a cab to the border. That's where he cut off his ankle monitors and dropped them into the bed of a passing pickup. He likes to imagine the authorities tracking them, wondering what he was doing.

Then he crossed into Mexico and started working his way to the coast.

Jessica Zak is a bail bondswoman in Austin. She's never met Dent, but she'd like to. On the advice of an attorney, Zak posted Dent's bond after the Austin DWI, and because she was told he was a celebrity and trustworthy, she didn't ask for a co-signer. When he ran, she was out $20,000. So she set about getting him back.

She hired private investigators to look for him in Arkansas, posting outside the home of his elderly mother. She had more people —at times, eight total—searching in Dallas and Austin. She says everyone they talked to said Dent owed them money or had screwed them over somehow. In all, Zak spent more than $15,000 to get back her $20,000 bond.

"It wasn't even about the money," she says. "He was just such a pompous ass."

When they tracked him to Mexico, Zak hired a woman to message Dent on Facebook and try to lure him back. Dent says that he knew what was going on from the first message, that he was "just having some fun with it." Zak is convinced otherwise.

"If he says he didn't fall for it, he's lying," she says. "He cried to her. He lied to her. He even sent pictures of his junk."

Over time, Zak says, the woman she hired began to fall for Dent. There were secret conversations and hurt feelings, and the woman started having marriage trouble. Zak became concerned.

"He is such a good con man," Zak says. "I think she believed she was going to live on the beach with a famous writer."

The bondswoman says she finally convinced someone in Homeland Security to look into the case. She says they were close. They had pictures of Dent's condo. They knew right where he was.

She sighs.

"Then the hurricane hit."

Randy Galloway says he wanted to visit Dent in the Collin County jail, but he didn't know what he'd say.

"He's probably one of the biggest wastes of talent in our business," Galloway tells me. "Being with Dent was a total trip, but he was one of those guys who had no stop sign. Everybody has some kind of stop sign. But if it's booze, if it's women, if it's cocaine, if it's gambling, Jim just didn't have a stop sign."

Most of the people Dent used to drink with haven't spoken to him in more than a decade, but they have similar thoughts: "He never got out of the fast lane." "The same thing that made him successful probably destroyed him."

Dent's book sales will probably pick up a little with the release of the movie based on *Courage Beyond the Game* later this year. He insists that *Twelve Mighty Orphans* would make an even better film.

The second time I visit him at the jail, he's gone before the judge for sentencing. Soon, he'll be shipped away to prison. He got eight years for the DWI involving his girlfriend and 10 years for the one at Walgreens, and another 10 years for jumping bail, but all of his sentences will be served at the same time. Because Dent's vehicles were declared deadly weapons in his DWI charges, he has to serve at least half of the 10 years before he's eligible for parole. People at the jail seem to think it's a good deal.

"Five years," the same sergeant as last time says, shaking his head, "for 10 DWIs?"

Dent says he's focused on finishing the book. He starts writing every day at 7:00 a.m. "It's the best time of the day, because the dumbasses are asleep," he says. He usually goes until noon, unless there's a visitor or laundry to do. He takes an hour break and then writes again until five. He says his hand cramps all the time, but "I play with the pain."

He's sent me the first 100 pages. Like most of his books, there are some interesting details and some entertaining stories—and a few awkward clichés. He writes about the glitz and excess surrounding the Cowboys, and about girlfriends who tempt him away from the keyboard with a glass of wine—or show up at his home in nothing but a winter coat and lingerie.

In the parts he sent me, he explains that of his 10 DWIs, four were the result of blackout drinking, pure indulgence. The other six came after someone upset him and he drank too much to deal with it. Dent is a smart man. He says the right things: "I take full responsibility," and "I have no one but myself to blame." But the pages I saw didn't have much in the way of contrition or remorse.

There have been other profiles of Jim Dent through the years, some of which also feature interviews with him behind bars. And toward the end, there's always some moment where he promises that he's done drinking for good. People who like him want to believe him, but at this point in his battle with alcohol, he's certainly the underdog. If he were a character in a book someone else was writing, he probably wouldn't be a hero.

He says he's found Christ now. He's excited to talk about his plans for when he gets out. He says he met a guy in jail who has a rich brother who is interested in publishing his memoir and maybe turning some of his other books into movies. Dent says he's talked to people about speaking at churches, about sharing his long, sordid story. He says he wants to use his talents to help people, and he knows committing to speeches might help keep him sober.

A few seconds later, he reminds me that in all of his DWI arrests, he never hurt anyone else. Aside from a tollbooth, he says, there was never any serious property damage.

"I've had one car wreck, and it was my car," he says. "I know I've had a slew of DWIs. There were some mitigating circumstances. The brother-in-law called the cops, and he shouldn't have. I got in an argument, and my girlfriend was saying the wrong things to me —" He interrupts himself. "I know I shouldn't have the number of DWIs I have, and I take full responsibility."

"There was always alcohol, though," I say. "That was a factor in every one of your arrests, right?"

He pauses for a moment to think about what I've said.

"Well," he says. "It's more my state of mind."

L. JON WERTHEIM AND KEN RODRIGUEZ

Smack Epidemic

FROM SPORTS ILLUSTRATED

ROMAN MONTANO HAD barely learned cursive when he was asked to sign his first baseball. Parents of teammates had watched him dominate game after game in Albuquerque's Little League during the summer of 2000, mowing down batters and belting home runs. The autograph requests were mostly facetious, but what they signified was clear: the kid was going somewhere.

The next few years only confirmed that notion. Roman grew to 6'6" and 250 pounds. He made a mockery of the weight room at Eldorado High and ran the 40-yard dash in 4.9. As a sophomore defensive lineman he was honorable mention All-State in Class 5A. He also joined the basketball team his senior year, giving in to the pleadings of the coach, and was instantly the Eagles' best player. And after high school, when he trained with the legion of MMA fighters based in Albuquerque, they encouraged him to compete as a heavyweight.

Baseball, though, was always his favorite sport—"the most funnest," as he had put it to the *Albuquerque Tribune* when he was 12. He once struck out all 18 batters in a Thunderbird League game. The towering righty was Eldorado High's ace, his fastball reaching the 90s. The second starter? Ken Giles, now a flame-throwing Phillies reliever. "You're talking about a guy with a ton of potential: size, natural ability, attitude," Giles says. "Everyone wanted to be him, but everyone wanted to be around him too. The first word I would use to describe Roman is *lovable*."

A foot injury his junior year didn't derail Roman. He needed minor surgery on a small bone, but he popped some OxyContin and after a few weeks was back on the mound. His senior year Roman planned to lead Eldorado to a state title and then declare for the 2008 major league draft (the Braves had expressed the most interest in him), spurning about 20 Division I scholarship offers. Before the season, though, Roman committed one of those judgment-deprived acts for which teenagers are known. He and some friends used a stolen credit card at a mall. They got caught. The school found out. Though it was Roman's first offense, he was kicked off the team.

Humiliated, angry, and depressed, Roman thought back to the numbing effect of the OxyContin. His prescription had run out, but that wasn't much of an impediment. In the upscale Northeast Heights—more *High School Musical* Albuquerque than *Breaking Bad* Albuquerque—painkillers were competing with marijuana and alcohol as the party drug of choice. "There are pill parties," says Roman's younger brother, Beau. "[Pills are] so easy to get. They're everywhere."

Roman was soon in the grip of Oxy. He lost interest in baseball. He showed up high for graduation. JoAnn Montano and her husband, Bo, who owns a wheel-alignment and body-shop business, figured their son was just floundering—until JoAnn caught him using. She took him to an addiction center, and he was prescribed Suboxone to treat his opioid dependency.

Roman, though, couldn't fully kick his habit. Before graduation he had switched to a cheaper substance that offered the same high at a lower price: heroin.

At first Roman smoked "black" (black-tar heroin), a relatively crude version of the drug that was easy to obtain. Then he began using intravenously. But he hid his addiction well. He stayed on Suboxone, took up competitive bodybuilding, and started training at an MMA gym. He had a job selling phones for Verizon. "He looked so healthy, a big, strapping guy, not like a junkie," says Bo. "He was back doing his athletics. We thought the addiction was behind us. We didn't know how cunning and how manipulative this drug is."

On May 2, 2012, Roman was supposed to lift weights with his father in the morning. Roman didn't show up, and texts to him went unanswered. His fiancée, Mikaila Lovato, couldn't find him either.

In the evening two chaplains went to the Montanos' house,

asking for Roman's next of kin. They said that Roman had been found slumped in the driver's seat of his car behind a FedEx store, a syringe in his arm, the motor running. He was 22 and dead from a heroin overdose.

It is, by any measure, an epidemic. Heroin is not new or chic, but its use and abuse are spiking. According to data from the U.S. Centers for Disease Control and Prevention (CDC) and the National Center for Health Statistics, heroin-overdose deaths rose gradually from 2000 to '10 but then almost tripled in the following three years to 2.7 deaths per 100,000 people. Heroin use cuts across demographics. Young, old. Male, female. Wealthy, indigent. Urban, rural, and, most of all, suburban. But public authorities devoted to prevention and law enforcement, from the Drug Enforcement Agency (DEA) to the CDC, have been struck by a growing concentration in an unlikely subset of users: young athletes.

About a decade ago Jack Riley, the DEA's chief of operations, recognized that high school athletes were becoming "unwitting customers of the cartels," which target people susceptible to prescription-drug abuse. The number of addicts and overdose victims has grown substantially since then. "In the athletic arena, if anything can be likened to a weapon of mass destruction, it's heroin," Riley says. "It is that pervasive now."

While hard data for heroin use among young athletes are difficult to come by, the anecdotal evidence is abundant and alarming. A seven-month *SI* investigation found overdose victims in baseball, basketball, football, golf, gymnastics, hockey, lacrosse, soccer, softball, swimming, tennis, volleyball, and wrestling—from coast to coast. Riley saw this as a volunteer in a youth basketball league in St. Louis. He coached a player who, years after suffering an injury, succumbed to a heroin overdose. The cartels, Riley says, "have developed a strategy, with the help of street gangs, to put heroin in every walk of life. They recognize how vulnerable young athletes are."

To understand the increasingly busy intersection of heroin and sports, it's essential first to understand the general path to the drug. According to the U.S. Substance Abuse and Mental Health Services Administration, a full 80 percent of all users arrive at heroin after abusing opioid painkillers such as OxyContin, Percocet, and Vicodin. And according to the National Institute of

Drug Abuse, one in 15 people who take nonmedical prescription painkillers will try heroin within the next 10 years. While opioid painkillers can cost up to $30 per pill on the black market, heroin, which is molecularly similar, can be purchased for $5 a bag and provides a more potent high. "It's an easy jump," says Harris Stratyner, a New York City addiction specialist.

Studies have shown that while cumulative pain levels remained constant among Americans, prescriptions for pain medications more than quadrupled between 1999 and 2010. As the sports industry expands each year—and the stakes on rinks, fields, and courts grow higher—young athletes face enormous pressure to manage their pain and play through injuries.

A University of Michigan (UM) researcher uncovered a startling number in a 2013 national study: by the time high school athletes become seniors, approximately 11 percent will have used a narcotic pain reliever such as OxyContin or Vicodin—for nonmedical purposes. What's more, UM researcher Philip Todd Veliz, who conducted a 2013 longitudinal study of 743 male and 751 female adolescents in southeast Michigan that was published in the *Journal of Adolescent Health,* told *SI* that "male adolescent athletes who participated in competitive sports across the three-year study period had two times greater odds of being prescribed painkillers during the past year and had four times greater odds of medically misusing painkillers (i.e., using them to get high and using them too much) when compared to males who did not participate in competitive sports."

Moreover, "sports that involve high levels of contact (e.g., football) tend to socialize youth to view pain, violence and risk as normative features," Veliz said, and these "may influence risky behavior both on and off the playing field. In other words, participants in contact sports learn to view their body as an instrument that can be easily gambled with, even if it would involve permanent damage."

Consider Patrick Trevor. In the spring of 2009, Patrick was a sophomore lacrosse goalie at Rumson–Fair Haven, a well-regarded New Jersey high school with many students whose parents take ferries to jobs on Wall Street. A teammate's fluke shot in practice shattered Patrick's right thumb. He had two immediate concerns: easing the pain and getting back on the field. A future college scholarship, after all, was on the line. The doctor who examined

Patrick prescribed Roxicodone (Roxy in the vernacular), a cousin of OxyContin.

Patrick quickly became addicted to the medication and even took to crushing and snorting his pills. But he reckoned that playing high was better than playing in pain—which was better than not playing at all. "Us athletes," he says, "we'll do anything in order to keep playing." Within a few years Patrick had made the transition to heroin. His Roxy prescription had lapsed; his fondness for the high had not. At first he illegally purchased pills from friends; then he ventured into the worst pockets of Newark to get his heroin fix. College lacrosse had become the least of his concerns.

Patrick was arrested and spent a short time in jail. He went to several rehab facilities before finding success at the Dynamite Youth Center in Brooklyn. He proudly says his clean date is October 2, 2012. He was struck by how many athletes he saw at such a small facility. "Hockey, football, lacrosse," he says. "[Heroin is] a big thing in sports."

How big is difficult to say. "This should be on people's research agenda," Veliz says, lamenting the lack of reliable statistics. "Because this is actually happening."

More than a decade ago Amber Masters played soccer for Esperanza High in Anaheim despite a hyperextended right knee. ("I had to," she says. "We had college scouts there.") Colliding with another player, she tore tissue in the same knee. Surgery ended her season, and she became dependent on the opiate-based painkiller Norco.

When the prescription expired, she wanted to keep experiencing the feeling Norco gave her. A friend introduced her to Oxy. As Amber, once a gifted forward, chased a painkiller high, her soccer career imploded. Academic probation kept her off the team as a junior, and by the time she returned as a senior, she was not the same player. College recruiters disappeared. "I didn't really care," she says. "I had the party scene."

She first took heroin the summer before she enrolled at Orange Coast College in Costa Mesa, California. "I was addicted from the first hit I took," she says. Within a year she had dropped out of school, become a dealer ("I was my best customer," she says), and introduced her younger brother, Adam, to the drug. Amber became a mother. She eluded the law, but Adam was less fortunate. He went to jail for possession of narcotics. Then, on April 13, 2012, he died from an overdose. "That sent my addiction into a hard-core downward spiral," Amber says.

More trauma followed. Amber says her parents, Jerry and Ginger, sent her to rehab, kicked her out of the house when she relapsed, and refused to let her visit her daughter. (Ginger contends that she and Jerry set ground rules that Amber refused to obey. "She chose to leave," Ginger says.)

The separation was a sobering jolt to Amber. "I had a waking-up moment," she says. "I knew it was only a matter of time before I would die and leave my daughter behind." She entered rehab. Today she works in the billing department of an addiction recovery center in Irvine, California. She says she's been clean since October 19, 2012.

It's disturbing enough that athletes such as Masters come to heroin through painkillers prescribed after an injury. But *SI*'s reporting revealed a shocking contributing factor: families consistently said that they received no warning from physicians about the addictive power of the opioid painkillers they prescribed. Patrick Trevor recalls that the doctor who prescribed Roxy for him jokingly said, "You got the good stuff." Trevor adds, "I didn't really put two and two together until later . . . when I was a full-blown heroin addict. I knew painkillers were not good, but I didn't know how crazy addictive they were."

In 2014 the CDC issued a report headlined "Physicians Are Fueling Prescription Painkiller Overdoses." The study found that doctors were engaging in "dangerous" and "inappropriate" prescription practices. "Anyone who is giving a kid an opioid prescription without serious oversight and supervision is out of their mind," says Joe Schrank, a New York City–based drug counselor and former USC offensive lineman. "That stuff is like kryptonite."

If there is an epicenter for the heroin-in-sports crisis, it's Albuquerque (population 550,000), a high-altitude city less than 300 miles from the Mexican border. A report by the New Mexico health department found that the drug-overdose death rate in the state jumped by more than 60 percent between 2001 and '10, and in New Mexico's Youth Risk and Resiliency survey one in 10 youths admitted to using opiate-based prescription drugs to get high. In Albuquerque at least eight athletes have died from heroin or painkiller overdoses since '11. (The very week in April that *Sports Il-lustrated* visited the city to report this story, a former local baseball star, James Diz, died of an apparent heroin overdose at 23.)

Cameron Weiss was a strapping wrestler and football special-teams player at La Cueva High. In 2010, his sophomore year, he broke his left collarbone making a tackle in practice and required surgery; months later he fractured his right collarbone while wres-tling. He went on pain medication (Percocet and hydrocodone) and was soon ditching school and failing the AP classes he had been mastering. He confessed to his mother that he was addicted to heroin. Because of a federal law that prevents doctors from pre-scribing buprenorphine, a component of Suboxone, to more than 100 patients at a time, Jennifer Weiss-Burke had to call 80 physi-cians before she could get her son an appointment for a Subox-one prescription. On the drive to the doctor's, Cameron went into severe withdrawal. He was "combative, sweating, in a ton of pain," Jennifer says. "He was throwing up. He looked horrible."

Cameron's body had come to need the sustained opioid intake. Once he received the Suboxone, his withdrawal symptoms van-ished. "After 15 minutes it was like he was normal again—laugh-ing and happy," says his mother. But then she learned the reality of addiction: sobriety can be fleeting. Soon her son was using again. "It was a living hell," she says. He died of a heroin overdose at 18.

Lou Duran can relate. She watched her son, Michael, make the varsity baseball team at Sandia Prep as an eighth-grader and, two years later, become addicted to OxyContin after he strained his knee playing soccer. Michael hardly fit the profile of an addict: He spent hours hitting balls in a batting cage with teammates. He excelled academically. Owing to his blend of intelligence and ath-leticism, Lou called him her "Einstein jock."

Because of his addiction, though, his baseball career unraveled. He was kicked out of private school, went to public school, and then dropped out. After earning his GED, he went to San Diego City College, but he quickly transferred to New Mexico State in Las Cruces. Then he began using heroin. He went to rehab and attended therapy, only to relapse five times. Lou and her husband, Michael Sr., rode waves of terror followed by temporary relief. They witnessed their son's excruciating withdrawals and fleeting stretches of sobriety. Finally, in early 2011, Michael seemed to have broken free of the drug.

On February 1, the evening of a historic winter snowstorm, a white Audi TT pulled up to the Durans' house in subzero temperatures. Michael, 19, gave the driver cash he had stolen from his mother's purse. The driver handed him a bag of heroin. From a distance Michael Sr. recognized trouble. "Get in the house now," he barked to his son. Turning to the driver, he said, "Get out of here while you still can." The Audi sped away.

Michael had been scheduled to deliver an antidrug speech that evening at Eldorado High. He was going to address a seminar for concerned family members and students organized by Healing Addiction in Our Community, telling them about his struggle with painkillers and heroin: how he had been a standout baseball player who took his first drug at 15; how he revived two friends who had overdosed; how he wound up in jail. The winter blast, though, closed roads and postponed the speech. When Michael went inside his house, he gave his parents a persuasive story: the guy in the car was a friend who had stopped by to check up on him. Michael went upstairs to his bedroom.

Lou remembers the silence when she knocked on Michael's door the next afternoon. She remembers kicking it open and scanning the room. Her eyes flashed across an unmade bed, an empty couch, a television turned on, and she was relieved. Then, as she turned to leave, she found Michael's body.

Later Michael Sr. discovered notes from the antidrug speech his son was supposed to have given. One of the bullet points: *Lucky to be here today at all because I've cheated death more times than I can count.*

When her son became an addict in 2010, Jennifer Weiss-Burke began an awareness and advocacy group for relatives and friends of drug-dependent children. The group—Healing Addiction in Our Community, which Michael Duran was to have addressed the night he died—has grown to 50 members. It includes several families of young athletes who have overdosed on opioids. Weiss-Burke is also cofounder and executive director of Serenity Mesa, a long-term treatment center for young people in recovery from drug and alcohol addiction, which opened on May 26.

Nearby, the Durans continue to grieve. After her son died, Lou went through his text messages, found his dealer's phone number, and tracked down his address. She gave the information to the

DEA and FBI. "A week later," she says, "he was arrested." Lou now works at Turning Point Recovery Center, a local treatment facility.

On Albuquerque's northeast side, the Montanos' business, the Wheel Align It II body shop, doubles as a shrine to Roman. The office walls are covered with photos of him on the mound, standing next to UFC fighters, alongside Ken Giles. Giles learned of Roman's death while in the minors—"I lost it for a good week," he says—and now has the letters RM written with permanent marker on each of his major league gloves.

Bo Montano, a former wrestler who still carries himself like an athlete, has an elaborate tattoo on his right forearm in which Roman's initials are framed by the words SO OTHERS MAY LIVE. Like the Durans and Jennifer Weiss-Burke, Bo and JoAnn Montano honor their deceased son by involving themselves in drug treatment and prevention. Through churches and schools around Albuquerque, they lead a 12-step recovery program for addicts and alcoholics and introduce them to sponsors. The Montanos also make a point of hiring recovering addicts at the body shop. "It helps us more than it helps them," says Bo. "It gives us some peace."

Sitting on stools inside the shop this spring, the Montanos recounted these successes. But they stopped short of telling a story that's too tidy. Their saga, finally, is a contemporary tragedy. They replayed the final few years of their son's life, wondering what subtle signs or symptoms they missed. "[Roman] was fighting the best he could, but the drug had control," said Bo. "If things are going great, you use [heroin] to celebrate. If things are going bad, you use it to numb."

JoAnn, blinking back tears, said, "You know what really breaks my heart? My son knew he was meant to be an athlete. Sports was his first addiction. He just ran into another addiction that was so much more powerful."

STEVE FAINARU AND MARK FAINARU-WADA

The Most Dangerous
Man in Football

FROM ESPN: THE MAGAZINE

ONE DAY IN APRIL, the NFL asked Chris Borland to take a random drug test. The timing of this request was, in a word, bizarre, since Borland, a San Francisco 49ers linebacker, had retired a month earlier after a remarkable rookie season. He said he feared getting brain damage if he continued to play.

Borland had been amazed at the reaction to his decision, the implications of which many saw as a direct threat to the NFL. And now here was an email demanding that he pee in a cup before a league proctor within 24 hours or fail the test. "I figured if I said no, people would think I was on drugs," he said recently. That, he believed, "would ruin my life." As he thought about how to respond, Borland began to wonder how random this drug test really was.

What did the NFL still want with him? Nobody could have held out much hope that he'd change his mind. On Friday, March 13, when Borland retired via email, he attached a suggested press release, then reaffirmed his intentions in conversations with 49ers officials. Instead of announcing Borland's retirement, the team sent him a bill—an unsubtle reminder that he'd have to return most of his $617,436 signing bonus if he followed through. That Monday, Borland, knowing he was forgoing at least $2.35 million, not to mention a promising career, made the announcement himself to *Outside the Lines*. He has since elaborated on the decision to everyone from *Face the Nation* to Charlie Rose to undergraduates at Wisconsin, where he was an All-American.

Borland has consistently described his retirement as a preemptive strike to (hopefully) preserve his mental health. "If there were no possibility of brain damage, I'd still be playing," he says. But buried deeper in his message are ideas perhaps even more threatening to the NFL and our embattled national sport. It's not just that Borland won't play football anymore. He's reluctant to even watch it, he now says, so disturbed is he by its inherent violence, the extreme measures that are required to stay on the field at the highest levels, and the physical destruction he has witnessed to people he loves and admires—especially to their brains.

Borland has complicated, even tortured, feelings about football that grow deeper the more removed he is from the game. He still sees it as an exhilarating sport that cultivates discipline and teamwork and brings communities and families together. "I don't dislike football," he insists. "I love football." At the same time, he has come to view it as a dehumanizing spectacle that debases both the people who play it and the people who watch it.

"Dehumanizing sounds so extreme, but when you're fighting for a football at the bottom of the pile, it *is* kind of dehumanizing," he said during a series of conversations over the spring and summer. "It's like a spectacle of violence, for entertainment, and you're the actors in it. You're complicit in that: you put on the uniform. And it's a trivial thing at its core. It's make-believe, really. That's the truth about it."

How one person can reconcile such opposing views of football —as both cherished American tradition and trivial activity so violent that it strips away our humanity—is hard to see. Borland, 24, is still working it out. He wants to be respectful to friends who are still playing and former teammates and coaches, but he knows that, in many ways, he is the embodiment of the growing conflict over football, a role that he is improvising, sometimes painfully, as he goes along.

More than anything, Borland says he doesn't want to tell anyone what to do. This is the central conflict of his post-football life. He rejected the sport, a shocking public act that still reverberates, in tremors, from the NFL to its vast pipeline of youth leagues. Yet he's wary of becoming a symbol for all the people who want to end —or save—football.

We trailed Borland for five months as he embarked on a journey that drove him deeper into the NFL's concussion crisis and forced him to confront the sport in ways he avoided while playing. One day in June, he returned to Archbishop Alter High School in Kettering, Ohio, to visit with his old coach, Ed Domsitz. "We're in a period now where, for the next 10 or 15 years, many of us, we need to figure out a way to save this game," said Domsitz, a southwest Ohio legend who has coached for 40 years.

Jovial and gray-haired, Domsitz was standing on the Alter practice field, a lake of synthetic green turf. He tried to recruit Borland to his cause.

"Why don't you come back and coach the linebackers?" Domsitz asked. "We need to teach these kids the safe way to tackle."

"Some of my best tackles were the most dangerous!" Borland responded, laughing.

"You're exactly the kind of people we need," the coach insisted.

Borland lowered his head, embarrassed. "I can't do that," he said, almost inaudibly. "Maybe I could be the kicking coach."

Later, away from Domsitz, Borland explained: "I wouldn't want to be charged with the task of making violence safer. I think that's a really difficult thing to do."

In the months following his retirement, Borland has offered himself up as a human guinea pig to the many researchers who want to scan and study his post-NFL brain. He has met with the former vice chief of staff of the U.S. Army and with mental health experts at the Carter Center in Atlanta. He has literally shrunk, dropping 30 pounds from his 248-pound playing weight while training for the San Francisco Marathon, which he ran in late July.

As the Niners reported to training camp in July, Borland was examining the Book of Kells, a 1,200-year-old manuscript, at the Trinity College Library in Dublin, the start of a six-week European vacation.

In many ways, Borland is like any bright, ambitious recent college graduate who is trying to figure out the rest of his life. In other ways, he's the most dangerous man in football.

On that day back in April, Borland stared hard at his iPhone, pondering what to do about the NFL's summons to a post-retirement drug test. The league says it reserves the right to test players—even after they've retired—to ensure that they don't dodge a test, then return. But given the stakes, and the NFL's dubious history on concussions, it occurred to Borland that maybe, just maybe, he was being set up.

"I don't want to be a conspiracy theorist," he says. "I just wanted to be sure." Borland agreed to submit a urine sample to the NFL's representative, who drove in from Green Bay and administered the test in the Wisconsin trainer's room. Then he hired a private firm for $150 to test him independently. Both tests came back negative, according to Borland.

"I don't really trust the NFL," he says.

Toward the end of his rookie season, Borland read *League of Denial,* our 2013 book chronicling the NFL's efforts to bury the concussion problem. After his last game, he contacted us through former St. Louis Cardinals linebacker David Meggyesy, who also walked away from the NFL, in 1969. Meggyesy wrote a bestselling memoir, *Out of Their League,* in which he described football as "one of the most dehumanizing experiences a person can face." Borland, a history major at Wisconsin, had met Meggyesy during his senior year, after hearing him give a guest lecture titled "Sports, Labor and Social Justice in the 21st Century."

It's tempting to draw parallels between Borland and Meggyesy, both of whom reject the NFL's easy narrative of cartoon violence and heroic sacrifice. Late in his pro career, Meggyesy was benched for his political activism. At Wisconsin, in 2011, Borland was punished with extra conditioning for skipping class to protest Republican governor (and current presidential candidate) Scott Walker, who was trying to limit collective bargaining for public employees. Borland marched with three cousins, one a teacher, and carried a sign that read, RECALL WALKER.

But there are significant differences between the two men. Meggyesy linked his retirement to the politics of the antiwar and civil rights movements. Borland, a more reluctant activist, is concerned primarily with public health. "I'm not really interested in fighting anything," he says. "But there are former players who are struggling. And certainly there are kids that are gonna play in the future. So if my story can help them in any way, I'd like to find a way to do that."

Borland reached out to us back in February because, as he contemplated retirement, he hoped to speak with researchers who appeared in *League of Denial.* One was Robert Stern, a neurology professor at Boston University, the leading institution for the study of chronic traumatic encephalopathy, or CTE. Over the past decade, the disease has been found in the brains of 87 out of the 91 dead NFL players who were examined.

"I'm concerned to the point of contemplating retirement, despite only playing one year in the pros," Borland wrote Stern in an email. They arranged to speak by phone on March 13. According to Borland, Stern told him that he could already have brain damage "that might manifest later"; damage that could worsen as a result of "a thousand or 1,500 hits every fall for 10 years." Stern says he also cautioned Borland that the science was still limited. "He said if there was an increased risk of him not being able to play with his kids, he didn't want to take that risk," Stern recalls.

Borland says his conversation with Stern sealed his decision. He retired later that day.

Borland told Stern that he hoped to use his experience "to help science." His participation in concussion research has become a big part of his journey to find a meaningful role for himself after football. He is a highly coveted research subject because he is neither old nor dead and because he was recently exposed to NFL-grade head trauma.

One of his first post-retirement stops was a meeting with Stern.

"This is going to be a weird day for you," Stern told Borland as he began a day of testing on April 30 at the Boston University School of Medicine.

Bolted to the front of the red-brick building was a metal sign that read, TRUTH ABOVE EVERYTHING. Stern sat behind his desk in his office in a coat and tie. Like many concussion researchers, he has a complicated relationship with the NFL. Stern, who once accused the league of a "cover-up," says he now has a pending application for a $17 million CTE study funded by the NFL through the National Institutes of Health.

On this April day, Stern still seemed floored by Borland's decision.

"One of the things you asked me was, 'What do we know? What are the risks?' And I think I said about 100 times during our conversation: 'I just don't know!'" Stern told Borland, who wore jeans and multicolored Hoka running shoes and sipped coffee from a paper cup. "A decision to stop having exposure to repetitive hits to your head is, in my mind, a really, um, *unbelievable* decision. Not necessarily the right decision for everyone. I just wanted to make sure we're on the same page again."

"Absolutely," Borland said. "I understand correlation isn't causation and I'm just removing myself from the risks. I know I could be wrong."

"I guess better safe than sorry," Stern said.

"Exactly."

Borland was ushered into a separate room, where a graduate assistant peppered him with questions about his employment and concussion history.

Borland had said previously that he had two diagnosed concussions—one that knocked him out during eighth-grade soccer, another while playing football his sophomore year at Archbishop Alter.

"Some people have the misconception that concussions occur only after you black out when you get a hit to the head or to your body," the graduate assistant told him. "But in reality, concussions have occurred any time you've had any symptoms for any period of time." She ticked them off: blurred vision, seeing stars, sensitivity to light or noise, headaches, dizziness, etc.

"Based on that definition, how many concussions do you think you've had?" she asked.

Borland paused.

"I don't know, 30?" he said finally. "Yeah, I think 30's a good estimate."

The exam lasted most of the day. When Stern contacted him later, he told Borland that BU could detect no current effects from his decade of playing tackle football.

Over the next two months, Borland turned over his brain to the scrutiny of several researchers—some traditional, some not. After undergoing exams at UCLA and Johns Hopkins University in Baltimore, on May 13 he flew to Orange County, California, to see Dr. Daniel Amen, the psychiatrist who heads the Amen Clinic in Costa Mesa. Amen has treated hundreds of NFL players, many of whom swear by him. His methods are unproven, though, and some people in the medical community regard him as a quack. Borland wanted to see for himself.

Upon arriving, he found himself trailed by cameras for a show that Amen, wearing black jeans, a black T-shirt, and pancake makeup, was apparently trying to sell to TV. The medical exam included a visit to the clinic's director of research, a UCLA neurobiology PhD (and a former model, whom Amen said he initially included in his NFL study to attract subjects). She slipped a rubber cap over Borland's head to measure his brain's electrical activity. As the cameras rolled, Amen's wife, Tana, dressed in a red cocktail dress, declared to a bemused Borland, "What I really want to say to you is: You are a brain warrior. You're a brain warrior!"

That kind of thing happens a lot to Borland. He's so polite, so eager to be helpful, he finds himself in uncomfortable situations. "I think this whole world of brain injury and football is more political than I anticipated," he says. "And I don't want to be a part of that in any way." Borland turned down a request to promote the upcoming Will Smith movie, *Concussion,* and has rejected numerous endorsements. "I don't want to monetize head injury in football," he says. "I think that attacks your legitimacy to a certain degree."

Two weeks after he visited Amen, Borland drove the two hours from the Bay Area to Sacramento to participate in a fund-raiser for a paralyzed semipro player. He found himself in the middle of a sad pep rally that, oddly, showcased potential concussion remedies while celebrating the sport that causes the injury. Tables manned by people touting treatments like "CranioSacral Therapy" and "Bowenwork" touch stimulation lined the half-filled ballroom of the Red Lion hotel.

"*Who's got it better than us?*" shouted an auctioneer, trying to fire up the crowd with the slogan made famous by former 49ers coach Jim Harbaugh.

"Nobody," the fans responded tepidly. The bidding on a Borland-signed football stopped at $500, at which point Borland, wearing tan slacks and a solid blue tie, hurled it softly to the winner. The man told Borland that he appreciated the "bravery" of his decision to retire—then asked for the ball to be made out to his nephew, who was just starting to play high school football.

Borland wondered whether he was the only one attending the event who saw its irony. "You don't have to promote the game to help people who have been hurt by it," he said.

Part of the confusion is that, even though he walked away from the NFL, football people—fans, players, coaches—still consider him one of them. They find it inconceivable that someone who was so tough and played the game so hard doesn't buy into the hype, which Borland, somewhat derisively, calls "the overwhelming tide of marketing about how great and awesome football is." Borland scoffs at the oft-repeated clichés about football's unique ability to impart wisdom. "It's too bad Gandhi never played football," he said one afternoon. "Maybe he would have picked up some valuable lessons."

Borland himself once seemed as if he might have been created in an NFL factory.

He grew up in Kettering, a Dayton suburb, which he described in a paper for a UW history course as "a top down, planned neighborhood of mostly white middle-class people." Borland's father, Jeff, who played linebacker for a year at Miami (Ohio), is a plain-speaking investment adviser. Zebbie, Borland's ebullient mom, teaches cooking classes at a local market. He is the sixth of seven children (one girl, followed by six boys) who routinely battered one another in a variety of neighborhood contests until night fell and their tree-lined street twinkled with fireflies.

The Borlands are a tight-knit family of independent thinkers, with political views that run the spectrum from red to blue. "We'll get together and talk politics for six hours on a Friday night—yelling, cussing at each other—and the next day everybody will be fine," says Mark Borland, a Dayton attorney and the third-oldest Borland sibling. "It's almost a time-honored tradition on the holidays."

Chris went through childhood known as Little Borland, quiet and shy but also freakishly athletic and physical. "He came out ready to fight," says Joe Borland, a U.S. Army JAG officer who is 12 years older than Chris. Jeff forbade the boys to play tackle football until they turned 14, partly out of concerns about concussions. "I was always big on technique and the fundamentals," he says. "And that didn't necessarily get coached by dad coaches in pee-wee leagues." Chris played basketball and soccer through eighth grade, excelling against older boys, but he yearned for more contact. "Once he gets a taste of football, he's gonna love it," Jeff told Zebbie.

At Archbishop Alter, Borland did love to hit, but he was known as much for flights of improvisational genius. He played running back almost exclusively until his senior year, when Domsitz, his coach, created the Borland Rule, installing him on defense at rover whenever opposing teams crossed the 50. Borland's most memorable play, still a local legend, came against Fairmont, Alter's crosstown rival. On third and short, he launched himself over the line, turned a somersault in midair, and pulled down the running back from behind as his feet hit the ground. The play has been viewed nearly 222,000 times on YouTube.

Borland was ignored by top Division I schools, who saw him as small and unremarkable. Ohio State was 80 miles up Interstate 70, but the Buckeyes weren't interested, and neither, really, was Borland. He pinned his hopes on Wisconsin, his grandfather's school. Joe took control of his little brother's recruiting.

Bret Bielema, now at Arkansas, was the coach at Wisconsin when Borland showed up at a camp in Madison. "I sat and watched him for three days, and he must have made 20 interceptions, made every play known to man, punted 60 yards, kicked 30-yard field goals," Bielema recalls. "I just sat there with my jaw dropped."

When the camp ended, Bielema invited Borland, his brother Joe, and their sister, Sarah, to his office. When Bielema offered Borland a scholarship, Borland leaped out of his chair to hug the startled coach. Borland, of course, would later walk away from millions, but at the time he was so excited to play football for nothing that he celebrated in the stadium parking lot with a standing backflip.

"It's intoxicating, it's a drug, a drug that gives you the most incredible feeling there is," Borland was saying. "Outside of sexual intercourse, there's probably nothing like it. But fun is the wrong word for it. I don't consider football fun. It's not like a water park, or a baseball game."

It was early July, and Borland sat on the patio of the Wisconsin student union, sipping a tall beer on a warm night. The school sits between two lakes, Mendota and Monona, and boats bobbed in the shimmering water. Borland graduated in 2013, but he frequently returns to Madison.

Borland's football addiction, as he calls it, flourished on the turf at Wisconsin's Camp Randall Stadium, and ultimately, his disillusionment with the sport began there. An unknown when he arrived, he left as the Big Ten Defensive Player of the Year. Undersized, with stubby *T. rex* arms, he bludgeoned people, once hitting a Michigan State receiver so hard, Clowney-style, he separated him from his helmet and do-rag. Borland forced 15 career fumbles, one shy of the FBS record. He seemed to play in a state of ecstasy:

Matt Lepay, a Badgers broadcaster, looked over at practice one day and saw Borland catching rapid-fire passes from a JUGS gun with his feet.

Bielema left Wisconsin for Arkansas at the end of Borland's junior year. He became emotional as he described receiving a handwritten letter from Borland. On one side was a list of all of Borland's accomplishments. "On the other side," Bielema said, choking back tears, "he wrote, 'None of these things would have been accomplished if you hadn't given me a chance.'"

Off the field, Borland was hard to pin down—complex, quietly opinionated, a voice of conscience in the locker room. "I've tried to describe Chris to other guys, because guys want to know about him, and it's tough," says Mike Taylor, who played linebacker alongside Borland. "He doesn't really do anything for himself. And everything he's done is thought out—the pros and the cons. He doesn't put people down. If there's a joke, he'll laugh, but if it's too harsh, he'd be the one to say, 'Hey, that's not funny, you shouldn't say that.' And guys would listen or shut up and say they were sorry. That's who he was." In the fall semester of his senior year alone, Borland put in 125 hours at local hospitals and schools, according to Kayla Gross, who organized volunteer work for Badgers athletes. "It will probably go down in history as the most volunteer hours ever" by an athlete at the school, she says.

In fact, Borland was leading something of a double life. Publicly, he was a football star, happy and fulfilled. Privately, he was taking an increasingly critical look at his sport.

Borland began at Wisconsin as a wedge buster on kickoffs, a task he compared to "bowling, but it's people doing it." After blowing up a wedge against Wofford, he couldn't remember the rest of the game, including his own blocked punt, which led to a touchdown. That night, unable to eat, his head pounding, Borland had a teammate wake him up every few hours, fearing he'd lapse into a coma. He never told the coaches or trainers. That Monday, he was named Co–Big Ten Special-Teams Player of the Week. "That's one of those things where, when you step away from the game and you look at it, it's like, 'Oh my god,' you know?" Borland says. "But it makes sense to you when you're 18 and you've dedicated your life to it and the most important thing to you is to get a good grade on special teams."

Near the end of his freshman year, Borland discovered Toradol, the controversial painkiller used widely in college and the pros. "It was life-changing," he told the BU researchers, chuckling, when they took his medical history. The U.S. Food and Drug Administration warns that Toradol should be used sparingly, for severe acute pain. Borland, who had shoulder surgery three times while at Wisconsin, said he would sometimes use the drug every other game.

Some of Borland's teammates were worse off, and that concerned him more. Taylor, his close friend, was also one of the best linebackers in the nation, twice All-Conference, a future pro. But it became harder and harder for Taylor to stay on the field. In 2011, he tore his meniscus on a blitz against Minnesota. The Monday after the game, he had knee surgery to remove half of it.

The next Saturday, with Wisconsin fighting for the Big Ten title, Taylor played against Illinois. "I remember that morning I was thinking, 'This is f—ing stupid. What am I doing?'" he recalls. "They shot Toradol in my ass. And I remember covering up my knee with bandages, just so I couldn't see blood. The first half was shaky for me. If you watch the game film, it's like, 'This dude should not be playing football.'"

Taylor says no one tried to stop him. "I think it was mostly my fault," he says. "I was waiting for them to say, 'Hey, you're out of here. This is kind of sad. And not smart.' But I was kind of in a position to dictate. I guess the coaches had trust in me." He thinks he took another shot of Toradol at halftime.

"After the game, I finally took everything off, and there was just blood dripping down," he says. "The hair was matted down because of all the compression on it, the tape, the glue, and there was still blood coming down. I remember the coaches coming by, going, 'Great game! Can't believe what you just did!'"

The next season, Taylor developed a hernia but continued to play. Wisconsin faced Stanford in the Rose Bowl that year. "I'm just laying on the table before the game, buck naked, just taking shots of s— I don't even know," he says. "Taking pills, putting straps on, putting Icy Hot on. People were coming in and looking at me like I'm a f—ing robot, like I'm dead."

Taylor had surgery after that season. After recovering, he signed with the Seattle Seahawks, but he is currently unable to play because of a bone condition in his hip and has been waived. He is 25 and has had 10 surgeries. (Wisconsin declined to comment specifically on Borland or Taylor but said in a statement that injured athletes are allowed back on the field only after medical staff deem them "fit to return." The school added, "The limited usage of Toradol is administered by our team physicians and closely monitored.")

Taylor says he and Borland often joked about their injuries. "You might be in so much pain that you'd just be laughing because it was so stupid what we were doing," he says. "I think after a while, Chris just thought, 'This is stupid, this is stupid, this is stupid.' And it got to the point, with his head, where there was just too much stupid going on. And he finally left."

Asked whether he thought Taylor's characterization was fair, Borland replied: "Yeah."

"People make the analogy to war a lot, and I have two brothers in the Army," Borland says. "Getting a TBI [traumatic brain injury] and having post-traumatic stress from war, well, that's a more important cause. Football is an elective. It's a game. It's make-believe. And to think that people have brain damage from some made-up game. The meaninglessness of it, you draw the line at brain damage."

Borland rarely shares his concerns with other players, not wanting to preach or judge. The public nature of his decision is the most uncomfortable part for him. "I think sometimes people don't know how to act around me now," he says. "Sometimes I feel almost like I'm consoling people, you know? Like, 'Hey, it's gonna be okay.'"

He has come to dread public events connected to football, where people are likely to tiptoe around his decision, as if he has an illness, or, worse, they lecture him about football.

On July 9, Borland drove in his family's Honda Accord from Madison to Chicago for a UW fund-raiser. The night was warm, and Wisconsin alums filled the terrace of the Chicago Club, overlooking Lake Michigan. "I'm not ready for this," Borland said as he walked off the elevator to the murmur of hundreds of people.

In a corner, attendees struck the pose next to Ron Dayne's Heisman Trophy. The tables were covered with UW football helmets, white and Badgers red, and four cheerleaders mingled in the crowd.

Borland had just arrived when he ran into a prominent alum, Wade Fetzer.

"Soooo," Fetzer said. "You're going through a big transition."

"Yeah," Borland said.

"But this is a huge issue. And you brought it to a head!"

Borland went straight to the bar and ordered a vodka and lemonade. People descended on him, friends, old teammates, and soon he was at ease. As part of the event, Lepay, the Badgers broadcaster, interviewed Wisconsin athletic director Barry Alvarez, who coached the football team for 16 years. Lepay asked Alvarez about the college football playoff system, the search for a replacement for retiring basketball coach Bo Ryan, the importance of recruiting good students. There was no mention that one of the finest football players in the school's history had recently abandoned the sport.

Later, as the evening wound down, we asked Alvarez about Borland. He sounded slightly defensive. "It was never an indictment against football," he said. "He just chose not to play, and I respect that decision. But there was never an indictment of football."

For his part, Borland seemed sad as he described the conflict he has created.

"On one level, it's great to see everybody, and these are my best friends in the world," he said. "And then on another level, there is this issue at hand. I'm the human representation of the conflict in their mind. And that might never change."

Shortly after he was drafted by the 49ers in the third round last year, Borland attended the annual rookie orientation put on by the NFL. The league tries to prepare young players for what to expect on and off the field, and it brought in two prominent retired players to give the rookies advice.

"Get yourself a fall guy," Borland says one of the former players advised. The former player, whom Borland declined to name, told the rookies that if they ran into legal trouble, their designated fall guy would be there to take the blame and, if necessary, go to jail. "'We'll bail him out,'" Borland says the former player assured them.

Borland was appalled. "I was just sitting there thinking, 'Should I walk out? What am I supposed to do?'" he recalls. He says he didn't leave the room because he didn't want to cause a scene, but the incident stayed with him.

Borland's only connection to the NFL now is through his friends and his bank account. His financial situation isn't desperate, but it's not what many people think it is. The 49ers paid him $420,000 in salary last year (the NFL minimum) plus his $617,436 signing bonus. Minus taxes and contributions to his charitable trust, he took home about $550,000—but still has that bill for more than $463,000 of his signing bonus. Borland, who led the 49ers in tackles last year, used a performance bonus to pay the first installment and still owes more than $300,000, due over the next two years. (It helps that Borland is the Donald Trump of frugality. Despite grossing well over $1 million last year, he rented a room in a Silicon Valley condo for $800 a month. One night he was FaceTiming with his mother, who got a glimpse of the bare walls, the reading lamp on the floor. "Chris, are you in the hospital?" she asked.)

In his own quiet way, Borland is presenting a counternarrative to the one presented every week during football season—the narrative created by five TV networks, including ESPN, and myriad websites, publications, and talk shows . . . the narrative that only $10 billion in revenue can buy. Whether you agree with him or not, the effect is like stepping into a different reality.

Shortly after he retired, Borland was invited to attend the National Summit on Sports Concussion in Los Angeles. Once he accepted, the organizers used his name ("Chris Borland, former NFL player") to promote the event. Borland told them to stop. He didn't want to be seen as endorsing the idea that football can be made safe.

The morning of the conference, about 150 trainers, neurosurgeons, and biomedical engineers gathered in a large room at the Renaissance Hotel. Borland, reluctantly, had agreed to make a few remarks to kick off the event, along with Ryan Nece, the former Tampa Bay linebacker.

Nece exhorted the researchers to make football safe. "It is our responsibility to use our expertise and our experiences to find ways to make the game safer, better, stronger, and more exciting," he told them. "Because of the power in this room, that can happen."

No, it can't, Borland told the researchers, contradicting Nece and, by extension, one of the main reasons behind the conference. "I made a decision a few months ago to walk away from football based on not only what I'd come to learn but also what I'd experienced," he said. "The game may be safer; you can make an argument about that. My experience over my five years at Wisconsin and my one year in the NFL was that there were times where I couldn't play the game safely. There are positive measures we can take . . . but on a lead play, on a power play, there's violence."

Borland says distancing himself from the sport has helped him see it more clearly. And he is more disturbed by what he sees. One night, before he drove to Stanford to hear Meggyesy speak, we joined Borland for dinner at a Palo Alto taco joint, Tacolicious. He wore a hoodie and jeans and looked like a grad student. (The only vestiges of Borland's NFL body are his calves, which still resemble footballs, in size and shape.) The conversation turned to Meggyesy's exposé of the NFL and its characterization that pro football is dehumanizing.

The following exchange occurred:

Question: "Do you agree?"

Answer: "Well, the combine is about as much as a human being can be treated like a piece of meat in 21st-century America. You walk onstage in your underwear. You walk room to room, where sometimes five doctors are pulling on different parts of your body while you're in your underwear and talking about you like you're not there. So, yeah. I mean, it's like cattle. They're in the cattle business. It's how well your body can perform."

Question: "But you obviously love the sport. So how do you reconcile that feeling with the parts that you love?"

Answer: "I think by compartmentalizing. I would say, 'This comes along with it.' At times I would think, 'How can I slam this guy in his face and then be a gentleman Monday through Saturday?' By compartmentalizing and then going to that place on game day. But I don't think there's any such thing. If you're violent, you're violent."

Question: "Do you think the game brings out things in ourselves that are already there?"

Answer: "I don't know if Aristotle's cathartic theory—that we're still really hunter-gatherers, with fangs and eyes in front of our skulls—I don't know if [football] finds an outlet for that or it promotes that. If it's natural, maybe we should express it in other ways, not necessarily partaking in the violence. Because that's what the game is sold on. I don't know if we should promote that. I don't think we should bury it either, but maybe we should find another way to express our physical nature."

For now, that's as close as Borland will come to saying football should be banned. But he thinks the NFL's current mantra—making football safer—is silly and pointless. Once you admit that, he believes, it's merely a matter of how much risk you're willing to take by playing.

The concussion that led Borland to retire came on a routine play, and that's precisely his point: unlike riding a bike or driving a car, where head injuries occur by accident, in football the danger increases by doing everything right. During a preseason practice, he stuffed the lead blocker, six-foot-four, 293-pound fullback Will Tukuafu. Borland—five inches shorter and 50 pounds lighter—buried the crown of his helmet into Tukuafu's chin and stood him up. He walked away dazed for several minutes. He began to wonder how many times his brain would be subjected to the same injury and what the lasting effect might be. "It raised the question, 'When will it stop?'" he says.

In February, Borland's sister, Sarah, his oldest sibling, sent him an article on Boston University researcher Ann McKee, who warns that "sub-concussive" hits—the kind that occur on every play—might be the primary cause of brain damage in football.

"I'm way ahead of you," Borland wrote back.

Now, five months after his historic decision, Borland finds himself whipsawed by football's various stakeholders. It can leave him indecisive and, at times, uncertain where to turn. "It's not a fun thing to do, completely miserable, really," he said one day. "You just catch s— constantly, for the most innocent things." When the BU-affiliated Sports Legacy Institute recently asked him to endorse its campaign to eliminate heading in youth soccer, Borland agonized over the decision. Eventually, he agreed because "personally it makes a lot of sense to me. I just don't want to be that guy who rains on everyone's parade. I love sports so much and grew up playing every sport under the sun, and it was pure bliss. To fundamentally change a sport or to encourage people to do that, it's a little intrusive."

He says he knows some people probably blame him for contributing to the "pussification" of football. "I think in the eyes of a lot of circles, especially within football, I'm the soft guy," he says. "But I'm fine with being the soft, healthy guy."

Both of Borland's parents seem done with football. "I'm just watching car crashes; I don't even see the game," Jeff says. Zebbie says she recently read a book set in ancient Rome and "it was so similar to the football stadium, with all the fans cheering in the background and bringing the gladiators in. And I thought, 'We're just repeating history, over and over again.' It's an American pastime, but it's hurting people. So it's not worth it anymore to me." The question is how far their son will be willing to go.

"I'm conflicted," Chris Borland says. "I don't want to tell a 16-year-old who's passionate about playing football to stop, or his parents who are passionate to stop. But I don't know if I'll have my kids play either. I don't think it's black-and-white quite yet." Recently, a friend of Borland's mother sought guidance from him on whether her son should play football. Borland said he was comfortable providing information but not advice. "I'm not going to help people parent their children," he says. "I took the stance personally to not do it; I walked the walk. But it's not my place to tell anyone else what to do."

His father isn't so sure. "Somebody sooner or later is going to ask him, 'Yes or no?'" Jeff says. "Just, 'Yes or no?' And you are going to have to answer it."

On July 30, as the 49ers prepared to open training camp, Borland touched down in Cork, Ireland. He was planning to spend six weeks in Europe. He carried with him one pair of black pants (which he was wearing), six shirts, six pairs of underwear and socks, stuffed into a black backpack with his iPod (nano), laptop, journal, and a Kindle, on which he was reading *The Metamorphosis*, the Franz Kafka novella.

Borland walked to a nearby Travelodge, pausing to take a picture of a life-size statue of Christy Ring, a local hurling legend. There will be no statues built for Borland, of course, and that seems fine with him. Informed that the Travelodge was booked, he decided to walk five miles into Cork, which is not unlike landing at LaGuardia Airport and deciding to walk into Manhattan.

Nights in Cork are brisk. Borland, who had no jacket or sweater, cloaked himself in a beige British Airways blanket he had taken off the plane. He spent the entire night walking the charming Irish city, listening to Van Morrison, crossing the River Lee, climbing the hills dotted with row houses bathed in pastels, a sensation he described, euphorically, as "floating."

Borland said it's a coincidence he decided to leave the States at the exact moment our fevered obsession with football begins anew. But you have to wonder. Had Borland stayed in football, he would have been a big part of the 49ers' fall story; you could have written it in your sleep. Now someone else will have to replace Patrick Willis, who retired a week before Borland, and someone will write *that* story. Borland, meanwhile, was in Europe, alone and anonymous.

Borland paused when he was asked what he wants the rest of his life to be. "That's the hardest question in the world," he said one afternoon while eating lunch in Edinburgh, Scotland. "It's like, 'What's the meaning of life?' I just want to be honest. There's no worldly possessions that really excite me. I don't need prestige. I just want to do something where I can feel confident that I'm making the world a better place."

During the summer, Borland was driving from California to Ohio when he picked up an audiobook of Jimmy Carter's *Beyond the White House: Waging Peace, Fighting Disease, Building Hope.* The book mentioned Rosalynn Carter's mental health initiative. Borland was so moved he cold-called the Carter Center in Atlanta and arranged a meeting, which he called "one of the best days of my life." He is cutting short his trip to attend a September symposium there.

It seems clear that Borland is seeking a role at the intersection of football and mental health, at least for the time being. That is not good news for the NFL. Not everyone will agree with Borland. People will call him soft and accuse him of trying to ruin the national sport. But many will listen. Last December a poll conducted by Bloomberg Politics revealed that 50 percent of Americans would not want their sons to play football. Borland's decision has loomed over a spate of recent early retirements, including Patriots offensive lineman Dan Connolly and 49ers offensive tackle Anthony Davis, who said he was taking at least one year off. It's hard to ignore a man who walked away from millions of dollars simply because he thought football was bad for his health and, in the end, morally suspect. What parent wouldn't stop to listen, if only for a moment?

And, as anyone can see, the non-football life agrees with him. "This is like a movie, like it's not even real," he said, standing next to the remains of a 16th-century castle on the Scottish coast in the late afternoon. Rain, pouring out of slate clouds, lashed the Firth of Clyde and the deep green hills, but everything was somehow cast in an unearthly glow.

The night before, Borland had been out drinking in Dublin. He found himself at a packed oval-shaped bar, Millstone, near Trinity College, sampling ales and whiskey. Behind him was a friendly, low-key bachelor party, and soon he was introduced to the group. One man, a Brit named Matt, bought him a glass of Midleton Very Rare, an expensive Irish whiskey, and explained that he worked for TaylorMade, the golf manufacturer.

"So, what is it that you do?" Matt asked Borland.

Borland paused.

"I'm between jobs," he replied.

DAN BARRY

Meet Mago, Former Heavyweight

FROM THE NEW YORK TIMES

GREENWICH, CONN. — Mago is in the bedroom. You can go in.

The big man lies on a hospital bed with his bare feet scraping its bottom rail. His head is propped on a scarlet pillow, the left temple dented, the right side paralyzed. His dark hair is kept just long enough to conceal the scars.

The occasional sounds he makes are understood only by his wife, but he still has that punctuating left hand. In slow motion, the fingers curl and close. A thumbs-up greeting.

Hello, Mago.

This is Magomed Abdusalamov, 34, also known as the Russian Tyson, also known as Mago. He is a former heavyweight boxer who scored four knockouts and 14 technical knockouts in his first 18 professional fights. He preferred to stand between rounds. Sitting conveyed weakness.

But Mago lost his 19th fight, his big chance, at the packed Theater at Madison Square Garden in November 2013. His 19th decision, and his last.

Now here he is, in a small bedroom in a working-class neighborhood in Greenwich, in a modest house his family rents cheap from a devoted friend. The air-pressure machine for his mattress hums like an expectant crowd.

Today is like any other day, except for those days when he is hurried in crisis to the hospital. Every three hours during the night, his slight wife, Bakanay, 28, has risen to turn his six-foot-three body —210 pounds of dead weight. It has to be done. Infections of the gaping bedsore above his tailbone have nearly killed him.

Then, with the help of a young caretaker, Baka has gotten two of their daughters off to elementary school and settled down the toddler. Yes, Mago and Baka are blessed with all girls, but they had also hoped for a son someday.

They feed Mago as they clean him; it's easier that way. For breakfast, which comes with a side of crushed antiseizure pills, he likes oatmeal with a squirt of Hershey's chocolate syrup. But even oatmeal must be puréed and fed to him by spoon.

He opens his mouth to indicate more, the way a baby does. But his paralysis has made everything a choking hazard. His water needs a stirring of powdered food thickener, and still he chokes —eh-eh-eh—as he tries to cough up what will not go down.

Mago used to drink only water. No alcohol. Not even soda. A sip of juice would be as far as he dared. Now even water betrays him.

With the caretaker's help, Baka uses a washcloth and soap to clean his body and shampoo his hair. How handsome still, she has thought. Sometimes, in the night, she leaves the bedroom to watch old videos, just to hear again his voice in the fullness of life. She cries, wipes her eyes, and returns, feigning happiness. Mago must never see her sad.

When Baka finishes, Mago is clean-shaven and fresh down to his trimmed and filed toenails. "I want him to look good," she says.

Theirs was an arranged Muslim marriage in Makhachkala, in the Russian republic of Dagestan. He was 23, she was 18, and their future hinged on boxing. Sometimes they would shadowbox in love, her David to his Goliath. You are so strong, he would tell her.

His father once told him he could either be a bandit or an athlete, but if he chose banditry, "I will kill you." This paternal advice, Mago later told the *Ventura County Reporter,* "made it a very easy decision for me."

Mago won against mediocre competition, in Moscow and Hollywood, Florida, in Las Vegas and Johnstown, Pennsylvania. He was knocked down only once, and even then, it surprised more than hurt. He scored a technical knockout in the next round.

It all led up to this: the undercard at the Garden, Mike Perez versus Magomed Abdusalamov, 10 rounds, on HBO. A win, he believed, would improve his chances of taking on the heavyweight champion Wladimir Klitschko, who sat in the crowd of 4,600 with his fiancée, the actress Hayden Panettiere, watching.

Wearing black-and-red trunks and a green mouth guard, Mago

went to work. But in the first round, a hard forearm to his left cheek rocked him. At the bell, he returned to his corner, and this time, he sat down. "I think it's broken," he repeatedly said in Russian.

Maybe at that point, somebody—the referee, the ringside doctors, his handlers—should have stopped the fight, under a guiding principle: better one punch too early than one punch too late. But the bloody trade of blows continued into the seventh, eighth, ninth, a hand and orbital bone broken, his face transforming.

Meanwhile, in the family's apartment in Miami, Baka forced herself to watch the broadcast. She could see it in his swollen eyes. Something was off.

After the final round, Perez raised his tattooed arms in victory, and Mago wandered off in a fog. He had taken 312 punches in about 40 minutes, for a purse of $40,000.

In the locker room, doctors sutured a cut above Mago's left eye and tested his cognitive abilities. He did not do well. The ambulance that waits in expectation at every fight was not summoned by boxing officials.

Blood was pooling in Mago's cranial cavity as he left the Garden. He vomited on the pavement while his handlers flagged a taxi to St. Luke's–Roosevelt Hospital. There, doctors induced a coma and removed part of his skull to drain fluids and ease the swelling.

Then came the stroke.

It is lunchtime now, and the aroma of puréed beef and potatoes lingers. So do the questions.

How will Mago and Baka pay the $2 million in medical bills they owe? What if their friend can no longer offer them this home? Will they win their lawsuits against the five ringside doctors, the referee, and a New York State boxing inspector? What about Mago's future care?

Most of all: is this it?

A napkin rests on Mago's chest. As another spoonful of mush approaches, he opens his mouth, half-swallows, chokes, and coughs until it clears. Eh-eh-eh. Sometimes he turns bluish, but Baka never shows fear. Always happy for Mago.

Some days he is wheeled out for physical therapy or speech therapy. Today, two massage therapists come to knead his half-limp body like a pair of skilled corner men.

Soon, Mago will doze. Then his three daughters, ages two, six, and nine, will descend upon him to talk of their day. Not long ago, the oldest lugged his championship belt to school for a proud show-and-tell moment. Her classmates were amazed at the weight of it.

Then, tonight, there will be more puréed food and pulverized medication, more coughing, and more tender care from his wife, before sleep comes.

Good-bye, Mago.

He half-smiles, raises his one good hand, and forms a fist.

SAM BORDEN

He's the Last Boxer to Beat Floyd Mayweather Jr., and He So Regrets It

FROM THE NEW YORK TIMES

PAZARDZHIK, BULGARIA — The man who beat Floyd Mayweather Jr. lives across the street from a burned-out coffee hut with a giant banana painted on its back wall. Around the bend, leaning in the tall grass, is a corroded shed holding ancient farming equipment. Every so often a horse trots down the craggy road, pulling a splintered cart and a rider toward the center of one of this country's poorest towns.

Late Tuesday morning, the man who beat Mayweather, Serafim Todorov, stood on the curb here. He was in front of the seven-floor concrete apartment building where he, his wife, his son, and his pregnant daughter-in-law live in a modest first-floor unit. Todorov talked with his son, Simeon. He watched a horse clop by. He smoked a cigarette. Then he went inside, sat in a chair, and, like a teakettle perched on a glowing stove, steamed to a rolling boil as he remembered what happened in Atlanta 19 years ago.

The victory by Todorov, then 27, over Mayweather, then 19, in the featherweight semifinals of the 1996 Olympic boxing tournament was the last time Mayweather lost in the ring. A few months later, Mayweather turned professional and began a career that has produced 47 consecutive victories and hundreds of millions of dollars in earnings. On May 2 in Las Vegas, Mayweather will have a long-awaited showdown with Manny Pacquiao in what many are calling the richest fight in boxing history.

Yet for Todorov, now 45, the stark gap between his life and Mayweather's since their match—the loser is worth an estimated $280 million, and the winner does not even own a flat-screen TV—is not what roils him. It is the circumstances behind his life's unraveling that have made him sour.

And in a curious twist, Todorov believes he and Mayweather may have actually been wronged by the same man.

For years, boxing fans—particularly Americans—speculated that Todorov's victory over Mayweather was, at least in part, a product of suspect judging. Todorov does not discard this theory. "It's possible, absolutely," he said.

But Todorov's real fury stems from what happened in the Atlanta final—the match after his win over Mayweather—when, he believes, he was the one unfairly beaten. He detailed the unspooling that followed: a fallout with his federation, a failed attempt at switching nationalities, missed opportunities abroad, and unhealthy offers to work in the Bulgarian underworld.

Today, while Mayweather is preparing to make as much as $180 million for one fight, Todorov is trying to live on a pension of about 400 euros, about $435, a month. Slumped in a chair, Todorov gestured toward the window that looked out at the coffee hut with the banana on it. All of this, he said, all of this struggle can be traced to what happened in Atlanta. If that seems strange —remember, this is the fighter who won—then consider this other bizarre reality:

The man who beat Floyd Mayweather wakes up every morning wishing he had lost.

Suspect Judging

The fight between Mayweather and Todorov took place on a Friday, two days before the closing ceremony of the Atlanta Games, at the basketball arena on Georgia Tech's campus. It began with a flurry of punches, as if the opening bell had twisted a cap off both fighters' fizzing emotions. As Todorov watched a YouTube video of the bout, his lips curled into a tiny smile.

"He was 19, remember," Todorov said through an interpreter. "My experience was much stronger. I beat all the Russians, all the Cubans, some Americans, Germans, Olympic champions. I was making fun of them in the ring. British, French—I beat them all."

He nodded. "I was very smart. I was a very beautiful and attractive fighter to watch. You must be an artist in the ring. I was an artist."

Hyperbole aside, Todorov's basic assessment is accurate: Mayweather was a teenager, a Golden Gloves champion, sure, but one who had to overcome a hiccup in Olympic qualifying just to make the United States team. He had shown little on the international stage.

Todorov was a three-time world champion and a two-time European champion as an amateur, and the kind of boxer who would occasionally toy with his opponents by feinting and dodging their attacks before reaching around to tap them on the back of the shoulder. "No, no," he would taunt them, "I'm over here."

Todorov, who grew up in Peshtera, a southern town, learned boxing at a young age—his uncle taught him to fight when he was eight—and he quickly developed into a prodigy, a whirling master of the ring whose fundamentals were flawless. Footwork was always his specialty, and even this week, despite having not trained for years, he fell easily into a fighter's sharp, staccato prowls and bounces when asked for a short demonstration.

Todorov's weakness was his focus. He liked women and he liked rakia, the fruit brandy popular in many of the Balkan countries. His coach, Georgi Stoimenov, who discovered Todorov as a teenager and worked with him throughout his career, tried his best to control Todorov but found it difficult.

"At competitions, the other coaches would be sleeping in their own rooms; I would sleep in Serafim's room," Stoimenov said. One time, he said, he locked Todorov in his room only to come back and find he had jumped out the window.

Where did Stoimenov find Todorov? "A few floors below with the women's athletics team."

Todorov does not deny his flaws. Before the Atlanta Games, he said, he trained for only about three weeks, and even during that period found time to take breaks to go drinking with his friends. He still dominated at the Olympics, shredding his first three opponents by a combined score of 45–18. He said he had done little scouting on Mayweather other than watching his quarterfinal match.

"It was just like any other fight, to be honest—I had beaten much stronger fighters," Todorov said.

But Mayweather surprised Todorov in the first two rounds. Todorov feinted and used a lot of one-punch attacks while Mayweather pattered in combinations. The fighters went to the final round with Todorov trailing by a point, 7–6.

Still, Todorov was confident—"I was not afraid to go after him" —and the last three minutes were a mess of flailing blows. Two body shots gave Todorov the lead, 8–7, but Mayweather had a couple of flurries that did not earn him points. (These were among the sequences that critics of the judging raised afterward.) Mayweather finally tied the score with about a minute left.

Todorov came back with a hook to the body for 9–8 and another shot to the head for 10–8 and then held off Mayweather, barely, as the bout finished. In the ring, neither fighter immediately knew who had won because the scoring system was designed to keep the result secret until it was announced.

At the time, the rules called for five judges to watch the fight and press a button if they saw what they deemed a scoring blow; when three of the five judges pressed their buttons within a second of one another, a point was awarded to the fighter landing the punch. No one involved in the fight, including the judges, was supposed to know the score at any given time, though in practice most corners had a spy who would find a TV in the arena, which showed the score to viewers, and then signal to members of his camp whether their boxer was ahead or behind.

This system presented a number of problems—including its reliance on the reaction time of judges of varying ages—and has since been changed, but in Atlanta both Todorov and Mayweather said afterward that they believed they should have been awarded more points. When the decision was announced, the referee initially raised Mayweather's arm before realizing his mistake and raising Todorov's.

Mayweather's backers thought that Emil Jetchev, a Bulgarian who was the longtime chairman of the international referees' and judges' commission, had influenced the judges to favor his countryman, Todorov.

That was not a new accusation; South Korean and American boxers similarly suspected Jetchev at the 1988 Olympics in Seoul.

And Todorov agreed with the theory, but for his own reason: he blames Jetchev for his loss in the gold medal match, contending he was unfairly beaten, 8–5, by Somluck Kamsing of Thailand. Todorov said his first clue had come just before the final, when Jetchev entered his locker room and emphasized that if he wanted to win, he must knock out Kamsing.

"He never did this, never before," Todorov said, shaking his head.

"Why did he come to tell me this? I beat this Thai guy on points, so many points, in a pre-Olympic tournament. And Jetchev knows that I am a technical guy, that I am not Mike Tyson. So what he was doing was clear: He was saying, 'You are going to lose.'"

Jetchev was not available to comment on Todorov's accusation. A longtime associate who had worked closely with him for years said Jetchev, 87, was in failing health and no longer giving interviews. But even if he were, Todorov said he would not be interested in hearing an explanation or a denial. To him, those few days reflected the moment his career began to disintegrate.

After the semifinal, Mayweather did not seem outwardly upset at the decision, and Todorov did not gloat. It was a typical Olympic result—which is to say it was debatable, if not suspicious—but after a few moments in the ring, the boxers went back to the locker rooms and were ushered to doping control. This, Todorov said, is where he made the biggest mistake of his life.

A Chance of a Lifetime

The doping control room in the arena at Georgia Tech was a generic multipurpose area, Todorov recalled, and he sat in a chair toward the front. Mayweather sat behind him. The two boxers waited for their turn to provide a sample.

Suddenly, there were three other men in the room, Todorov said. Todorov could not understand what was written on their credentials, but it quickly became clear that two of the men were involved in promoting professional boxing. The third acted as an interpreter.

The interpreter sat next to Todorov. He said that the men had been impressed by Todorov and wanted to sign him to a professional contract. "They saw my style, they saw me in the ring, they saw that I was white," Todorov said, grinning at the memory. "There will never be another white boxer like me, and they knew this. They wanted me to stay."

The terms of the contract were familiar to Todorov, he said, because he had been approached by Australian promoters after he won the 1991 world championship in Sydney.

In Atlanta, Todorov recalled, he smiled as the interpreter checked off the perks. A big signing bonus. A house. A car. A new life and big fights in front of big crowds. The other two men leaned in, one of them holding a pen. But Todorov pushed it away.

"Without considering, I said no," he said. "I just said it quick, like that. No."

He looked down. "You know what happened next? The two men went over to Floyd and started talking in English."

Todorov is not foolish enough to think the men went to Mayweather only because he had rejected their offer, but the image remains burned in his memory all the same. It could have been him, he thinks now. It should have been.

Two days later, he received the visit from Jetchev just before the final against Kamsing. Angel Angelov, who worked in Todorov's corner, remembered Todorov being nearly apoplectic on his stool after the first round of the final, shouting at his coaches that the judges were not scoring his points and looking "as though he knew there was nothing he could do." He lost, 8–5.

After his defeat, Todorov spent two days in a perpetual stupor as he waited for his flight home. "I didn't stop drinking the entire time," he said. "I just wanted to drink myself to death."

He felt betrayed. He had brought much attention and adulation to Bulgarian boxing over the years, but now he felt only bitterness. With the 1997 world championships approaching, he met with officials from the Turkish federation and accepted an offer to change his affiliation and fight for Turkey.

The deal was not as rich as the one from the American promoters, but it was substantial. If Todorov won the gold medal, the officials told him, he would receive a reward of $1 million. All that was needed to process the nationality switch in time was approval from the Bulgarian federation.

"The deal was done," Todorov recalled. "And then I got a call telling me that it was off. Jetchev had asked the Turkish federation for a transfer fee of $300,000 at the last second."

He stood up, pacing. "So I couldn't go. But I also wasn't going to fight for Bulgaria. And so that was it for me. It was over."

Struggling to Move On

Todorov was 28. He could have had another Olympics in him, a few more world championship tournaments too. Instead he put away his gloves, save for a handful of professional bouts over the next few years that offered the chance of a quick payday.

As Bulgaria muddled through the economic difficulties of its transition after the fall of communism, Todorov drifted aimlessly. He had a few jobs—as a driver, in a grocery store, at a sausage factory—but nothing stuck. His wife, Albena, worked in a supermarket too, but could not find anything consistent. Both are now unemployed.

About 15 years ago, Todorov moved here, to the apartment across from the coffee hut with the banana on the wall. There are drug dealers and underworld bosses on the street, Todorov said, and some of them approached him about working for them. He could be a captain, they told him, a leader. The money would be good.

He turned them down.

"There is a lot of cheating here, a lot of negative things," he said. "I don't like this. But there is also no boxing gym, no training. I don't talk to people a lot here. I don't get involved in anything. I don't need a lot of friends. I just try to relax."

That is harder than it sounds. Even 19 years later, it does not take much for Todorov's brow to furrow and his glare to sharpen, because the regret hangs heavy. Albena wishes her husband had called her after the promoters made their offer. "It could have changed our lives and the lives of our children," she said, her eyes wide. Todorov cannot hide his disappointment.

If he had lost to Mayweather, he said, he would have surely continued fighting in an attempt to reach an Olympic final. He would not have wondered about the chance to stay in America, or about a subsequent betrayal against Kamsing. "Instead, it all happened and I wanted to hope that things here could get better," he said. "It was stupid. I came back and I found hell."

Early Tuesday afternoon, Todorov walked through a scraggly garden near the middle of Pazardzhik. He moved quickly, his head down and his shoulders slumped and his feet shuffling along the cracks in the concrete. As he crossed a street, two young men waiting at the red light leaned out their car windows.

"Sarafa!" they shouted, using a nickname for Todorov. There were smiles on their faces, and one of the men pantomimed a quick flurry of punches in the air. Todorov turned and gave a weak wave as the light turned green and the men drove off.

"They remember," Todorov said, but there was no joy in his voice. Then the man who beat Floyd Mayweather walked on.

BRETT POPPLEWELL

Stopping the Fight

FROM SPORTSNET

USED TO BE the warrior was the noble, set apart from those he swore to protect by his acceptance of violence and by a code of conduct that kept him honorable. Medieval knights called this chivalry; to the samurai it was the way of the warrior. It didn't matter what he accomplished day to day, all that mattered was that when the time came, he entered the battle and fought like he was already dead. That's what made him noble. That's what made him selfless.

Kevin Westgarth knows this. Not because he is a student of history and war but because he is one of hockey's discarded enforcers. A wandering samurai who now finds himself alone and bleeding in a Belfast arena.

Barely a minute has passed since he threw his last punch, cracked a man's helmet, and ripped the skin from the mangled remnants of his reconstructed knuckle. The residual sounds of the brawl—bloodthirsty shouts and chants—echo through the stands, bouncing off the boards and rafters and finding their way into the corner of the dressing room where Westgarth sits, chest heaving, blood pumping out of that knuckle.

He unclenches his fists, stretches out his fingers, and wipes the blood from his pads. Not long ago, he was cruising through the neutral zone, looking for a pass, when all of a sudden he was lying on his back, his legs taken out by a player on the opposing team. He was back on his skates in a matter of seconds, driving a quick jab to his agitator's face. The gloves were off before the other team's enforcer got close enough to take the first punch, but that enforcer was quickly down, tripped up on a stick and turtled on the ice while Westgarth threw five rapid rights to the back of his head, splitting his helmet. The crowd was just getting into it when the refs intervened, pulling Westgarth off and ushering him into this room to reflect on what got him here.

He doesn't realize he's being watched until a question is lobbed from the shadows.

"Does it hurt?"

The initial response is a reflexive "nah" that serves as a shield meant to deflect the question. But he's slowly lowering that shield, has been for days. Looking at the missing scar tissue that used to make up his knuckle, he becomes more honest. "It always hurts a little."

A trainer rushes in with a bag of ice to drape over the wound.

"Back in the NHL, there'd be a doctor here by now," Westgarth says, repositioning the ice while his eyes search the room for a towel to ease the sting of frozen plastic on the hole in his hand. "I didn't start that fight. The first guy slew-footed me. That's pretty much the most disrespectful thing you can do out there."

Westgarth bears no ill will to the helpless enforcer he just punched five times in the back of the head. "He was just doing his job," Westgarth says of the man who came to the agitator's aid and got pummeled for his courage.

There's a code to this game, a code that Westgarth generally embodies. But tonight it's been broken, first by the dishonorable man who tripped him and then by Westgarth himself. And though he's not yet ready to admit it, he'll soon concede that he wishes none of this had to happen.

The muffled cheers of 6,000 fans announce the end of play. They stomp on the bleachers above the dressing room, which will soon be rushed by the rest of Westgarth's team. But for now he sits quietly with that bag of ice. He's been here before, watching, listening, and waiting to join them in victory. That's how it was when he won the Stanley Cup. He's on his feet when the others come in, quicker to congratulate them on the win than they are to salute him for the fight. He had a big part in that 6–3 win, scored one of his team's goals before getting a game misconduct for doing exactly what his coach and teammates expect him to do.

As he removes his pads, his thoughts turn to his wife, who was in the stands reliving a decade's worth of anxiety when he dropped the gloves. He knows part of her wonders how different their life would be had he become a surgeon like he'd planned instead of the guy who risks his brain and his future every time he clenches his hands into fists. Regardless, this has been a good night, even if it is about to end with his wife reminding him that he didn't come all the way to Northern Ireland to keep on fighting. He'd stop it all if she ever asked him to. But she never has and will probably never have to. Because if Kevin Westgarth has his way, that fifth right that reinjured his knuckle will be the last punch he ever throws.

A slow breeze rolls off the North Channel, cooling the streets of Belfast as hockey fans exit the Odyssey Arena, make their way down a cobbled lane, and head back to the many corners of a town trying to put its history of violence behind it. Somewhere out in the city, restless drug dealers fighting over turf are busy planting a pipe bomb on a car. But their activities do not impact the men, women, and children who seem united as they head back into their segregated Catholic and Protestant neighborhoods. This is no-man's-land, a chunk of repurposed soil on the banks of the River Lagan, a sanctuary where the neutral teal of a hockey sweater has replaced the sectarian colors of years past. Unlike soccer and rugby, bound and tainted by old allegiances, hockey serves a unique purpose here because even though it is a violent sport, it was imported to this town to give fans from across the old divide something to cheer for. And so Kevin Westgarth and the rest of the Belfast Giants view themselves as peacekeepers as well as hockey players—a particularly interesting concept to Westgarth, who has believed himself a peacekeeper since the age of 17, when he first propelled his fists into another boy's head.

It is nearly midnight as Westgarth retires to his apartment next to a small Protestant enclave where years of bloodshed are commemorated in murals of gun-toting paramilitaries in front of the Union Jack. Not exactly the environment in which he thought he'd celebrate his 31st birthday, but it's there that his wife, Meagan, wakes him in the morning with pancakes before he changes the gauze on his hand, says good-bye, and makes his way to a ferry bound for the Scottish coast.

Because he is now—and perhaps forever will be—the last pure NHL enforcer to get his name on the Stanley Cup, he is interrupted on that ferry by fans, teammates, and journalists as he fetches a coffee or pockets an apple from the canteen. There's an awkwardness to this moment in Westgarth's life, which he explains when he says that as far as hockey players go, he is unremarkable. His 16 points in 169 NHL games isn't exactly a figure that attracts much attention back home. And yet he knows in many ways he's unique. He's had a privileged view of some of the moments that have changed the game over the past decade. He can say what the fallout was after Todd Bertuzzi broke Steve Moore's neck or after Colton Orr pulled George Parros face first to the ice, because he had to live in it. He can describe the human impact advanced analytics have had on people's understanding of the game because he's a casualty of it. He can describe both the difficulty of brokering the deal to end the 2012–13 lockout and what it was like to go to sleep knowing the next day you might have to take one of Brian McGrattan's fists to your face. Westgarth is more than just the last of the enforcers. He is a Princeton grad who gave up the orthopedic scalpel for the hockey stick. A selfless figure who found purpose standing up for every single member of the Los Angeles Kings, and who may be one of the smartest men to have ever played the game. That's why his former bosses, Brian Burke and Dean Lombardi, believe him destined to someday run his own NHL franchise or perhaps succeed Donald Fehr as head of the NHLPA. That's why a camera crew is trailing the bearded warrior as he struggles to find his place in a changing world. They're listening, along with his teammates, as he explains the lineage of the British Crown and why, in 1536, Henry VIII ordered the dissolution of the monasteries, leaving abandoned buildings similar to the one they'll soon pass along a Scottish highway en route to their next hockey game.

So, when he says he has little time for advanced analytics and the statisticians who say his role is obsolete, those listening wonder if Westgarth, a guy who sometimes wears a Stanley Cup ring two fingers over from the one lined with old scars from Cody McCormick's teeth, might know more about hockey than the whiz kids helping to make executive decisions for teams around the league.

But that's a fight Westgarth does not wish to have. Not on his birthday. Instead, he says: "My entire career has been a statistical anomaly." When he's alone enough to fully articulate his thoughts, he describes how an A+ student who was never the best player on his team defied the odds and spent five years in the NHL. Then he reveals what it's like to wake up and realize you're one of the last remaining soldiers in a dishonored war. "There's a solace in reflecting on a career that shouldn't have happened," he says. "Scoring an NHL goal—it's almost a statistical impossibility to get to do that. If you lace up a pair of skates in Canada, your percentage chance of getting to that is almost zero.

"I have always felt some type of responsibility over the people I'm close to—teammates, friends, family. I'm lucky to be a big guy. In hockey, that pays dividends. To be able to intimidate. It served me very well and I hope it served my teammates well."

The son of veterinarians, Westgarth was five when he started playing organized hockey in Amherstburg, Ontario, where he tried as best he could to emulate Cam Neely, his childhood idol and the archetypal power forward. At 13, when most players destined to make the NHL begin taking off, he was getting cut from AAA teams. By 16, a growth spurt made him one of the bigger kids in his grade and changed how he played the game.

He has filed the photographic memories of his first bare-knuckle brawl next to obscure statistics about Icelandic alcoholism and facts about what concussions can do to the human brain. "I threw one punch," he recalls of that first fight in junior. "He threw one too and he kind of fell down. I fell on top of him and got off the ice and was just like, 'Holy crap. I did it. I am still here.'"

Soon, he was dropping the gloves every time he tried out for a new team. "It was a way to get me noticed," he says.

He was playing travel hockey on the same team as his older brother when scouts from Princeton visited Chatham, Ontario, to check out Brett Westgarth's game. After they saw the younger Westgarth score a couple of goals and get into a fight, they suggested he come play for them as well. As Westgarth puts it: "I think they saw me as somebody who had SAT scores that could actually get into the school. I got accepted into Princeton in their engineering school. I deferred for a year and realized I didn't really want to go into engineering and transitioned to essentially premed and wound up in psychology. It was incredibly interesting, trying to figure out what goes on between our ears."

There was no fighting in college hockey, which allowed Westgarth to concentrate on the less martial elements of the game. But he knew that if he was to have any career after Princeton, his knuckles needed to get bloodied. Off the ice, he took up boxing with his brother and spent his summers sparring in the shadow of Tommy Hearns at the Kronk Gym in Detroit. There was an art and a science to the way men fought in the ring, which he admired. It gave the violence a sense of order and purpose, and would eventually bring discipline and skill to the way he fought on the ice.

She was struggling when he found her on campus. Alone by a piano, trying to play the one song she remembered from her childhood. He sidled up next to her on the bench, put his fingers on the keys, and played the rest of the song by memory. That's how Kevin Westgarth met his wife.

Meagan Cowher, daughter of former Pittsburgh Steelers coach Bill Cowher, had grown up surrounded by burly men who made their living smashing each other. But the boy sitting next to her seemed different. Well-read and fascinated by psychology and medicine, he could quote from *Moby Dick* and enjoyed the sound of a violin. It turned out he was the quintessential gentleman, stood up when she entered and exited the room, and impressed his future father-in-law by the way he held his daughter's coat, pushed in her chair, and adhered to a code of conduct most men neglect. She'd always imagined herself as a career woman and believed she'd fallen in love with a future doctor. She knew he'd been training to fight, but had no idea that she was destined to spend the next decade following his fists wherever they took him. Nor did she understand that he'd already begun training his mind in preparation to become an NHL enforcer.

Westgarth had picked up a copy of *The Code: The Unwritten Rules of Fighting and Retaliation in the NHL*. He read it night after night, learning that the code had existed since the game's earliest days. It was an inescapable force on the ice, described as "a living, breathing thing among us." It made good men do violent things to ensure everyone answered for their actions—"You play hard physically in order to get yourself more space out on the ice, but you don't take advantage of guys who aren't in a position to defend themselves." Whenever two heavyweights got into a fight, it was to finish something they generally didn't start. It was the end result of a series of on-ice events that had rendered the game unplayable. When it was over, and the enforcers were bloodied and penalized, everybody else could get back to the game. That's how the code worked. It's what let Gretzky be Gretzky. But it wasn't the enforcer's duty to protect just the superstars; the enforcers were there to protect the code itself. And to them, the code was the game.

Dean Lombardi, the GM who signed Westgarth to the L.A. Kings and later became a mentor, is an intellectual who views himself as a general, his team as his army and his enforcers as his most selfless soldiers. On the ice, he employed Westgarth to lead the battle when no one else could. To stand alone in front of 17,000 people and fight with no shield and no way to blame his teammates if he lost or was injured. Off the ice, he came to see Westgarth as "a throwback to the ancient times of the warrior class."

"He's not the archetype of the enforcer," Lombardi says. "In all of them, you've got this survival instinct that 'I've got to do this to feed my family.' You've got that *American Sniper* mentality that 'I love my teammates and I want to protect them.' Somewhere in there, you've got to find the justification as well as the will. But Westy went beyond that. There was an intellectual approach that motivated him beyond the barbarian approach."

Westgarth wasn't the first enforcer to be the best-educated player in his team's dressing room, but no matter the lineage or how he rationalized the violence, there was nothing he could do to prepare Meagan for watching it. The first time she saw him fight, she was sitting with his family. "It was me, his dad, his brother, and his mom, and before the puck dropped, both his dad and his brother stood up and started clapping. They knew Kevin had lined up right next to a fighter. I had no idea what was going on.

"When he is fighting, my heart starts to beat in my chest very, very quickly. I feel like it's a mini–anxiety attack. My palms start to get a little sweaty and I can't watch. I don't watch. I sit in my seat just staring down, waiting for everyone to calm down, which lets me know that it's done. Then I can finally take a breath."

Westgarth fought more than 60 times in 224 games with the Manchester Monarchs, the Kings' American Hockey League affiliate. Midway through his second season in Manchester, his right hand began to change as a result of countless bare-knuckle impacts with helmets, shoulder pads, teeth, orbital bones, and skulls. He fought through the pain as his hand became increasingly deformed. It took two surgeries to repair the knuckle and a third to reattach a tendon in his pinky. He can no longer straighten that finger but can give a very detailed description of that last surgery, during which he sat awake and watched out of sheer curiosity.

In January 2009, Westgarth made his NHL debut with the Kings when he was called up for a game against the Minnesota Wild, whose ranks included the most feared enforcer of them all: Derek Boogaard. The NHL had already become somewhat fight-shy after the 2004 Bertuzzi incident that led to criminal charges and demonstrated that coaches could be legally implicated for sending their players out to assault members of the opposing team. No longer able to tap their fighters on the shoulder and tell them exactly what to do, coaches left their enforcers to figure things out for themselves. Looking back on that night in Minnesota, Westgarth recalls how uneasy and naive he was about all that was going on around him. "Raitis Ivanans was another enforcer in L.A., and we were on the same line," he says. "I was there to possibly be his replacement. I turned to him and I'm like, 'I kind of want to get into a fight and show what I can do. What do you think?' And he's like, 'No, no, don't worry about it.' A minute later, he's on the ice getting into a fight with Boogaard. I learned a little something that day: everybody is worried about their own job, which you have to be."

The following season, he broke David Koci's jaw. He soon took Ivanans's job and began accumulating the battle wounds to show for it.

He can tell you the origin of each scar on his face. The dent under his left eye was originally from a puck but got reopened by Steve MacIntyre and McGrattan. The line that cuts through his right eyebrow is from a minor-league bout with Guillaume Lefebvre. The flattened spot on his beak is from the time John Scott broke his nose. His bloodied face made the *L.A. Times* after that fight. Despite their obvious presence, he doesn't see the scars when he looks in the mirror. And when others ask about them, he makes clear they're all worth bearing for having lived his dream.

Though there is no physical blemish that commemorates the ultimate culmination of that dream, there is an emotional wound that Westgarth keeps well hidden. Five years after he signed with the Kings, he sat in his gear in the team's dressing room, scratched from the playoff roster, watching the in-house TV feed as men he'd protected during the regular season scored goal after goal against Martin Brodeur in the 2012 Stanley Cup final. By the time he got on the ice the game was already won, but no one made him feel he wasn't part of that victory. When it was his turn to hoist the Cup, his wife was beside him. It was the last time he suited up as a King.

Four months into the current NHL season, Kevin Westgarth is lost in the corridors of a Scottish hockey arena, carrying his own gear and wondering how long it will take to find where he's going. Blood seeps through the gauze on his bandaged knuckle as he searches for the visitors' dressing room in the Braehead Arena on the outskirts of Glasgow. Soon he will pull on his Belfast Giants sweater and mark his birthday by trying, as best he can, to play not like the warrior he is, but like the power forward he always wanted to be. Tonight, though, he and his team are destined for defeat. In the dressing room after the final whistle, some of the Giants remove their pads and throw them against the walls, cursing the referees and looking, for a moment, like they might light all of Scotland on fire. But Westgarth is not one of these men. Though he, too, is angry, he channels his inner Zen, or perhaps his future diplomat, and tells those most enraged by the loss that they must recover and move on.

Standing at the bar inside a Scottish pub following the game, Westgarth sips a pint of Guinness as a few hard-core Giants fans —men and women who took the ferry to Scotland with their team —note his presence and encircle him from behind. He knows they are there. Can hear them whispering as they pull out their markers in hope he'll sign their Kevin Westgarth sweaters.

As the biggest name this team has employed since Theoren Fleury ignited these supporters back in 2005, Westgarth has a following he never had in the NHL. And though he is appreciative of his new fan base, he remains cognizant that back home, his former teammates are carrying on without him. Sipping his last postgame drink and counting the minutes until a 2:00 a.m. bus will return him to a ferry back to Belfast, he explains that sometimes it's hard to lament the battle when you're a casualty of a greater defeat.

There's a precedent to his declining fortune that Westgarth knows as well as any student of conflict. The last vestige of Japan's samurai class disappeared after the Second World War. But the respect for their kind had been eroded for generations; victims of their own failure to evolve and of political efforts to discredit their sacred status. He covers his mangled knuckle as he explains that

politics are as much responsible for the disappearance of the enforcers as modern analytics or any other external force currently
changing the game. "Hockey," he says, "is always going to be violent. Not just a contact sport but a conflict sport. People have died.
If you ask any of the enforcers, they will say they know what they're
getting into and gladly accept those risks to play this game."

There is a view, shared by some, that the enforcer's extinction
was inevitable after the 2012–13 lockout. For Westgarth, that's a
frustrating thought because as a key member of the 31-player ne-
gotiating committee, he spent six months working on the current
collective bargaining agreement that brought hockey back to the
fans. And so he wonders if there was anything he could have done
to try to stave off the elimination of his role.

But the truth may be that all of this was foretold before Westgarth dropped his gloves for the very first time. Says Lombardi:
"I can remember when Harry Sinden and the last of those GMs,
the icons like Cliff Fletcher and Bobby Clarke—even within those
guys, there was a recognition that the days of the pure gunslinger
were going to come to an end. That's not something that happened overnight. That evolved."

Westgarth could see this happening. On January 13, 2013, one
day after the collective bargaining agreement was signed, he became property of the Carolina Hurricanes, having requested the
trade so he could get a chance at more ice time.

The urge to rebrand himself as anything but a gunslinger became paramount the next season on October 1, 2013, when he
sat at home watching as his friend and fellow Princeton alumnus
George Parros engaged Colton Orr in an ill-fated bout that saw Orr
pull Parros chin-first to the ice. The impact left Parros motionless
and looking, for a moment, as if he were dead. Soon, Westgarth's
fear for his friend was joined by fear the incident would further
the argument that neither Parros nor Orr nor any other enforcer
had a place in this game. What Westgarth failed to understand was
the effect that fight had on his wife, sitting next to him struggling
to not picture her husband's face on the unconscious man being
stretchered off the ice.

By Christmas, Westgarth had played just 12 games with the
Hurricanes. He was feeling lost and disengaged from the battle
when he was granted refuge by Brian Burke, the Harvard-educated
lawyer and vocal champion of the enforcer's role who still clung

to the view that "large hostile individuals are useful on a hockey rink." Burke had turned the Calgary Flames into one of the last bastions of the warrior class and put Westgarth on a line next to McGrattan, who'd inherited the title of heavyweight champion of the league after Boogaard overdosed on the painkillers to which he'd become addicted.

Westgarth's season was on an upward trajectory into March when, in his third fight as a Flame, he raised his fists against Edmonton's Luke Gazdic at center ice. That's when all his wife's earlier fears became a reality.

Listening to Westgarth retell the details of that fight is like listening to a chess master analyze his own defeat. To Westgarth, everything was going fine until he made an ill-timed and ultimately costly move. "It was a pretty good fight. I'm having trouble getting free and I distinctly remember hitting him right in the middle of the visor . . . I made a terrible mistake, a slow, lazy change to get my left free, and I let go of his right arm. He came across and hit me in the side of the head and down I went."

At that moment, Meagan was across town in a friend's kitchen, the game on in the background. Suddenly, everything stopped. She found herself staring at the television as her husband lay stricken on the ice, his mouth guard spat out by his side, a referee motioning for help while the Edmonton crowd cheered louder.

Her eyes grow misty as she recounts what it is like to watch your husband get knocked out over and over on instant replay by a punch he didn't see coming. "I got in the car and I'm driving as fast as I can to get there because I just want to see him with my own eyes and make sure he's okay.

"I walked into the arena and outside the dressing room he's just kind of sitting there by himself. The game's still going on, the arena's still full of people, and he's just sitting there waiting for the game to finish so that he can see his teammates and let them know that he's okay.

"He gave me a big hug and kiss and said, 'I'm sorry. I messed up.' We sat on folding chairs and watched the game. I was there with him for only about 15 minutes and went back to the hotel, because for him, it was weirdly isolating. I knew he would probably rather be in his locker room with some of his teammates trying to feel more normal."

To have sustained just one concussion in more than 100 bare-knuckle fights makes him one of the luckiest of all enforcers. He is thankful that his physical toll has been almost entirely confined to the battering ram that is his right hand. Just as he is thankful that the postconcussion syndrome he suffered after that fight in Edmonton lasted only about a week. He was back in the Calgary lineup 11 days later, and though he fought three more times with the Flames, he redoubled his efforts to convince himself and others that he could actually play, closing the last half of the season with seven points, including four goals, one of which he chipped past Henrik Lundqvist.

But not even Burke could keep him with the Flames when the season was over. Westgarth traveled north to the same ice on which he was concussed and tried out for the Edmonton Oilers. He made his final stand in the NHL on October 2, 2014, landing more than a dozen punches against Vancouver's Tom Sestito in a preseason scrap. Three days later, he sat in Edmonton GM Craig MacTavish's office inside Rexall Place, listening as MacTavish said, "I don't think we're going to need you." The Oilers had already packed up his equipment by the time he left that meeting. An hour and a half later, they had him on a plane, heading home to his wife.

Before long, almost every other enforcer in the NHL would have a similar experience. Soon, even McGrattan was relegated to the AHL.

As he stands in the hills of Braniel looking down on Belfast, Westgarth's scraggly beard and tweed cap give him the air of an Irish shepherd as he expounds on what got him here. He says he had a sense of finality when he was cut from the Oilers, a realization that his NHL career was over. But finality takes a while to get used to. Soon, he was being courted by a Canadian coach working in a land with two hockey rinks and a 14-year connection to the game. His wish to find himself led him to pack up his gear and come to the island of his grandmother's youth. He's here now playing hockey, but also contemplating doing an MBA alongside his wife. No longer interested in becoming an orthopedic surgeon, he spends his downtime wondering if maybe he should follow Lombardi's advice and become a lawyer, or if he should work toward becoming what Burke believes him to be: a future NHL GM. It is the urge to change with the changing world that sets him apart from other enforcers like McGrattan and Orr—discarded warriors who continue to cling to the belief that one day their masters will remember that hockey is a game of honor, not stats, and return them to their place in the NHL.

"I know there's no going back," Westgarth says. Just as he knows there's no way to re-create the same energy he felt every time he got into a fight on an NHL rink. Nor a way to place a statistical value on the comfort his presence used to give the players he was there to protect. "I will take the pride of being an enforcer to the grave with me. It was something I really worked hard at. If people find that off-putting or kind of unsavory, then they don't know enough about it. To me, it's the most selfless thing. It was done for my teammates."

There's a sadness that comes with being the last of one's kind, which Westgarth laments when he explains: "Heavyweight enforcers were usually the guys everybody liked the most—gregarious and a good time to be around. That was always the strange duality of their existences on the ice.

"I don't think I would have ever made it without fighting. Every single practice, I was out there trying to make my skating better, trying to improve as a player. At the end of the day, without fighting, I wouldn't have been there in the first place. I wish I could play hockey like Patrick Kane and dangle around everybody and score goals and win the game and that's the end. I don't think that's in my nature."

Inside the Giants dressing room, Westgarth ponders his future while also regaling his teammates—many of them older than him; the majority of them Canadians who never reached the NHL —with tales of what it was like to have lived not just his dream, but theirs as well. Future cops, coaches, and students themselves-, they're all looking to a life beyond the game. And yet they sit and listen like children as he recounts how when he hoisted the Cup above his head, he could feel the bell bend in his hand. Every member of this team is thankful for his presence here. Not just for the stories he shares, but for the ones they will one day be able to pass on about the time they played hockey alongside a Cup winner. To those clinging to the end of their careers, Kevin Westgarth is validation. A man who, like them, is trying to play as well as he can for as long as he can. None of them understands that he is torn between the needs of this team and city, the hopes of his wife, and his increasing understanding that a hockey career is just a window of time. All the while, he reflects on the damage that the battles caused. Not to his hand, his head, or to the faces of the men he left concussed or convulsing on the ice, but to his mother and wife who never wanted to see him fight. And though he's bothered by that damage, there is no relinquishing the pride he took from his many victories and defeats. Especially not when the wound of being dishonored and cast out of the NHL is as raw as the hole on his knuckle. There's a bitterness there, but also a strange satisfaction in having been one of the NHL's last enforcers.

"It's somehow comforting," he says. "To go out with an entire group of players that I've always respected. I wish it hadn't happened, but it's maybe minimal solace to be on the front lines of the last hurrah."

Regardless of his lost place in the North American game, Westgarth still means something here. Especially to the Giants and their growing horde of fans. That's why they're packing this arena and why his face appears on the Jumbotron. In this unlikely place, Westgarth has regained his role, safeguarding this team's stars— men whose names mean little back home but who mean everything to the team's quest for another championship. Here, Kevin Westgarth, the warrior whom Dean Lombardi, Brian Burke, and Craig MacTavish ultimately deemed unnecessary, has emerged as an inspiration to the children of conflict who have become his greatest fans. Here, he is not just needed, he's wanted. Even the politicians—loyalist and republican alike—are willing to stand before TV cameras and cheer his name while his coach urges him to settle in and lead the Giants to glory.

There's an irony to Westgarth's newfound place that seems lost on everyone except him. The day after his birthday, Westgarth, along with his wife and teammates, wanders freely through Belfast's streets on a pub crawl, venturing in and out of bars and neighborhoods where the lone Northern Irish member of the team—their backup goaltender—dares not go. His absence is a sobering reminder of a fragile détente, of why armed police in bulletproof Land Rovers patrol past concrete and metallic walls that still divide the former stomping grounds of the Irish Republican Army from those of their unionist foes. Here, where the maintenance of peace sometimes requires police to carry machine guns and erect checkpoints to screen civilians for bombs, the toll of the fight has left people exhausted. And there lies the irony. For in this city, Kevin Westgarth—human casualty of the NHL's own newfound détente—is still expected to fight.

And yet he, too, has become exhausted from battle.

Though he has accumulated 20 points in 30 games, he has barely fought, which is problematic because whether he likes it or not, that's still part of why he's here—to enforce the code. And now he has broken it, along with that defenseless man's helmet. Not because he wanted to please his coach, but because he followed the advice his father gave him before coming out here: "I hope you don't have to fight anymore. But if you do, I hope you beat the crap out of them so they leave you alone."

Seated with his armor hanging on a hook behind him, Kevin Westgarth explains for the last time what it's like to be a roaming samurai searching for peace. "To be feared," he says, "is helpful in this line of work. If you can win the fight without throwing a punch, you're way better off. I have the hands to prove it."

Content to end his career as a Giant, Westgarth makes his final preparations to move beyond the game. Because he knows that fear alone will not guarantee him peace on this ice. For the longer he stays, the more likely he is to be followed. Soon, men like McGrattan and Orr and the rest of the wayward enforcers might be brought in to arm this league. Then the code will become spectacle. And for Kevin Westgarth, that's not worth fighting for.

MICHAEL ROSENBERG

A Woman Fell from a Stadium

FROM SPORTS ILLUSTRATED

THE PHONE FELL FIRST. Glenn Israel heard it hit concrete a
few feet away from him and crack. He looked up and saw a young
woman sitting on a railing 45 feet above him, crying.

Everybody in the vicinity that day was just passing through. A
full NFL stadium feels like an enormous party, with thousands celebrating in the same way. But it is also like a small city. On this 2013
day, four days before Thanksgiving, O.co [Oakland] Coliseum was
filled with the dreams, job stresses, loves, addictions, plans, undi-
agnosed diseases, appetites, and relationship woes of more than
60,000 people.

The Oakland Raiders had lost to the Tennessee Titans, 23–19.
In an indoor batting cage near the Raiders' locker room, Oakland
coach Dennis Allen was beginning his postgame press conference
with an injury report.

Israel had just posed for a photo with his friend Donnie Navidad by the Al Davis Memorial Flame, named for the late Raiders
owner. Former Raiders star Bo Jackson had lit the flame before
the game, and Navidad wore his Jackson jersey, hoping to get an
autograph. He never got one, so on their way out, he and Israel
asked a woman there to take their photo.

Navidad walked back toward her to pick up his camera. Israel
did not join him, because he has a bum ankle, and the fewer steps
he takes, the better. He was walking toward the parking lot when
the phone landed.

Fans saw other fans looking toward the sky, and they looked up
too, at the horror unfolding above Section 300. The woman was

dangling now, her arms spread back behind her, clinging to the railing. Even if she wanted to pull herself back up, the physics were almost impossible.

"No, no, no!"

"Don't jump! Don't jump!"

A fan named Tom Rodriguez heard the screams and looked up. By day, Rodriguez sells spray-on protective coating for the beds of trucks, but when he attends Raider games he is a temporary celebrity because of his outfit: white mask, silver mohawk helmet, and full Raiders uniform, including pants and pads. Fans kept stopping him to take his photograph, which is why he was still by the flame instead of in the parking lot when the phone dropped. He ripped off his mask and helmet to prepare to catch the woman.

Navidad was standing next to Rodriguez. He glanced back at Israel and said: "Do you think she's gonna jump?"

Israel said, "She's coming down right now."

She plummeted 45 feet in less than two seconds. Rodriguez reached to his right to save her, but he had no chance. He was too far away, and she was falling too quickly.

Navidad was her only hope. Forty-three years earlier, Navidad was in Marine boot camp, crawling under a wire screen as rounds of gunfire exploded over his head, learning to react immediately to the unforeseen, and here it was, in the form of a woman's body descending toward him at 35 miles per hour. He tried to brace himself and fall backward as she landed on him, to absorb the shock. She ricocheted off him and landed a couple of yards away, where she landed on concrete.

Blood pooled around her head. Rodriguez stood over her and thought she might be dead. Navidad appeared to be knocked out.

Police rushed to the scene. So did Israel, who got Navidad's attention and asked him simple questions. *What's my name? How many fingers am I holding up?* Navidad answered correctly. His left arm was quite bruised, and his ankle would bother him for a month, but those were his only injuries.

The woman had no identification on her. Nobody in the crowd knew who she was. Navidad thought he heard her say a single word, ever so gently, right before she hit him: *"Momma."*

She was rushed to Highland Hospital in Oakland with major neck, spine, and facial injuries and admitted as a Jane Doe. Police picked the pieces of her phone off the concrete, got the number off the SIM card, and ran it through several law-enforcement and public databases and contacted the phone's service provider, and turned up a name: Brittany Nicole Bryan of San Jose. Twenty years old.

Navidad was a local-news hero, celebrated in that brief window before TV stations move on to the next day's show. He read a few stories about the incident and was stunned by the reader comments. People wrote that if this woman wanted to die, he should have let her. Or he should have sold movie rights and made money off it.

Or, on an ESPN.com story: "You know your team sucks when your fans can't even wait to get home before they off themselves." And: "The lady should have just finished the job and not exposed kids or other people to her mental illness."

Tom Rodriguez read the comments too, and the man who attended the game in full costume got so angry that he posted a comment himself:

> To all you dumb people who are talking smack about us losing, when I was there trying to help save a young girls life with the man who got hurt, people shouldn't be talking SMACK. This was serious and you wouldn't know or feel the same if you were in the same situation, I was there when she fell on the man next to me . . . It was not something to JOKE about because we lost the game. I am just happy that they are both alive. So Keep Your Stupid Comments to your SELF.

They did not Keep Their Stupid Comments to Themselves, because Brittany Bryan was not even a real person to them, just an anonymous character on the Internet, grist for the sarcasm mill. Even her family did not know what happened; her boyfriend, who had been at the game, thought she went home, and her mother and sisters assumed she was with her boyfriend.

Her sister Vicky came home from a Mexican vacation with a gift for Brittany (small turtle and fish figurines) and a more expensive one for herself (a silver and turquoise bracelet), and looked forward to seeing Brittany. Her sister Bernadette saw a headline about a woman jumping off the Coliseum after the Raiders game and clicked on another story. The next day, they learned their sister was in the hospital and might die there.

Brittany always thought of herself as Daddy's girl, and with this father, who wouldn't't? Larry Bryan was 10 kinds of fun, eager to make the kids laugh, desperate to make them feel loved. He treated Brittany's older sisters, Bernadette and Vicky Fox, like they were his own daughters, even though they have a different father. On Christmas, gifts covered the entire living-room floor, and adventure always seemed just a few minutes away. Larry was the rare gambler with the reputation for winning more than he lost, and he loved taking his family to Las Vegas, or to a hotel in San Jose to swim and play video games. Sometimes he would look them in the eye and wink.

Even his job seemed fun: buying and selling jewelry and other collectibles. Sometimes he would drive the kids to antique stores to sell a necklace or two. They were stunned when he was arrested on New Year's Eve, 2006, for multiple burglaries. The accusations followed a pattern: Larry broke through windows of million-dollar homes or sliced open screens. He stole jewelry, watches, foreign currency, and a few other valuables, and left the electronics. That day, 14-year-old Brittany watched her mother Joy bury a brown bag in the backyard. Joy would be found guilty of being an accessory and concealing stolen property.

The court sentenced Larry to 37 years in prison. Brittany quickly entered a program that would allow her to graduate from high school early so she could get a job. Larry worried about her future. Her sisters tried to take care of her, but Brittany thought they were acting like her parents instead of her sisters. She became an emotional wall, giving one-word answers to innocuous questions.

At 16, she became pregnant, and she waited five months to tell her family, so nobody would try to talk her into an abortion. When Brittany finally shared the news, Bernadette took her to the restaurant where Brittany worked and gave her an informational packet about adoption. Brittany understood the impulse—adoption might be best for her *and* the baby—but decided to keep the baby, a girl named Lyla, born a week before Brittany turned 17. She wanted Larry to meet Lyla. He never did. He died in jail, in his sleep, after battling heart problems. He was 58.

Now here she was, 20 years old with no wallet on her, just another Jane Doe to Internet commenters but Brittany Bryan to her family. Doctors induced a coma to help save her life. A few weeks later, she woke, with no idea how she ended up in the hospital. Bernadette told her she dropped off the top of the Coliseum after the Raiders game. Brittany searched the Internet for local news reports about it, and she heard newscasters talk about a young woman attempting suicide and a heroic ex-Marine saving her life, and she thought: "Why did this happen to me? I was so happy."

Brittany Bryan sits outside a Starbucks in San Jose, California. Almost a year has passed. The book she has been reading is on the table: *The Peter Principle: Why Things Always Go Wrong.*

She feels better now than she did a few months ago, partly because a piece of her skull is no longer embedded in her abdomen. Doctors put it there as part of a craniotomy, a procedure that allowed them to perform brain surgery while retaining the bone from her skull.

"It looked like I was pregnant on half of my stomach," she says. "I could feel it and it was really hard. I couldn't talk because I had a breathing tube in my throat. I was pointing at it, like: 'What's going on?' They were saying, 'It's your head.' Imagine how I'm feeling. 'What do you mean *it's my head?* How did it get down there?'"

Her sisters kept vigil at the hospital, sleeping on a cot in Brittany's room. The hospital gave her a computer-generated assumed name, Paul 51, in case the media tried to find her. Family members had to show their driver's licenses to prove they were on an approved visitors list, so they could go in and see a woman who looked like a stranger. Bernadette recognized only her eyelashes, which are distinct. Everything else looked as computer-generated as the name Paul 51.

Brittany's right hand was broken, her left heel was shattered, and bones in her face were fractured. Doctors gave teaspoons of hope surrounded by piles of caveats: *We can't promise this will work. Don't get your hopes up.*

They said even if she survived, she might never seem like herself again. But she does. She emerged from the coma and the surgeries physically whole, or as close to whole as anybody could dream. Oakland's Highland Hospital is known for treating trauma victims, often because of gunfire and other violent crimes in Oakland, but even at Highland, Brittany's case stood out. Doctors from other floors of the hospital visited her and called her "the miracle patient." The moment her breathing tube was removed, she looked at the family members in the room and noticed who wasn't there.

"I miss Lyla," she said, and she started crying.

Her embarrassment was overwhelming. She was reluctant to

talk to anybody. How do you explain dropping 45 feet off the top of a stadium? Her friends didn't know about the incident (the media had not used her name) and they wondered why she was ignoring them. Finally she told a few: "I had a really bad accident." This is how she refers to it, as "my accident."

Suicide? Her family was skeptical. It never occurred to her that the woman might be her sister. Vicky wondered if there was "some hidden, severe depression that we had no idea about," but she saw Brittany every day and thought she had never been happier. Her relationship with her new boyfriend seemed strong. She loved being a mom.

Yet there she was at Highland, literally shattered and also drugged and confused. The idea that she attempted suicide was so far-fetched in her mind that she wondered if somebody had pushed her. But she didn't remember what happened, let alone why.

"All these people, not just the news reporters, all these people that were talking about it were just so sure of themselves," she says. "There are 100 witnesses saying the same thing, and it's them against me and how I feel."

Somehow, her phone still worked after the fall. But for three weeks, she couldn't remember the lock-screen code. Then one day it came back to her: 8779. She could use the phone to make calls, but the screen was broken, and eventually she just bought a new one.

The moments before the accident have come back to her too —not all of them, certainly, but enough to give her some sense of what happened. She gave her wallet to her boyfriend so she wouldn't have to hold it in the restroom. She got lost coming out of the restroom, which was not as unusual as it sounds. She is one of those people who is known, within her family, for her almost comically awful sense of direction. She once came out of the restroom at a San Jose Sharks game and couldn't remember where her seat was, and it happened at a San Francisco Giants game too, but she found her way back to her seat.

This time, Brittany couldn't figure out where to go. She had been consuming alcohol all day, starting with Jell-O shots at a pregame tailgate, and she was drunk and disoriented. She tried calling and texting her boyfriend but couldn't get through.

As she stood in a concourse area behind section 144, a man named Kimani Crum saw her crying and tried to help. She said she was looking for her boyfriend, her cell phone was dead, and she did not know where her seat was. Crum gave her some suggestions on how to find her boyfriend and left.

She tried to call her mom to pick her up. Her phone was dying. She looked for a place to charge her phone as thousands rushed out of the stadium. Somehow she ended up at Section 300, which is half a football field and two levels away from Section 144. Section 300 was also closed, which may have been appealing to her. She has anxiety in crowds sometimes.

Once she got past a rope barrier blocking off the stairway, there was nobody to stop her. Police would find a single set of fresh footprints in the dust along the edge of the tarp covering the seats.

She remembers "climbing some kind of stairs . . . it's kind of a blur." She may have walked upstairs because everybody else was going down, and this was a chance to get away, or maybe she was just hoping to get a better signal in the postgame cellular haze.

Down by the Al Davis Memorial Flame, Crum looked up and saw her climbing over the railing. He realized this was the same woman he had tried to help.

What was she thinking as she sat there? She wishes she knew. She has heard that when people are drunk, they don't hear words like "don't," and perhaps her ears filtered that out of the crowd's pleas: *Jump!* . . . *Jump!* She may not even have realized she was four stories above concrete. She may have let go of the railing out of frustration, or to feel momentarily free. She will probably never know.

The last thing she remembers was wishing her mother Joy would take her home. This would explain the only word that Navidad heard her say before she landed: "*Momma.*"

Some witnesses said she jumped and others said she fell, but she thinks she was too drunk to know the difference. This is the one thing she knows for sure: whatever she did, she never would have done it sober. Rodriguez, who watched her fall, insists that if she had pushed herself away from the railing, she would have sailed past him and Navidad.

Brittany's best friend's mother is a recovering alcoholic, and before the accident, Brittany would sometimes join her at Alcoholics Anonymous meetings. She did not talk much, because she was a drinker, and "I didn't want to be a hypocrite. It was just nice and refreshing to hear other people's stories, just to listen."

After her fall, she thought about joining a support group for people with traumatic-brain injuries, but decided that wasn't right for her. She prefers the AA meetings, and hearing stories there convinced her that alcohol triggered the incident at the Coliseum. She says she is not an alcoholic. She says she did not get drunk often, even before the accident, and never felt compelled to drink every day. But like many 20-year-olds, once in a while she would drink with her friends, especially at a concert or sporting event, with no limit in mind and no worries about consequences.

Her story is not one of addiction. It's about impairment, and it is an uncommon variation of a common theme. Two nights after Brittany sat for her *SI* interview, St. Louis Cardinals outfielder Oscar Taveras climbed in his car in the Dominican Republic with a blood-alcohol level of .287, more than five times the National Transportation Safety Board–recommended limit of .05. Taveras drove into a tree, killing himself and his girlfriend, Edilia Arvelo. And last summer, after former Auburn tight end Philip Lutzenkirchen died in a one-car accident, tests showed his blood-alcohol level was 0.377, which may explain why he decided to get in a car with a driver whose blood-alcohol level was 0.17. The driver also died.

It is harder to understand a woman dropping off the top of a football stadium, unprompted by anyone else. But alcohol-related deaths occur every day to people who are not driving and are not alcoholics. According to a 2012 study by the Centers for Disease Control in the United States, four drunk pedestrians a day are killed by cars.

"It could be your first time drinking," Brittany says. "Anything can happen."

Her story may be hard to believe, but at least one man understands how alcohol can push a person outside the bounds of normal behavior. In the 1980s, Donnie Navidad was a Marine reserve, training at the Pohakuloa Training Area in Hawaii, drinking boilermakers with his Marine pals: a shot of Wild Turkey with Schlitz malt liquor, and why stop at one or two?

"I'd try to outdrink the rest of my partners," he said. "Some of the craziest s—. You're drunk, but you just keep drinking."

Navidad would climb palm trees on the Big Island until he was

30 or 40 feet above the ground. He easily could have fallen, broken his back or his neck, and been a different character in one of these stories.

"You know, you do crazy stuff when you're drinking," he says. "It kind of dares you. It gives you that feeling, to dare you to do it no matter what the outcome is."

Glenn Israel injured his ankle in the Navy, moving 500-pound bombs around flight decks during a 10-year stint. He served in Vietnam, which is precisely what Donnie Navidad envisioned doing when he tried to enlist in the Navy out of high school in 1970. Donnie's dad had been a Navy man. But the Naval recruiter asked him to wait a week, and so he joined the Marines instead after taking a one-page test that would change his life, and eventually save Brittany Bryan's.

His wife Lora says he "thinks like a Marine and acts like a Marine," from his serious nature to his ability to always make her feel safe. Sometimes it's like he just walked out of boot camp last week. He can still make a Swiss harness seat out of rope, a skill you don't need in daily American life, because "[t]here are things that are in you that will never leave you." But there is one thing this Marine never did.

Ask Navidad if he served in Vietnam, and his choice of words is telling: "I didn't get to go." Lora thinks that bothered him; he was a Marine, but he never really did what Marines were trained to do. Then one day he posed for that photo by the Al Davis Memorial Flame, and the Navy vet told the Marine: *She's coming down right now.*

"You are trained to react under those kinds of conditions," Navidad says. "It's just a reaction. You are in a civilian mode, you are enjoying life, and you see this body falling . . . are you going to let this human life splatter in front of you? Come on. Had I let that happen, I'm a wreck."

When Brittany left the hospital, she sent Donnie a thank-you note and a picture of her and Lyla. The picture sits on a shelf in the Navidads' house alongside family photos. Lora says the placement was intentional.

"When you save somebody's life, you are kind of bonded to that person," she says. "To him she is, and will be, a very important part of his life forever."

After a Raiders-Chargers game in October, Donnie pointed up to where Brittany had dangled. His brother could not believe anybody survived. He is right to be amazed. Brittany probably hit Donnie with at least 1,500 pounds of force.

Lora has seen a different Donnie since the accident. He is more outwardly compassionate, more conscious of the people around him, more outgoing because of the attention. The decision that could have killed him brought him peace. "He is much better for it," she says. Israel agrees: "He's mellowed out a lot since that happened."

Donnie is proud he saved Brittany's life, but he still wishes he could have saved it *better,* more cleanly: "The only thing that really bothers me out of this whole ordeal is I didn't get to block her into my body. She bounced." In the first moments afterward, he wondered if he had failed. He saw the blood around her head and asked his friend Israel, "Is she going to be okay?"

She is okay. More than okay. She says she truly was happy before, but she was also coasting, finding excuses not to go back to school or pursue a more ambitious career.

"Honestly, I feel a little bit better than I did," she says. "I'm just happier. I feel like it taught me a lot."

The girl who wouldn't share anything with her sisters just opened her life to *Sports Illustrated.* Bernadette and Vicky say they are closer than ever, they talk about everything, and they all dote on Lyla, who is four years old now and has a sense of humor that reminds them all of Larry, especially when she looks adults in the eye and winks.

In September, Brittany celebrated her 21st birthday in San Francisco with her sisters and a few friends. She wore the silver and turquoise bracelet that Vicky bought in Mexico; Vicky decided, after the accident, that she would rather give it to Brittany than keep it for herself. They went to the Tonga Room and Hurricane Bar, where Brittany drank her ceremonial first legal drink. Then they went back to their room at the Omni, where they danced and sang. Brittany drank a single glass of champagne, resisted any more, and felt lucky.

Brittany just started classes at San Jose City College. She is thinking about becoming a nurse. She would not have considered that career before the accident because she was scared of administering shots. But some of the nurses at Highland brought her such comfort and joy, and she wants to bring that to others. The nurses told her she can get accustomed to needles. One of them showed her proper technique: pinch the skin a little harder than you think is necessary, then insert the needle, and the patient barely feels any pain at all.

JOHN BRANCH

Hold On, Boys

FROM THE NEW YORK TIMES

THE 1,000-FOOT CLIFFS of Zion National Park that border the open range of Smith Mesa glowed orange and red, like hot coals. The sun slinked low on the opposite side of a wide sky.

Bill Wright, 60, stopped his pickup on the dirt road last spring, dusty from drought. He walked west, weaving through green junipers, scraggly shrub live oak, flowering barrel cactus, and dried cow pies. His pointed boots left a string of meandering arrows in the red sand.

The boys were off riding saddle broncs on the professional rodeo circuit's Texas swing—somewhere between Austin, Nacogdoches, and Lubbock, Bill could never keep up. Billy's wife, Evelyn, was at home, two hours north in Milford, Utah, teaching at the elementary school. Bill was alone, living in a camper, eating from a skillet, surrounded by silence and 20,000 acres of rugged rangeland hiding a few hundred of his cattle.

The sand gave way to stair-stepped rocks, like risers on which enormous choirs might perform, until the last one dropped off several hundred feet. The canyon below was a deep and jagged cut in the forever landscape of southern Utah, as if carved by impatient gods with a dull knife. The Wrights have been running cattle in the area for more than 150 years, since great-great-grandparents arrived beginning in 1849 during the Mormon migration.

"My boys will be the sixth generation," Bill said. His mouth never opened very far when he spoke. And Cody's boys will be the seventh.

Cody Wright is the oldest of seven boys among Bill and Evelyn's

13 children. The boys, ages 18 to 37 and similarly built—like a litter of puppies, Bill said—are a posse of the world's best saddle-bronc riders. Taut-muscled and not too tall, they are able to muster the guts, strength, and balance to ride a bucking horse like few others, as if genetically gifted to do so. A Wright boy has won the saddle-bronc world title every even-numbered year since 2008.

Cody won twice, in 2008 and 2010. Jesse, now 25, won in 2012. Jesse's twin, Jake, was second in 2013. In 2014, those three and a fourth Wright boy, Spencer, 24, qualified for the sport's most prestigious event, December's National Finals Rodeo—a record for one family.

But rodeo careers can end without warning, as quick as the next try at an eight-second ride. So the boys, most with families to support, increasingly plug their rodeo earnings into Bill's modest ranching business. While they crisscross tens of thousands of miles to more than 100 events a year across the West, Bill shepherds the growing herd back home in Utah.

From a distance, at a time of urbanization and connectivity, rodeo and ranching may seem anachronistic notions—quaint and sepia-toned from an America that no longer exists. To the Wrights, rodeo and ranching represent not the past, but the present and the future. The hope is that the combination can sustain the expanding Wrights for several more generations.

"Rodeo's not something that everybody's going to be able to do," Bill said. "Where ranching possibly is."

He stared into the canyon. His eyes, squinty pinches beneath the low brim of a tan cowboy hat smudged with grit, were trained over a lifetime of spotting specks of black and brown moving amid red soil and green brush.

That such a gorge was created by moving water felt like a myth. Beyond an occasional trickle through a cluster of green ferns deep in the shadows, there was little moisture now. Not in this drought.

That was a main reason that Bill wanted to gather his cattle earlier than usual, even before most of his children and 30-some grandchildren arrived for the family's annual roundup on Memorial Day weekend. He needed to move the herd 100 miles to the north, to the high-elevation summer range in the Tushar Mountains near Beaver, Utah, where there were plants to eat and water to drink.

In May, Bill sold 102 yearlings, born the previous spring and still growing. "I normally would have kept them until September," Bill said. "But prices were so damn high, and things looked so bleak, we decided to do it now. I got more out of them cattle selling them this year at 600 pounds than I did last year at 850 pounds."

Beef prices were at record highs. Demand was rising. The number of cattle in the United States was at its lowest number since 1951.

"I sold a steer for $2.53 a pound," Bill said. It was a price he had never seen. "When I was a boy, my dad bought cattle for 22 cents a pound. I remember we bought it once for 33 cents, then had to sell it at 22 cents. We lost $20,000 on 100 head of yearlings."

Today's high prices did not quash the anxiety of pinning the livelihoods of the family's future generations on a few hundred cattle. The number of cattle operations in the United States shrinks as the average size grows. The Wrights' operation is bigger than about 90 percent of those around the country, government statistics show, but a herd of 200 calf-bearing cows is barely enough to earn a living for Bill and Evelyn. ("Behind every successful rancher," Evelyn said, "is a wife who works in town.") The business will have to expand exponentially to provide for their children and grandchildren.

Land is the biggest impediment. Like most ranchers in the West, the Wrights lease most of their grazing pastures through a patchwork of permits from the Bureau of Land Management or the United States Forest Service. Each permit dictates how many cattle can graze on a particular parcel, and for how many months of the year.

Bill's father had one of the first permits sold in the aftermath of the Taylor Grazing Act of 1934, meant to prevent overgrazing on tens of millions of acres of public range in the West. These days, permits can cost tens or hundreds of thousands of dollars. Bill has eight permits, some bought with hefty bank loans.

More and more, though, he pays cash, with help from the boys.

Last year, Jesse bought a permit for summer. A few years before, Cody earned a $100,000 payday at the Calgary Stampede and splurged with the winnings—on cows, practically doubling Bill's herd.

"One of these days I'm going to nail him down and figure out what I've got," Cody said. "I know I have at least 78 cows. If I don't, he's been selling 'em off."

Farther down the Virgin River, near Mesquite, Nevada, is a rancher named Cliven Bundy—"a good, hard-working ranchman," Bill said.

Last spring, Bundy was at the center of a standoff with the land management bureau. The conflict went back two decades, over permits the government wanted to rescind to protect the threatened desert tortoise. Bundy refused to give up his permits.

The debate simmered for years. When the government came last spring to confiscate the cattle, hundreds of armed, antigovernment demonstrators showed up. The showdown became a national proxy over the power of the federal government and the rights to public lands. Authorities left after a couple of tense weeks, the matter unresolved.

"My personal feeling is, it was the government trying to bully people around," Bill said.

It is why Bill wants to someday buy enough private land to ranch on his own. He has little hope that it will happen on the land that Bill's ancestors homesteaded. Bill and some siblings still own about 1,200 acres on Smith Mesa, while the rest of the rangeland is leased. When Bill was a boy in nearby Hurricane, Utah, he helped clear some of the land of its trees, making room for crops and livestock. Family members are buried in a dusty cemetery in Virgin, a few miles away.

Now Bill ponders a big move—selling the land and all his permits, and finding a huge parcel somewhere cheaper than next to a national park.

"My dad and I talked about it a lot," Bill said. "We always said if we could better ourselves, we wouldn't be sentimental. Things have changed so much. This ground seems to be worth more as scenic land than agricultural land."

It was late May when the boys took a break from the rodeo circuit. Each morning, they climbed onto horses and descended into the canyon, looking for flashes of movement and listening for grunts and murmurs of cattle hidden in the prickly thicket among the cliffs and boulders. For hours, they nudged small herds north into a box canyon with no obvious exit.

The boys, alone or in pairs, emerged from the abyss at dusk, trailing cows and calves that trekked single file up a steep trail, as sure-footed as mountain goats, diagonally toward the canyon rim. One evening, a riderless horse lost its balance and tipped backward. It tumbled downhill in sliding and bouncing somersaults, 50 feet deeper into the canyon. It crashed into a stand of trees, shaking them furiously. Everything went still, except for a dust cloud that rose gently, like campfire smoke.

Back at camp, Dutch ovens pulled from the fire were filled with chicken, others with peach cobbler. There were bowls of salad and corn. Surrounded by children and grandchildren, eyes closed, Bill offered a prayer. He asked the Heavenly Father to bless the family, the animals, the land, and "this great nation." A one-room cabin that his parents built in the 1940s stood nearby.

He was told about the horse, which, miraculously, seemed uninjured.

"It ain't the first time that's happened," Bill said between bites. Just a year before, Spencer was atop a horse that tumbled; he was thrown against a tree and was knocked out. "When I was a boy, we lost a cow over the edge. And I did it again a few years ago, lower in the wash."

The boys were scattered across the starlit desert, coaxing their day's find into a vast pasture where hundreds of cattle were collected over several days. By the time they got back to camp, the Dutch ovens were cold, and the coals in the fire burned a dusty orange. Most everyone was in bed.

Memorial Day was Branding Day, a family holiday. The campsite percolated to life. The cool morning air hinted at hot. The forecast called for 95 degrees.

Men, horses, and dogs nudged the herd in clumps toward the corral, the guttural bovine dissents carrying half a mile. Cody recruited young boys to gather wood to feed two fires, then buried irons deep in their coals. He drove three stakes deep into hard dirt nearby. Each held one end of a long, black inner tube. At the other end was a metal harness that looked like a medieval contraption.

Boys loitered nearby on horseback, coiled ropes in their hands. Bill gave a nod. Calves were lassoed by their back feet and dragged toward one of the three stations. The heads were wrestled into the harnesses and the calves, moaning and wild-eyed, were stretched long onto their sides.

Like a pit crew to a racecar, a team converged on the animal. Someone with an ear punch tagged an ear with an identifying colored marker. Two with needled syringes injected vaccines. Someone called out "steer!" if the calf was male.

Castration was quick. Bill tugged on the scrotum, sliced away the testicles, and dug his fingers inside the steer. He pulled out bands of tissue and sliced again. Young boys sprayed the area with an antiseptic. Some years, they collect the testicles to fry and eat later. This year, though, the pen of the corral was left littered with dirt-covered testicles. They looked like pearl onions.

Someone else with a knife carved a gash into the tip of each calf's ear, an identifying marker, usually causing a spritz of red blood. A white-hot branding iron was pressed hard against the animal's hip. Flesh and hair sizzled, smoked, and sometimes flamed. A putrid scent filled the dusty, cacophonous air.

"It smells like money," someone said.

Each calf took little more than a minute, never more than two. Released, they clambered to their feet and scampered in search of their mothers.

A few hours later, the corral empty and silent, the nearby pasture serenely dotted with cattle grazing on thinning grass, Bill knelt in the dirt and scribbled numbers on a box with a pencil. His hands were stained in blood.

Bill stared at hash-mark tallies of cows, heifers, steers, and bulls, plus the 108 calves branded, tagged, and inoculated. "How can I be 60 short?" he asked himself.

He remembered that he had already moved 36 cows north to the mountains, to get a jump-start on summer amid the drought here in the desert. But he was still short 24. They were sprinkled somewhere among the tens of thousands of acres of canyons and pastures around him.

The rest of the family would pack up and leave later in the day. The boys would head into the heart of the summer rodeo circuit. Bill would be left alone, again.

"Next few days," he said, "I'm going to be back and forth, looking for these cows."

Hours on the Road, Seconds in the Saddle

The black road unspooled beneath the headlights like a treadmill. Painted dashes on the pavement rolled past in a silent parade of blurs. There was no horizon; through the cracked windshield of the Dodge truck, sky and desert were painted the same charcoal hue. Las Vegas was six hours of darkness away.

"Rusty?" Cody called through the back window to his 18-year-old son in the camper. "You guys check in for your flight in the morning?"

The day started at dawn, back home in Milford, Utah, where most of the Wrights live. Cody, his brother Spencer, his son Rusty, and another saddle-bronc rider from Utah named Brady Nicholes drove three hours to Las Vegas, then another six hours through the Mojave Desert, over the Tehachapi Mountains, and into the vast San Joaquin Central Valley to Clovis, California, near Fresno.

Now and again, they spotted a familiar pickup with an over-size camper riding piggyback. Inside were the twins Jake and Jesse, brothers of Cody and Spencer.

Cody was the oldest, by a long way, in both age and experience. He had a scar under his right eye and a gap between his front teeth. Like all the Wrights, despite being born and raised in Utah, he had a hint of a drawl—not Southern so much as rural. His rodeo results are louder than his personality.

"He's the kinda guy, when he goes to 31 flavors," his mother said, "he comes out with vanilla."

The two loads of Wrights arrived 45 minutes before the rodeo began, as the leaden sky poured a cold rain. In front of a scattered crowd, Spencer scored an 84, good enough for second and a $4,281 check. Jesse's 78 earned him $744. Cody's 77 earned $93. Rusty's 74 was out of the money, and Jake bucked off.

The boys were gone by the time the rodeo ended. The pickups escaped the muddy parking lot and split in different directions, toward different rodeos. Cody's truck arrived in Las Vegas about three in the morning. The four men slept for a few hours in the airport parking lot, flew to Houston, drove three hours to a rodeo in Corpus Christi, Texas (only Spencer, $2,940 for second, earned money), drove back to Houston, slept in the rental car, flew to Las Vegas at dawn to retrieve Cody's truck, drove five hours to Lakeside, California, for another rodeo (Rusty got $1,518 for second, Spencer $231 for seventh), and then drove eight hours back to Milford.

It was 35 hours of driving, two flights, three time zones, and three rodeos in three days. Cody, a two-time world champion, winner of more than $2 million in career prize money, earned $93.

"I've made a pretty good living rodeoing," he said. "But I've done it hard."

Bill Wright, Cody's father, was 12 when he rode a bull and won $40 at a county fair in Hurricane, Utah. He did all the rodeo events as a teenager.

Riding a bull is like being in an eight-second car accident. Bareback riding—broncs without a saddle—is filled with neck-snapping, back-bending whips and jerks.

But saddle-bronc riding was Bill's favorite. More poetry than chaos, it is the classic rodeo event, depicted in the cowboy silhouette on the Wyoming license plate. It is balance and technique, rhythm and guts.

"I just think it's a little more fulfilling," Bill said. "Don't know if it's harder to learn, but I think it's more of a skill. You have to work harder at it."

Cody was in grade school when he found Bill's old chaps and spurs in the rafters. Bill was soon putting 20,000 miles on his truck every year driving Cody and his younger brothers to 40 rodeos a year. They rode bareback and bulls. Slowly, surely, the Wright boys each settled into bronc riding, leaving the other events behind.

"I mighta had something to do with that," Bill said. "Once you got it learned, it's not near as hard on your body. Besides, my dad said cowboys ride horses—saddle horses. It used to bug him, bareback riding. He'd say, 'Cowboys don't ride bareback.'"

Cody was in high school when Bill and Evelyn moved the family from Hurricane about two hours north to Milford (population 1,400), in search of a smaller town and better schools. The backyard has a wide-angle view of the Mineral Mountains and a rodeo arena, where the boys—mostly the grandchildren now—practice on a ragged collection of bucking horses that Bill keeps.

It was fall now. The sunlight was flat, not warm enough to offset the chill of a persistent wind that blew across the valley. Milford, founded as a mining town and train stop, has dozens of wind turbines dotting the horizon. Metal signs at the edge of town along Highways 21 and 257 declare Milford the home of Cody Wright, world champion. Jesse's name was added after 2012.

Cody was outside his house, south of town amid the hayfields, not far from where Jesse and Jake have homes too. There were goats in a nearby pen and a half-dozen horses in the field. His Dodge pickup was gone, replaced by a newer version. Cody sold it with 560,000 miles on it.

"But the engine was pretty new," he said. "It only had 300-some on it."

Cody's five-year-old daughter, Lily, was on a horse, spurring it to a full sprint. One of his sons, 11-year-old Statler, was atop a mechanical bucking machine.

Cody turned on the power, low. The thing hummed and heaved, and Statler bobbed up and down comfortably in the saddle. One hand clenched a thick rein, the other waved over his head.

"The only thing that needs to move is from your knees down, plus your hand as the horse bobs its head," Cody said. "But you have to keep the rein tight."

A bucking saddle is different from a riding saddle. There is no horn between the legs, and the stirrup leathers come out of the front, not straight down the side. The saddle attaches to the bucking horse in two places. A flat strap is tied to rings on a wide, multi-roped cinch under the horse's chest, just behind its front legs. Another strap, snugged with buckles, wraps around the horse's belly in front of its hind legs.

The thin end of a six-foot rein ties to a halter on the horse's head. The other end is a thick, loose weave, almost frayed, to give the rider something meaty and soft to hold with a clenched fist.

The key calculation for every ride is how much rein to have—too tight, and a drop of the horse's head might pull the rider over; too loose, and the rider exits off the back.

The career of a bucking horse can last a decade or more, and it builds a reputation for how it bucks, skips, spins, hesitates, and tosses its head. The Wrights record all their rides in a worn ledger to tell future riders how much rein to give a particular bronc. One fist past the front edge of the saddle is a little. Three fists are a lot.

When the gate swings open, the horse bounds out sideways. For a markout, the first requirement in a ride, a rider's feet must be above the horse's shoulders when the horse lands on its front feet the first time. The other main rule: no touching the horse with the off hand. As in bull riding and bareback riding, the cowboy must hold on for eight seconds to receive a score. No points, no money.

Rider and animal each get half the score, on a scale that adds to 100. The bronc is judged for how high and hard it bucks. The cowboy is judged by how well he stays in control above the chaos. The rein should be tight, the seat in the saddle, the legs churning together in time with the ups and downs of the horse below.

"When the front feet hit the ground, and the back feet are kicked up, your feet should be forward, so it's like you're standing," Cody said.

Clinging for dear life excites the crowd but dulls the judges. Keeping the toes pointed out, the spurs against the animal, is point-adding showmanship. A score above 90 is rare. Anything above 80 is usually in the money.

In 2014, Cody, by the count of the Pro Rodeo Cowboys Association, earned $111,093 in 98 rodeos, good for second among saddle-bronc riders. The goal every year is finishing in the top 15 to qualify for December's National Finals Rodeo, a 10-night, big-stakes event where a rider can double or triple his season's winnings.

The cutoff for the top 15 in 2014 was about $60,000 in season earnings. More than 200 golfers made more than that on the PGA Tour.

Expenses eat the winnings quickly. Cody spent $11,040 on rodeo entry fees and about $20,000 on gas. He put 90,000 miles on the truck and replaced tires twice. When he took his family along in the summer, he took his worn motor home—more repairs, more mouths to feed, fewer people to share the costs of gas or do the driving.

"If you don't make $65,000 or $70,000, I don't think you can break even," Cody said. "Depends on how many guys you travel with."

Cody remained a perennial threat to win a world title despite being the oldest of the top riders by several years. For now, the financial certainty is better in rodeo than in the ranching business that Bill is building.

"I can't figure out for sure if I could stop rodeoing and just do ranching," Cody said. "I don't know if I could quit doing it and not take away from Dad. He enjoys it, and I like seeing him enjoy it."

His father is one reason to keep at it. His sons are another.

"I never gave it a thought that I'd still be riding when Rusty was riding," Cody said.

They spent the year together, Cody showing his son how the vagabond world of rodeo works. Rusty ranked 30th with $30,124 in official earnings and was named 2014 rookie of the year.

And now Ryder is only a year or two away, and he looks to be as good as Rusty. And behind him is Stetson, a junior high champion, then Statler, practicing atop the mechanical bucking horse.

As Cody moves toward ranching, his own sons move into rodeo. The road unspools toward an unseen horizon.

Like wind through a desert canyon, the cheers and groans of 17,000 fans rushed through the hard bends of the arena hallway and into the locker room. They swirled and faded, leaving behind only the faintest of echoes.

Cody Wright sat alone.

Minutes before, the other 14 saddle-bronc riders vying for the world championship grabbed their saddles and reins and shuffled out, wordlessly. They wore cowboy hats on their heads, dirty boots on their feet, worn leather chaps on their hips, and silver belt buckles the size of salad plates on their flat bellies. Their footsteps were deadened by carpet, but their spurs jangled.

One would win the $19,002.40 first prize rewarded for each of 10 go-rounds over 10 nights of the National Finals Rodeo in Las Vegas. A night later, one would be declared world champion.

It might have been Cody. But two nights before, trying to dismount after the eight-second buzzer and before either of the pickup men arrived on horseback to assist, Cody slid off the back of a lurching bronc named Camp Fire. The knob at the top of the humerus bone of his left arm snapped out of the socket of his shoulder.

He winced. Only his wife, mother, and oldest son, sitting in Section 112 of the Thomas & Mack Center, understood that a wince on Cody's face meant something serious. Cody held his left arm snug to his body and walked directly to the medical room. He sat on a table, his shirt off, his dislocated left shoulder hanging with a dull ache. An IV pumped painkiller into his veins. Doctors yanked. Cody reflexively tensed. Another dose, another yank. An ambulance was called.

"He's all right," Jesse said. "But I'll bet he's a sore sucker tomorrow."

Cody, his left arm taped to his body in a sling, his jeans and belt buckle undone at the waist, was helped to a gurney. Propped up, with a drunken look on his face, he was taken up an elevator and out an arena door. Fans stopped and stared and pointed as he was loaded into an ambulance.

About the time that Cody was drugged fully unconscious at the hospital, his humerus yanked back into the socket with an audible pop, Spencer Wright, more than 13 years younger, stood backstage at the South Pointe Casino, tugging on a longneck Coors Light.

The South Pointe is a 25-story hiccup amid the low sprawl on the southern end of Las Vegas, several miles from the neon clash of the Strip. The winner of each night's seven events—bareback riding, calf roping, steer wrestling, saddle-bronc riding, tie-down roping, barrel racing (the only women's event), and bull riding —is called onstage at the South Pointe and, in front of hundreds of fans, awarded an enormous belt buckle and a bottle of whiskey.

Spencer had won for the second time in the first seven go-rounds. The emcees called Spencer out of the darkness, and he shuffled into the spotlight. Bill, Evelyn, Jake, and CoBurn Bradshaw, a promising saddle-bronc rider married to the youngest Wright daughter, trailed in support.

As usual, Spencer's expression hinted at bewilderment. Eyebrows slightly raised, the outside edges of his eyes slightly curled beneath his strawberry-blond shag, he wore the sad countenance of a caged puppy.

"Poor Spencer," one of the two emcees said. "He just hates this."

The night before, when Jake won, Jake bit off the cap of the whiskey bottle, tossed it into the crowd, and took a swig. Spencer's whispered replies to questions could barely be heard. The soundman turned up the volume of the microphone.

"He's 23," an emcee said. "We just told him he's won 68 grand this week, and he does this."

He shrugged, comically. The crowd laughed. Spencer smiled a perfect smile. Three of his teeth were fake and new, replacing three knocked out when Spencer was run over by the pickup man's horse in Walla Walla, Washington, a few months back.

Days before, Cody was the Wright expected to contend for the world title. He was positioned third with three go-rounds left, but his chances were as tattered as his shoulder. He would finish in ninth, with season winnings of $130,393.86.

Jesse, the 2012 champion, had arrived to Las Vegas with $77,495, but he was cursed with ordinary horses and scores. He would finish the season in eighth place, with $134,502.22.

In 2013, Jake held the lead through eight rounds, but a missed mark in Round 9 cost him the world title and left him second. He barely got to Las Vegas in 2014, needing the season's final rodeo to qualify for one of 15 slots in 14th place, with $59,795 in season earnings. Then he won Round 6 and finished in the money—top six—every remaining night to end up fifth in the world, with year-long winnings of $155,420.44.

Spencer arrived in Las Vegas last December as the afterthought. He was the 2012 rookie of the year, 29th in the standings, but his 2013 season was washed out by injuries. He spent 2014 traveling in the father-and-son shadow of Cody and Rusty. His $60,265 in winnings was enough to qualify him for the National Finals Rodeo in 13th place.

But once he reached Las Vegas, as if immune to pressure, he strung together solid, moneymaking rides. He won the fourth go-round with 84 points on Mata Fact. Through six rounds, Spencer, Cody, and Cort Scheer were the only riders to score every night —no buckoffs or blown markouts—putting them in position to claim the rank-altering bonuses that go to those with the highest average score over 10 rides.

"No one's even paying attention to Spencer," Bill said before Round 7. "He's sneaking up there and no one's noticing."

And then on the night that Cody got hurt, Spencer won again, an 85-point ride on Pretty Boy, after being introduced by the public-address announcer as the "redheaded Wright brother."

"Look at the leaderboard!" the announcer shouted minutes later, when Jake scooted between Spencer's 85 and Jesse's 78 in the night's standings. "Spencer Wright! Jake Wright! Jesse Wright! Utah, you're second to none!"

Cody returned to the empty arena at 10 the next morning. His shoulder might require surgery and, either way, would surely knock him off the rodeo circuit for a month or two. Cody wanted to know if it could withstand three rides in three days first.

Cody went to the locker room and sat in his saddle on the floor. He clenched the reins with his left hand and jerked upward as hard as he could, trying to simulate a ride. Something popped deep inside.

The next night, he was alone in the locker room again, watching the ninth go-round unfold on television without him.

"I woulda come out to the chutes," he said, "but I didn't want anybody huggin' me."

He sat in a folding chair, his left hand tucked into a jacket pocket that he used like a sling, and stared at a television bolted high in the corner. Between rides, he stood and checked the night's matchups of rider and horse, taped to the wall. He knew the horses better than any other rider. He knew which ones were likely to drop their heads or spin to the left or hop out of the chute with a stutter step.

The sound of the crowd snaked down the corridor and foreshadowed the result on television, delayed by a few seconds. A rider would disappear from the television screen and reappear, in person, in the locker room. Most were expressionless. A few were angry. Cody chatted them up. He is a bit of a big brother to everyone.

"That horse come in flat, Bradley?" he said to start one conversation.

On television, Spencer clung to Pony Man, 1,200 pounds of jerks and kicks that bucked off Jake in Round 4. It was raining outside, where the livestock was kept, and Spencer's saddle slid back and forth on Pony Man's back—"Look at that saddle!" Cody said to no one—but Spencer managed to keep his feet moving in time and his free hand aimed at the rafters, like a waiter holding an invisible tray. He scored an 81.5 and took the night's lead.

Moments later, he entered the room dragging his saddle and reins.

"He was soaking wet," Spencer said. "I thought I had it on. I pulled it tight. Kept hitting my back cinch."

Jake beat Spencer with an 82 on a horse called Let Er Rip. But he was flipped off at the buzzer and landed on his head with the bounce of a pogo stick. He shuffled away to cheers, headed straight to the medical room.

Slowly, the locker room refilled with cowboys and chatter, the adrenaline evaporating back into ease. Beers were cracked. Cigarettes were lit. One more solid ride, and Spencer would win the unlikeliest of Wright championships.

"I'm going to go check on Jake," Cody said. He found his brother facedown and shirtless on an examination table, a large bag of ice on the back of his neck.

"Been 15 minutes yet?" Jake mumbled.

Cody laughed.

"About two," he said. "You got frostbite yet?"

X-rays the next morning found a compression fracture in Jake's vertebrae, between the shoulder blades. Doctors told him he would miss the next two months, at least, of the rodeo circuit.

"I don't get paid for watchin'," Jake said.

He would ride the final night, a bolt of pain darting through his back with each buck, and earn a $3,064.90 paycheck for a 78 score.

Around Christmas, Jake overturned an all-terrain vehicle while pulling youngsters through the snow. He already had plans for surgery on a bone spur in one hand, but broke the other, and had the operations at the same time.

"If he'd a got throwed out of that and got that thing on top of him, he's looking at paralyzation," Bill said in January, somewhat annoyed. "But he's like a cat in a cage—put him in a room, he paces around. He just can't set."

Cody rode the final night too. He wore a straitjacket of a brace that tied his left arm to his body. It was a strong ride, but he was so worried about his shoulder that he missed his markout and got no score.

"Nothing hurt but my pride," he said outside his camper in the arena parking lot. He smiled. Within a week, he had shoulder surgery, and was told he would miss the first three months of 2015.

In Chute 1, Spencer leaned back in the saddle, clenched the fat rein with his left hand, and held his right over his head. He gritted his teeth and nodded. The gate swung open.

Lunatic From Hell skipped out, and Spencer held the heels of his boots hard against the horse's neck. The animal surged across the dirt in heaving bursts. Spencer pumped his legs in time, twice clenching the horse's wide middle to hang on. The buzzer sounded. The score came: 79.

Only Cort Scheer, a 28-year-old from Nebraska, could beat him for the world title. But Scheer never found rhythm aboard Big Fork, scored a 71, and finished second in the world standings.

Jake ambushed Spencer in the hallway. The other riders, including Scheer, congratulated him in the locker room by spraying him with cheap beer.

The world champions of the seven rodeo events were introduced during a ceremony of stirring music and pyrotechnics. No family had ever had three world champions in rodeo. Bill's hat was tugged low, shading the tears in his eyes. Two rows of Wrights in Section 112 stood and cheered.

"I'm speechless," Spencer stammered softly into the microphone, and the crowd laughed. "I'm glad to have my brothers. I love them. And I love my parents."

He was off to another rodeo the next week, not sure what to do with his 10-day winnings of $145,123. He considered a house in Milford, but instead bought 10 older cows from Bill's herd, and then another 48 head.

By then, Bill was on horseback in the Tushar Mountains near Beaver, Utah, where he kept the herd through the summer and fall. About a month earlier, he found a calf alone, shivering in the cold. He loaded it in his truck and brought it home to Milford. It was placed near the fireplace, and children and grandchildren took turns petting it and nursing it with formula. It died after a couple of days.

Bill figured he still had about a dozen cattle missing in the mountains. He needed to get them down to the relative warmth of Smith Mesa before the snow got too deep, and spent most of a month doing it.

"I'm still short a couple of head," he said in late January. "They could be dead, or they could be pocketed up somewhere. You just don't know."

He was down at Smith Mesa, alone, fixing a tractor tire. He wanted to plant a few hundred acres of grain, most of it rye, on the family land, to supplement the herd's diet across the sandy, rugged terrain.

Some late-summer storms had filled the ponds, but Bill wasn't so sure that the drought was over.

"They said we're not that far from normal—86 percent of normal, I think they figured," he said. "But it seems like we're dry. We don't have any snowpack. There isn't a stitch of snow."

He said he hadn't talked to Jake in a while, and was meaning to call Cody, and had hoped to get a little help from Spencer with the tractor tire. But Spencer was with Jesse, Bill thought, and probably with CoBurn too, traveling to some rodeos.

They had been to Odessa, but Bill wasn't exactly sure where they were now. Maybe Denver.

ALEXANDRA STARR

American Hustle

FROM HARPER'S MAGAZINE

MOST NIGHTS DURING the early summer of 2011, Chukwue-
meka Ene would slip out the back door of a bungalow in Jackson, Mississippi, and make his way to a nearby convenience store.
He didn't mind the Deep South's steamy heat; it reminded him
of the climate in his hometown of Enugu, Nigeria. Ene was 17
years old, but at six feet three inches tall, he might easily have
been mistaken for a man in his twenties. This was particularly true
when his broad features took on a brooding expression—and in
Jackson, he wasn't smiling much. Back at the house, two younger
Nigerian boys were waiting for him to return with the three loaves
of white bread he ritually procured during these expeditions. The
boys slept together on the floor of the living room, with one pillow
shared among them. Formal meals were limited mostly to sporadic
drive-throughs at fast-food restaurants.

That left Ene and his companions—lanky teenagers whom I'll
refer to by their nicknames, Ben and Dixon—perpetually hungry.
They had arrived in the United States just a few weeks earlier, hoping to be groomed for college athletic scholarships, and their days
were spent on intensive basketball drills and pickup games at the
Jackson YMCA.

Ene had discovered the sport at the age of 15, when he stum-
bled across a game in a local park on his way to visit a cousin. He
was mesmerized by the boys hustling back and forth, yelling for
the ball. After the game wound down, he took a few tentative shots
of his own—and the next day, he returned and joined in the play,
shredding a pair of flip-flops in the process. Basketball quickly

became an obsession. When Ene wasn't in class, he was playing with a local high school team or at the park. Sometimes he even slept there, near the court. Passions ran high: once, after an argument over a call, an opponent jumped Ene on his walk home and stabbed him in the hand, just below his thumb. After a trip to the hospital for stitches, Ene returned the following day and worked on dribbling with his nondominant hand.

His prowess at alley-oop passes soon earned him a nickname: Alley. He also won a spot in Nigeria's national basketball program, beginning with its under-16 team. According to Ene, his slavish devotion to the sport infuriated his father, particularly when the tournament schedule required him to miss school. The more Ene learned about the economics of the sport, however, the more convinced he became that it could serve as a social conveyor belt. His family wasn't well off; they lived in a village on the outskirts of Enugu and operated a poultry farm. But a satellite dish beamed ESPN into their living room, and during marathon viewing sessions Ene learned how transformative basketball had been for a figure like Michael Jordan, catapulting a kid from small-town North Carolina to global stardom.

Ene's dreams of life in the United States were further burnished by the ongoing migration of his teammates. In one season alone, half a dozen boys on the roster left for the United States, scooped up by scouts and coaches on the hunt for tall, talented players. Ene's former teammates posted photographs of themselves on Facebook, decked out in Nike high-tops and jerseys, dunking with one hand. Their departures and glamorous reappearances on the Web nagged at him. So when a teammate told Ene about Sam Greer, a man who reportedly brought Africans to the United States to play high school and college basketball, Ene sent an email. He received a terse reply: "Send me a clip so I can see if you can play."

Greer must have liked the video Ene passed along, because he told the teenager he would take him on. He also asked him to identify other, taller, younger kids who were good players. Ene sent clips of Ben (six feet eight inches) and Dixon (six feet nine inches), both of whom he had met at the park. Greer scooped them up as well. He sent all three boys the paperwork they would need for their visas, and coached them in advance of their consular interviews. "By GODS grace," Ene wrote Greer, "everything will go well."

It didn't. Instead, Ene was to learn that in the unsparing economy of youth basketball, he was little more than a commodity. Players destined for a professional career, or even a spot on a powerhouse college team, are lavished with attention and often slipped cash and gifts. The others are generally cast aside. This rejection would be devastating for any young person—but when foreign players are deemed poor bets, as Ene ultimately was, they're often left to fend for themselves, halfway across the world from their families, in a country with no formal safety net for undocumented foreigners.

It was in the 1980s, with the rise of the seven-foot Nigerian center Hakeem Olajuwon, that U.S. basketball mandarins began looking to Africa for talent. Olajuwon starred at the University of Houston before going on to a Hall of Fame career with the Houston Rockets and the Toronto Raptors. Like many Africans, Olajuwon was originally a soccer aficionado; he didn't convert to basketball until his teens, when a fellow student pressed him to play for the school's team. His ball-handling skills eventually brought him renown, and Guy Lewis, then the coach at the University of Houston, offered Olajuwon a scholarship. Yet the Nigerian center wasn't initially treated as a prized recruit: when he first landed in Houston, in 1980, no one even bothered to pick him up at the airport.

The other African star of the era was Dikembe Mutombo, who was born in the Democratic Republic of the Congo, starred at Georgetown during the 1980s, and went on to play for several NBA teams, becoming one of the best defenders in the history of the league.

The second wave of players from the continent didn't replicate these successes. In fact, Africans accounted for two of the most notorious draft busts in recent NBA history: Michael Olowokandi, from Nigeria, and Hasheem Thabeet, from Tanzania, both of whom went on to disappointing (and, in Olowokandi's case, prematurely truncated) careers.

One reason Africans haven't made a bigger mark on U.S. basketball is that soccer is still the dominant sport on the continent. Africans tend to take up hoops as teenagers, by which time their elite American counterparts will have dedicated hundreds or even thousands of hours to the sport. An infinitesimal number of people have the innate gifts, as Olajuwon did, to compensate for a late start. The NBA has attempted to raise the sport's visibility in Africa through its Basketball Without Borders camps, which have been held for the past dozen years in Johannesburg, and more recently in Dakar. A handful of NBA players and scouts also sponsor their own camps. For example, Luc Mbah a Moute, a forward for the Philadelphia 76ers, holds an annual showcase in Cameroon, his home country, where he spotted the latest star African import, a seven-foot center named Joel Embiid, who now plays for the same team.

Still, despite these institutionalized paths to the United States, most Africans are recruited through informal channels. Teenagers do a lot of importuning: American coaches often find their email inboxes clogged with missives from African players seeking opportunities abroad. But enterprising coaches have also developed their own recruiting networks. Eric Jaklitsch, for instance, is an assistant coach at Our Savior New American, a private Lutheran school in Centereach, Long Island. He has assembled one of the country's finest high school basketball teams in part by plucking players from Africa—where he has yet to set foot. Instead, he relies on scouts like Tidiane Dramé, the self-anointed "King of Mali," who helped to identify Cheick Diallo, a towering Malian power forward. Diallo was one of six African players on the school's 2014–15 roster—a number that has prodded some observers to dub the team "Our Savior Few Americans."

Sam Greer appears to have assembled his own web of contacts in Africa. In a phone conversation, he told me that he first visited the continent decades ago, as part of a Christian ministry raising awareness about AIDS. According to a longtime coach in Memphis, Greer was then a local "runner"—a street scout who identified players in and around the city. It seems that Greer upgraded from regional scouting to international recruitment by amassing an insider's knowledge of African basketball. Indeed, Ene had marveled that the American recruiter was as conversant as any local fan with the Nigerian team's junior roster.

Greer says that he has brought approximately 250 foreign players to the United States. He also claims that recruiting isn't his day job: he told me that he works for the federal government, though he gave no indication of his duties or whether they had helped him to target African players. (Officials at the U.S. Citizenship and Immigration Services and the Department of Homeland Security say he isn't on their payrolls.)

In any case, Greer's emails to Ene convey an insider's savvy about both the technical process of obtaining a visa and the image the boys would need to project to U.S. Embassy staff. He explained to Ene that the key bit of documentation the boys would need for their applications was a letter from a school superintendent in Corinth, Mississippi, confirming that they would be attending high school and would stay with a host family who was covering their fees. These letters arrived in Nigeria in March 2011. They made the boys eligible for I-20s: certificates they could use to apply in turn for F-1 visas, which would allow them to live and study in the United States until they graduated from high school.

There are no official records of how many Africans come to the United States to play sports, since recruits aren't required to identify themselves as such. (Greer instructed his charges not to breathe a word about basketball when they visited the U.S. Embassy in Abuja.) But athletes are much more likely to apply for the F-1 than for the J-1, a cultural-exchange visa with stricter requirements. In 2013, 4,132 F-1 visas were granted to Nigerians, compared with 640 J-1s.

Ene was elated when he received word that his F-1 application had been successful. "Life is going to start," he remembers thinking. "I'm going to be good." Ene's father, however, was appalled by his son's plan to leave Nigeria, especially because it was facilitated by a sport he reviled. When it became clear that Ene was leaving, his father renounced his parental rights and refused to pay a penny for the airline ticket, forcing his son to solicit donations from friends and relatives.

Despite this showdown, Ene didn't dwell on the fact that his sole contact in the United States was a complete stranger. "It was America," he later recalled. "What could go wrong?" He might have seen warning signals in Greer's emails, which were laced with admonishments that can be read either as concern for the boys' safety or as preemptive assertions of control. "Remember I will be the person to handle everything for you, and no one will control you I promise that," he wrote in one email, "so when in America you must tell me everything that goes [on]."

Greer's insistence on being the boys' primary custodian, even as he was sending them to live and train with other people, spoke to his knowledge of elite youth basketball. The payoff for identifying talent and securing a young player's loyalty can be enormous, especially if that player blossoms into an NBA star. Sometimes the payoff is direct: successful pros may share part of their windfall with the people who guided them. Other times it is indirect, but no less lucrative: coaches and agents have been known to provide gifts, cash, and jobs to recruiters who deliver top players to their rosters or client lists.

Reaping such rewards, however, depends on a tight personal connection with the player. Serving as a father figure, or even just a buddy with a bulging wallet, may be enough. But with foreign players, marooned in a strange land with little in the way of cash or connections, this sense of indebtedness can be established in more formal ways. Which may be why Greer wrote Ene before he arrived: "I want to make sure for no reason any one get guardianship but me because I really don't trust to [*sic*] many people in America." Ene, too, would soon come to share that sense of wariness about other people's motives.

The YMCA in Jackson has a spartan quality. The windows don't admit much light, and the floor could use a coat of polish. What impressed me, during my visit one April afternoon, was the players. For a quarter of an hour, I watched members of Omhar Carter's MBA Hoops team run a layup drill, and no one missed a single basket. The standout was a fifth grader named Mason Manning, whose hands moved so swiftly they resembled a blur of butterfly wings. (I later found a YouTube clip in which he calmly dribbles two balls between his legs; it had more than 40,000 views.)

MBA Hoops is considered by many the best Amateur Athletic Union team in Mississippi. The AAU, founded in 1888, is nonprofit, mostly volunteer, and—well, amateur. Yet the word is something of a misnomer, because the organization has a noticeable patina of professionalism. Teams operate year-round, flying across the country to play in tournaments and showcasing children as young as six. The exposure the AAU circuit provides makes participation de rigueur for any player with hopes of landing a college scholarship or embarking on a professional career. Virtually every U.S.-born NBA star—including the past two MVPs, Kevin Durant and LeBron James—played for AAU teams. And companies like

Adidas, Nike, and Under Armour are eager to donate shoes, uniforms, tournament entry fees, and cash for expenses.

This puts extra pressure on AAU coaches to constantly enlist new talent. And that pressure helps explain why Omhar Carter was receptive to a pitch he received in early 2011 from Greer, whom he hadn't previously encountered, to house and coach three Nigerian players, two of whom were over six and a half feet tall. According to Carter, Greer described himself as the middleman for any African player coming to the Deep South. "Now that I look back on it," Carter told me, "with him being in Memphis, I should've looked into it a bit more."

That June, Carter and Greer picked up the boys when they arrived at Memphis International Airport. Carter drove the boys directly to Mississippi and left them at a female friend's house in Jackson. Once they had dropped their bags, their host said that they would be sleeping on the floor of the living room. Ben and Dixon asked Ene in their native Ibo whether they should protest, but Ene shook his head. Carter, he figured, must still be setting up a separate bedroom in his own home. Give it time, he counseled.

The next morning, according to Ene, Carter picked up the boys and drove them to the gym without providing breakfast. Apparently there had been some confusion about who would feed them. Over the next few days, Carter treated the boys to an occasional fast-food meal, but not surprisingly, given their long hours at the gym, they were always hungry. And so Ene began his nocturnal shopping expeditions, buying bread and occasionally cookies and Gatorade with funds left over from the collection he'd taken up to pay for his plane ticket. While this was going on, the boys were settling into a routine of high-tempo drills in the morning and games against college athletes at night. They practiced for other coaches too, in sessions that felt like unacknowledged tryouts.

To Ene, the situation began to resemble a form of servitude. It wasn't just the dearth of food or proper beds, but the lack of autonomy. The boys had no access to a computer, so they couldn't communicate with their parents or with Greer. And Ene was increasingly desperate to make contact, because Carter had taken possession of their passports. (Carter told me that he held the documents to keep them from being stolen, but his charges saw it as a way of exerting control.)

When Carter brushed away Ene's complaints about the passports, Ene bought a SIM card for his Nigerian phone at the convenience store. He called Sam Greer. "Get us out," he said, "or I'll go to the police." The scout counseled against involving outside authorities and said that he would settle things with Carter. Soon enough, Carter returned the passports and drove the boys to Corinth High School—which they were supposed to be attending in the first place. There they toured the facilities and played for the coach but were never formally enrolled.

Before the summer was over, Greer said he would remove the boys from Carter's care. Chris Threatt, the varsity head coach at McClellan Magnet High School in Little Rock, Arkansas, would host them instead. Greer bought the boys train tickets from Jackson to Memphis. When they arrived, he treated them to burgers and apologized for what he later described to me as "the buzz saw" they had encountered in Mississippi.

While his team finished practicing, Omhar Carter and I sat down at a wooden table in the lobby of the Jackson Y. Grunts emanated from the weight room nearby. Although Carter looked like he, too, had put in his time there, he didn't come across as intimidating. Rather, he was gracious and good-humored. During drills with the team, he had mixed flashes of toughness with playfulness, teasing one of his players when the boy took off his shirt. "Really, Marie?" he asked. "Is that necessary?" Marie, it turned out, was from Nigeria, as was another player, whom Carter identified as Emmanuel. The two boys had been easy to spot during practice; they towered over the others.

Emmanuel and Marie were the first African players Carter had taken on since Ene, Ben, and Dixon had left. He had sworn off coaching foreign players for a while after the mess with Greer's recruits, and signed up Emmanuel and Marie only after meeting them through an African student at a local college. The two were still enrolled at a high school in Florida but were in Jackson to train during spring break.

Carter disputed Ene's claim that the three boys weren't cared for during their time in Mississippi. He said that he had provided breakfasts for his players in hotel-buffet quantities, with pancakes, bacon, and sausage, and that the boys had stayed in his house for a time, where they had their own room and their own beds. In his account, the homestay at his friend's house was comfortable too: Carter described a living space with a "huge bed, a big, huge couch," bookshelves, and a television.

He attributed Ene's disgruntlement to the role the boy had been forced to assume. It was Greer, Carter told me, who had presented Ene as a kind of uncle—the caretaker of the two younger, taller, more desirable recruits. "No one wanted him," Carter said. "It was a package deal." He also felt that the boys had made little effort to integrate themselves into his team. "They would always go off into a circle and they would talk in their language," he recalled. Their insular behavior frustrated him, since he was providing them with clothing, coaching, housing, food, and transportation. But their ultimate allegiance seemed to be to Greer. "At the end of the day," he told me, "whatever Sam said, went."

Carter and Greer haven't spoken since. After one of Carter's current Nigerian players distinguished himself at a local tournament, however, Greer apparently contacted the boy's father. Carter pulled out his cell phone and read me some of Greer's messages, which had been forwarded to him by the family: "I got a call about the two boys who were in Florida. But they are hiding out in Mississippi. Those boys can go to jail if they get caught." Greer meaningfully noted that he had a friend who worked at the Student and Exchange Visitor Information System, the government program that supervises I-20s. "It's no problem with me," he continued. "But there seems to be some funny business." The players had been freaked out by the implication. "If you are from Africa and you hear that Homeland Security is going to pick you up," said Carter, "that's scary."

Greer's veiled warning to the Nigerian boy's father was likely an effort to poach the players. According to Carter, Greer recoups the money he spends bringing kids over to the United States by sending them to college teams that pay him a fee. "It's like an auction," Carter told me. "Each kid is an item to sell."

Such poaching isn't unusual, especially at the AAU level, because landing a superstar player can be extraordinarily lucrative. (After recruiting and grooming the future NBA star Tyson Chandler, an AAU coach named Pat Barrett was rewarded with a reported $200,000 when his protégé signed with the Chicago Bulls.) Nor is it uncommon for a player to compensate members of the network that embraced him as a teenager. In 1997, as an 18-year-old rookie with the Toronto Raptors, Tracy McGrady signed a $12 million endorsement deal with Adidas—which stipulated payments of $900,000 apiece to his high school coach and the scout who had discovered him.

Generally, however, the payoff for AAU coaches comes from agents, colleges, or pro scouts seeking to curry favor with a recruit. Sometimes these bribes are cash transactions; other times, they take the form of career advancement. Though the NCAA made efforts to curb the practice in 2010, colleges have long recognized that they can reel in top freshman prospects by hiring their AAU coaches. In 2006, for example, Kansas State lured a coach named Dalonte Hill away from the University of North Carolina at Charlotte, in what appeared to be a blatant attempt to land Michael Beasley, whom Hill had coached during his AAU days. The strategy worked. Beasley ditched an offer from UNC Charlotte and signed with Kansas State. By 2008, the university was paying Hill a reported $420,000 per year.

"America is not the place I thought it was."

Three years after receiving that text message from Ene, Chris Threatt still remembered it word for word. Greer had put Ene in touch with the McClellan High coach, presumably to bolster the case for taking in the three Nigerians. Threatt had two teenage daughters and years of experience at McClellan, whose varsity team won the Arkansas state championship in 2010. "I get satisfaction from helping," Threatt told me. If the Nigerian teenagers were in distress—and showed the promise Greer had touted—taking them in seemed like the natural thing to do.

For two months, the three boys lived with Threatt in Little Rock. According to Ene, it was a decided upgrade from Mississippi. They were fed, had their own beds, and attended church with the coach's family on Sundays. A collection taken up from the congregation paid for clothes and school supplies.

The boys were soon joined by a fourth Nigerian player and Greer recruit, whom I'll call Kelvin. To relieve the crowding, they were divided among three households: Kelvin was placed in the home of an acquaintance of Threatt's, while Ene was sent to live with one of Threatt's assistant basketball coaches. Kelvin, Ben, and Dixon landed spots on Team Penny, one of the best AAU programs in the South. Threatt took an assistant-coaching position with the team and began driving the boys to and from Memphis on weekends for practice and tournaments.

Soon, though, the boys received stunning news: because they had neither been registered at Corinth High School nor had their I-20 forms transferred to their new school, they were in the United States illegally. The three host families proposed to set things right by adopting their guests. Threatt told me the offer sprang principally from altruism, and noted that adoption would have shielded the boys from deportation and allowed them to receive health insurance. This was particularly important for the three Team Penny players, who would be at greater risk of injury.

There were, however, legal barriers to the adoptions. And for Ene in particular, returning to Nigeria was no longer a possibility, given the fallout with his father. He hoped to attend college, and had maintained a 3.86 GPA at McClellan, but as a foreign student, he found it difficult to apply for financial aid. His visa status barred him from playing on the high school basketball team, which meant that he had no way to attract attention from college coaches. Greer arranged a tryout for Ene, at LeMoyne-Owen College, in Memphis, but nothing came of it. Ene remembers the days after graduation as agonizing. "I was just sitting around, doing nothing," he said. When an aunt offered to let him live with her in New York City, he quickly boarded a Greyhound bus from Little Rock to Queens.

Back in Arkansas, the other boys' relationships with their host families deteriorated, then became openly hostile. An anonymous tip to the National Human Trafficking Resource Center led agents from the Department of Homeland Security to visit the home where Kelvin was staying, on January 1, 2013. The agents determined that he had not in fact been trafficked, but they confirmed that he wanted to leave. The following day, they interviewed Ben and Dixon, who also said they wanted out. All three were transported to a juvenile-immigration shelter in Chicago, and are now in foster care in Michigan.

Threatt was shaken by this denouement. "The police came to my *house*," he said. He added that one of the younger boys had consistently defied his host parents' rules. Notes made by the DHS agents buttress his argument, describing the coach and another host parent as disciplinarians but finding no evidence of abuse.

At least one DHS agent speculated that the homestays blew up because the players weren't racking up impressive stats on the court. It's not an easy proposition to land a spot on Team Penny's roster, but the boys were regarded as aspirational prospects at best, unlikely to attract attention from major college programs, let alone the NBA. "They weren't getting the result they wanted," Ene said. "Maybe that's why things changed a little at the end."

People who bring athletes over from Africa tend to cast themselves as Father Flanagans. Greer, for example, told me he's in it "to help kids." But given the rewards of landing a tall, talented player, there is obviously potential for exploitation. George Dohrmann, the author of *Play Their Hearts Out* (2010), argues that the NBA should acknowledge that the AAU is a cesspool and impose more rigorous supervision. European soccer, in which professional teams run their own academies to identify and train the rising generation of talent, could serve as a model. If this system were transferred to the United States, a young star in New York would play for the Knicks' academy team, under the oversight of high school athletics regulations, and be given the chance to work his way up to the team's roster. If he turned out not to be NBA caliber, he could still pursue college or play abroad.

Ohio has taken the step of barring foreign students on F-1 visas from playing high school sports. "We believe the F-1 is ripe for abuse," Deborah Moore, an associate commissioner for eligibility at the Ohio High School Athletic Association, told me. The prohibition followed in part from a 2001 incident in which a scout from the Central African Republic recruited at least nine athletes to play soccer and basketball for Dayton Christian High School, in Miamisburg, then filled out the prospective students' F-1 visa applications with the names and addresses of host families who were unaware that they were being listed. Foreign students who move to Ohio without their parents and want to play sports must now have a J-1 visa unless they've been adopted by an American citizen.

Nevertheless, Moore said, people keep trying to skirt the regulation. In fall 2013, the athletic director at Talawanda High School, in Oxford, Ohio, received a visit from a towering Nigerian student and his purported guardian, who wanted to enroll the teenager and have him play basketball there. When the guardian was informed that the boy was ineligible, he soon found a willing school in a different state.

Farther south, Sam Greer's African scouting has continued unabated, and he reportedly landed a big score from Ene's hometown of Enugu: Moses Kingsley, a six-foot-ten-inch forward who entered the University of Arkansas in 2013 as a top-fifty recruit. Kingsley had the smooth ride of a truly elite player. He attended Huntington Prep, a basketball powerhouse in West Virginia, and apparently forged a close relationship with his host family in Proctorville, Ohio. "Miss my Host Family!" he tweeted in July 2013. "Miss the good laughs."

Things got even worse for Ene a few months later, when his aunt's landlord pointed out that the young man wasn't listed on the lease, and he was forced to move out. Now he had nowhere to go. Through a search on the Web, he found a Harlem nonprofit called African Services Committee (ASC) and showed up there hauling two bags. "It was like he was going to board a flight," said Jessica Greenberg, an attorney with the organization, who immediately suspected that Ene was homeless. She phoned around but was unable to find him a bed — the 19-year-old would have to spend the night at a men's shelter.

He returned to the ASC office the next morning with a shell-shocked look on his face. The staff had warned Ene to keep his belongings close at hand, so he had clung to his baggage all night long. Another attorney, Kate Webster, called Covenant House, a center for homeless youth, and insisted that they provide a bed for him. "We are talking about a trafficking victim," she said.

Meanwhile, Ben and Dixon were being assisted by the Polaris Project, an anti-trafficking nonprofit. Ene called the organization so frequently to check up on his former companions that the receptionist came to recognize the sound of his voice. He displayed similar initiative in fixing his visa status. After one of his initial consultations at ASC, Webster left him at a computer while she went to make some photocopies. "I figured he would download a video game," she said. Instead, when she returned a few minutes later, she found him researching the U visa, which is reserved for immigrants who have been the victims of a crime. "Maybe," he asked her, "I would be eligible for this?"

In the end, Webster counseled Ene to put in a petition for Special Immigrant Juvenile Status. Originally created in 1990 for undocumented children in foster care, it was later expanded to include kids who could prove they had been the victims of abuse, abandonment, or neglect at the hand of a parent or guardian. In 2013, one of the most traumatic experiences of Ene's life—his father's official renunciation of his parental rights—resulted in his receiving a green card.

The moment you see Ene's wingspan, it becomes clear why Sam Greer wanted to bring him to the United States. Its breadth was on ample display one afternoon in late March of last year, when he was asked to keep early arrivals out of the main foyer of Covenant House, where recruiters like Modell's Sporting Goods and the U.S. Army had set up booths as part of a job fair. He executed the assignment zealously, arms wide. "It's not time yet," he told a group of teenagers jostling to get by. "Just trying to get hired, man," a boy said. Ene was implacable: "That's why we are *all* here."

While Covenant House doesn't generally hire interns for its Career Development department, an exception was made for Ene. He spent his mornings helping residents prepare résumés and conduct job searches, then went to work as a security guard at a Queens library in the evenings.

In June, he arranged for another Nigerian basketball player whom he knew from pickup games in Enugu to live at Covenant House. Through the boy's Facebook posts, Ene learned that he had been brought over by a scout to compete in an AAU tournament in Georgia. On arrival, the player had discovered he would not be placed with a host family. Instead, he spent months sleeping in a poorly ventilated gym.

That yet another Nigerian had been coaxed to the United States with false assurances deeply riled Ene. "It's like modern slavery," he said. "It's not slavery where they put a chain on your hand or your neck. But it's people trying to use you." He didn't attribute this behavior to racism per se—after all, everyone who had been involved in his transplantation to the American South, including Greer, Carter, and Threatt, was black. Nor did he hold Greer or Threatt responsible for his ill treatment. "You can't put them all in the same shoe," he insisted, while rejecting the implicit argument that any experience in the United States was a step up from what awaited Nigerians back home. "What kind of good life are they giving us, telling us to sleep on the floor?" he asked me. "I didn't take it like a good life."

By late summer, Ene still hadn't had the chance to talk at length with the new Nigerian at Covenant House. He was working 12-hour days and saving money for college. He no longer harbored dreams of a basketball scholarship. "I still like the game," he said. "But it's a dirty business. I don't want to get involved in it again."

STEVE RUSHIN

Ruck and Roll

FROM SPORTS ILLUSTRATED

AT FIRST GLANCE the Rugby World Cup is the greatest celebration of national stereotypes since It's a Small World opened at Disneyland. Italian fans came dressed as pizza slices, Welshmen wore sheep's clothing, Aussies arrived in striped prison jumpsuits, and every French fan was reduced to a beret and a baguette. Step up to a stainless-steel urinal trough at a stadium in England or Wales over the last six weeks, and you saw English knights dropping chain-mail trousers, Tonga supporters parting grass skirts, and kilted Scotsmen fartin' through tartan.

When Canada played Italy during the group stages of the tournament, a man in a bear costume—presumably standing in for the whole of Canada—ran onto the pitch at Elland Road stadium in Leeds and was promptly tackled by security guards. His head rolled but was quickly retrieved, and the man was allowed, for dignity's sake, to wear the bear's head when frog-marched off to detention, a faraway look in his unblinkable eyes.

Even the players play dress-up. Two years ago this Halloween week, a member of the Scottish national team, Ryan Wilson, walked into a fast-food restaurant in Glasgow at 2:00 a.m. dressed as Batman. When he attacked a man inside Barbeque Kings, a second player—Ally Mclay, dressed as Tweedledee—confronted Wilson with the now famous phrase, "Leave it, Batman." Wilson/Batman then assaulted Mclay/Tweedledee in front of various witnesses, among them a minion from *Despicable Me* and a giant red crayon.

Of all the stereotypes offered at the 2015 Rugby World Cup,

the most persistent are attached to the players themselves, most of whom are presumed by much of the world to be hard-drinking hard men playing through pain for national pride. You expected the Australians to play AC/DC's "Back in Black" at an ear-shattering volume during practice at London's Twickenham Stadium, while the team bus, festooned with wallabies, waited outside—and that's precisely what you got.

But if this Saturday's World Cup final between Australia and New Zealand at Twickenham reveals anything, it will be national character more than these national caricatures. New Zealand, the reigning World Cup champion, is the odds-on favorite to win the Webb Ellis Cup, and if the All Blacks are the only thing the world knows of New Zealand, well, they still make a fine national hood ornament. "The All Blacks," as Ireland international Mike Gibson once said, "are the national virility symbol."

The Haka, the All Blacks' pregame Maori war dance, remains a fearsome sight, though less so when performed by the happy drunks packed elbow-to-elbow inside The Eel Pie pub, a short walk from Twickenham Stadium, which is on Rugby Road, not far from the world's most famous rugby pub, The Cabbage Patch, itself a stone's throw from The William Webb Ellis, yet another rugby pub, named for the so-called inventor of rugby, whose rules were first codified just 90 miles north of here at Rugby School, in Rugby, England, a phrase—Rugby, England—that's been a redundancy throughout October.

Twickenham is ground zero of world rugby, its high street closed to traffic on match days, its front gardens given over to grilled meats, Cub Scouts painting New Zealand and Australian flags on faces, a lone bagpiper in a Slipknot shirt knocking out a stirring rendition of the theme from *Star Wars,* tips thrown into his upturned tam-o'-shanter.

And so it will go on Saturday, as fans walk that green mile to the stadium with equal parts joy and foreboding. To see the All Blacks doing the Haka inside Twickenham, and the flames shooting up from the sidelines like hellfire, and 82,000 fans counting down to kickoff—ten, nine, eight, as if reading the final seconds on the doomsday clock—is to be seized by the sudden sense of impending apocalypse that precedes every World Cup rugby match.

English novelist Julian Barnes has written of *le reveil mortel,* the "wake-up call to mortality," those moments when you are abruptly reminded that you are destined to die. "My wake-up call frequently shrills at the start of a sports event on television," Barnes wrote, "especially, for some reason, during the Five (now Six) Nations rugby tournament."

Mercifully the bottled violence about to be unstoppered before these games is undercut by the crowd, whose costumes build a sense of conviviality among rival supporters, many of whom wear split scarves—featuring both teams—and split outfits: A bagpiper in a corked Australian outback hat, for instance, or a Wales jersey paired with a Japanese hachimaki bandana.

The entire rugby-playing world became fans of Japan when that latecomer to the sport stunned South Africa 34–32 in a group stage match on September 19. It was the biggest upset in rugby history. So historic was this Miracle on Rice that the Brave Blossoms' victory over Samoa two games later was witnessed by 25 million people in Japan, hosts of the next World Cup, in 2019. That's 20 percent of the nation and the largest domestic audience ever to watch a rugby match on TV.

Between those wins against South Africa and Samoa, Japan lost to Scotland without winger Akihito Yamada. That's because Japan had followed its victory over the Springboks with a recovery swim in the sea off Brighton, where Yamada was stung on the foot by the poisonous spine of a weever fish. "It hurt like crazy," Yamada said. "I'm never going in the ocean again."

It was the first and last admission of physical pain during the entire tournament, which began on September 18 with a field of 20 countries. As a chalked-up sandwich board outside one pub read, FOOTBALL IS 90 MINUTES OF PRETENDING YOU'RE HURT, RUGBY IS 80 MINUTES OF PRETENDING YOU'RE NOT.

That sign makes a fair point, as every single injury at the Rugby World Cup was described as a "knock" or a "niggle" or a nuisance. It seemed as if most of the Wales roster was felled by serious injury during the World Cup, but the team advanced to the quarterfinals anyway. The players began to sound like Monty Python's Black Knight, protesting that every limb amputation was but a flesh wound.

After a group stage win over Fiji on October 1, Wales forwards coach Robin McBryde said of two key players, "Dan Lydiate and Bradley Davies are a bit battered, but they are fine." McBryde, a former international hooker, was also the winner of Wales's Strongest Man Competition in 1992, so his pain tolerance may be higher than most, especially when you consider that the "fine" Lydiate needed a plate inserted into his left eye socket. "So he's fine now," said Wales head coach Warren Gatland, inevitably.

All of this is to say that the Rugby World Cup is not the more famous FIFA World Cup, and it is quite keen to make that distinction clear. No sport has inspired as many aphorisms as rugby, the best known of which goes, "Soccer is a gentleman's sport played by hooligans; rugby is a hooligan's sport played by gentlemen." But there's also this one, spotted on a T-shirt at Twickenham: IF I WANT TO SPEND 90 MINUTES WATCHING MEN STRUGGLE TO SCORE, I'LL GO TO THE PUB.

Spoiler alert: That guy is going to the pub anyway. Indeed, he was standing in line at one of the stadium's many bars—The Sin Bin, maybe, or possibly The Third Half—where fans are given convenient cup holsters that allow them to carry away as many as six beers in each hand.

As if to underscore that this sport isn't that other sport, rugby fans are allowed to drink beer in their seats, a privilege not afforded to England's soccer supporters. As with most hard-earned rights—free speech and freedom of assembly come to mind—the right to drink in one's seat is exercised robustly and conspicuously at Twickers. At halftime of the Scotland-Australia quarterfinal, with the Bravehearts holding an improbable one-point lead that wouldn't last, the in-house emcee interviewed a kilted man in the front row, an exchange that was broadcast on the Jumbotron to 77,110 spectators. "Can you keep it up in the second half?" the interviewer wanted to know.

"Are we talkin' about the rugby?" replied the man, as the emcee hastily pulled the microphone away.

Built in 1909 on the site of a former cabbage patch, Twickenham Stadium reached a pinnacle of perfection in 1974, when an Australian accountant named Michael O'Brien streaked onto the pitch at halftime of an England-France match. After disporting in the altogether for a bit, he was finally caught by three London policemen, one of whom—history records him as constable Bruce Perry—placed his bobby helmet over O'Brien's meat and two veg. An American photographer named Ian Bradshaw captured the moment for posterity. Even in captivity, O'Brien looked so proud

—so smugly self-satisfied—that the helmet most likely would have remained in place even had Perry stopped holding it.

This year, in addition to the headless bear in Leeds, a South Africa supporter ran onto the pitch at Villa Park in Birmingham and tried to join a ruck in jeans and a Springboks shirt, but he was summarily taken down by Samoa tackler Vavao Afemai. "I don't know if he was drunk or just an idiot," said halfback Kahn Fotuali'i, unaware that these things are seldom an either-or proposition, and that pitch invaders are usually both at the same time.

The signs on the platform at the Twickenham train station welcomed the world with these words: TWICKENHAM — HOME OF ENGLAND RUGBY. "Not anymore," said a 10-year-old boy in a Scotland jersey, disembarking there with his dad and grandfather before the Scotland-Australia quarterfinal on October 18. The boy posed for a photograph beneath the sign while making a loser's "L" on his forehead.

The host nation had long since crapped out of the Rugby World Cup in the group stages, just as England has done at the last cricket and soccer World Cups too, and is likely to do at the next Quidditch World Cup. Eclipsed in the sports they invented and exported, England fans either threw themselves behind another rugby team or longed for happier times.

En route to the quarterfinals at the last World Cup, in New Zealand in 2011, some England players enjoyed a night out in Queenstown, and photos posted to social media showed them posing with the human projectiles of a bar's "dwarf-tossing" spectacle. The bar manager assured the tabloids that England players behaved impeccably that night, defending the team with this memorable quote: "They were great lads, not throwing the midgets."

In fairness to England, the U.S. also went out in the group stages this year, losing all four of its matches, including a 64–0 squeaker to South Africa. But America is a developing rugby nation, likely to improve. "The U.S. will be much better in 20 years' time," said an Englishman in his twenties on a postgame train from Twickenham, urging an American to look on the bright side. "And now you have a sport that isn't rubbish to watch." After a moment of reflection he said, "It's not the rugby that makes your country a laughingstock. It's the guns."

As for England, they will always have the memory of 2003, when Jonny Wilkinson's late kick in Sydney won them the World Cup, making Wilko the beau ideal of the English sportsman or—in the words of one English friend—"what David Beckham was supposed to have been."

In rugby you're never far from a withering reference to soccer. When Scotland fullback Stuart Hogg appeared to dive in the hope of being awarded a penalty in an early-round match against South Africa at St. James' Park—usually the home of Newcastle United of the Barclays Premier League—Welsh referee Nigel Owens dressed him down in public. "If you want to dive like that again," Owens said, in comments picked up by a microphone, "come back here in two weeks and play."

The rugby referee is God, or at the very least, Dad. In the 38th minute of the Scotland-Australia quarterfinal, during a rare break in play, one Scotland player asked South African referee Craig Joubert for permission to tie his own boot. "Do it quickly, yeah," Joubert sighed.

The referee is seldom criticized, even when he gets things terribly wrong, as Joubert would do at the end of that match. Under a gunmetal sky, in a curtain of rain, Scotland lost on a last-second penalty kick that Joubert mistakenly awarded. "He's refereeing in front of millions of people, so I understand," Scotland back-row David Denton said afterward. "But it's affecting us for the rest of our lives, and affecting a nation."

While rugby's code forbids acknowledgment of physical pain —"We're unbreakable," said Bravehearts captain Greig Laidlaw— the same is not true of emotional turmoil. Denton, Scotland's 6'5" loose forward, met his family immediately after the loss to Australia, and the tears were copious. "We could have filled a bathtub," he said, a shiner starting to form beneath his left eye.

Scotland—and every other team in the tournament—aspires to express its national values through rugby. "There's so much humility to them," coach Vern Cotter said of his team. "There's no egos in the squad," said Denton. Given one last chance to blame the referee for his team's loss, he said only, "In this case, fortune didn't favor the brave."

These verities—of courage, respect, humility, and perseverance —were impossible to ignore, even when overshadowed by, say, that man in the star-spangled bikini, cheering on the Eagles in Leeds.

When Wales, depleted by the countless injuries they refused to acknowledge, also succumbed late to favored South Africa in another quarterfinal at Twickenham, Gareth Thomas, once Wales's captain and now a television analyst, said of the squad, "What they've done in this World Cup has highlighted how three million people live their lives."

With that in mind, many English fans suddenly became Scottish or Welsh, pairing England shirts with tartan tams or dragon hats. And it wasn't only the English. Rory Steinle was wearing a Wales jersey while standing outside the White Swan pub, overlooking the River Thames, on a gorgeous match-day Saturday in Twickenham. He's Australian, he said, from Sydney, but his father is Welsh and his mother is Scottish. Steinle also brought "a new Australia jersey that fits me better," he said, plucking at his Wales shirt, which was from the 2011 World Cup. "I'm expanding."

A lower-division rugby player in Sydney, Steinle has broken both hands, both shoulders, a leg, and several ribs playing rugby. Forty-eight hours earlier his girlfriend, Chelsea Hancock, fell near the pinnacle of a mountain in Scotland and broke her leg. "She's back in the hotel room with her leg in the air," said Steinle, who could empathize. "The first year we dated, I was in hospital 10 times."

He said all of this in a matter-of-fact manner. If the 31-year-old could still shrug his shoulders, no doubt he would have. "It's rugby," he said, a phrase that came up frequently, as when he said by way of parting, "When you see some 200-pound piece rush up to the referee to say, 'I'm sorry about that penalty, sir, I didn't mean it'—that's rugby."

And then he was on his way, with thousands of other fans, making the 15-minute walk to Twickenham Stadium, past The William Webb Ellis and the world-famous Cabbage Patch, in front of which Springbok fans were playing street rugby, replete with tackles. They passed food trucks and front gardens, where vendors sold a dizzying variety of rugby-nation foods—Cornish pasties, bangers and mash, Braai, biltong, boerewors, and burgers.

Inside Twickers, players pulled at one another by the back of their shorts, revealing miles of what Americans call plumber's crack and Brits call builder's bum. Beyond these superficial differences of a common language, the world was otherwise in harmony. The uprights looked like tuning forks, and everyone thrummed at the same frequency. "The World in Union" was the slogan of this World Cup, a play on words referring not just to international brotherhood but to the game of rugby union, as distinct from rugby league. The differences are hardly worth going into, except to quote Tom David, the former Wales international, who once said, "The main difference between playing league and union is now I get my hangovers on Monday instead of Sunday."

When Scotland was eliminated from the World Cup, its magnificently bearded flanker, Josh Strauss, pronounced himself "gutted" but said he would nevertheless "go out with the boys and have a little fun—I think everyone deserves it."

Like Strauss, aka The Beard That's Feared, few were eager to leave the World Cup, with its pubs and pies and camaraderie, its lineouts and knock-ons and kickoffs.

On his final night in London, one spectator woke in the pre-dawn darkness—*le reveil mortel* often visits him in hotel rooms in the middle of the night—and turned on the TV. The former All Blacks star Ali Williams was being interviewed on a replay of the BBC show *Extra Time*. Asked if anger was a motivation for playing international rugby, Williams suggested it was something like the opposite. "To put yourself in pain is probably [how] I'd put it," he said, describing rugby as a joyful willingness—an eagerness—to open oneself to the certainty of physical peril.

"I'll be vulnerable here to injury; I'm going to just go through it," Williams said of his mind-set, and this open invitation to injury, in the service of something larger than oneself—well, that's rugby. "I loved it," he said. "[I] miss it." Anyone who attended the World Cup, and was suddenly headed home, felt exactly the same way.

CHRIS JONES

There's Somebody Ruthless on the Way

FROM ESQUIRE

MOST OF THE TIME, Conor McGregor wins fights with his fists. He has won once with elbow strikes, and he has won once by submission. But the other 15 times he has professionally beaten another man bloody—most recently Dennis Siver, whom he picked apart in Boston in January—it has been with his hands. His coach, an Irish mixed martial artist named John Kavanagh, has studied the physics of human combat and collision for decades, and even he can't explain why the five-foot-nine McGregor can hit as hard as he does. The hardest hitters usually have long arms, which McGregor does, and they usually have big fists, which McGregor does, but there's something else in him, some mysterious and extraordinary combination of desire and angle and speed, that makes his punches land like bombs.

McGregor, who is also extremely Irish, has an upright stance when he fights, a style that is both entrancing to watch and almost comically traditionalist. "He looks exactly like the Notre Dame logo," says Dana White, the president of the Ultimate Fighting Championship, referring to the university's ornery bare-knuckled leprechaun. Watching McGregor fight brings to mind ancient words like *fisticuffs* or *donnybrook*. He makes the delivery of knockouts look like some time-honored craft that occupies the space between art and science, like barrel making or leatherwork. A former plumber, he makes fighting seem like a trade.

When ordinary men land a punch, it lands with a blow, a seismic shock, like a hammer's thud. Most punches blemish. When McGregor lands a punch, his fists behave more like chisels, like awls. His punches cut. They don't bruise the skin; they break it. By the second round of their fight, Dennis Siver didn't look as though he'd been battered so much as he'd been glassed. His face was full of tiny holes.

Whatever reason McGregor's punches are different, they have made him his sport's newest darling, the culmination of a two-year rise from obscurity to headliner to crossover star. He will fight Brazilian champion Jose Aldo for the UFC's featherweight belt in July, and White believes it will be his organization's biggest fight of the year, "a global event," in large part because of McGregor's ability to seem more giant than he is.

But the 26-year-old McGregor doesn't want to be regarded as peerless in only a single facet of his occupation — as just a puncher. "I don't look at a man who's expert in one area as a specialist," he says. "I look at him as a rookie in ten other areas. If you can box, what happens if I grab hold of your legs? If you put me face-to-face with Floyd Mayweather — pound-for-pound boxing's best — if I fought Floyd, I would kill him in less than 30 seconds. It would take me less than 30 seconds to wrap around him like a boa constrictor and strangle him."

McGregor sees the human body the way he sees fights, the way he sees this New York bar in which he's sheltering from the cold, the way he sees existence: each is a collection of openings and avenues, roadblocks and hurdles. He always sits, as he is sitting now, with his back to a corner; he has scouted the exits; he has several routes of possibility mapped out in his cartographer's brain, every available advance and retreat. "I have a self-defense mind," he says. "I've had it all my life."

The way even the most successful still covet, McGregor dreams of possessing the ultimate trapdoor, of mastering the decisive submission that would finish any opponent: the rear naked choke. He has never managed to apply it during a UFC fight. He talks about it the way any of us talks about an object of desire that eludes us.

"It's the most dominant submission," he says almost wistfully. It isn't an arm or a knee bar or an ankle lock, each of which leaves its victim the opportunity to survive, however slight. And it isn't a punch that can be slipped or countered. The rear naked choke is almost a metaphor for the consequences of our most calamitous mistakes. "You can do nothing to me, but I can do whatever the fuck I want to you," McGregor says. "I have complete control."

He's not sure he's making himself plain enough. He wants you to understand the feeling of true hopelessness, the sensation of every last door closing to you. He wants you to hate that feeling, which will make you appreciate more deeply the moments you are free. His longtime girlfriend, Dee Devlin, sitting beside him in the bar, does her best to explain his intentions. "He wants you to be better than you are," she says.

So under the bright lights of a photo studio, he strips down to his underwear and jumps on you from behind. You feel his weight lean into you, 170 pounds walking around—he can cut more than 20 pounds in the week before weigh-ins—his pectorals fitting into the tops of your shoulders like puzzle pieces. His broad chest is painted with a giant tattoo of a gorilla eating a human heart. It's not some cartoonish representation of a human heart, either, but an illustration ripped out of a medical textbook, with ventricles and veins. It is a drawing of your heart, and now you can feel his, beating through the ink and into your back.

McGregor's legs hook around your waist, anchored in place by his huge ass. "Glutes are a motherfucker," he says. "Glutes are power." The sole of his left foot presses against the point of your hip; the heel of his right foot digs into your groin. Almost by instinct, your hands find that leg and try to remove it, but legs beat arms almost every time, the way arms beat necks. His right arm wraps around your throat, his thickly veined forearm locked under your chin. His left arm crosses over his right wrist and tucks behind your head. And then he begins to pull back his right arm while he pushes forward with his left.

It doesn't hurt. That's the wrong word. You're uncomfortable. McGregor knows the feeling. The last time he lost a fight, the sixth bout of his career, back in 2010, it was in 38 seconds, and it was to a choke. He was so averse to the sensation, he tapped out before he lost consciousness, one of the great regrets of his life. "That ate me alive," he says. "After that, I said I was going to fight to the death. You're going to have to kill me."

The rear naked choke is oblivious to such resolutions. Your

body, like nearly everything you do with it, has imperfections that can seem like evolutionary carelessness. There are the few square inches of your liver that lie exposed, wide open under your ribs, a four-lane expressway to your central nervous system. There are the underengineered flying buttresses of your knees, waiting to snap. And there is your carotid artery, conveying massive volumes of your blood to your brain, close enough to the surface of your neck that you can see and feel it coursing, as though a salmon might run up it. Because that artery means life, it also means death. There is no way for you to strengthen it, to shield it, to mitigate the effects of pressure put upon it. Now McGregor squeezes, in two directions at the same time—again pulling with his right, pushing with his left—his arms like the blades of dull scissors. Your eyes are drawn down, leading the way for the rest of you, to the tattoos on his left wrist: a mustachioed gentleman in a top hat, and one of McGregor's principal mantras: SLOW IS SMOOTH, SMOOTH IS FAST. He doesn't have to squeeze very hard, and he doesn't have to squeeze very long.

One second, two seconds, three seconds . . .

"Once the blood cuts from the brain, it's over," McGregor whispers.

It is. You are.

McGregor has lived his entire life in pursuit of the opposite sensation: *limitlessness*. For as long as he can remember, he has been obsessed with movement and its endless opportunities. He has studied animals for their advantages—gorillas, lions, crocodiles—and in Kavanagh's Dublin gym, he tries to find their secrets in himself. Kavanagh has given him a key to the place, because McGregor will get the urge, as irresistible as a choke, to move at all hours of the day and night, slithering and monkey-stalking across the mats. Devlin routinely wakes up to find her man shadowboxing in front of the mirror at four in the morning. He doesn't lift weights or put in carefully apportioned session work like most fighters. "Machines don't use machines," he says, "and I am a machine." He doesn't recognize most of the modern walls we have built around ourselves. "*Ritual* is another word for fear, manifested in a different way." He doesn't believe in time, or at least he won't submit to it; he recognizes that clocks exist, but he sees no reason to obey their demands. He eats when he wants, he sleeps when he wants, but mostly he moves when he wants. For McGregor, death would be stillness—if he believed in death.

"Even in death, they say your vision, you can see everything," he says. "It's almost like you're evolving to the next stage. It's like a different plane of existence, just another form of movement, now we're moving through the fucking universe or I don't know what the fuck. Think of what's out there."

In some ways, it's hard to bear McGregor's company, and not just because he might decide to choke you out at any moment. He is so confident and self-possessed, so in command of his body and seemingly of his fate, he fills you with doubt about yours. Most of our social interactions are based on the premise that we've all agreed to follow certain rules. McGregor has not agreed to those rules, he will not, which is unnerving because it makes his behavior unpredictable—you find yourself saying, "You can't do that" or "You must do this," and he does and doesn't do it—but also because he makes you wonder why you've agreed to those rules yourself. He walks down the middle of streets; he eats the way storms consume coastlines. He is exhausting as a lunch partner, just as he is inside the octagon. In both instances, he is an igniter of brutal self-examination, the most unflattering mirror.

"You tell someone the truth about themselves and they crumble," he says.

"It's life," Devlin says of her boyfriend's ability to create fissures. Their relationship predates his career as a professional fighter by two weeks. His loves are intertwined. "It's our life," she says. "It's not like it's on and then it's off. It's just the way he is."

He has been fighting in some capacity since he was a child, born a challenging presence. "I seem to have a face—I seem to attract attention somehow," he says. "For some reason, people want to try to come at me. They want to hit me. I just wanted people to leave me alone, basically. I didn't get into this to be somebody. I got into it to feel comfortable in uncomfortable situations."

He began by kickboxing and then boxing. Then he discovered jujitsu and its system of levers, how to beat a man even when you're trapped on your back just by applying a little pressure where pressure isn't normally applied. "It fascinated me," he says. "It fascinated me then, and it fascinates me now."

Then he sat in the stands at UFC 93 in Dublin in 2009. "That's when I could reach out and touch it," he says. He was still an apprentice plumber then, one foot in each world. To hear him tell it, he went back to a damp building site and looked at the masters, men old and shivering before their time, and he made the choice, as though it were a choice, that he would no longer abide. He put down his tools, because machines don't use machines, and walked away. He saw in fighting a nearly perfect freedom, a way to translate his love of boundless physical expression—in a sport where so long as you don't stick your fingers into eyes or open cuts, you're pretty much good to go—into that rarest of lives, he and Dee, soaring together, never to be caged again. "No matter what was going on in my life, good or bad, I always knew—we knew—that we would end up here," he says. "It was inevitable in my head."

He uses *inevitable* more than most people. For McGregor, his certainty about his rise, and its continuing, isn't bravado. He is doing you the favor of letting you glimpse a future that only he has seen. It's almost as though he can't help it, as though his jaw is just one more pressure-release valve through which he can vent his bottomless reserves of spiritual anarchy. Ask him about his reputation for trash talk and this is what he says, uninterrupted, it seems, even by breaths:

"Trash talk? Smack talk? This is an American term that makes me laugh. I simply speak the truth. I'm an Irish man. We don't give a fuck about feelings. We'll tell you the truth. People ask me a question about somebody, I tell them the truth. I don't have anything bad to say about Jose Aldo. It's pretty plain and simple. His time is up. It's done. There's somebody ruthless coming to get him. There's somebody cold coming to get him. I can look at him dead in the eye and say, *It's done. You're over now. You're a champion that nobody gave a fuck about.* Nobody cared about him before I came along. Nobody cared about the division before I came along. He's a decision machine. He can barely finish his dinner, never mind his opponent. And he's fought bums. He's fought little small bantamweights and he still can't put them away. Now he's coming in against a monster of a featherweight who hits like a truck. It's over for him. I don't need to say jackshit else. July is a wrap. It's *inevitable.*"

Only two years ago, Dana White went to Dublin to accept an award from Trinity College. It seemed as though everywhere he went, every bar, every street corner, he heard Conor McGregor's name. White has been told about a thousand secret talents over the years; he has assessed an army of local heroes. You will never know their names. But White heard McGregor's name enough that it made him wonder. He flew back to Las Vegas and asked his matchmakers about this Irish kid. They told him McGregor had fought a little, nothing especially noteworthy—14 fights, mostly against unknowns, mostly knockout wins, a couple of submission losses. Still curious, White brought his unlikely prospect out to the desert. He remembers driving up the Strip in his Ferrari and Mc-Gregor's energy competing with the engine and the lights. White signed him to a five-fight deal without ever seeing him fight.

"He's a penny stock that couldn't have worked out better," White says. "He's one in a million. He has that thing that you can't teach people, whatever it is that makes people gravitate toward you. He has that more than any fighter I've ever met. He makes you believe everything he believes."

Maybe it is a choice whether we abide. Maybe we don't have to be there at nine o'clock sharp. Maybe we don't die.

Conor McGregor has been damaged. It was during his first fight in America, in Boston in August 2013. In the second round against Max Holloway, McGregor emerged from a scramble on the ground with an unfamiliar feeling: he couldn't find his feet. Because he really believes what he believes, he still went on to win the fight, but he had torn the anterior cruciate ligament in his left knee. It's a devastating injury for any athlete, but for someone like Mc-Gregor, it was especially cruel. He was built flawed like the rest of us after all.

He was told to sit still. He didn't listen. "People will study my recovery," he says. He found new ways to work out, shedding the last of his conventional weights and routines. He pressed his body against itself, refusing every invitation to idleness. He did push-ups against hotel-room sinks. He did single-leg squats. He came back and won his next three fights: TKO (first round, 18 significant strikes landed); TKO (first round, nine); and most recently, against Siver, TKO (second round, 64). Each was the performance of the night; each made him more popular; each made him more certain. "I learned a lot more about how important balance is, how important control of the body is," McGregor says. "From the moment I open my eyes, I'm trying to free my body. I'm trying to get looser, more flexible, to gain control. Movement is medicine to me."

He studied footage of his fights and of animals hunting other animals, and he became closer to one of them than one of us. If he was a breed apart before his knee was blown out, he was his own species after, better than he was. White tore up his contract, and then he tore it up again. In McGregor's fight against Aldo, he will see a cut of the pay-per-view for the first time. Because its outcome is inevitable, and because he has a self-defense mind, he has already begun thinking of what will come next. "I'm interested in movement, and I'm interested in money, and I'm interested in the movement of money," he says. "If I win that belt and we do a million pay-per-views, we can rip up that motherfucker right there and do what the fuck we want."

"Someone like him, the money just rains down," White says. "He's going to get everything he's ever wanted."

Earlier that freezing day in New York, McGregor and Devlin had walked into a Christian Louboutin store in the Meatpacking District. McGregor is a stylish man; for him, clothes are another means of applying pressure to other men. He tried on several pairs of sneakers, ridiculous sneakers, the sort of clown shoes that would get the shit kicked out of a kid who wore them to the wrong school. He got stuck on a pair of gleaming white high-tops studded with rainbow hunks of plastic, little pyramids and diamonds that fought with the smooth red soles for his eye's dubious attention.

"They're fucking out there," he said, looking at himself in a mirror. "Wouldn't see no one back home wearing a pair of these."

He looked at them some more, turning, convincing himself.

"If you like them, get them," Devlin said.

"If someone says something—*whap*," he said, and he began firing off kicks in the middle of the store, the taken-aback employees looking at him and his cauliflower ears anew, doing all the mental arithmetic that men do when they're ranking themselves within the orders of other men. "Just snap them in the face," McGregor said, kicking again at the mirror.

"I don't know about them, I have to say," Devlin said.

"If I'm not going to wear 'em out of the store, I'm not getting 'em," he said. Then he nodded to himself. "I'm wearing 'em out."

Devlin laughed and paid for the shoes: $1,700. The leather

boots McGregor had worn into the store went into the bag. The new sneakers went out into the snow and slush. They flashed like sirens.

Then a strange thing happened. A family with young daughters walked up to McGregor and asked for his picture. Then a construction worker broke from a road site and asked for one too. Then a small crowd began to assemble in the cold on the cobblestones, inexplicably drawn to this man, to this machine, wearing shoes that somebody could wear only if he were somebody. McGregor was surrounded, just like that, made captive by his otherness.

He is aware of the irony. "If you're not in the humor of it, it can be heavy," he says, back in his corner of the bar. "People can become familiar with it, like they've known you all your life. That's weird for me. The reason I got into the game was so that people would leave me the fuck alone." He stops, his flashing black eyes looking at how many of the faces in this room are looking back at him. "It's backfired on me," he says.

And then McGregor is what he so rarely is: he is still, and he is quiet. You get the sense that he's recalculating, looking for different exits. He says he has not wondered once whether he might lose to Aldo—"If I entertain things, they tend to come true," he says—but sitting there, in the silence, he feels as though he has it in him, whatever the result, to disappear one day, maybe on a day not all that distant from today. He knows we'll swallow him alive if he stays; even he can't fight all of us off. The only way he'll have complete control is if he leaves. Maybe that's the future he's seen for himself all along, a great train robber's last big score before he makes good his final escape, vanishing into the jungle with his girl.

"We're the only animal that wakes up and doesn't stretch," he says, coming around.

"Look at your dog," Devlin says.

"Wake up and stretch," McGregor says. "Start there."

Start there and end up with everything you've ever wanted. To demonstrate, he announces that he's going back to his fancy hotel and falling into his cloud of a bed. It's three o'clock in the afternoon.

He won't sleep well. He hasn't worked out in two days, and he's edgy about it, as though he's taking his gifts for granted, as though he's forgotten those dark times when he felt trapped. He'll wake up at two in the morning and start prowling around his hotel room, padding across the thick carpets like a jewel thief, climbing the furniture, scaling the walls, walking upside down across the ceiling, learning how to move through the universe.

A few hours later, you'll wake up, the shadow of his arms still pressed around your neck. You'll get out of bed, and you'll stretch.

WRIGHT THOMPSON

The Greatest Hitter
Who Ever Lived On

FROM ESPN: THE MAGAZINE

CLAUDIA WILLIAMS FOUND comfort wearing her dad's favorite red flannel shirt. It smelled like him. Time frayed the threads, pulled apart seams, and years ago the shirt went into a safe. She keeps many things locked away. In a closet next to her garage, her father's Orvis 8.3-foot, 7-weight graphite fly rod leans on a wall. His flies are safe too, and she can see his hands in the bend of the knots. She feels closest to him fishing but has been only once or twice since he died. Nearby, pocketknives rust at their hinges. His old leather suitcase is there too, in its final resting place after years of trains, ballparks, and hotel rooms.

Her husband, Eric Abel, comes home from running errands. He'd been through the safes and the storage unit they keep filled to its 10-foot ceiling, hunting for the flannel shirt. She is laughing in the kitchen, a lazy Sunday morning. Eric takes a breath and enters the room. "First of all, Claudia," he says slowly, "let me apologize; I don't know what we've done with that shirt."

Suddenly quiet and hiding now, she says, "I don't wanna think about it," as one more piece of her father slips away.

She is hiding from loss, and from regret, hiding from her family's past, which is always operating the strings of her daily life. Whenever she lets herself go back, she ends up at the same place: the beginning. Ted Williams's mother gave him nothing but a name, and as soon as he grew old enough,

he gave it back, changing Teddy on his birth certificate to the more respect-
able Theodore. He longed to rewrite the facts of his life. His father drifted on
the edge of it. His mother, May, was obsessed with her work at the Salvation
Army, abandoning her own kids, and the descriptions of his lonely life exist
in many accounts, most notably biographies by Ben Bradlee Jr. and Leigh
Montville. San Diego neighbors would watch Ted and his younger brother
Danny, eight and six, sitting alone on the front porch late into the night.
The anger that dominated both their lives started there, on those lonely
evenings outside 4121 Utah Street, waiting for their mom to come home.
May Williams never saw her son play a major league game, even though
she lived through his entire career. When she died, 11 months after he hit
a home run in his final at-bat, he went through her things and gathered
up family photographs. He tore them into pieces and threw the pieces away.

That was 1961, and he never wanted family to hurt him again. He
lived most of the next 41 years as a kind of island. He died in 2002 and is
frozen at 7895 East Acoma Drive in Scottsdale, Arizona. Claudia and her
brother, John-Henry, supported cryonics; older half-sister Bobby-Jo wanted
her father cremated and sued her siblings in the courts and fought them
in the media. Ted Williams gave his three children the name he'd made
famous, and when he died, their battle turned a solemn passing into a late-
night punch line. Death exposes everyone, and it exposed Ted Williams,
stripping away the armor he'd created as a boy on Utah Street, revealing
what he'd tried so hard to hide: he came from damaged people, and he left
damaged people behind.

Claudia Williams, now 43, rarely tells anyone about her relation to
Ted Williams. Her coworkers at the Crystal River, Florida, medical
center where she's a nurse are only now finding out on their own.
It was two years before her best friend knew. If people do know,
she tests them constantly, to make sure they don't like her for her
dad's name. She recently stopped to pick up swim fins from a
workout partner, and he said he was having an office party and invited her in. Instead, she sat in her car in the parking lot, stewing,
wondering whether he just wanted to show off "Ted's daughter,"
and finally she drove away, enraged, leaving the fins behind.

Upon occasion, she curses exactly like he did, stringing together blistering oaths, a kind of profane poetry: "that whore of a
bitch f—ing c— of a bimbo," say, of a nurse who spoke to reporters about the family. Claudia is beautiful and familiar, her face

a combination of her mother's *Vogue* model cheekbones and her father's all-American jaw. When she is up, laughing with a goofy smile and light in her eyes, you cannot get close enough to her, and when she is down, spiraling into a darkness only she can see, you cannot get far enough away. With no children of her own, she's destined to remain a daughter. She's young because her dad was much older than her mom—Ted, the eternal player, tossed Dolores Wettach a note across the first-class cabin of an international flight, introducing himself simply as a fisherman—starting Claudia's lifelong struggle to hold tight to something slipping between her fingers. "I hate time," she says.

She lives in a sprawling Florida community popular among retirees whose first resident and primary pitchman was her father. He's everywhere. Her country club membership number is 9. Every day, she drives on Ted Williams Memorial Parkway. She turns from West Fenway Drive onto Ted Williams Court in her black Acura, the Euro club music rattling the rearview mirror.

"You should look at the lyrics," she says as the stereo plays. The songs bleed together into a singular anthem of loneliness and loss. *This will be my monument / This will be a beacon when I'm gone / You're everywhere I go / I promise I won't let you down / It's not over, not over / Not over, not over, yet.* The lines speak to the two competing desires governing her life: she wants to be close to a father she didn't really know for much of his life, but she wants to escape his shadow too.

She left home at 16, moving to Europe to finish high school, working as a nanny, training for triathlons, living in France, then Switzerland, then Germany, any place where nobody'd ever heard of Ted Williams. In letters home, she described being adrift, telling her dad she felt "like a lost athlete looking for a sport." She cooked hot dogs in a gypsy circus. Her father offered her money, but she refused it. In this stubbornness, she found the emotional stability sought but never discovered by her brother, who died 11 years ago from leukemia. "I surpassed John-Henry quicker because I got away," she says.

She never asked for anything. Her dream was to attend Middlebury College in Vermont. When she didn't get in, Ted called the governor of New Hampshire, who pulled some strings. The reconsidered acceptance letter made her weep with rage because she knew what had happened. She told Middlebury no. Her friends at Springfield College didn't realize her father was Ted Williams until she asked some guys who played baseball to teach her to throw; the Red Sox had requested she toss out a first pitch as a surprise to her father, and she didn't want, as she told them, "to throw like a girl." Her brother lobbed one wild, but Claudia kicked her leg and delivered a strike. Ted beamed, a reward she seldom got while he lived and craves now that he's gone.

"I think I'm just looking for him to still be proud of me," she says.

She trained for a triathlon and then devoted her life to making the 2000 Olympic team, falling just short. Around 2005, she started playing tennis with some older ladies in the neighborhood. Then the Williams kicked in: she moved up the USTA ratings, 3.5 to 4.0, then, she says, she became the best 4.0 in Citrus County, then the top-ranked 4.0 player in the state. Hooked, she decided to play at the local junior college. For a season, at 37 years old, she competed against teenagers. After her father died, she received a sponsor's exemption to run the Boston Marathon in his memory; she turned it down, trained, and ran fast enough to qualify on her own. "I don't know who has to say, 'You did well,'" says Abel, who was the Williams family attorney when he met Claudia.

When she decided to be a lifeguard, she completed the most advanced open-water rescue training. After deciding to make jewelry, she took classes to become a master craftsman. She learned how to skydive, and after having to deploy the backup chute on her first solo jump, she went back up again: *I'll show you, sky!* Her workout routines—miles in a pool and on a treadmill, hours daily in a gym—break the alpha dogs who try to hang with Ted's daughter. She makes them earn their story. In the past few years, she studied nursing, and even that hasn't been enough, so now she's studying biology and statistics, prerequisites for graduate school. Her top choice is Duke, and in her application essay she talked about her life as a frustrated athlete without a sport. She talked about the influence of her father, but she never mentioned that the father in question was Ted Williams.

This story began two years ago, when I reached out to Claudia about meeting at her home in Hernando. The timing never worked for her because she struggles to look past her obsessions: nursing school and a book she wrote about her father, which started as a stocking stuffer about lessons she learned and turned into a cathartic exploration of the person she's still trying to be. Finally she said yes. The first visit lasted a week in the fall of 2014, and we made paella and she told funny stories about her dad—he'd call the public phone in European hostels and boom at unsuspecting travelers, "Is CLAUDIA WILLIAMS there? This is her FATHER! OL' TED WILLIAMS!"—and she got melancholy later and said, "We need to laugh more."

She let me poke through the family's filing cabinets, its safes, her dad's hospital records, anything I wanted—she could prove, she said, that her father agreed to be frozen. We talked for hour upon hour. To her, the many accounts of Ted Williams are all fatally flawed because most people didn't understand that the two famous acts of his life—ballplayer and fisherman—occurred only because he was hiding from the third and final act of his life: fatherhood. He'd been raised by an erratic and absent mother. He had a cousin who was murdered by her husband, and a criminal brother who died young and angry. He hid in the hyperfocus required by baseball and fishing; most nights after ball games, he returned to the hotel where he lived—he never purchased a home in Boston—and tied fishing flies alone. He preferred to spend off-seasons in the woods or on the water. Once, he arrived late to spring training because he lost track of time while hunting wolves in a cold northern forest, and the media focused so much on the process story of the tardiness that nobody seemed to notice the window Williams had briefly opened into his truest self: he sought peace in the wilderness with wolves.

Ted Williams hated his childhood home, leaving before graduation the same as Claudia, never going back. His lifelong feud with the press began when a writer asked rhetorically in a column what kind of boy didn't go home in the winter to visit his mother. How could he be expected, then, to create a family when he despised his own so much?

"I was for s— as a father," he confided once to a cousin.

On the day his only son, John-Henry, was born, Ted was salmon fishing in Canada. He'd been retired for eight years. That night, like always, he wrote in his fishing log. Ted wrote about the water temperature (70–72 degrees), his friends who came up to fish, and details of the trout and arctic char he caught while casting for salmon. He never mentioned a pregnant Dolores, and he never mentioned the boy.

To the public, he was a success, but to himself, he was a failure, consumed with shame and regret. Bobby-Jo came into the world first, in the middle of his career. When she was young, he got so mad at her that he spit a mouthful of food in her face. Ted drove her back to her mom's house in Miami once, and when they arrived, it transpired that Bobby-Jo had forgotten her keys, and Ted, raging, kicked her out of the car and left her standing alone there in the dark, exactly as his mother had done to him.

Instead of Bobby-Jo becoming the first Williams to graduate from college, which Ted wanted as desperately as he wanted to hit a baseball, she got pregnant. Rather than tell her father, she slit her arm from the wrist to the elbow. She entered a psych ward, which he paid for, and got an abortion, which he paid for, and when her scars taunted him—physical proof that he'd become his mother—he paid for plastic surgery too. He couldn't buy her peace. Doctors diagnosed manic depression, and she moved from booze to pills, cheating on her husband with the neighbor and giving herself another abortion with drugs and alcohol. Doctors gave her electroshock therapy. She threw plates and knives. Her voice turned childlike whenever she spoke to him, a thin "Daddy." She asked for money and begged for help. She never held a job. At the funeral for Williams's longtime girlfriend, Louise Kaufman, Claudia recognized her half-sister, Bobby-Jo, whom she'd never met, simply by seeing a familiar wave of fear register on Bobby-Jo's face at the sound of Ted's voice: he boomed in the next room, sucking up all the oxygen, and two women, born 23 years apart, flinched.

"You must be Bobby-Jo," Claudia said.

"Claudia?" she replied.

Ted talked with Bobby-Jo moments later.

"Hi, Daddy," she said.

"Are you still smoking?" he asked.

"I'm down to one pack a day," she said.

"Jesus," he said, then he walked away.

By the time Eric Abel came into the Williams inner circle as the family attorney, Ted had already excommunicated Bobby-Jo. At Ted's request, Abel wrote her out of the will, and Abel said over the nine years he spent around Williams, he heard him mention Bobby-Jo maybe three times, and every time he called her a "f—ing syphilitic c—."

He called Claudia a "c—" too, and a "fat bitch," and told John-Henry he was the "abortion I wanted." They tried to understand his rages, and why they'd even been born. "I mean, he had [me] at 53 years old," Claudia says, her voice wavering. "Right from the start, we knew we weren't gonna have much time, you know? The lessons that he had to teach us, we didn't have the time to learn . . . We're desperately trying—I say 'we' like John-Henry's still around—but we're desperately trying to figure out what made him tick."

Their mom, Dolores, and Ted didn't last long. He got his freedom, fishing every day. She got the kids. Claudia remembers growing up with a mother increasingly bitter over her failed love affair, on a Vermont farm without a television, isolated by their environment and the fame of their absent father. The children created their own world, and only they understand what it felt like to live in it. All they had was each other, and both longed to decode their dad, and maybe find themselves in the process. Whenever they'd ask questions about his childhood, or his life, he'd scowl and grumble, "Read my book."

Claudia loves dragons. She especially loves movies about dragons. On the living room cabinet, there's a ceramic statue of Toothless, the star of the animated movie *How to Train Your Dragon*. She got it as a gift. Her voice changes and her eyes and face soften when she says "Toothless." A few years ago, she and Eric's teenage daughters from his first marriage went to see a movie called *The Water Horse*, about a boy who raises a Loch Ness Monster—which is close enough to a dragon for Claudia—then releases the beast to save its life. It is named Crusoe, and as the movie ended, Eric's girls looked over and saw Claudia weeping, shoulders rocking up and down, distraught over the boy taking the dragon out to sea.

"You were sobbing," says Eric's daughter Emma, now 22, grinning as she tells the story. Claudia smiles.

"My heart hurt," she says.

That night, after Eric cooks steaks and Emma bakes sugar cookies, everyone piles onto the sofa for movie night. Claudia picks *How to Train Your Dragon,* bringing another round of catcalls and laughter. Everyone settles in, and the movie starts.

"Toothless!" she coos.

"He's real to you, isn't he?" Eric asks, kindly. No one is laughing now, and Claudia reaches for Eric's hand from time to time. Every now and again, she sighs. The story is about a boy trying to live in the shadow of his powerful and domineering father—about a child searching for his place in the world. Watching her watch a dragon movie makes it all make sense.

Sitting on her couch, she cries when the dragon saves the little boy.

"You won't always be there to protect him," a character in the movie tells the father, and Claudia smiles, turns to Eric, and says, "John-Henry would've loved this movie."

John-Henry Williams loved frogs.

He loved anything small and weak. During storms, driving up the hill toward their house in Vermont, he'd jump out of the car in the pouring rain, trying to get the frogs to move before they died beneath the wheels of the car. Like any damaged person, he took his protection too far. He saved a wild duck he found, and countless other birds. If they bit him, he'd tap their beaks to scold them, as if they loved him with the same intellectual fervor he loved them. Claudia still remembers Bangor the Cat. Driving back from visiting Ted's compound in Canada, Dolores and John-Henry stopped in Maine to spend the night in sleeping bags at a rest stop. In the night, he heard a kitten crying, and after searching for and finding her, he tucked the cat, fleas and all, into his bag. At home, he brought her back to health and felt hurt when she wanted to roam outside. Always scared of being abandoned, he fit a dog harness on a long leash and tied Bangor to his bed. Claudia tried to get him to release the cat, but he refused to listen.

He protected Claudia too. The first time they visited Ted in Florida together, he made sure she knew not to annoy him, advising her to use the bathroom before leaving the airport. At Ted's place in Islamorada, in the Keys, she got a terrible sunburn. Terrified of Ted raging at them, John-Henry quietly fed her ice chips and got her ginger ale when she vomited from sun poisoning. She was about nine. He was 12. John-Henry rubbed Vaseline on her shoulders and told her not to cry.

That was three decades ago. There is only one picture of John-Henry in her house. It hurts too much. When he got leukemia a year after Ted died, she donated bone marrow, and when he needed another transplant and her blood count was too low, she begged the doctors to try anyway. She screamed at them in the blood lab. An agnostic, she stopped in a church near the Los Angeles hospital and got on her knees and begged. It was the first and only time she has prayed. She asked God to take her instead. John-Henry died on a Saturday, and as he requested, his body was suspended at Alcor too, in the same tank as his dad.

Eleven years he's been gone.

"Grief is weird," Claudia says, riding at night through the dark neighborhoods around their house. "The first seven years, any time I would have a break, any fun, one moment—inevitably, guilt. Just horrible guilt. Like I didn't deserve to be happy."

"I'm the one who reached down to keep pulling you up," Abel says, driving. "Still do. I love you. When you laugh—"

She interrupts him. A heavy rain is falling, blurring the streetlights reflecting off the asphalt, and she looks out into the glare of the headlamps and sees something move.

"Did you see the frog?" she says suddenly. "You gotta watch for him!"

"No," he says.

"I don't know if you ran over him," she says.

"Did I hit one?" he asks.

She starts slapping his arm.

"*Stop! Stop!*" she cries.

He presses hard on the brakes, and she gets out. In the rain, in the glow of their house, she shakes her foot along the pavement, clearing a path, making sure no frogs get caught beneath the tires of the approaching car.

A mile away, a secret remains locked in one of Ted Williams's safes.

On a shelf above a Desert Eagle .44, his fishing logs tell a different story from the one he gave his fans and his children. In public, he seemed to revel in the solitary pursuit of baseball greatness, then fishing greatness, but really, his lonely existence was a self-imposed exile, not because he didn't want to know his children but because he was scared of hurting them, and of being hurt.

Something happened to Ted Williams in the years after his son came into the world. "What's incredible as an observer was to watch him in love with his kids," says Abel, now 52. "The vulnerability of having love for your children. You could see it just gnaw. It was everything against his grain to succumb to this outside influence of children. Love had control over him. He felt vulnerable. A vulnerability he never had in his life. I think he *hated* that vulnerability of feeling guilt."

In his logs, John-Henry and Claudia began to make appearances.

First, just simple mentions, when they were little: "Claudia, John Henry took canoe ride to Gray Rapids." Soon Ted gave them praise that would never reach their ears. By 1979, when they were 10 and seven, he practically gushed in his upright, loopy handwriting. On June 14, he wrote about his son: "His casting is better than I expected so he must have been practicing some. After an aching rest and a few blisters on his casting hand, he is getting a little uninterested. Finally he got his first fish. A grilse. Enthusiasm revived. 3 grilse, caught his first salmon. 10 pounds. Big day in a young fisherman's life."

Claudia and John-Henry would have given anything to know this. It might have changed their lives. Near the safe in his old house is a note Ted saved, dated December 10, 1983, when Claudia was 12. It's a contract she wrote—the Williams family loves handwritten contracts—with her mother at a Howard Johnson's somewhere: "When I grow up I will never have a child. If I do I will pay my mom 1,000 dollars."

Less than a year later, Ted sat before a stack of posters, doing one of the bulk signings familiar to all famous athletes. At some point during the session, instead of signing his name, he wrote a note to Claudia, one he knew she'd discover someday. He signed the rest, and the whole box went into storage. She found the note three years ago, 10 years after he died, going through memorabilia. Trembling as she held the poster in her hand, she finally read the words she wanted so badly to hear as a child: "To my beautiful daughter. I love you. Dad."

*

Ted wanted to change. Trouble is, nobody knew how to start to repair something so completely broken. It began with Claudia. About 20 years ago, she graduated from college. He asked her what she wanted as a gift, and she said she wanted time. The three of them flew together to San Diego and drove up the Pacific Coast. It was a do-over. So many firsts happened on that trip. She and her brother saw the house on Utah Street. The three of them laughed, and they asked Ted questions, and he told stories and asked them questions too. For years, she'd thought her father had stopped maturing when he became famous at 20, and now they'd both reached his emotional age, equals and running buddies for the first time. He never lost his temper or spun off in a rage. He wasn't angry, and they weren't scared.

They visited Alcatraz, and Ted used a Walkman for the first time, befuddled by the technology, and they all laughed. Something happened to Ted Williams's face when he laughed; most pictures show him stern, in concentration, but when he giggled, his jowls would hang and his eyes would squint and he looked, for just a moment, nothing like one of the most famous men in America. He looked anonymous and happy. When the boat docked back at Pier 39, they walked down the boards looking for dinner. A man at a card table was reading palms. Claudia saw him first, and she and John-Henry dragged their father over.

The fortune-teller sat on a low stool. He traced his finger over the old man's wrinkled palm. Ted laughed and made a joke about it feeling good, and the inside of his hand was soft, the calluses he cultivated during baseball long gone smooth. John-Henry snapped photos, forever documenting every moment he spent around his dad. Claudia leaned in and watched. Everything that would happen began in these moments, but none of them could see the future, not even the fortune-teller.

He looked up at the old man.

"You have heavy burdens you're still carrying," he said. "It's time to let them go."

Ted Williams tried to follow that advice. He really tried.

Nine months after that trip, he had a stroke. His health declined steadily for nearly the next nine years. John-Henry and Claudia cared for him every day, and every day they discovered new levels of understanding and knowledge. They sought out anything that might buy him more time—no matter how experimental, unorthodox, or just plain weird. They paid $30 a pill for vitamins and pumped oxygen-rich air into his room. They tried bee pollen and acupuncture and hired a therapist to work through his anger. John-Henry bought a dialysis machine so Ted could get the treatment at night. Nothing worked.

Father and son had epic fights, bad enough that the caretakers called protective services. Investigators came to the house and interviewed both men, asking whether Ted was being made to sign autographs against his will, before determining there was no abuse. John-Henry wanted to control his father—his latest Bangor—and his father rebelled. About once a year, Abel would get called to the house to mediate a bizarre dispute, usually about Ted showering to ward off infection, or taking his medicine regularly.

"You could see an internal struggle," Abel says. "'Goddamn, that's my son. He loves me, I love him. F—. I wanna say no so goddamn bad. Everything about me says no. But I love him.' You could just watch it rage."

Even now, Abel laughs about the scene he'd find upon entering the house. "Dad, you have to take this medicine," John-Henry would be saying. "You have to take these pills."

"I'm not taking this s—," Ted would growl, seething. "F— you."

Abel would write up a contract on a napkin or a piece of scratch paper, which is what Ted liked, and negotiate a settlement: Ted agreed to take the pills every day, and John-Henry agreed to let him shower only four times a week. Both would sign it, and the crisis would be averted.

Even as he fought him, Ted knew John-Henry was struggling to find his place in the world. He worried about his son. Once, when Abel was flying to San Diego to meet with the Upper Deck baseball card company, Ted pulled him aside.

"See if you can help John-Henry get a job," Williams asked. "I know Claudia will be fine."

The guilt Ted carried slipped away when he did something to help his kids. Looking back, Claudia wishes she'd let him get her into Middlebury, because it was the only thing he knew how to do. In those last years, she taught him how to be a father to a daughter. When Claudia went through a breakup, instead of keeping her pain a secret like she'd done as a teenager, she explained how to comfort her.

"Please don't be mad," she said. "Just please listen to me. I'm hurting."

She could hear him grinding his teeth.

"What the hell do you want me to do about it!" he yelled. "I can't do a f—ing thing!"

"Just tell me you love me," she said.

"JESUS CHRIST!" he yelled. "I love you more than you'll ever know."

The outside world slipped away, and the universe shrank to the three of them: a dad looking for absolution, a son who needed a dad to show him how to be a man, a daughter who'd always craved a family, which they at long last became. A strange family, to be sure, but a family nonetheless, with a patriarch who'd found escape from his guilt and his shame in the company of his children.

"He never thought he was gonna be a good father," Claudia says. "He'd given up on it. Thought he wasn't very good at it. And we actually showed him that not only was he good at it, we wanted him and we said, 'You can do this, Dad.' And once he realized 'I can be good at this, and these kids want to learn from me,' we had run out of time."

Then John-Henry read a book about cryonics.

Ted's house is full of secrets about his son too, windows into a desperate but curious mind at work. In the long row of filing cabinets, a drawer holds a blue folder marked "Alcor." It's thick, jammed with newsletters, receipts, contracts, and John-Henry's handwritten notes taken during a visit to the cryonics facility.

He filled six yellow legal-sized pages, jotting down the price for freezing just the head ($50,000) and the price for the entire body ($120,000), making charts and decision trees plotting the potential repercussions of cryonics. On a page, he drew a horizontal graph, with a line drawn down the middle, dividing the plan into actions he'd take before convincing his father and what he'd need to do after. In big letters, he wrote "Make Claudia co-petitioner" and circled it. She agreed. "I didn't want John-Henry to lose his father," she says. "He needed him so badly. He was still learning, he was still—he was still—what is it? Evolving? Becoming a man in his father's eyes? He needed more time."

The literature John-Henry took home from Alcor, one of the country's two major cryonics companies, worked in his imagination; he purchased every book they offered, according to credit card receipts. The most important thing he read was the origin text of cryonics, a book by science fiction writer and professor Robert Ettinger titled *The Prospect of Immortality.* Ettinger wrote that the freezer always trumped the grave, and with nothing to lose, why not take a chance? Children who buried their parents were described as murderers. Ettinger also made many other wild and foolish predictions about what science would bring to the world in his lifetime, so the book, like the Bible, is believable to those who want to believe. On page 5, Ettinger seemed to be speaking directly to John-Henry: "The tired old man, then, will close his eyes, and he can think of his impending temporary death as another period under anaesthesia at the hospital. Centuries may pass but to him there will be only a moment of sleep without dreams."

Around the long kitchen table, John-Henry began to make his case.

Ted did not want to be frozen at first. His will, which he wrote near the end of the fishing act of his life, made his wishes very clear. He should be cremated, his ashes "sprinkled at sea off the coast of Florida where the water is very deep."

Four years passed between John-Henry's purchasing the books and requesting membership documents from Alcor. Ted's health declined, more every day. John-Henry kept saying cryonics provided a chance for them all to be together again one day.

"What does Dad think?" Claudia asked.

"He thinks it's kooky," John-Henry says. "But he is interested. I can tell."

They spent hours around the dining table, and every so often John-Henry would bring it up. Sometimes Ted would curse and walk away. Other times he'd listen.

These private discussions would eventually become public, fitting into an existing narrative. John-Henry Williams, a six-foot-five ringer for his handsome father, had long lived in the zeitgeist as a bumbling son who took and took without ever standing on his own. In the definitive biography of Ted Williams, by Ben Bradlee

Jr., John-Henry is shown as a terrible businessman and a cheat, someone who lied so often—inviting his dad to a college graduation where he didn't actually graduate, claiming to make his college baseball team when he never tried out—that he lied about Ted's wanting to be frozen too. This depiction of her brother by an author she cooperated with haunts Claudia, who believes her dad knew better, and she feels like the only one left to defend John-Henry.

After Ted died, friends told reporters that Williams disagreed with his son's obsession. The stories and biographies quote staff members and associates who say Ted continued to want his remains scattered in the Atlantic, and in the end, Bradlee seemed to conclude that Ted did not want to be frozen. Abel goes into the study and comes back with the book. He opens it on the kitchen counter, the pages full of his notes, some passages marked with a check if he feels they're accurate, other quotes highlighted, and some with sharp, angry pen strokes when he's aggrieved, the margins littered with "not true" and "bulls—" and "lie." Bradlee spent a decade reporting, and while Claudia and Eric say he got many things about Ted's military and baseball careers right, they say he allowed unreliable people to give opinions couched as facts when discussing the inner workings of the Williams clan, which has forever been a complicated tribe in which truths are perceptions and history keeps repeating itself: Bobby-Jo died five years ago, of advanced liver disease, killed by the same bad habits as her mother.

The clean cryonics narrative of Bradlee's book doesn't match the messiness of that long family dispute. Claudia has spent considerable time looking for documents that would prove she was in the hospital for the signing of the informal contract. Bradlee's book strongly suggests, without ever saying so directly, that she was lying about being there. She says she visited the hospital so many times that all those trips ran together, but she remains steadfast: Ted signed a piece of paper. The argument remains frustrating for everyone: Claudia can't prove they followed her father's wishes, and Bradlee can't prove they didn't. Nobody quoted is without an agenda, whether fueled by anger, misunderstanding, jealousy, or love. Nobody is unaffected. Nobody is clean. It's a mess, all of it. Ted Williams left behind so many unanswered questions that two of his children went to the extreme edges of science to find more time for them to be answered, while his third child went to equal extremes to stop them. At the end, jealous and estranged, Bobby-Jo raged, leaving bizarre voice mails on Abel's answering machine: "This is Barbara Joyce Ferrell. I live right behind you. Prepare thyself, sir."

Bobby-Jo lashed out, and Claudia hid, and John-Henry got as close as he could. He pushed and explained his idea, working cryonics into those dinner-table evenings. One night, Ted looked at Claudia and asked, "Are you in on this too?"

"Who knows what the future will bring?" she said, and John-Henry argued some more. Ted, exhausted and struggling to keep his eyes open, sort of laughed, then his son helped him to the recliner where he slept. Months passed, and after trying every other option available to buy time, only surgery would help Ted. First, he needed a heart catheterization, and doctors worried he might not survive even that preliminary procedure. Most people his age wouldn't risk a series of operations. In her book, Claudia writes what her father told the doctor. "Doc, if you can give me any extra time with these guys, let's do it," he said. "I've had a great life, and what the hell, if I die, maybe I'll die on the table. I'd like to have some more time with my two kids."

The doctor nodded and scheduled the surgery. Claudia began to cry, and Ted's voice cracked when he tried to comfort her, as she'd taught him to do.

"It'll be all right," he said.

According to Claudia, that's when John-Henry returned to the Williams family favorite: the nonbinding, casually written contract. She says Ted sighed, agreed to go along with their wishes, and signed a piece of paper agreeing to be frozen. He knew he might not live through his procedure, and at the end of his life, he'd finally put aside his own wishes for theirs. For comedians and baseball fans and biographers, cryonics was a joke or a disgrace, but inside the Williams family, it was a profound act of love, a conscious attempt to undo the cycle of pain both felt and caused.

"If it means that much to you kids," he said, "fine."

She and Eric fell in love during the horrible siege after they froze her father, who died of cardiac arrest almost two years after signing the note. She was trapped in his house by television trucks and reporters shouting questions. Claudia, then 30 and an elite athlete, paced the halls like a wild animal. Days passed without her manic exercise routine, which she used to exhaust herself into a kind of peace. Finally Eric realized she needed to escape, so he put her in the back seat of his car, covered her with blankets, and snuck her past the cameras. They drove to a nearby park, where she could run until she felt tired enough to stop thinking.

That was 13 years ago, and while people still remember something about Ted's head being frozen, the daily onslaught is over. Claudia and Eric are moving back into Ted's old house, not wanting to sell it and not wealthy enough to maintain two homes. It's empty now, under renovation, sitting low and wide on a hill, beneath the grove of live oak trees. Claudia and Eric pull into the drive, the gate with the red number 9 closing behind them.

Her mood founders when she stands in the towering great room, cold and unfurnished now, except for row upon row of almost empty bookshelves rising toward the ceiling. The only thing left is a frayed set of Ted's beloved *Encyclopedia Britannica,* which he bought after retiring, spending hours scouring them for the knowledge he felt ashamed not to have. When he was an old man, Harvard begged him to come and receive an honorary degree. He refused, over and over again, never feeling as if he belonged in a place with such educated people. "I don't think [Ted] at the end of his life felt like he accomplished anything," Abel says. "Ted had that constant insecurity."

The house is empty inside, dangling wires and pencil marks on the walls indicating where a range will go. Ted's white Sub-Zero fridge with the wood-paneled front is unplugged in the corner. The kitchen brings back so many memories. The wires and the hoses and the sawdust on the floor amplify how much those memories have faded. The dining table used to be there, by the window. Training for triathlons after she came home from Europe, every weekend Claudia would ride her bike here from Tampa.

"Daddy would sit right here," she says, laughing. "He would see me coming up the road. He'd be waiting for me right here. When I walked into the house, there'd be a hot dog on the table."

She didn't like hot dogs, but she loved to see her father smile, so she ate them every time.

"He thought I needed salt," she says, then switches to her flaw-less Ted Williams impersonation, a chin-jutting bass drum: "Yup, isn't that GOOD? That's a good hot dog, isn't it? OL' TED WIL-LIAMS, HUH? YOU WANNA 'NOTHER ONE?"

Her spirit lightens when she does his voice, everything lit from the inside. They spent hours at that table, talking, playing the games he never got to play as a kid—*As I was going to St. Ives, I met a man with seven wives*—and debating religion and the nature of life and death.

"Those late nights when it was clear he didn't have much time left . . . ," she says, trailing off, the light gone.

She has lost her father to old age and her brother to leukemia. Every year, she plants a tree in their memory, and leaving her dad's house one day, she sees that one of John-Henry's trees is dying. Reminders of grief surround her, and now her mother is fading too. One afternoon, she gets a frantic phone call and rushes to her mom's bedside less than a mile away. The live-in caretaker is crying. Claudia, a nurse, listens to the plodding thumps of a tired heart. She checks her mom's blood pressure: 86/60 and dropping.

"Mom, you want to go to the hospital?" Claudia asks.

"No," Dolores Williams says.

"Even if it means saving your life?"

"No."

Her mom stabilizes, and Claudia heads home. The rain pounds the roof of her car. Soon she will face herself alone, as her father faced the world stripped of the soothing focus of baseball and fish-ing. Tears roll down her cheeks. She sighs hard; rattling almost, jagged on the edges, a noise so full of pain that people who hear it feel compelled to protect her.

"Our time is running out," she says. She feels lonely. She's a young woman living among retirees with only a few friends. Every-one she has ever loved except for Eric is gone or almost gone, and she's sure she'll outlive Eric.

"Who's gonna take care of me?" she sobs.

There is a possibility.

Before John-Henry died, he froze some of his sperm, and as executor, she controls it. As she parks her car and goes into the house, she's deciding whether to share an idea that has been gain-ing momentum and fervor.

"The legacy deserves to go on," she says finally, crying harder than before.

John-Henry had asked her to keep the family alive. "You have to have a child," he told her.

The idea is strange, yet mechanically quite simple: she'd need a surrogate mother and a name. Back at home, all of it piles up, hurt stacked upon hurt, so what started as sadness about her mom became fear and desperation over the family coming to an end with her, and she's just dissolving in her high-ceilinged kitchen, coming apart. This is the vision greeting Eric when he walks in from work: his wife, her face red and puffy, sobbing so hard she's struggling to breathe. When she sees him, she stretches out her arms. Eric rushes toward her.

"Mom's having a bad day," she tells him. "She's tired. It makes me angry, of course. She's the only thing I have left."

She asks him again about creating and raising Ted Williams's grandchild.

"That's still something, right, on the table that you and I might do?" she asks, hopeful. "We might do that?"

Normally he's not keen on the idea.

"Yes," he says.

"We might?" she says, sounding vulnerable and shaky, like she's grasping for something beyond not only her reach but even her ability to name it. She's searching, searching for a father, for a purpose, for a child, searching for the chance to complete what her dad started in the last decade of his life. That's the hope and the promise of whatever life remains in John-Henry's sperm. Doctors told her there's enough genetic material for one chance at insemination, and as long as it remains frozen, some part of her brother, and her father, remains alive with it. She also has considered using her egg and Abel's sperm to create a child, going back and forth between the ideas. She's searching for a way to break the Williams cycle—either by letting it die with her or by being the first good parent in generations—and she's searching for something much more elusive too. She never saw her father's body, and nothing forced her to really accept his disappearance from her life. Every culture has deeply symbolic rituals for burying and mourning the dead. With Ted's remains in stasis—they didn't hold a memorial service, not even a small, private one—she hasn't moved past grief into acceptance and peace. With time, she's come to regret not having a funeral. She's searching for how to say good-bye, or maybe a way to move on, which often feels like the same thing.

Before Claudia drove me back to the airport, Abel quietly asked me to keep in touch because she didn't meet many new people and really struggled with good-byes. I left wondering what kind of life awaited her. Maybe she'd just find ways to exhaust herself, and find obsessions to occupy her mind, day after day, year after year, never breaking free of her father and never feeling as if she had honored his memory either. But something happened in the months after our first visit.

It started with her book, *Ted Williams: My Father.*

She stepped out of the shadows and did readings. The Red Sox hosted her in Boston, and a big crowd showed up, and people cried when she shared her memories, her joys, and her pain. One at a time, they said she'd shown them a side of Ted Williams they'd never known. She did an interview in the Fenway stands, sitting in the red seat marking the longest home run ever hit in the ballpark, off the bat of her dad. She got lost in thought, staring down at the tiny home plate, feeling a strange connection. She walked past the hotel where he lived, long ago turned to luxury condos. His presence seemed real. The people most affected by her book were the fans who idolized her dad, now going through the same struggles of aging and illness he had.

She got a letter from Jimmie Foxx's daughter.

"You are our voice," it said.

Seeing the joy she brought to the elderly, long her favorite group of people, reminded her of an old man she treated as a student nurse. He was difficult, so she tried talking to him about baseball.

"I love the Red Sox," he said.

"Me too," she replied.

"I was there at Fenway Park when Ted Williams hit his last home run," he said. "It was a bright, sunny day, and I was there."

"I was told it was a cold and overcast day," she said, then did something she never does. She told him she was Ted Williams's daughter. He beamed, and the next day, everything about him seemed different, and not just because he wore Red Sox gear head to toe. He smiled, and seemed lighter. It's the same look her father got when she'd care for him in the last years of his life. Those memories, and the reaction of the elderly readers, finally pointed her toward her long-sought purpose.

As part of her application and interview process at Duke—still a long shot, but her dad taught her to try to be the greatest—she said she wanted to specialize in gerontology. "It wasn't until I cared for my elderly father as his health declined," she wrote on her application, "that I discovered my true calling."

Now she just needed to get into a graduate program, do years of studying, and open her own nurse-practitioner's office. Every patient who walked through the door would get treated like Ted Williams. She didn't want to waste another moment. She felt time rushing away.

The last two weeks before finding out, she swam miles in the pool and pounded out sets in the gym. Finally an email from Duke arrived asking her to log on to its website for the school's decision.

She opened the link and started to read the letter.

"Congratulations," it began.

Claudia grinned when I walked back into her house the day after she was accepted to Duke. Standing around the kitchen, she and Eric told the story of what happened when she opened her letter. Eric rushed home and found her sitting at the computer, quiet and solemn, validated for perhaps the first time in her life. Soon she'll be studying online for a master's degree from one of the greatest universities in the world. Even in her moment of triumph, something worried her, a neurotic fear. "Do you think they accepted me because of Dad?" she asked. "Or do you think they accepted me because of me?"

Everyone who knew Ted Williams knows that his daughter's going to Duke would mean more to him than his home runs and war medals combined.

"Daddy would be so proud," she said.

"I think he knows," Eric replied.

The house felt different than before, desolation replaced by hope. A Louisville Slugger leaned in the same cabinet as Toothless the Dragon, the first bit of baseball memorabilia in the living room. The renovations on Ted's house are complete. She and Eric will move in soon. Once she gets her nurse-practitioner's office open and running, she is still planning to use John-Henry's sperm or her egg to create a baby. Ted's old study would make a perfect nursery. A tire swing already hangs from a thick branch of an oak tree, plenty of room to run and play in the shade. The child could start a new future for the Williams family, built on love, or become a casualty of the cycle that shaped Claudia's life, and her father's life before that. She's hoping for a boy.

DON VAN NATTA JR. AND
SETH WICKERSHAM

The Patriot Way

FROM ESPN: THE MAGAZINE

HIS BOSSES WERE FURIOUS. Roger Goodell knew it. So on
April 1, 2008, the NFL commissioner convened an emergency session of the league's spring meeting at The Breakers hotel in Palm
Beach, Florida. Attendance was limited to each team's owner and
head coach. A palpable anger and frustration had rumbled inside
club front offices since the opening Sunday of the 2007 season.
During the first half of the New England Patriots' game against
the New York Jets at Giants Stadium, a 26-year-old Patriots video
assistant named Matt Estrella had been caught on the sideline, illegally videotaping Jets coaches' defensive signals, beginning the
scandal known as Spygate.

Behind closed doors, Goodell addressed what he called "the
elephant in the room" and, according to sources at the meeting,
turned over the floor to Robert Kraft. Then 66, the billionaire Patriots owner stood and apologized for the damage his team had
done to the league and the public's confidence in pro football.
Kraft talked about the deep respect he had for his 31 fellow owners and their shared interest in protecting the NFL's shield. Witnesses would later say Kraft's remarks were heartfelt, his demeanor
chastened. For a moment, he seemed to well up.

Then the Patriots' coach, Bill Belichick, the cheating program's
mastermind, spoke. He said he had merely misinterpreted a league
rule, explaining that he thought it was legal to videotape opposing
teams' signals as long as the material wasn't used in real time. Few

in the room bought it. Belichick said he had made a mistake—"my mistake."

Now it was Goodell's turn. The league office lifer, then 49 years old, had been commissioner just 18 months, promoted, in part, because of Kraft's support. His audience wanted to know why he had managed his first crisis in a manner at once hasty and strangely secretive. Goodell had imposed a $500,000 fine on Belichick, a $250,000 fine on the team, and the loss of a first-round draft pick just four days after league security officials had caught the Patriots and before he'd even sent a team of investigators to Foxborough, Massachusetts. Those investigators hadn't come up empty: inside a room accessible only to Belichick and a few others, they found a library of scouting material containing videotapes of opponents' signals, with detailed notes matching signals to plays for many teams going back seven seasons. Among them were handwritten diagrams of the defensive signals of the Pittsburgh Steelers, including the notes used in the January 2002 AFC Championship Game won by the Patriots 24–17. Yet almost as quickly as the tapes and notes were found, they were destroyed, on Goodell's orders: league executives stomped the tapes into pieces and shredded the papers inside a Gillette Stadium conference room.

To many owners and coaches, the expediency of the NFL's investigation—and the Patriots' and Goodell's insistence that no games were tilted by the spying—seemed dubious. It reminded them of something they had seen before from the league and the Patriots: at least two teams had caught New England videotaping their coaches' signals in 2006, yet the league did nothing. Further, NFL competition committee members had, over the years, fielded numerous allegations about New England breaking an array of rules. Still nothing. Now the stakes had gotten much higher: Spygate's unanswered questions and destroyed evidence had managed to seize the attention of a hard-charging U.S. senator, Arlen Specter of Pennsylvania, who was threatening a congressional investigation. This would put everyone—players, coaches, owners, and the commissioner—under oath, a prospect that some in that room at The Breakers believed could threaten the foundation of the NFL.

Goodell tried to assuage his bosses: he ordered the destruction of the tapes and notes, he insisted, so they couldn't be exploited again. Many in the room didn't believe it. And some would con-

clude it was as if Goodell, Kraft, and Belichick had acted like partners, complicit in trying to sweep the scandal's details under the
rug while the rest of the league was left wondering how much glory
the Patriots' cheating had cost their teams. "Goodell didn't want
anybody to know that his gold franchise had won Super Bowls by
cheating," a senior executive whose team lost to the Patriots in a
Super Bowl now says. "If that gets out, that hurts your business."

Just before he finished speaking, Goodell looked his bosses in
the eye and, with dead certainty, said that from then on, cheaters
would be dealt with forcefully. He promised the owners that all 32
teams would be held to the same high standards expected of players. But many owners and coaches concluded he was really only
sending that message to one team: the New England Patriots.

Seven years later, Robert Kraft took the podium on the first day
of the Patriots' 2015 training camp and, with a mix of bitterness
and sadness, apologized to his team's fans. "I was wrong to put
my faith in the league," he said. It was a stunning statement from
the NFL owner who has been Roger Goodell's biggest booster and
defender.

Goodell had just upheld the four-game suspension he had lev-
eled in early May against quarterback Tom Brady for a new Patriots cheating scandal known as Deflategate. An NFL-commissioned
investigation, led by lawyer Ted Wells, after four months had concluded it "was more probable than not" that Brady had been "at
least generally aware" that the Patriots' footballs used in the AFC
Championship Game held this year had been deflated to air pressure levels below what the league allowed. Goodell deemed the
Patriots and Brady "guilty of conduct detrimental to the integrity
of, and public confidence in, the game of football," the league's
highest crime, and punished the franchise and its marquee player.

Kraft was convinced Brady was innocent, but he "reluctantly"
accepted the punishment, in large part because he was certain
Goodell would reduce, or eliminate, his quarterback's four-game
suspension, the way business is often done in the NFL. Kraft had
good reason to believe Goodell might honor a quid pro quo:
throughout Goodell's nightmare 2014 season of overturned player
discipline penalties, bumbling news conferences, and a lack of
candor, Kraft had publicly stood by the commissioner—even as
he privately signaled deep disappointment in Goodell's perfor-

mance and fury at the judgment of his top lieutenants, according to sources. After Goodell had upheld Brady's punishment, on the basis mainly of his failure to cooperate by destroying his cell phone, Kraft felt burned and betrayed.

Now the owner of the defending Super Bowl champions was publicly ripping the league. To anyone casually watching Deflategate, the civil war pitting Goodell against the Patriots and their star quarterback made no sense. Why were the league's premier franchise, led by a cherished team owner, and Brady, one of the NFL's greatest ambassadors, being smeared because a little air might have been let out of some footballs?

But league insiders knew that Deflategate didn't begin on the eve of the AFC Championship Game.

It began in 2007, with Spygate.

Interviews by *ESPN: The Magazine* and *Outside the Lines* with more than 90 league officials, owners, team executives, and coaches, current and former Patriots coaches, staffers, and players, and reviews of previously undisclosed private notes from key meetings, show that Spygate is the centerpiece of a long, secret history between Goodell's NFL, which declined comment for this story, and Kraft's Patriots. The diametrically opposed way the inquiries were managed by Goodell—and, more importantly, perceived by his bosses—reveals much about how and why NFL punishment is often dispensed. The widespread perception that Goodell gave the Patriots a break on Spygate, followed by the NFL's stonewalling of a potential congressional investigation into the matter, shaped owners' expectations of what needed to be done by 345 Park Avenue on Deflategate.

It was, one owner says, time for "a makeup call."

In August 2000, before a Patriots preseason game against the Tampa Bay Buccaneers, Jimmy Dee, the head of New England's video department, approached one of his charges, Matt Walsh, with a strange assignment: he wanted Walsh to film the Bucs' offensive and defensive signals, the arm-waving and hand-folding that team coaches use to communicate plays and formations to the men on the field. Walsh was 24 years old, a lifelong New Englander and Patriots fan. He was one of the few employees Belichick retained that season, his first as the team's coach. The practice of decoding signals was universal in football—a single stolen signal can change a game—with advance scouts jotting down notes, then matching the signal to the play. The Patriots created a novel spying system that made the decoding more dependable.

Walsh later told investigators that, at the time, he didn't know the NFL game operations manual forbade taping signals. He would later recall that even Dee seemed unsure of "what specifically it was that the coaches wanted me to film." Regardless, Walsh complied, standing on the sideline with a camera aimed at Tampa Bay's coaches. After the game, he gave the Beta tape to Dee.

Not coincidentally, the Bucs were also New England's opponent in the regular-season opener. A few days before the game, Walsh told Senate investigators, according to notes of the interview, a backup quarterback named John Friesz was summoned to Belichick's office. Offensive coordinator Charlie Weis and a professorial, quirky man named Ernie Adams were present. Adams was—and still is—a mystery in the Patriots' building, a socially awkward amateur historian of pro football and the Vietnam War who often wore the same red, hole-ridden Patriots sweater from the 1970s. He had a photographic memory, and Brady once said that Adams "knows more about professional football than anyone I ever met."

Adams's title was football research director, the only known person with that title in the NFL. He had made a fortune in the stock market in the 1980s, and the joke was that the only person in the building richer than Adams was Kraft. Belichick and Adams had been friends since 1970, when they were classmates at Phillips Academy, a New England prep school. Adams introduced himself to Belichick because he recognized his name from a little-known scouting book published in 1962 by his father, Steve Belichick.

When Bill Belichick became coach of the Browns in 1991, he hired Adams to be a consigliere of sorts. Owner Art Modell famously offered $10,000 to any employee who could tell him what Adams did. In short, in Cleveland and in New England, Adams did whatever he wanted—and whatever Belichick wanted: statistical analysis, scouting, and strategy. Years later, Walsh recalled to Senate investigators that Adams told old stories from the Browns about giving a video staffer an NFL Films shirt and assigning him to film the opponents' sideline huddles and grease boards from behind the bench. The shared view of Belichick and Adams, according to many who've worked with them, is this: the league is lazy and incompetent, so why not push every boundary? "You'd want Bill and Ernie doing your taxes," says a former Patriots assistant coach. "They would find all the loopholes, and then when the IRS would close them, they'd find more."

Days before the Tampa Bay game, in Belichick's office, Friesz was told that the Patriots had a tape of the Bucs' signals. He was instructed to memorize them, and during the game, to watch Bucs defensive coordinator Monte Kiffin and tell Weis the defensive play, which Weis would relay over the radio headset system to quarterback Drew Bledsoe. That Sunday against the Bucs, Walsh later told investigators, the Patriots played more no-huddle than usual, forcing Kiffin to signal in plays quickly, allowing Weis sufficient time to relay the information. Years later, some Patriots coaches would point to the score—a 21–16 Bucs win—as evidence of Spygate's ineffectiveness. But as Walsh later told investigators, Friesz, who did not respond to messages to comment for this story, told Walsh after the game that the Patriots knew 75 percent of the Bucs' defenses before the snap.

Now the Patriots realized that they were on to something, a schematic edge that could allow their best minds more control on the field. Taping from the sideline increased efficiency and minimized confusion. And so, as Walsh later told investigators, the system improved, becoming more streamlined—and more secretive. The quarterbacks were cut out of the process. The only people involved were a few coaches, the video staff, and, of course, Adams. Belichick, almost five years after being fired by the Browns and fully aware that this was his last best shot as a head coach, placed an innovative system of cheating in the hands of his most trusted friend.

As the Patriots became a dynasty and Belichick became the first coach to win three Super Bowls in four years, an entire system of covert videotaping was developed and a secret library created. "It got out of control," a former Patriots assistant coach says. Sources with knowledge of the system say an advance scout would attend the games of upcoming Patriots opponents and assemble a spreadsheet of all the signals and corresponding plays. The scout would give it to Adams, who would spend most of the week in his office with the door closed, matching the notes to the tapes filmed from the sideline. Files were created, organized by opponent and by coach. During games, Walsh later told investigators, the Patriots' videographers were told to look like media members, to tape over their team logos or turn their sweatshirt inside out, to wear credentials that said Patriots TV or Kraft Productions. The videographers also were provided with excuses for what to tell NFL security if asked what they were doing: tell them you're filming the quarterbacks. Or the kickers. Or footage for a team show.

The cameramen's assignments differed depending on the opponent. For instance, Walsh told investigators that against Indianapolis he was directed to take close-ups of the Colts' offensive signals, then of Peyton Manning's hand signals. Mostly, though, the tapes were of defensive signals. Each video sequence would usually include three shots: the down and distance, the signal, and, as an in-house joke, a tight shot of a cheerleader's top or skirt. The tape was then often edited, sources say, so that Adams's copy contained only the signals, in rapid fire, one after another. According to investigators, Walsh once asked Adams, "Are the tapes up to standards?"

"You're doing a good job," Adams said. "But make sure that you get everyone who's giving signals, even dummy signals."

As much as the Patriots tried to keep the circle of those who knew about the taping small, sometimes the team would add recently cut players from upcoming opponents and pay them only to help decipher signals, former Patriots staffers say. In 2005, for instance, they signed a defensive player from a team they were going to play in the upcoming season. Before that game, the player was led to a room where Adams was waiting. They closed the door, and Adams played a compilation tape that matched the signals to the plays from the player's former team, and asked how many were accurate. "He had about 50 percent of them right," the player says now.

During games, Adams sat in the coaches' box, with binoculars and notes of decoded signals, wearing a headset with a direct audio line to Belichick. Whenever Adams saw an opposing coach's signal he recognized, he'd say something like, "Watch for the two-deep blitz," and either that information was relayed to Brady or a play designed specifically to exploit the defense was called. A former Patriots employee who was directly involved in the taping system says "it helped our offense a lot," especially in divisional games in which there was a short amount of time between the first and second matchups, making it harder for opposing coaches to change signals.

Still, some of the coaches who were with the Patriots during the Spygate years debate the system's effectiveness. One coach who was in the booth with Adams says it didn't work because Adams was "horrible" and "never had the calls right." Another former coach says, "Ernie is the guy who you watch football with and says, 'It's going to be a run!' And it's a pass. 'It's going to be a pass!' And it's a run. 'It's going to be a run!' It's a run. 'I told you!'"

In fact, many former New England coaches and employees insist that the taping of signals wasn't even the most effective cheating method the Patriots deployed in that era. Several of them acknowledge that during pregame warm-ups, a low-level Patriots employee would sneak into the visiting locker room and steal the play sheet, listing the first 20 or so scripted calls for the opposing team's offense. (The practice became so notorious that some coaches put out fake play sheets for the Patriots to swipe.) Numerous former employees say the Patriots would have someone rummage through the visiting team hotel for playbooks or scouting reports. Walsh later told investigators that he was once instructed to remove the labels and erase tapes of a Patriots practice because the team had illegally used a player on injured reserve. At Gillette Stadium, the scrambling and jamming of the opponents' coach-to-quarterback radio line—"small s—" that many teams do, according to a former Pats assistant coach—occurred so often that one team asked a league official to sit in the coaches' box during the game and wait for it to happen. Sure enough, on a key third down, the headset went out.

But the truth is, only one man truly knows how much Spygate, or any other suspect method, affected games: Belichick.

He had spent his entire adult life in professional football, trying to master a game no coach could control. Since he entered the league in 1975, Belichick had witnessed the dark side of each decade's dynasties, airbrushed away by time and lore. Football's tradition of cheating through espionage goes back to its earliest days, pioneered by legends such as George Halas. And so when it came to certain tactics—especially recording signals of a coach "in front of 80,000 people," Belichick would later say, a practice that he claimed other teams did and that former Cowboys coach Jimmy

Johnson once confessed to trying himself—Belichick considered it fair game. He could call an offensive or defensive play whenever he wanted, based on a suggestion from Adams or not, and never have to explain why to anyone. "Remember, so much of this is the head coach's prerogative," says a former Patriots assistant coach. (Belichick, Adams, and Dee declined to comment for this story through the Patriots, who made several officials available to talk but not others.)

A former member of the NFL competition committee says the committee spent much of 2001 to 2006 "discussing ways in which the Patriots cheated," even if nothing could be proved. It reached a level of paranoia in which conspiracy theories ran wild and nothing—the notion of bugging locker rooms or of Brady having a second frequency in his helmet to help decipher the defense—was out of the realm of possibility. There were regular rumors that the Patriots had taped the Rams' walk-through practice before Super Bowl XXXVI in February 2002, one of the greatest upsets in NFL history, a game won by the Patriots 20–17 on a last-second Adam Vinatieri field goal. The rumors and speculation reached a fever pitch in 2006. Before the season, a rule was proposed to allow radio communications to one defensive player on the field, as was already allowed for quarterbacks. If it had passed, defensive signals would have been unnecessary. But it failed. In 2007, the proposal failed once again, this time by two votes, with Belichick voting against it. (The rule change passed in 2008 after Spygate broke, with Belichick voting for it.) The allegations against the Patriots prompted NFL executive vice president of football operations Ray Anderson to send a letter to all 32 team owners, general managers, and head coaches on September 6, 2006, reminding them that "videotaping of any type, including but not limited to taping of an opponent's offensive or defensive signals, is prohibited from the sidelines."

But the Patriots kept doing it. In November 2006, Green Bay Packers security officials caught Matt Estrella shooting unauthorized footage at Lambeau Field. When asked what he was doing, according to notes from the Senate investigation of Spygate that had not previously been disclosed, Estrella said he was with Kraft Productions and was taping panoramic shots of the stadium. He was removed by Packers security. That same year, according to former Colts GM Bill Polian, who served for years on the competition committee and is now an analyst for ESPN, several teams complained that the Patriots had videotaped signals of their coaches. And so the Patriots—and the rest of the NFL—were warned again, in writing, before the 2007 season, sources say.

Looking back on it, several former Patriots coaches insist that spying helped them most against less sophisticated teams—the Dolphins and Bills chief among them—whose coaches didn't bother changing their signals. Even when they had the perfect play teed up, sometimes the system would fail, owing to human error. Several opposing coaches now say they wish they had messed with Belichick's head the way he had messed with theirs. You want to tape signals? Fine. We'll have three guys signaling plays and disguise it so much that Ernie Adams has to waste an entire day trying to decode them, then change them all when we play.

At the time, though, only one head coach actually did: Eric Mangini.

On September 9, 2007, in the first game of the season, Estrella aimed a video camera at the New York Jets' sideline, unaware he was the target of a sting operation. Mangini was entering his second year as the Jets' coach. Belichick had practically invented Mangini: In January 1995, he saw potential in a 24-year-old Browns PR intern and moved the fellow Wesleyan alum into football operations. Belichick hired Mangini to be his assistant when he coached under head coach Bill Parcells for the Jets in the late '90s, and soon became a father figure of sorts to Mangini, whose father had died when he was young. Then, in 2000, Belichick brought Mangini to New England as defensive backs coach, promoting him to defensive coordinator in 2005.

In 2006, Jets GM Mike Tannenbaum, one of Mangini's best friends and another Belichick charge, wanted to hire the 34-year-old Mangini as head coach. Mangini took the job over the objections of Belichick, who hated the Jets so much that he barely mentioned his tenure there in his official Patriots bio. Belichick revoked Mangini's key card access and didn't allow him to pack up his office. The tension was raised later that year, when the Patriots accused the Jets of tampering and the Jets countered with an accusation that the Patriots had circumvented the salary cap. Mangini, who is currently the defensive coordinator for the San Francisco 49ers and who declined to comment for this story, knew the Patriots inside and out and would tweak his former boss by using his tricks against him, like having a quarterback punt on third-and-long at midfield, one of Belichick's favorite moves.

Then there was the videotaping. Mangini knew the Patriots did it, so he would have three Jets coaches signal in plays: one coach's signal would alert the players to which coach was actually signaling in the play. Still, Mangini saw it as a sign of disrespect that Belichick taped their signals—"He's pissing in my face," he told a confidant—and wanted it to end. Before the 2007 opener, sources say, he warned various Patriots staffers, "We know you do this. Don't do it in our house." Tannenbaum, who declined comment, told team security to remove any unauthorized cameramen on the field.

During the first half, Jets security monitored Estrella, who held a camera and wore a polo shirt with a taped-over Patriots logo under a red media vest that said: NFL PHOTOGRAPHER 138. With the backing of Jets owner Woody Johnson and Tannenbaum, Jets security alerted NFL security, a step Mangini acknowledged publicly later that he never wanted. Shortly before halftime, security encircled and then confronted Estrella. He said he was with "Kraft Productions." They took him into a small room off the stadium's tunnel, confiscated his camera and tape, and made him wait. He was sweating. Someone gave Estrella water, and he was shaking so severely that he spilled it. "He was s—ting a brick," a source says.

On Monday morning, Estrella's camera and the spy tape were at NFL headquarters on Park Avenue.

Considering how the NFL currently conducts its investigations or reviews of its investigations—outsourcing the legwork, allowing it to take months to complete, making the findings public, and almost always losing if the inevitable appeal is heard by an independent arbitrator—it's striking that the Spygate inquiry lasted only a little over a week, and that Goodell's findings stuck. The day after the game, September 10, the Jets sent a letter to the Patriots asking them to preserve any evidence because they had sent an official grievance about the Patriots' spying to the NFL, says Robyn Glaser, vice president of the Kraft Group and club counsel of the Patriots. Kraft told Belichick to tell the truth and cooperate with the investigation, and the coach waived the opportunity to have a hearing. On September 12, Goodell spoke on the phone with Belichick for 30 minutes, sources say. Belichick explained that he had misinterpreted a rule, which the commissioner did not believe to be true, sources say, and that he had been engaged in the practice of taping signals for "some time." The coach explained that "at the most, he might gain a little intelligence," Goodell would later recall, according to notes. Belichick didn't volunteer the total number of games at which the Patriots had recorded signals, sources say, and the commissioner didn't ask. "Goodell didn't want to know how many games were taped," another source with firsthand knowledge of the investigation says, "and Belichick didn't want to tell him."

The next day, the league announced its historic punishment against the Patriots, including an NFL maximum fine for Belichick. Goodell and league executives hoped Spygate would be over.

But instead it became an obsession around the league and with many fans. When Estrella's confiscated tape was leaked to Fox's Jay Glazer a week after Estrella was caught, the blowback was so great that the league dispatched three of its executives—general counsel Jeff Pash, Anderson, and VP of football operations Ron Hill—to Foxborough on September 18.

What happened next has never been made public: The league officials interviewed Belichick, Adams, and Dee, says Glaser, the Patriots' club counsel. Once again, nobody asked how many games had been recorded or attempted to determine whether a game was ever swayed by the spying, sources say. The Patriots staffers insisted that the spying had a limited impact on games. Then the Patriots told the league officials they possessed eight tapes containing game footage along with a half-inch-thick stack of notes of signals and other scouting information belonging to Adams, Glaser says. The league officials watched portions of the tapes. Goodell was contacted, and he ordered the tapes and notes to be destroyed, but the Patriots didn't want any of it to leave the building, arguing that some of it was obtained legally and thus was proprietary. So in a stadium conference room, Pash and the other NFL executives stomped the videotapes into small pieces and fed Adams's notes into a shredder, Glaser says. She recalls picking up the shards of plastic from the smashed Beta tapes off the floor and throwing them away.

The Patriots turned over what they turned over, and the NFL accepted it. Sources with knowledge of the investigation insist that the Patriots were "borderline noncompliant." And a former high-level Patriots employee agrees, saying, "The way the Patriots tried to approach it, they tried to cover up everything," although he refused to specify how. Glaser adamantly denies that assertion, saying all the Patriots' evidence of stolen signals was turned over to the league that day. On September 20, Glaser says, the team signed a certification letter promising the league that the only evidence of the videotaping of illegal signals had been destroyed two days earlier and that no other tapes or notes of stolen signals were in the team's possession. The letter does not detail the games that were recorded or itemize the notes that were shredded.

And that was it. The inquiry was over, with only Belichick and Adams knowing the true scope of the taping. (After the season, Belichick would acknowledge the Patriots taped a "significant number" of games, and according to documents and sources, they recorded signals in at least 40 games during the Spygate era.) The quick resolution mollified some owners and executives, who say they admired the speed—and limited transparency—in which Goodell carried out the investigation. "This is the way things should be done . . . the way they were done under Pete Rozelle and Paul Tagliabue," a former executive now says. "Keep the dirty laundry in the family."

But other owners, coaches, team executives, and players were outraged by how little the league investigated what the Patriots' cheating had accomplished in games. The NFL refused to volunteer information—teams that had been videotaped were not officially notified by the league office, sources say—and some executives were told that the tapes were burned in a dumpster, not crushed into pieces in a conference room. The NFL's explanation of why it was destroyed—"So that our clubs would know they no longer exist and cannot be used by anyone," the league said at the time—only made it worse for those who were critical. "I wish the evidence had not been destroyed because at least we would know what had been done," Polian says. "Lack of specificity just leads to speculation, and that serves no one's purpose—the Patriots included."

The view around much of the league was that Goodell had done a major favor for Kraft, one of his closest confidants who had extended critical support when he became the commissioner the previous summer. Kraft is a member of the NFL's three-person compensation committee, which each year determines Goodell's salary and bonuses—$35 million in 2013, and nearly $44.2 million in 2012. "It felt like this enormous break was given to the Patriots," a former exec says. They were also angry at Belichick —partly, some admit, out of jealousy for his success but also because of the widespread rumors that he was always pushing the envelope. The narrative that paralleled the Patriots' rise—a team mostly void of superstars, built not to blow out opponents but to win the game's handful of decisive plays—only increased rivals' suspicions. After all, the Patriots had won three Super Bowls by a total of nine points. Although Belichick admitted to Kraft that the taping had helped them only 1 percent of the time ("Then you're a real schmuck," Kraft told him), the spying very well could have affected a game, opponents say. "Why would they go to such great lengths for so long to do it and hide it if it didn't work?" a long-time former executive says. "It made no sense."

The Patriots' primary victims saw Spygate, and other videotaping rumors, as confirmation that they had been cheated out of a Super Bowl—even though they lacked proof. The Panthers now believe that their practices had been taped by the Patriots before Super Bowl XXXVIII in 2004. "Our players came in after that first half and said it was like [the Patriots] were in our huddle," a Panthers source says. During halftime—New England led 14–10—Carolina's offensive coordinator, Dan Henning, changed game plans because of worries the Patriots had too close a read on Carolina's schemes. And, in the second half, the Panthers moved the ball at will before losing 32–29 on a last-second field goal. "Do I have any tape to prove they cheated?" this source says. "No. But I'm convinced they did it."

No player was more resolute that Spygate had affected games than Hines Ward, the Steelers' All-Pro wide receiver. Ward told reporters that Patriots inside information about Steelers play calling helped New England upset Pittsburgh 24–17 in the January 2002 AFC Championship Game. "Oh, they knew," Ward, now an NBC analyst who didn't return messages for this story, said after Spygate broke. "They were calling our stuff out. They knew a lot of our calls. There's no question some of their players were calling out some of our stuff."

Some of the Steelers' defensive coaches remain convinced that a deep touchdown pass from Brady to Deion Branch in the January 2005 AFC Championship Game, which was won by the Patriots 41–27, came from stolen signals because Pittsburgh hadn't changed its signals all year, sources say, and the two teams had played a game in the regular season that Walsh told investigators he believes was taped. "They knew the signals, so they knew when it went in what the coverage was and how to attack it," says a former Steelers coach. "I've had a couple of guys on my teams from New England, and they've told me those things."

When Spygate broke, some of the Eagles now believed they had an answer for a question that had vexed them since they lost to the Patriots 24–21 in Super Bowl XXXIX: how did New England seem completely prepared for the rarely used dime defense the Eagles deployed in the second quarter, scoring touchdowns on three of four drives? The Eagles suspected that either practices were filmed or a playbook was stolen. "To this day, some believe that we were robbed by the Patriots not playing by the rules . . . and knowing our game plan," a former Eagles football operations staffer says.

It didn't matter that the Patriots went 18–1 in 2007. Or that they would average more wins a season after Spygate than before. Or that Belichick would come to be universally recognized as his generation's greatest coach. Or that many with the Patriots remain mystified at the notion that a historic penalty was somehow perceived to be lenient. The Patriots were forever branded as cheaters — an asterisk, in the view of many fans, forever affixed to their wins. The NFL was all too aware of the damage baseball had suffered because of the steroids scandal, its biggest stars and most cherished records tarnished. After Spygate made headlines, rumors that had existed for years around the NFL that the Patriots had cheated in the Super Bowl that had propelled their run, against the Rams, were beginning to boil to the surface, threatening everything. "I don't think fans really want to know this — they just want to watch football," the Panthers source says. "But if you tell them that the games aren't on the level, they'll care. Boy, will they care."

In January 2008, in the middle of the playoffs, Arlen Specter, the senior United States senator from Pennsylvania, bumped into Carl Hulse, a *New York Times* congressional reporter, on Capitol Hill.

Hulse asked Specter which team he thought would win the Super Bowl, which would eventually feature the New York Giants and the undefeated Patriots.

"It all depends," Specter jokingly replied, "if there is cheating involved."

Specter told Hulse he was troubled by the NFL's lightning-quick investigation and by the destruction of the tapes and the notes. Twice during the previous few months, he had written letters to Goodell seeking additional information about Spygate. Twice the commissioner had not replied.

That disclosure led to a story in the *Times*, putting Spygate, and all of its unanswered questions, front and center two days before the Super Bowl. Only then did Goodell reply to Specter. Unsatisfied, Specter told the *Times*, "The American people are entitled to be sure about the integrity of the game." Even more intriguing to Specter, there were fresh reports that Matt Walsh, working as an assistant golf pro in Hawaii at the time, had not been interviewed by the NFL the previous September. The reports suggested Walsh had additional information—and possessed videotapes—of the Patriots' spying.

Specter was at the time the ranking Republican on the Senate Judiciary Committee. A former Philadelphia district attorney, he had cut his investigative teeth as a lawyer for the Warren Commission, and two decades earlier he had gone after the NFL for its antitrust exemption. Specter was now 77 years old and undergoing chemotherapy to treat non-Hodgkin's lymphoma, the complications from which would claim his life in October 2012. One of his biggest political patrons was Comcast, the Philadelphia-based cable TV giant that was at the time locked in a dispute with the league over fees for carrying the NFL Network, a connection the senator vehemently denied had motivated his interest in Spygate.

Instead, Specter said he was motivated by curiosity about Goodell's own statements on the matter, according to hundreds of previously undisclosed papers belonging to Specter and interviews with former aides and others who spoke with him at the time. At his pre–Super Bowl news conference on February 1, 2008, Goodell insisted the Patriots' taping was "quite limited" and "not something done on a widespread basis," contradicting what Belichick had told him. Goodell was asked how many tapes the league had reviewed, and destroyed, the previous September. "I believe there were six tapes," the commissioner replied, "and I believe some were from the preseason in 2007, and the rest were primarily in the late 2006 season."

The Patriots had spied far more often than that, of course, but Specter didn't know it at the time. All he knew was that he didn't buy Goodell's explanation for destroying the tapes—that he didn't want to create an uneven playing field. "You couldn't sell that in kindergarten," Specter said.

Specter didn't have subpoena power, so he played hardball with the league, threatening to pursue legislation that would cancel its antitrust exemption. And so at 3:00 p.m. on Wednesday, February 13, 2008—10 days after the Giants upset the previously undefeated Patriots 17–14 in the Super Bowl—Goodell and Pash arrived at Specter's office, Room 711 of the Senate Hart Building on Capitol Hill. During the one-hour, 40-minute interview, the new details of which are revealed in Specter's papers and in interviews with key aides, Goodell was supremely confident, "cool as a cucumber," stuck to his talking points, and apologized for nothing, recalls a senior aide to Specter. Pash, who according to a source later that spring would offer to resign over how the Spygate investigation was handled, spent the interview "sweating, squirming."

Repeating what he had proclaimed publicly, Goodell assured Specter the destroyed tapes went back only to the 2006 season. But then he confessed something new: that the Patriots began their taping operation in 2000 and the destroyed notes were for games as early as 2002, "overwhelmingly for AFC East rivals," contradicting an assertion he made just two weeks earlier in public. The commissioner told Specter that among the destroyed notes were the Patriots' detailed diagrams of the Steelers' defensive signals from several games, including the January 2002 AFC Championship Game—in which Ward later alleged that the Patriots called "our stuff out."

When Specter pressed Goodell on the speed of the investigation and his decision to destroy evidence, Goodell became "defensive" and had "the overtone of something to hide" according to notes taken by Danny Fisher, a counsel on Senator Specter's Judiciary Committee staff and the lead investigator on the Spygate inquiry.

"No valid reason to destroy," Specter wrote in his own notes, which are archived as the Senator Arlen Specter Papers at the University of Pittsburgh.

Goodell assured Specter that "most teams do not believe there is an advantage" from the taping, a comment contradicted by the outraged public and private remarks of many players and coaches, then and now. "Even if Belichick figured out the signals," Goodell insisted, "there is not sufficient time to call in the play."

The senator seethed that Goodell seemed completely uninterested in whether a single game had been compromised. He asked Goodell whether the spying might have tipped the Patriots' Super Bowl win against the senator's favorite team, the Eagles. Goodell said that he had spoken with Eagles owner Jeffrey Lurie and then–head coach Andy Reid and that "both said the outcome of the [February] 2005 Super Bowl was legitimate," an assertion contradicted by the private feelings of many senior members of the team.

Then Specter moved to the most damning allegation still unresolved at the time: that the Patriots had taped the Rams' pre–Super Bowl walk-through.

The commissioner acknowledged that he first "got wind" of the widespread rumor the previous September, something he had not said publicly. But Goodell told Specter the NFL had found no hard evidence that New England had taped the walk-through, saying that the league interviewed the video staffs of the Patriots and the Rams. "Each said no taping went on, and if it had, the Rams' video staff surely would have reported it," the notes show.

After the interview, Specter was even more convinced that Goodell had neglected to look hard enough for the truth. And so he decided to investigate the things the NFL had chosen to ignore. "The league's explanations just didn't add up, and the senator's prosecutorial instincts wouldn't allow him to let it go," Fisher says.

After the meeting with Specter, Goodell told reporters he had no regrets about his decision to destroy the evidence.

"I think it was the right thing to do," he said. "I have nothing to hide."

Within days, Specter concluded that the NFL, the Patriots, and senior league officials were very much hiding from him. His calls and emails to 25 people from the Patriots, members of the competition committee, and other teams went unanswered; lawyers from white-shoe Manhattan law firms, including one representing the Patriots' videographers, declined to make their clients available for questioning. (The senator was able to reach one former Patriots scout, who told him to "keep digging.") In his 2012 book, *Life Among the Cannibals,* Specter wrote that a powerful friend—he wouldn't name the person—told him that if he "laid off the Patriots," there could be a lot of money for him in Palm Beach. Specter told the friend, "I couldn't care less."

So Specter turned to the one person who appeared willing to talk: Matt Walsh.

Since the Patriots had lost to the Giants in the Super Bowl, Walsh had emerged as a reluctant whistleblower in media stories. He had not been interviewed by the NFL and had kept eight previously undisclosed spying tapes and other material from his days in New England; he was fired in 2003 for performance issues. Walsh hinted that the cheating was more widespread than anyone knew—and, perhaps, that he possessed proof that the Patriots had taped the Rams' walk-through.

On May 13, 2008, after signing an indemnification agreement with the NFL, Walsh and his lawyer met for three hours and 15 minutes at league headquarters with Goodell, Pash, outside NFL lawyer Gregg Levy, Patriots lawyer Dan Goldberg, and Milt Ahlerich, the league's director of security. A source in the meeting says that Ahlerich asked the majority of the questions; Goodell was mostly silent. Afterward, Goodell told reporters that the information provided by Walsh was "consistent with what we disciplined the Patriots for last fall" and that he "was not aware" of a taped Rams walk-through and "does not know of anybody who says there is a tape." Hoping to end the matter forever, Goodell added that unless some new piece of information emerged, the league's interest in Spygate was closed.

That afternoon, Walsh and his lawyer, Michael N. Levy, flew to Washington and met with Specter and his staff for more than three hours. Walsh, who along with Levy declined to comment for this story, covered many topics; among them, that the public didn't know the great lengths that video assistants were told to use to cover up the videotaping of signals. Belichick had insisted that it was done openly, with nothing to hide.

"Were you surprised that Belichick said he had misinterpreted the rules?" Specter asked.

"Yes," Walsh said. "I was surprised that Belichick would think that because of the culture of sneakiness."

Walsh told Specter that the taping continued in the years after he left the team, by Steve Scarnecchia, his successor as video assistant, whom Walsh claimed to see taping opposing coaches' signals at Gillette Stadium from 2003 to 2005. Specter asked whether he had told Goodell about it. "No," Walsh said. "Goodell didn't ask me about that."

Then Specter turned to the alleged videotaping of the Rams' walk-through. Walsh confessed that after the Patriots' team picture, he and at least three other team videographers lingered around the Louisiana Superdome, setting up cameras for the game. Suddenly, the Rams arrived and started their walk-through. The three videographers, in full Patriots apparel, hung around, on the field and in the stands, for 30 minutes. Nobody said anything. Walsh said he observed star Rams running back Marshall Faulk line up in an unusual position: as a kickoff returner. That night, Walsh reported what he had seen to Patriots assistant coach Brian Daboll, who asked an array of questions about the Rams' formations. Walsh said that Daboll, who declined through the Patriots to comment for this story, drew a series of diagrams—an account Daboll later denied to league investigators.

Faulk had returned only one kickoff in his career before the Super Bowl. Sure enough, in the second quarter, he lined up deep. The Patriots were ready: Vinatieri kicked it into a corner, leading Faulk out of bounds after gaining one yard.

During the walk-through, the Rams had also practiced some of their newly designed red zone plays. When they ran the same plays late in the Super Bowl's fourth quarter, the Patriots' defense was in position on nearly every down. On one new play, quarterback Kurt Warner rolled to his right and turned to throw to Faulk in the flat, where three Patriots defenders were waiting. On the sideline, Rams coach Mike Martz was stunned. He was famous for his imaginative, unpredictable plays, and now it was as if the Patriots knew what was coming on plays that had never been run before. The Patriots' game plan had called for a defender to hit Faulk on every down, as a means of eliminating him, but one coach who worked with an assistant on that 2001 Patriots team says that the ex-Pats assistant coach once bragged that New England knew exactly what the Rams would call in the red zone. "He'd say, 'A little birdie told us,'" the coach says now.

In the meeting in Specter's office, the senator asked Walsh: "Were there any live electronics during the walk-through?"

"It's certainly possible," Walsh said. "But I have no evidence."

In the coming years, the Patriots would become baffled by those persistent rumors, which were mostly fueled by a pre–Super Bowl 2008 *Boston Herald* report—later retracted—that a team videographer had taped it. Some media outlets—including ESPN—have inadvertently repeated it as fact. According to Patriots spokesman Stacey James, "The New England Patriots have never filmed or recorded another team's practice or walk-through . . . Clearly the damage has been irreparable . . . It is disappointing that some choose to believe in myths, conjecture and rumors rather than give credit to Coach Belichick, his staff and the players."

After the Walsh interview, Specter again accused Goodell of conducting a "fatally flawed" investigation designed not to determine whether the taping affected a game. He complained to aides that the NFL had never publicly identified the "more than 50 people" in 11 days whom Goodell had claimed the league had interviewed. And Fisher says that Specter felt "stonewalled" by everyone connected to the NFL. And so Specter called for an independent investigation of Spygate, modeled after the inquiry by former Senator George Mitchell of the rampant use of steroids in major league baseball, or a transparent investigation led by a committee of Congress. Asked whether he was willing to say the NFL covered up, Specter hesitated. "No," he said. "There was just an enormous amount of haste."

But in his handwritten notes the day before, beneath Matt Walsh's name, Specter jotted the phrase, "Cover-up."

On the exact day that Specter called for an investigation, Goodell left a voice-mail message on Mike Martz's cell phone. The Super Bowl against the Patriots had derailed Martz's career as much as it made Belichick's. Martz's offense, dubbed the Greatest Show on Turf in 1999, was never the same, and in 2006, he was fired as the Rams' coach. After bouncing around the league, he was then the 49ers' offensive coordinator. Like a number of former Rams —especially Faulk and Warner, who now both work for the NFL

Network—Martz was deeply suspicious of whether the Patriots had videotaped the walk-through or his team's practices before the Super Bowl, even though he believes that the Rams' three turnovers were the main factors in the defeat.

Martz says now that he returned Goodell's call from the 49ers' practice field. During a five-minute conversation, Martz recalls that the commissioner sounded panicked about Specter's calls for a wider investigation. Martz also recalls that Goodell asked him to write a statement, saying that he was satisfied with the NFL's Spygate investigation and was certain the Patriots had not cheated and asking everyone to move on—like leaders of the Steelers and Eagles had done.

"He told me, 'The league doesn't need this. We're asking you to come out with a couple lines exonerating us and saying we did our due diligence,'" says Martz, now 64 years old and out of coaching, during a July interview at his summer cabin in the Idaho mountains.

A congressional inquiry that would put league officials under oath had to be avoided, Martz recalls Goodell telling him. "If it ever got to an investigation, it would be terrible for the league," Goodell said.

Martz says he still had more questions, but he agreed that a congressional investigation "could kill the league." So in the end, Martz got in line. He wrote the statement that evening, and it was released the next day, reading in part that he was "very confident there was no impropriety" and that it was "time to put this behind us."

Shown a copy of his statement this past July, Martz was stunned to read several sentences about Walsh that he says he's certain he did not write. "It shocked me," he says. "It appears embellished quite a bit—some lines I know I didn't write. Who changed it? I don't know."

Since Spygate broke, Martz says he has continued to hear things about the run-up to that Super Bowl. Goodell "told me to take him at his word," he says. "It was hard to swallow because I always felt something happened but I didn't know what it was and I couldn't prove it anyway. Even to this day, I think something happened."

No matter how angry owners and coaches were over Goodell's handling of Spygate, they were unified in their view that a congressional investigation posed a threat to the game itself. On June

5, 2008, Specter delivered a lengthy speech on the Senate floor, blasting the NFL's investigation, destruction of evidence, and lack of transparency. "The overwhelming evidence flatly contradicts Commissioner Goodell's assertion that there was little or no effect on the outcome of the game," he said. Once more, Specter called for "an objective, thorough, transparent investigation" of Spygate. But he knew then, his aides now say, that such an investigation was never going to happen.

The NFL had won. Barely.

Goodell moved on immediately—the same day as Specter's floor statement, actually—introducing a mandatory "Policy on Integrity of the Game & Enforcement of Competitive Rules" to be signed by owners, team presidents, general managers, and head coaches after each season, swearing they had "complied with all League competitive policies." The first thick paragraph detailing prohibited acts reads like a litany of Spygate-era acts and accusations, including "unauthorized videotaping on game day or of practices, meetings or other organized team activities" and the barring of "unauthorized entry into locker rooms, coaches' booths, meeting rooms or other private areas." At the same time, the league also relaxed its investigative standard of proof to the "preponderance of the evidence," making findings of guilt easier, and required the signees to cooperate with NFL investigations.

But Spygate's damage went far beyond rule changes and new disciplinary procedures. Belichick's reputation was so tarnished that he worried that Spygate would come up during his Hall of Fame consideration, people who know him say. Goodell was now suspect in many of his bosses' eyes after making the first of several conduct decisions that would ultimately draw unwanted criticism. And Kraft no longer owned what many considered to be the model sports franchise. Kraft would later say that he knew that Spygate wasn't "personal," that Goodell had done "what he thought was right for the league . . . even if his judgment isn't pure."

And yet, despite Spygate, Kraft's influence in the league grew, with Goodell and with business matters. During labor negotiations in 2011, Kraft emerged as the reasoned, respected voice among those who helped bridge the wide gulf between the players' union and the owners. As chairman of the league's broadcast committee, Kraft took the lead to hammer out long-term, record-shattering agreements with NBC, Fox, CBS, and ESPN. To some executives, Kraft was considered "the assistant commissioner," a nickname that a source says has always embarrassed him because it's not how he wants to be perceived. He was always as quick to praise and defend Goodell in public as he was during closed-door meetings.

Last autumn, though, Goodell suffered through his worst season as commissioner, one in which the publicity about the NFL and Goodell's leadership was almost uniformly negative for months. His mishandling of the Ray Rice domestic violence discipline caused commentators, including some at ESPN, to call for his firing. Some owners felt Goodell's handling was cause for his dismissal or, at the very least, his contract not being renewed beyond March 2019. One owner said, "We're paying this guy $45 million for this s—?"

Publicly, Kraft continued his role as Goodell's chief supporter, saying that the commissioner had been "excellent" on Rice. But sources say Kraft became deeply concerned last fall by the performance of Goodell. A close friend who saw him that October recalls Kraft saying, "Roger's been very disappointing in the way he has handled this. And I'm not alone in feeling like that." Kraft was also furious at the league's executives, from Pash to its public relations staff, and said they had failed to help Goodell. "Roger's people don't have a f—ing clue as to what they are doing," Kraft told his friend.

Another team's senior executive who frequently talks with owners says the owners last autumn were "really split. There are people who feel [Goodell] has made them a lot of money and they shouldn't do anything. Others think, 'He has embarrassed the league and if we had a better commissioner, we'd be making more money.'" All the negative headlines certainly haven't affected the league's bottom line—total revenues and TV ratings continue to shatter records. The NFL's annual revenue, racing toward $15 billion, is the most important metric that Goodell's bosses use to judge his performance, several owners and executives say.

Shortly before this past Thanksgiving, as the league awaited a former federal judge's decision on the appropriateness of the indefinite suspension Goodell had given to Rice, Kraft attended a fund-raising dinner and, reflecting a sense among some owners, confided to a friend, "Roger is on very thin ice." At the same time, according to another source, Kraft was still rallying support for the commissioner despite his increasing disappointments. Asked when the owners would likely discuss Goodell's performance, Kraft replied, "We're going to wait until after the Super Bowl."

And then, on the eve of the AFC Championship Game, as Kraft hosted Goodell at a dinner party at his Brookline, Massachusetts, estate, a league official got a tip from the Colts about the Patriots' use of deflated footballs.

Even the language of the tip seemed to echo suspicions shaped by the Spygate era. Ryan Grigson, the Colts' general manager, forwarded to the league office an emailed accusation made by Colts equipment manager Sean Sullivan: "It is well known around the league that after the Patriots game balls are checked by the officials and brought out for game usage, the ball boys for the Patriots will let out some air with a ball needle because their quarterback likes a smaller football so he can grip it better."

From the beginning, though, Goodell managed Deflategate in the opposite way he tried to dispose of Spygate. He announced a lengthy investigation and, in solidarity with many owners, outsourced it to Wells, whose law firm had defended the NFL during the mammoth concussions litigation. In an inquiry lasting four months and costing at least $5 million, according to sources, Ted Wells and his team conducted 66 interviews with Patriots staffers and league officials. Wells, who declined to comment, also plumbed cell-phone records and text messages.

A 243-page report was made public that applied the league's evidentiary standards—relaxed after Spygate—against Brady, while Belichick, who had professed no knowledge of the air pressure of his team's footballs and said this past January that the Patriots "try to do everything right," was absolved of any wrongdoing. Finally, Goodell and Troy Vincent, executive vice president of football operations, waited until the conclusion of the investigation before awarding punishment, rather than the other way around. Another legacy of Spygate—consequences for failing to cooperate with a league investigation—was used against the Patriots and, ultimately, Brady. Goodell upheld Brady's four-game suspension because the quarterback had asked an assistant to dispose of his cell phone before his March interview with Wells. That, in fact, was the only notable similarity between the two investigations: the order to destroy evidence.

Sources say that the Patriots privately viewed it all as a witch hunt, endorsed by owners resentful of New England's success and a commissioner who deferred too much authority to Pash and Vincent. Patriots executives were furious that a January 19 letter they received from NFL executive David Gardi contained two critical facts—details the league used as the basis for its investigation—that were later proved false: that during a surprise inspection at halftime of the AFC Championship Game one of New England's footballs tested far below the legal weight limit, at 10.1 psi, and that all of the Colts' balls were inflated to the permitted range. A source close to Brady views the targeting of him as resentment and retribution by opposing teams: "Tom has won 77 percent of his games—in a league that is designed for parity, that's a no-no."

But to the many owners who saw the Patriots as longtime cheaters, it really didn't matter that Goodell appeared eager, perhaps overeager, to show the rest of the NFL that he had learned the lessons of Spygate. One team owner acknowledges that for years there was a "jealous . . . hater" relationship among many owners with Kraft, the residue of Spygate. "It's not surprising that there's a makeup call," one team owner says. Another longtime executive says a number of owners wanted Goodell to "go hard on this one."

Kraft felt it firsthand in May. He had publicly threatened legal action against the NFL but then privately decided against it. Not long after arriving in San Francisco for the league's spring meeting, Kraft sensed that many owners wouldn't have stood with him anyway, sources say. They backed Goodell.

"The one that stunned him the most—the one that really rocked him—was John Mara," says a close friend of Kraft's. The Giants' president and CEO is a quiet, deeply respected owner whom Goodell often leans on for counsel. Mara had signaled to Kraft, "It's not there. We're not there with you on this. Something has to happen. The commissioner has to do his job." Mara insists that this account "is not true," but the next day at the spring meeting, Kraft announced he'd grudgingly accept the league's punishment against his team, proclaiming it was best for the league. After Kraft's announcement that he would accept the penalties, a number of owners, including Mara, thanked him for doing so, sources say.

Over the summer, Jerry Jones of the Cowboys and Stephen Ross of the Dolphins publicly backed Goodell's Deflategate investigation despite all of its embarrassments—from the flawed science to the questions of its independence to the inaccurate leaks reported by ESPN and other media outlets. Many other owners and executives, who feared alienating Kraft, did so privately, insisting that Goodell's willingness to take on the Patriots has helped him emerge in a stronger position with most of his billionaire bosses, managing the expectations of his 32 constituents with the savvy of a U.S. senator's son.

"Roger did the right thing—at last," one owner said after Goodell upheld Brady's punishment. "He looks tough—and that's good."

"Pleased," said another longtime owner.

"About time," an executive close to another owner said. "Overdue."

"The world has never seen anyone as good as Roger Goodell as a political maneuverer. If he were in Congress, he'd be majority [leader]," one owner says.

The makeup call carried public fallout. In his 40-page decision on September 3 that vacated Brady's suspension over Deflategate, Judge Richard M. Berman rebuked Goodell and the NFL, saying that the commissioner had "dispensed his own brand of industrial justice." Columnists, analysts, and even some NFL players immediately pounced, racing to proclaim that Goodell finally had suffered a crushing, perhaps legacy-defining defeat. From the Saints' Bountygate scandal through Deflategate, Goodell is 0-5 on appeals of his high-profile disciplinary decisions.

For his part, Goodell denied that Deflategate was connected to Spygate: "I am not aware of any connection between the Spygate procedures and these procedures [in Deflategate] . . . ," he said on ESPN's *Mike & Mike* radio show on September 8. "There is no connection in my mind between these two incidents."

During the same appearance, Goodell said he would consider reducing his role in the disciplinary process, a proposal raised by influential team owner Arthur Blank of the Falcons. "I am open to changing my role," Goodell said. "It's become extremely time-consuming, and I have to be focused on other issues. I've discussed this with owners."

Owners are still weighing the fallout of Deflategate. Brady's court victory was narrow; Berman ruled only on whether the league had followed the collective bargaining agreement, not on the quarterback's guilt or innocence. It didn't matter to them that the Patriots had accepted the league's punishment in May. For the second time in less than a decade, in the eyes of some owners and executives, Goodell had the Patriots in his hands and let them go. The league lost, again. The Patriots won, again.

And so it was that in mid-June, while Deflategate's appeal rolled on, Kraft hosted a party at his Brookline estate for his players and coaching staff. Before dinner, the owner promised "rich" and "sweet" desserts that were, of course, the Super Bowl champions' rings. On one side of the ring, the recipient's name is engraved in white gold, along with the years of the Patriots' Super Bowl titles: 2001, 2003, 2004, and, now, 2014.

A photograph snapped at the party went viral: There was a smiling Tom Brady, in a designer suit, showing off all four of his rings, a pair on each hand. On the middle finger of his right hand, Brady flashed the new ring, the gaudiest of the four, glittering with 205 diamonds—and no asterisks.

GRETEL EHRLICH

Rotten Ice

FROM HARPER'S MAGAZINE

I FIRST WENT TO Greenland in 1993 to get above tree line. I'd been hit by lightning and was back on my feet after a long two-year recovery. Feeling claustrophobic, I needed to see horizon lines, and off I went with no real idea of where I was going. A chance meeting with a couple from west Greenland drew me north for a summer and part of the next dark winter. When I returned the following spring, the ice had failed to come in. I had planned to travel up the west coast by dogsled on the route that Knud Rasmussen took during his 1916–18 expedition. I didn't know then that such a trip was no longer possible, that the ice on which Arctic people and animals had relied for thousands of years would soon be nearly gone.

In the following years I went much farther up the coast, to the two oldest northernmost villages in the world: Qaanaaq and Siorapaluk. From there I traveled with an extended family of Inuit subsistence hunters who represent an ice-evolved culture that stretches across the Polar North. Here, snowmobiles are banned for hunting purposes; against all odds, traditional practices are still carried on: hunting seals and walrus from dogsleds in winter, spring, and fall; catching narwhals from kayaks in summer; making and wearing polar-bear pants, fox anoraks, sealskin mittens and boots. In Qaanaaq's large communal workshop, 21st-century tools are used to make Ice Age equipment: harpoons, dogsleds, kayaks. The ways in which these Greenlanders get their food are not much different than they were a thousand years ago, but in recent years Arctic scientists have labeled Greenland's seasonal sea ice "a rotten

ice regime." Instead of nine months of good ice, there are only
two or three. Where the ice in spring was once routinely six to 10
feet thick, in 2004 the thickness was only seven inches even when
the temperature was −30 degrees Fahrenheit. "It is breaking up
from beneath," one hunter explained, "because of the wind and
stormy waters. We never had that before. It was always clear skies,
cold weather, calm seas. We see the ice not wanting to come back.
If the ice goes it will be a disaster. Without ice we are nothing."

Icebergs originate from glaciers; ice sheets are distinct from sea
ice, but they, too, are affected by the global furnace: 2014 was the
hottest year on earth since record-keeping began, in 1880. Greenland's ice sheet is now shedding ice five times faster than it did in
the 1990s, causing ice to flow down canyons and cliffs at alarming
speeds. In 2010, the Petermann Glacier, in Greenland's far north,
calved a 100-square-mile "ice island," and in 2012, the glacier lost a
chunk twice the size of Manhattan. Straits and bays between north-
west Greenland and Ellesmere Island, part of Canada's Nunavut
territory, are often clogged with rotting, or unstable, ice. In the
summer of 2012, almost the whole surface of Greenland's ice
sheet turned to slush.

What happens at the top of the world affects all of us. The
Arctic is the earth's natural air conditioner. Ice and snow radiate
80 percent of the sun's heat back into space, keeping the middle
latitudes temperate. Dark, open oceans and bare land are heat
sinks; open water eats ice. Deep regions of the Pacific Ocean have
heated 15 times faster over the past 60 years than during warming
periods in the preceding 10,000, and the effect on both glaciers
and sea ice is obvious: as warm seawater pushes far north, seasonal
sea ice disintegrates, causing the floating tongues of outlet glaciers
to wear thin and snap off.

By 2004 the sea ice in north Greenland was too precarious for
us to travel any distance north, south, or west from Qaanaaq. Sea
ice is a Greenlander's highway and the platform on which marine
mammals—including walrus, ring seals, bearded seals, and polar
bears—Arctic foxes, and seabirds travel, rest, breed, and hunt.
"Those times we went out to Kiatak and Herbert islands, up Politiken's Glacier, or way north to Etah and Humboldt Glacier," the
Inuit hunters said, "we cannot go there anymore." In 2012, the
Arctic Ocean's sea ice shrank to a record minimum. Last year, the
rate of ice loss in July averaged 40,000 square miles per day.

The Greenland ice sheet is 1,500 miles long, 680 miles wide, and covers most of the island. The sheet contains roughly 8 percent of the world's freshwater. GRACE (Gravity Recovery and Climate Experiment), a satellite launched in 2002, is one of the tools used by scientists to understand the accelerated melting of the ice sheet. GRACE monitors monthly changes in the ice sheet's total mass, and has revealed a drastic decrease. Scientists who study the Arctic's sensitivity to weather and climate now question its stability. "Global warming has fundamentally altered the background conditions that give rise to all weather," Kevin Trenberth, a scientist at the National Center for Atmospheric Research, in Boulder, Colorado, says. Alun Hubbard, a Welsh glaciologist, reports: "The melt is going off the scale! The rate of retreat is unprecedented." To move "glacially" no longer implies slowness, and the "severe, widespread, and irreversible impacts" on people and nature that the most recent report of the Intergovernmental Panel on Climate Change (IPCC) warned us about have already come to fruition in Greenland.

It was in Qaanaaq in 1997 that I first experienced climate change from the feet up. I was traveling with Jens Danielsen, headed for Kiatak Island. It was spring, and six inches of snow covered the sea ice. Our 15 dogs trotted slowly; the only sound was their percussive panting. We had already encountered a series of pressure ridges —steep slabs of ice piled up between two floes—that took us five hours to cross. When we reached a smooth plain of ice again, we thought the worst was over, but the sound of something breaking shocked us: dogs began disappearing into the water. Jens hooked his feet over the front edge of the sled, lay on the trace lines, and pulled the dogs out. Afterward, he stepped down onto a piece of rotten ice, lifted the front of the sled, and laid it on a spot that was more stable, then jumped aboard and yelled at the dogs to run fast. When I asked if we were going to die, he smiled and said, "*Imaqa.*" Maybe.

Ice-adapted people have amazing agility, which allows them to jump from one piece of drift ice to another and to handle half-wild dogs. They understand that life is transience, chance, and change. Because ice is so dynamic, melting in summer and reforming in September, Greenlanders in the far north understand that nothing is solid, that boundaries are actually passages, that

the world is a permeable place. On the ice they act quickly and
precisely, flexing mind as well as muscle, always "modest in front
of the weather," as Jens explained. Their material culture represents more than 10,000 years of use: dogsleds, kayaks, skin boats,
polar-bear and sealskin pants, bone scrapers, harpoons, bearded
seal–skin whips—all designed for beauty, efficiency, and survival in
a harsh world where most people would be dead in a day.

From 1997 to 2012 I traveled by dogsled, usually with Jens and
his three brothers-in-law: Mamarut Kristiansen, Mikile Kristiansen,
and Gedeon Kristiansen. The dogtrot often lulled me to sleep, but
rough ice shook me to attention. "You must look carefully," Jens
said. From him I began to understand about being *silanigtalersar-
put:* a person who is wise about things and knows the ice, who
comes to teach us how to see. The first word I learned in Greenlandic was *sila,* which means, simultaneously, weather, animal and
human consciousness, and the power of nature. The Greenlanders
I traveled with do not make the usual distinctions between a human mind and an animal mind. Polar bears are thought to understand human language. In the spring mirages appear, lifting
islands into the air and causing the ice to look like open water.
Silver threads at the horizon mark the end of the known world and
the beginning of the one inhabited by the imagination. Before
television, the Internet, and cell phones arrived in Greenland, the
coming of the dark time represented a shift: anxiety about the loss
of light gave way to a deep, rich period of storytelling.

In Qaanaaq the sun goes down on October 24 and doesn't rise
again until February 17. Once the hood of completely dark days
arrives, with only the moon and snow to light the paths between
houses, the old legends are told: "The Orphan Who Became a Giant," "The Orphan Who Drifted Out to Sea." Now Jens complains
that the advent of television in Qaanaaq has reduced storytelling
time, though only three channels are available. But out on the ice
the old ways thrive. During the spring of 1998, when I traveled
with Jens and his wife, Ilaitsuk, along with their five-year-old grandchild, installments of the legends were told to the child each night
for two weeks.

That child, now a young man, did not become a subsistence
hunter, despite his early training. He had seen too many springs
when there was little ice. But no one suspected the ice would disappear completely.

The cycle of thinning and melting is now impossible to stop. The enormous ice sheet that covers 80 percent of the island is increasingly threaded with meltwater rivers in summer, though when I first arrived in Greenland, in 1993, it shone like a jewel. According to Konrad "Koni" Steffen, a climate scientist who has established many camps on top of the Greenland ice sheet, "In 2012, we lost 450 gigatons of ice—that's five times the amount of ice in the Alps. All the ice on top has pulled apart. It used to be smooth; now it looks like a huge hammer has hit it. The whole surface is fractured."

In 2004, with a generous grant from the National Geographic Expeditions Council, I returned to Qaanaaq for two month-long journeys—in March and in July. The hunters had said to come in early March, one of the two coldest months in Greenland, because they were sure the ice would be strong then. They needed food for their families and their dogs. We would head south to Savissivik, a hard four-day trip. The last part would take us over the edge of the ice sheet and down a precipitous canyon to the frozen sea in an area they called Walrus El Dorado. It was –20 degrees when we started out with 58 dogs, four hunters—including Jens, Gedeon, Mamarut, and a relative of Jens named Tobias—and my crew of three. We traveled on *hikuliaq*—ice that has just formed. How could it be only seven inches thick at this temperature? I asked Jens. He told me: "There is no old ice, it's all new ice and very salty: hard on the dogs' feet, and, you'll see, it melts fast. Dangerous to be going out on it." But there we were.

After making camp we walked single file to the ice edge. The ice was so thin that it rolled under our feet like rubber. One walrus was harpooned. It was cut up and laid on our sleds. I asked about the pile of intestines left behind. "That's for the foxes, ravens, and polar bears," Mamarut said. "We always leave food for others." Little did we know then that we would get only one walrus all month, and that soon we would be hungry and in need of meat for ourselves and the dogs.

The cold intensified and at the same time more ice broke up. We traveled all day in frigid temperatures that dropped to what Jens said was –40, and found refuge in a tiny hut. We spent the day rubbing ointment onto our frostbitten faces and fingers, and eating boiled walrus for hours at a time to keep warm. A day later

we traveled south to Moriusaq, a village of 15, where the walrus
hunting had always been good. But the ice there was unstable too.
We were told that farther south, around Savissivik, there was no
ice at all. Mamarut's wife, Tekummeq, the great-granddaughter of
the explorer Robert Peary, taught school in the village. She fed
us and heated enough water for a bath. Finally we turned around
and headed north toward Qaanaaq, four days away. Halfway there,
a strong blizzard hit and we were forced to hole up in a hut for
three days. We kept our visits outside brief, but after even a few
minutes any exposed skin burned: fingers, hands, cheeks, noses,
foreheads, and asses. The jokes flowed. The men kept busy fixing dog harnesses and sled runners. Evenings, they told hunting
stories—not about who got the biggest animal but who made the
most ridiculous mistake—to great laughter.

Days were white, nights were white. On the ice dogs and humans
eat the same food. The dogs lined up politely for the chunks of
frozen walrus that their owners flung into their mouths. Inside the
hut, a haunch of walrus hung from a hook, dripping blood. Our
heat was a single Primus burner. Breakfast was walrus-heart soup;
lunch was what Aleqa, our translator (who later became the first
female prime minister of Greenland), called "swim fin"—a gelati-
nous walrus flipper. Jens, the natural leader of his family and the
whole community, told of the polar bear with the human face,
the one who could not be killed, who had asked him to follow, to
become a shaman. "I said no. I couldn't desert my family and the
community of hunters. This is the modern world, and there is no
place in it for shamans."

When the temperature moderated, we spent three weeks trying
to find ice that was strong enough to hold us. We were running out
of food. The walrus meat was gone. Because Greenlandic freight
sleds have no brakes, Jens used his legs and knees to slow us as we
skidded down a rocky creekbed. At the bottom, we traveled down
a narrow fjord. There was a hut and a drying rack: the last hunter
to use the shed had left meat behind. The dogs would eat, but we
would not—the meat was too old—and we were still a long way
from home. The weather improved but it still averaged 30 degrees
below zero. "Let's go out to Kiatak Island," Jens said. "Maybe we
can get a walrus there." After crossing the strait, we traveled on an
ice foot—a belt of ice that clung to the edge of the island. Where it

broke off we had to unhook the dogs, push the sleds over a 14-foot cliff, and jump down onto rotting discs of ice. Sleds tipped and slid as dogs leaped over moats of open water from one spinning pane to the next. We traveled down the island's coast to another small hut, happy to have made it safely. From a steep mountain the men searched the frozen ocean for walrus with binoculars, but the few animals they saw were too far out and the path of ice to get to them was completely broken.

A boy from Siorapaluk showed up the next morning with a fine team, beautifully made clothing, a rifle, and a harpoon. At 15 he had taken a year off from school to see whether he had the prowess to be a great hunter, and he did. But the ice will not be there for him in the future; subsistence hunting will not be possible. "We weren't born to buy and sell things," Jens said sadly, "but to live with our families on the ice and hunt for our food."

Spring weather had come. The temperature had warmed considerably, and the air felt balmy. As we traveled to Siorapaluk, a mirage made Kiatak Island appear to float like an iceberg. Several times, while we stopped the dogs to rest, we stretched out on the sled in our polar-bear pants to bask in the warmth of the sun.

North of Siorapaluk there are no more habitations, but the men of the village go up the coast to hunt polar bears. When Gedeon and his older brother Mamarut ventured north for a few hours to see whether the route was an option for us, all they saw was a great latticed area of pressure ice, polynyas (perennially open water), and no polar bears. They decided against going farther. We had heavy loads, and the dogs had not eaten properly for a week, so after a rest at Siorapaluk we turned for home, traveling close to the coast on shore-fast ice.

On our arrival in Qaanaaq, the wives, children, and friends of the hunters greeted us and helped unload the sleds. The hunters explained that we had no meat. With up to 15 dogs per hunter, plus children, the sick, and the elderly, there were lots of mouths to feed. Northern Greenland is a food-sharing society with no private ownership of land. In these towns families own only the houses they build and live in, along with their dogs and their equipment. No one hunts alone; survival is a group effort. When things go wrong or the food supply dwindles, no one complains. They still have in their memories tales of hunger and famine. Greenland has its own government but gets subsidies from Denmark. In the old days, before the mid-1900s, an entire village could starve quickly, but now Qaanaaq has a grocery store, and with Danish welfare and help from extended families, no one goes without food.

Back in town after a month on the ice, we experienced "village shock." Instead of being disappointed about our failed walrus hunt, we celebrated with a bottle of wine and a wild dance at the local community hall, then talked until dawn. Finally my crew and I made our rounds of thanks and farewells and boarded the once-a-week plane south. It was the end of March, and just beginning to get warm. When I returned to Qaanaaq four months later, in July, the dogsleds had been put away, new kayaks were being built, and the edges of paddles were being sharpened to cut through roiling fjord water. I camped with the hunters' wives and children on steep hillsides and watched for pods of narwhals to swim up the fjord. "*Qilaluaq*," we'd yell when we saw a pod, enough time for Gedeon to paddle out and wait. As the narwhals swam by, he'd glide into the middle of them to throw a harpoon. By the end of the month enough meat had been procured for everyone. In August a hint of darkness began to creep in, an hour a day. Going back to Qaanaaq in Jens's skiff, I was astonished to see the moon for the first time in four months. Jens was eager to retrieve his dogs from the island where they ran loose all summer and to get out on the ice again, but because of the changing climate, the long months of darkness and twilight no longer marked the beginnings and endings of the traditional hunting season.

The year 2007 saw the warmest winter worldwide on record. I'd called the hunters in Qaanaaq that December to ask when I should come. It had been two years since I'd been there, and Jens was excited about going hunting together as we had when we first met. He said, "Come early in February when it's very cold, and maybe the ice will be strong." The day I arrived in Greenland I was shocked to find that it was warmer at the airport in Kangerlussuaq than in Boston. The ground crew was in shirtsleeves. I thought it was a joke. No such luck. Global air and sea temperatures were on the rise. The AO, the Arctic Oscillation, an index of high- and low-pressure zones, had recently switched out of its positive phase —when frigid air is confined to the Arctic in winter—and into its negative phase—when the Arctic stays warm and the cold air filters down into lower latitudes.

Flying north the next day to Qaanaaq, I looked down in disbelief: from Uummannaq, a village where I had spent my first years in Greenland, up to Savissivik, where we had tried to go walrus hunting, there was only open water threaded with long strings of rotting ice. As global temperatures increase, multiyear ice—ice that does not melt even in summer, once abundant in the high Arctic—is now disappearing. Finally, north of Thule Air Base and Cape York, ice had begun to form. To see white, and not the black ink of open water, was a relief. But that relief was short-lived. Greenland had entered what American glaciologist Jason Box calls "New Climate Land."

Jens, Mamarut, Mikile, and Gedeon came to the guesthouse when I arrived, but there was none of the usual merriment that precedes a long trip on the ice. Jens explained that only the shore-fast ice was strong enough for a dogsled, that hunting had been impossible all winter. Despondent, he left. I heard rifle shots. What was that? I asked. "Some of the hunters are shooting their dogs because they have nothing to feed them," I was told. A 50-pound bag of dog food from Denmark cost more than the equivalent of 50 U.S. dollars; one bag lasts two days for 10 dogs.

Gedeon and Mikile offered to take me north to Siorapaluk. What was normally an easy six-hour trip took 12 hours, with complicated pushes up and over an edge of the ice sheet. On the way, Gedeon recounted a narrow escape. He had gone out hunting against the better judgment of his older brother. His dogsled drifted out onto an ice floe that was rapidly disintegrating. He called for help. The message was sent to Thule Air Base, and a helicopter came quickly. Gedeon and the dogs (unhooked from the sled) were hauled up into the hovering aircraft. When he looked down, his dogsled and the ice on which he had been standing had disappeared.

We arrived at Siorapaluk late in the day, and the village was strangely quiet. It had once been a busy hub, with dogsleds coming and going, and polar-bear skins stretched out to dry in front of every house. There was a school, a chapel, a small store with a pay phone (from which you could call other Greenland towns), and a post office. Mail was picked up and delivered by helicopter; in earlier times, delivery of a letter sent by dogsled could take a year. Siorapaluk once was famous for its strong hunters who went north along the coast for walrus and polar bears. By 2007 everything had changed. There were almost no dog teams staked out on the ice, and quotas were being imposed on the harvest of polar bears and narwhals.

At the end of the first week I called a meeting of hunters so that I could ask them how climate change was affecting their lives. Otto Simigaq, one of the best Siorapaluk hunters, was eager to talk: "Seven years ago we could travel on safe ice all winter and hunt animals. We didn't worry about food then. Now it's different. There has been no ice for seven months. We always went to the ice edge in spring west of Kiatak Island, but the ice doesn't go out that far now. The walrus are still there, but we can't get to them." Pauline Simigaq, Otto's wife, said, "We are not so good in our outlook now. The ice is dangerous. I never used to worry, but now if Otto goes out I wonder if I will ever see him again. Around here it is depression and changing moods. We are becoming like the ice."

After the meeting I stood and looked out at the ruined ice. Beyond the village was Kiatak, and to the north was Neqe, where I had watched hunters climb straight up rock cliffs to scoop little auks, or dovekies, out of the air with long-handled nets. Farther north was the historic (now abandoned) site of Etah, the village where, in 1917, a half-starved Knud Rasmussen, returning from his difficult attempt to map the uninhabited parts of northern Greenland, came upon the American Crocker Land expedition and the welcoming sound of a gramophone playing Wagner and Argentine tangos. Explorers and visitors came and went. Siorapaluk, Pitoravik, and Etah were regular stops for those going to the North Pole or to Ellesmere Island. Some, most notably Robert Peary, fathered children during their expeditions. The Greenlanders—and those children—stayed, traveling only as far as the ice took them. "We had everything here," Jens said. "Our entire culture was intact: our language and our way of living. We kept the old ways and took what we wanted of the new."

It wasn't until 2012 that I returned to Qaanaaq. I hadn't really wanted to go: I was afraid of what I would find. I'd heard that suicides and drinking had increased, that despair had become contagious. But a friend, the artist Mariele Neudecker, had asked me to accompany her to Qaanaaq so that she could photograph the ice. On a small plane carrying us north from Ilulissat she asked a question about glaciers, so I yelled out: "Any glaciologists aboard?" Three passengers, Poul Christoffersen, Steven Palmer, and Julian

Dowdeswell, turned around and nodded. They hailed from Cambridge University's Scott Polar Research Institute and were on their way to examine the Greenland ice sheet north of Qaanaaq. As we looked down, Steve said, "With airborne radar we can identify the bed beneath several kilometers of ice." Poul added: "We're trying to determine the consequences of global warming for the ice." They talked about the linkages between ocean currents, atmosphere, and climate. Poul continued: "The feedbacks are complicated. Cold ice-sheet meltwater percolates down through the crevasses and flows into the fjords, where it mixes with warm ocean water. This mixing has a strong influence on the glaciers' flow."

Later in the year, they would present their new discovery: two subglacial lakes just north of Qaanaaq, half a mile beneath the ice surface. Although common in Antarctica, these deep hidden lakes had eluded glaciologists working in Greenland. Steve reported, "The lakes form an important part of the ice sheet's plumbing system connecting surface lakes to the ones beneath. Because the way water flows beneath ice sheets strongly affects ice-flow speeds, improved understanding of these lakes will allow us to predict more accurately how the ice sheet will respond to anticipated future warming."

Steve and Poul talked about four channels of warm seawater at the base of Petermann Glacier that allowed more ice islands to calve, and the 68-mile-wide calving front of the Humboldt Glacier, where Jens and I, plus seven other hunters, had tried to go one spring but were stopped when the dogs fell ill with distemper and died. Even with healthy dogs we wouldn't be able to go there now. Poul said that the sea ice was broken and dark jets of water were pulsing out from in front of the glacier—a sign that surface and subglacial meltwater was coming from the base of the glacier, exacerbating the melting of the ice fronts and the erosion of the glacier's face.

The flight from Ilulissat to Qaanaaq takes three hours. Below us, a cracked elbow of ice bent and dropped, and long stretches of open water made sparkling slits cuffed by rising mist. Even from the plane we could see how the climate feedback loop works, how patches of open water gather heat and produce a warm cloud that hangs in place so that no ice can form under it. "Is it too late to rewrite our destiny, to reverse our devolution?" I asked the glaciologists. No one answered. We stared at the rotting ice. It was down there that a modern shaman named Panippaq, who was said to be capable of heaping up mounds of fish at will, had committed suicide as he watched the sea ice decline. Steve reminded me that the global concentration of carbon dioxide in the atmosphere had almost reached 400 parts per million, and that the Arctic had warmed at least five degrees. Julian Dowdeswell, the head of the institute at Cambridge, had let the younger glaciologists do the talking. He said only this: "It's too late to change anything. All we can do now is deal with the consequences. Global sea level is rising."

But when Mariele and I arrived in Qaanaaq, we were pleasantly surprised to find that the sea ice was three feet thick. Narwhals, beluga, and walrus swam in the leads of open water at the ice edge. Pairs of eider ducks flew overhead, and little auks arrived by the thousands to nest and fledge in the rock cliffs at Neqe. Spirits rose. I asked Jens whether they'd ever thought of starting a new community farther north. He said they had tried, but as the ice retreated hungry polar bears had come onto the land, as they were doing in Vankarem, Russia, and Kaktovik, Alaska. The bears were very aggressive. "We must live as we always have with what the day brings to us. And today, there is ice," he said.

Jens had recently been elected mayor of Qaanaaq and had to leave for a conference in Belgium, but Mamarut, Mikile, and Gedeon wanted to hunt. When we went down to the ice where the dogs were staked, I was surprised to see Mikile drunk. Usually mild-mannered and quiet, he lost control of his dogs before he could get them hitched up, and they ran off. With help from another hunter, it took several hours to retrieve them. Perched on Mikile's extra-long sled was a skiff; Mamarut tipped his kayak sideways and lashed it to his sled. Gedeon carried his kayak, paddles, guns, tents, and food on his sled, plus his new girlfriend, Bertha. The spring snow was wet and the going was slow, but it was wonderful to be on a dogsled again.

I had dozed off when Mamarut whispered, "*Hiku hina,*" in my ear. The ice edge. Camp was set up. Gedeon sharpened his harpoon, and Bertha melted chunks of ice over a Primus stove for tea. The men carried their kayaks to the water's edge. Glaucous gulls flew by. The sound of narwhal breathing grew louder. "*Qilaluaq!*" Gedeon whispered. The pod swam by but no one went after them. It was May, and the sun was circling in a halo above our heads, so

we learned to sleep in bright light. It was time to rest. We laid our
sleeping bags under a canvas tent, on beds made from two sleds
pushed together. The midnight sun tinted the sea green, pink,
gray, and pale blue.

Hours later, I saw Gedeon and Mikile kneeling in snow at the
edge of the ice, facing the water. They were careful not to make
eye contact with passing narwhals: two more pods had come by,
but the men didn't go after them. "They have too many young
ones," Gedeon whispered, before continuing his vigil. Another
pod approached and Gedeon climbed into his boat, lithe as a cat.
He waited, head down, with a hand steadying the kayak on the ice
edge. There was a sound of splashing and breathing, and Gedeon
exploded into action, paddling hard into the middle of the pod,
his kayak thrown around by turbulent water. He grabbed his harpoon from the deck of the kayak and hurled it. Missed. He turned,
smiling, and paddled back to camp. There was ice and there was
time—at least for now—and he would try again later.

In the night, a group of Qaanaaq hunters arrived and made
camp behind us on the ice. It's thought to be bad practice to usurp
another family's hunting area. They should have moved on but
didn't. No one said anything. The old courtesies were disintegrating along with the ice. The next morning, a dogfight broke out,
and an old man viciously beat one of his dogs with a snow shovel.
In 20 years of traveling in Greenland, I'd never seen anyone beat
a dog.

Hunting was good the next day, and the brothers were happy
to have food to bring home for their families. Though the ice was
strong, they knew better than to count on anything. We were all
deeply upset about the beating we had witnessed, but there was
nothing we could do. In Greenland there are unwritten codes of
honor that, together with the old taboos, have kept the society
humming. A hunter who goes out only for himself and not for the
group will be shunned: if he has trouble on the ice no one will
stop to help him. Hunters don't abuse their dogs, which they rely
on for their lives.

To become a subsistence hunter, the most honorable occupation
in this society, is no longer an option for young people. "We may
be coming to a time when it is summer all year," Mamarut said as
he mended a dog harness. Once the strongest hunter of the family

and also the jokester, he was now too banged up to hunt and rarely smiled. He'd broken his ankle going solo across the ice sheet in a desperate attempt to find food—hunting musk oxen instead of walrus—and it took him two weeks to get home to see a doctor. Another week went by before he could fly to Nuuk, the capital of Greenland, for surgery. Now the ankle gives him trouble and his shoulder hurts: one of his rotator cuffs is torn. The previous winter his mother died—she was still making polar-bear pants for her sons, now middle-aged—and a fourth brother committed suicide. "They want us to become fishermen," Mamarut said. "How can we be something we are not?"

On the last day we camped at the ice edge, the hunters got two walrus, four narwhals, and 10 halibut. As the men paddled back to camp, their dogs broke into spontaneous howls of excitement. Mamarut had opted to stay in camp and begin packing. In matters of hunting, his brash younger brother, Gedeon, had taken his place. Eight years earlier I had watched Gedeon teach his son, Rasmus, how to handle dogs, paddle a kayak, and throw a harpoon. Rasmus was seven at the time. Now he goes to school in south Greenland, below the Arctic Circle, and is learning to be an electrician. Mamarut and his wife, Tekummeq, have adopted Jens and Ilaitsuk's grandchild, but rather than being raised in a community of traditional hunters, the child will grow up on an island nation whose perennially open waters will prove attractive to foreign oil companies.

At camp, Mamarut helped his two brothers haul the dead animals onto the ice. One walrus had waged an urgent fight after being harpooned and had attacked the boat. Unhappy that the animal did not die instantly, Gedeon had pulled out his rifle and fired, ending the struggle that was painful to watch. The meat was butchered in silence and laid under blue tarps on the dogsleds. Breakfast was fresh narwhal-heart soup, rolls with imported Danish honey, and *mattak*—whale skin, which is rich in vitamin C, essential food in an environment that can grow no fruits or vegetables.

We packed up camp, eager to leave the dog-beater behind. It was the third week of May and the temperature was rising: the ice was beginning to get soft. We departed early so that the three-foot gap in the ice that we had to cross would still be frozen, but as soon as the sun appeared from behind the clouds, it turned so warm that we shed our anoraks and sealskin mittens. "Tonight that whole ice edge where we were camped will break off," Mamarut said quietly. The tracks of *ukaleq* (Arctic hare) zigzagged ahead of us, and Mamarut signaled to the dogs to stay close to the coast lest the ice on which we were traveling break away. We camped high on a hill in a small hut near the calving face of Politiken's Glacier, which in 1997 had provided an easy route to the ice sheet but was now a chaos of rubble. Mamarut laid out the topographic map I had brought to Greenland on my first visit, in 1993, and scrutinized the marks we had made over the years showing the ice's retreat. Once the ice edge in the spring extended far out into the strait; now it barely reached beyond the shore-fast ice of Qaanaaq. Despite seasonal fluxes, the ice kept thinning. Looking at the map, Mamarut shook his head in dismay. "Ice no good!" he blurted out in English, as if it were the best language for expressing anger. On our way home to Qaanaaq the next day, he got tangled in the trace lines while hooking up the dogs and was dragged for a long way before I could stop them. These were the final days of subsistence hunting on the ice, and I wondered if I would travel with these men ever again.

The news from the Ice Desk is this: the prognosis for the future of Arctic ice, and thus for human life on the planet, is grim. In the summer of 2013 I returned to Greenland, not to Qaanaaq but to the town of Ilulissat in what's known as west Greenland, the site of the Jakobshavn Glacier, the fastest-calving glacier in the world. I was traveling with my husband, Neal, who was on assignment to produce a radio segment on the accelerated melting of the Greenland ice sheet. In Copenhagen, on our way to Ilulissat, we met with Jason Box, who had moved to Denmark from the prestigious Byrd Polar and Climate Research Center to work in Greenland. It was a sunny Friday afternoon, and we agreed to meet at a canal where young Danes, just getting off work, piled onto their small boats, to relax with a bottle of wine or a few beers. Jason strolled toward us wearing shorts and clogs, carrying a bottle of hard apple cider and three glasses. His casual demeanor belies a gravity and intelligence that becomes evident when he talks. A self-proclaimed climate refugee, and the father of a young child, he said he couldn't live with himself if he didn't do everything possible to transmit his understanding of abrupt climate change in the Arctic and its dire consequences.

Jason has spent 24 summers atop Greenland's great dome of ice. "The ice sheet is melting at an accelerated pace," he told us. "It's not just surface melt but the deformation of the inner ice. The fabric of the ice sheet is coming apart because of increasing meltwater infiltration. Two to three hundred billion tons of ice are being lost each year. The last time atmospheric CO_2 was this high, the sea level was 70 feet higher."

We flew to Ilulissat the next day. Below the plane, milky-green water squeezed from between the toes of glaciers that had oozed down from the ice sheet. Just before landing, we glided over a crumpled ribbon of ice that was studded with icebergs the size of warehouses: the fjord leading seaward from the calving front of the Jakobshavn Glacier. Ice there is moving away from the central ice sheet so fast—up to 150 feet a day—and calves so often that the adjacent fjord has been designated a World Heritage Site, an ironic celebration of its continuing demise. Ilulissat was booming with tourists who had flocked to town to observe the parade of icebergs drift by as they sipped cocktails and feasted on barbecued musk oxen at the four-star Hotel Arctic; it was also brimming with petroleum engineers who had come in a gold-rush-like flurry to find oil. But the weather had changed: many of the well sites were non-producers, and just below the fancy hotel were the remains of several tumbled houses and a ravine that had been dredged by a flash flood, a rare weather event in a polar desert.

Neal and I hiked up the moraine above town to look down on the ice-choked fjord. We sat on a promontory to watch and listen to the ice pushing into Disko Bay. Nothing seemed to be moving, but at the front of stranded icebergs fast-flowing streams of meltwater spewed out, crisscrossing one another in the channel. Recently several subglacial lakes were discovered to have "blown out," draining as much as 57,000 gallons per minute and then refilling with surface meltwater, softening the ice around it, so that the entire ice sheet is in a process of decay. From atop another granite cliff we saw an enormous berg, its base smooth but its top all jagged with pointed slabs. Suddenly, two thumping roars, another sharp thud, and an entire white wall slid straight down into the water. Neal turned to me, wide-eyed, and said: "This is the sound of the ice sheet melting."

Later, we gathered at the Hotel Icefiord with Koni Steffen and a group of Dartmouth glaciology students. Under a warm sun we sat on a large deck and discussed the changes that have occurred in the Arctic in the past five years. Vast methane plumes were discovered boiling up from the Laptev Sea, north of Russia, and methane is punching through thawing sea beds and terrestrial permafrost all across the Arctic. Currents and air temperatures are changing; the jet stream is becoming wavier, allowing weather conditions to persist for long periods of time; and the movements of high- and low-pressure systems have become unpredictable. The new chemical interplay between ocean and atmosphere is now so complex that even Steffen, the elder statesman of glaciology, says that no one fully understands it. We talked about future scenarios of what we began to call, simply, bad weather. Parts of the world will get much hotter, with no rain or snow at all. In western North America, trees will keep dying from insect and fungal invasions, uncovering more land that in turn will soak up more heat. It's predicted that worldwide demand for water will exceed the supply by 40 percent. Cary Fowler, who helped found the Svalbard Global Seed Vault, predicts that there will be such dire changes in seasonality that food-growing will no longer align with rainfall, and that we are not prepared for worsening droughts. Steffen says, "Water vapor is now the most plentiful and prolific greenhouse gas. It is altering the jet stream. That's the truth, and it shocks all the environmentalists!"

In a conversation with the biologist E. O. Wilson on a morning in Aspen so beautiful that it was difficult to imagine that anything on the planet could go wrong, he advised me to stop being gloomy. "It's our chance to practice altruism," he said. I looked at him skeptically. He continued: "We have to wear suits of armor like World War II soldiers and just keep going. We have to get used to the changes in the landscape, to step over the dead bodies, so to speak, and discipline our behavior instead of getting stuck in tribal and religious restrictions. We have to work altruistically and cooperatively, and make a new world."

Is it possible we haven't fully comprehended that we are in danger? We may die off as a species from mere carelessness. That night in Ilulissat, on the patio of the Hotel Icefiord, I asked one of the graduate students about her future. She said: "I won't have children; I will move north." We were still sitting outside when the night air turned so cold that we had to bundle up in parkas and mittens to continue talking. "A small change can have a great effect," Steffen said. He was referring to how carelessly we underestimate the profound sensitivity of the planet's membrane, its skin of ice. The Arctic has been warming more than twice as fast as anywhere else in the world, and that evening, the reality of what was happening to his beloved Greenland seemed to make Steffen go quiet. On July 30, 2013, the highest temperature ever recorded in Greenland—almost 80 degrees Fahrenheit—occurred in Maniitsoq, on the west coast, and an astonishing heat wave in the Russian Arctic registered 90 degrees. And that was 2013, when there was said to be a "pause" in global heating.

Recently, methane plumes were discovered at 570 places along the East Coast of the United States, from Cape Hatteras, North Carolina, to Massachusetts. Siberian tundra holes were spotted by nomadic reindeer herders on the Yamal Peninsula, and ash from wildfires in the American and Canadian West fluttered down, turning the southern end of the Greenland ice sheet almost black.

The summer after Neal and I met with Koni Steffen in Ilulissat, Jason Box moved his camp farther north, where he continued his attempts to unveil the subtle interactions between atmosphere and earth, water, and ice, and the ways algae and industrial and wildfire soot affect the reflectivity of the Greenland ice sheet: the darker the ice, the more heat it absorbs. As part of his recent Dark Snow Project, he used small drones to fly over the darkening snow and ice. By the end of August 2014, Jason's reports had grown increasingly urgent. "We are on a trajectory to awaken a runaway climate heating that will ravage global agricultural systems, leading to mass famine and conflict," he wrote. "Sea-level rise will be a small problem by comparison. We simply must lower atmospheric carbon emissions." A later message was frantic: "If even a small fraction of Arctic seafloor methane is released to the atmosphere, we're fucked." From an IPCC meeting in Copenhagen last year, he wrote: "We have very limited time to avert climate impacts that will ravage us irreversibly."

The Arctic is shouldering the wounds of the world, wounds that aren't healing. Long ago we exceeded the carrying capacity of the planet, with its 7 billion humans all longing for some semblance of First World comforts. The burgeoning population is incompatible with the natural economy of biological and ecological systems. We have found that our climate models have been too conservative, that the published results of science-by-committee are unable to keep up with the startling responsiveness of Earth to our every footstep. We have to stop pretending that there is a way back to the lush, comfortable, interglacial paradise we left behind so hurriedly in the 20th century. There are no rules for living on this planet, only consequences. What is needed is an open exchange in which sentience shapes the eye and mind and results in ever-deepening empathy. Beauty and blood and what Ralph Waldo Emerson called "strange sympathies" with otherness would circulate freely in us, and the songs of the bearded seal's ululating mating call, the crack and groan of ancient ice, the Arctic tern's cry, and the robin's evensong would inhabit our vocal cords.

About Winning

FROM THE SUN

1

Our college rowing coach isn't easily excited, but when he is, he stands up in his boat, backlit by the suggestion of a sunrise, losing and then regaining his balance, flailing his arms, and hollering in that booming voice: *That's amazing! That's fucking amazing! You're flying!* His excitement is rare. It startles us, and we row faster. I hear his boat's engine rev as he accelerates to keep up.

2

Also he is impatient and mercurial and unreliable and petulant and manipulative and arrogant.

3

Well, it's true.

4

He calls me a pain in the ass. He says if he ever has to name a boat after me, that's what he'll call it: the *Pain in the Ass. What would you call my boat?* he asks, like it's a challenge. I say I can't think of anything, and his face falls. I can tell he is used to making an impression, even the kind of impression that would make me insult him right back.

5

The first time we lose, I dropped the stroke rate too low in the head wind—34 strokes per minute when it should have been a clean 36—which means he and I will both interpret the failure as my fault. As the girls and I carry the boat on our shoulders along the river, spectators who would have slapped our backs and beamed if we had gold slung around our necks just let us walk by. I understand now why he hates losing so much, why he refuses to let us do it: we are suddenly unremarkable, and we have made him unremarkable too. He is waiting at the trailer, using the canvas of our boat sling like a makeshift hammock. His belly spills over the sides of it, and he doesn't stand up as we set the boat on the rack and huddle around him. Our breathing has not yet quieted. I feel the raw burn of our 2K race in the back of my throat, the lactic acid lighting into my quads, and I realize this is how racing feels when the adrenaline of victory is not there to blunt it. His breathing is almost as heavy as ours. He is silent for a while, which makes our little movements feel loud, and then he looks right at me. *You are useless,* he says. *We could have won that race with a lawn gnome in your seat.* I feel something in me shatter, but I knew this was coming, and I do not cry. *You have done more to hurt this crew than anyone,* he says. The girls are squirming, and one of them says, *Coach—* He says, *Don't you dare contradict me,* and she does not.

6

In an especially tumultuous coaches' meeting, he fires his entire staff, including two volunteers. He points wildly at each person to be released. He fires the ceiling. He fires the trash bin. The novice coach cries. The 70-year-old technical trainer just shrugs and walks out. When, of course, he rehires everyone the next day, he does it with none of the same fanfare. He seems defeated.

7

Things he says and doesn't mean:
I'll make you girls dinner. I owe you. (He didn't.)
Your weight is not important. (It was, so we stopped eating.)
I promise. (Later: *It's not like I promised or something!*)
We won't row if the combined air and water temperature is lower than 50 degrees. (A freshman girl got hypothermia and frostbite.)
Easy row tomorrow. (Surprise five by 1K races to earn our seats in the boat.)

8

Oh, but when we win the national championship, he careens down to the medals dock and splashes water into our boat as we row up, as if he has simply forgotten to be middle-aged and angry. He keeps splattering water despite the photographers' protests, until we are all drenched in a strange sort of baptism. He nearly topples into the river, and the grandstand gasps collectively, but when he stands back up, he is radiating adrenaline. We can almost convince ourselves that he is proud of us, which is something we've never seen before. We awkwardly return his hugs as he makes his way from stern to bow and says to each of us the things we had long ago stopped hoping to hear.

9

Steve Redgrave, who won five Olympic gold medals for British rowing, stands at the podium to talk to our team. *They're not really made of gold,* he says. He and his teammate checked with a jeweler. They're sterling silver with gold coating. Now he lets his daughters run around the house with them. They're practically worthless, just emblems, really, these things we fight so hard for.

10

My teammates elect me the next team president. *You're not afraid of him,* they tell me, by way of explanation. According to deep-seated rowing tradition, the next boat bought for the crew will be named after me. I am proud of this, because in college rowing we know our predecessors not from their victories but from their surnames pasted on the bows of the boats in the dusty boathouse. The election results are announced at a rally in our college auditorium, and afterward I find him waiting outside, huddled against the chill, stuffed into a too-small windbreaker like an overpacked suitcase. I am smiling. I ask if we will call my boat the *Pain in the Ass.* He does not look up when he tells me he's killing the tradition; it's not going to happen. *You're not the right person to be president,* he says. *Your teammates made a mistake.* I say, *Coach, I can do it.* He says, *You will break.*

11

I agree to babysit his sons, whom I taught to row last summer. The pay is 10 bucks and anything I want from the fridge. He admits that the boys ask for me, and he doesn't sound thrilled about it. When he answers the front door, he squints at me and says, *Your hair looks less frizzy today,* and his wife appears behind him to admonish him for his lack of sensitivity before they head out for Italian. His sons are known among the girls on the team for pointedly ignoring babysitters, but the two of them have deemed me worthy of conversation (an endorsement that will prompt him to insist that they do it just to upset him). A few hours later he bursts into the living room, drunk and singing Italian folk songs in a surprisingly melodic baritone. Then he pulls me aside, turns serious, and asks how the boys were. His wife shouts from the kitchen, *No more rowing talk!* He yells, *We're not!* He turns back to me, and I say they were fine; we played basketball. He grins and tells me they both made the middle-school team this year, and their first game is next week. He will miss it because we have a race in California, and for a minute he looks as far away as those salty West Coast skies. *But we are going to win out there,* he says, brightening, and we do.

12

I ask him to go for a walk with me every Wednesday on my lunch hour. *To talk about the team,* I say. He grumbles but agrees, and we form a habit of circling the campus along the paved pathways. I pretend it is very important to me, and he pretends that it is not at all important to him. We argue, but we laugh. The contention between us feels amiable, and in those moments I believe I will prove him wrong about me. He starts to lose some weight, says the walking helps, that he's trying to stay healthy for his boys. He says I'm a damn strong athlete and that I am teaching him things, but he never says what they are. Some Wednesdays I show up at his office at our scheduled time and he's not there, and the receptionist smiles kind of sadly and gives me a mint.

13

A few of us on the crew go sledding over Christmas. The boathouse hill is too slick for it, and I smash my head so hard the pain radiates through my eyeballs. For a minute I can't speak. Our trainer says the impact caused a concussion, and she's not impressed. She says she would rather get a concussion herself than tell him I am injured, so I have to do it. Today. Before practice. I expect him to be mad at our recklessness, so I rehearse what I'm going to say. When I start to speak, he interrupts: *Don't come to me with problems; come to me with solutions.* We stare at each other, and as a solution I sit down on a rowing machine, and he nods and says, *That is the honorable thing.* Music pumps through the training center now, and he stands right behind me, where he can see my screen, and he doesn't move, even though my elbows hit him in the belly with every stroke. I feel a terrible ringing behind my eyes, and I think my skull is cracking open along its fissures like tectonic plates, so I drop the stroke rate, back off, slow down. He yells to all the girls rowing alongside me—though I can tell by the direction of his voice that he hasn't turned his gaze away from my screen—*You call this leadership? Your president is losing you another championship. Who is going to show her what it takes to win?* I take a breath and sprint, and I'm fast, fast enough to call it leadership after all. My elbows strike him harder, but he still doesn't move. When the 6K test is over, I drop the handle, which bounces up and bangs against the rowing machine, and then I vomit. *Don't drop the handle,* he says, and he walks away.

14

On the dock that day, after we won the championship, the thing he said to me when he hugged me was this: *When I call you a pain in the ass, it's a compliment. Kid, I wouldn't have you any other way.*

15

He complains of chest pain while the team is on the road, and I volunteer to drive him to the emergency room. An assistant coach (recently rehired) tosses me the keys to the team truck, where he sits shotgun and says nothing on the way, save to bemoan my driving skills, which compels me to take the turns more sharply, which doesn't help. When we arrive, they put him in a gown and on a gurney and take him to be examined. *You must be the rower,* a nurse says when she sees me in my spandex in the waiting room. *Go on in, but be careful. He's a little . . . cantankerous.* He doesn't like my seeing him like this, and I don't like it either. In the dimly lit labyrinth of wheeled stretchers and low voices, he is separated from neighboring patients by thin curtains. His gown doesn't cover his whole belly, and he looks like a big injured animal. He is crying, and his words trip over each other. *My wife is leaving me,* he says. *She's taking my sons!* Then, like an afterthought, *I have a blood clot.* I say, *Coach, I'm so sorry.* His eyes focus on me, and he hollers (the same way he does on the river when our propulsion per stroke is not quite enough), *Get away from me! Get the hell out of here!* until the nurses run over to make sure that I do, and when I am far enough down the hall that he cannot see or hear, I collapse against a wall and cry so hard my muscles convulse. A passing doctor stops, bends to set his hands on my knees, and says, *It's always hard to see our loved ones suffer.* I look up. The idea of loving my coach feels like an accusation. I want to spurn the very notion of it, but the doctor has a kind smile, and I can't think of how I would begin to explain. I draw shaky breaths and thank him. Then my teammates call to ask why I'm not back; they're waiting; it's time to row.

16

February feels dreary on the river. The oar rubs bloody blisters into my palms, and when we dock, he asks how I like starboard side. Because I will not admit how difficult it is, I just say that the water is nice—it is; it's glass—and he says, *You're a fighter, kid.* I say, *Sometimes I don't think I'm good for the team.* We are silent, and I think: Wait, that's not true at all. I don't believe that. Where did that come from? I realize it's something he has told me over and over, and I think he realizes this too, because he takes a moment to wipe the sweat from his brow and squints against the gray sky. *Have you ever stopped trying?* he asks. We both know I have not.

17

I see him walking out of a building downtown. It's a psychiatrist's office. He asks me not to tell anyone.

18

The truth is I really was a pain in the ass. I asked too many questions. I fought back. I remembered the promises he didn't keep. When he trusted me to hold a 36, I let him down.

19

His director criticizes him for the way he treats his rowers, for his disregard for anyone's opinions but his own: Maybe 4:00 a.m. is too early to practice. Maybe the team shouldn't drive through the night to races in other states. Everyone tries to be gentle with him but nothing changes. He yells and stomps and storms, and he is hated, but his boats are faster than anyone else's. Parents cringe at the comments he makes over the loudspeaker. Other teams report him. Officials give him warnings. The university gives him warnings. I have to sit in on the meetings because I am the team president, but I am silent: the honorable thing. *You won't make me leave,* he says. It's not just about winning, they tell him.

20

Tomorrow's championship represents the completion of my collegiate rowing career—four years of morning training and fast boats and winning records. I never missed a practice, and if the world is fair, he will thank me or at least he won't compare me to a lawn gnome, and I will believe that we got somewhere together. I'm polishing these hopes from my seat in the hotel lobby when he plops onto the couch next to me and asks how I feel about being done. Then, without waiting for my answer, he says, *You see, I taught you not to quit no matter what, and that is a lesson you can take anywhere.* I nod and then promptly take that lesson across the street to a pub, where I order a beer, even though it's almost midnight and we race in eight hours. The bartender recognizes my rowing jacket and says he's a former rower himself. I mention the race tomorrow, and he seems to understand what it means to be drinking the night before a championship. He tells me the story of Xeno Müller, a Swiss rower with two Olympic medals to his name who was sitting at a starting line to qualify for the 2004 Athens Olympics when, moments before the buzzer for a race he almost certainly would have won, he calmly rowed himself back to the docks and put his boat away. *You can quit,* the bartender tells me. *Just like that.* I draw circles in the condensation of my glass and wonder what it would be like to let someone else mark the rate and shoulder the weight of the outcome. And yet. I know I'll wake up in the morning and pull as hard as I can into whatever head wind drives across the river this year and have the right to say, *I didn't quit!* to the man who spent four years telling me I would, and who would have been happier if I did, but who will now claim even the tiny sliver of accomplishment that I earn by proving him wrong.

Contributors' Notes

Notable Sports Writing of 2015

Contributors' Notes

CHRIS BALLARD is a senior writer for *Sports Illustrated* and the author of four books. He lives in the Bay Area, where he was a visiting lecturer at the UC Berkeley Graduate School of Journalism in 2016. This is his fifth appearance in *The Best American Sports Writing*.

DAN BARRY is a columnist and reporter for the *New York Times*. He has reported from all 50 states on various events, including the World Trade Center attack and the aftermath of Hurricane Katrina, and won many journalism awards, including a share of a Pulitzer Prize for investigative reporting. He is the author of four books: a memoir; a collection of his "About New York" columns; *Bottom of the 33rd: Hope, Redemption, and Baseball's Longest Game*, which received the 2012 PEN/ESPN Award for Literary Sports Writing; and *The Boys in the Bunkhouse: Servitude and Salvation in the Heartland.*

SAM BORDEN, the European sports correspondent for the *New York Times*, has received five APSE awards in writing and is the author of two books: *The Complete Idiot's Guide to Soccer Basics* and *Ace in America* (with Mark Feinsand and Peter Abraham), a biography of the former Yankees pitcher Chien-Ming Wang. He is a native of Larchmont, New York, and received a bachelor's degree from Emory University in 2001 and a master of fine arts in creative writing from Fairfield University in 2013. A soccer aficionado, he is a certified amateur and collegiate referee and also enjoys poker and other card games.

JOHN BRANCH is a California-based sports reporter for the *New York Times*. In 2013 he was awarded the Pulitzer Prize in feature writing for his tale of a deadly avalanche, titled "Snow Fall," and was a finalist the previous year for his story about the late NHL enforcer Derek Boogaard, who died of a painkiller overdose and was found to have CTE, the degenerative brain disease. He lives near San Francisco.

JOHN BRANT is a longtime writer-at-large for *Runner's World* and contributes to numerous national publications. His most recent book is *The Boy Who Runs: The Odyssey of Julius Achon,* published in 2016. This is Brant's sixth appearance in *The Best American Sports Writing.* His story in the present volume was guided and edited at *Bicycling* magazine by Lou Mazzante and Bill Strickland. In March 2016, Zilong Wang, the subject of Brant's profile, set out by bicycle on a "Journey to the East," a three-year trek that will take him across the U.S., Eurasia, and mainland China on "a pilgrimage around the globe in service to the ecological and spiritual awakening of our time." Zilong is chronicling his progress at http://www.journeye.org/.

WILLIAM BROWNING is a University of Mississippi graduate. He began his career as a reporter for the *North Mississippi Herald* in Water Valley, Mississippi. He has worked for newspapers in Wyoming and Florida, mostly covering crime and the military. In 2011 he received an APSE award. His story "A Long Walk's End" was cited by Longform.org and named a Longreads.com number-one story of the week. He and his wife, Joy, have a dog and two cats.

MATT CALKINS has been a sports columnist at the *Seattle Times* since August 2015. Previously, he was a columnist at the *San Diego Union-Tribune,* and before that, the Trail Blazers beat writer for the *Vancouver Columbian.* Born and raised in the San Fernando Valley, Calkins graduated from Loyola Marymount University in 2004.

KIM CROSS is a *New York Times* bestselling author and journalist who sold her Jamis Six-Fifty B mountain bike to pay for the fact-checking of *What Stands in a Storm,* a narrative nonfiction account of the biggest tornado outbreak on record. Her work has appeared in *Outside, Southwest, Garden & Gun, Popular Mechanics,* the *Tampa Bay Times,* and ESPN.com. She teaches advanced reporting at the University of Alabama and cofounded the Archer City Story Center in a one-stoplight Texas town. She will fact-check the hell out of your fishing story (kimhcross.com).

GRETEL EHRLICH'S essays, short stories, and poems have appeared in many anthologies, including *Best Essays of the Century, Best American Essays, Best Spiritual Writing, Best Travel Writing,* and *The Nature Reader.* Her work has appeared in *Harper's Magazine, The Atlantic,* the *New York Times Magazine,* the *New York Times* op-ed page, the *Washington Post, Time, Outside, Audubon,* and many other publications. Her books include *A Match to the Heart, This Cold Heaven,* and *Questions of Heaven.*

STEVE FAINARU is coauthor with his brother, Mark Fainaru-Wada, of the book *League of Denial: The NFL, Concussions, and the Battle for Truth*. Before joining ESPN as an investigative reporter, he served as a war correspondent for the *Washington Post*, where he won a Pulitzer Prize in international reporting in 2008.

MARK FAINARU-WADA joined ESPN in November 2007 as an investigative reporter for ESPN's Enterprise Unit. Previously, at the *San Francisco Chronicle*, he and his colleague Lance Williams earned a string of national honors —including the George Polk, Edgar A. Poe, Dick Schaap Excellence in Journalism, and Associated Press Sports Editors Awards—for their work on the BALCO steroids case. Fainaru-Wada is coauthor with Williams of *Game of Shadows: Barry Bonds, BALCO, and the Steroids Scandal That Rocked Professional Sports*.

STEVE FRIEDMAN is the author of four books, coauthor of two, and a two-time finalist for the National Magazine Award in feature writing. He grew up in St. Louis, graduated from Stanford University, and lives in New York City. This is his ninth appearance in *The Best American Sports Writing*. More at Stevefriedman.net.

CHRIS JONES worked for *Esquire* from 2002 until 2016, first as a contributing editor and later as a writer at large. He served the same two men for those 14 years: David Granger, *Esquire*'s editor in chief, and his deputy, Peter Griffin. They were perfect editors: generous, kind, careful, brave. In January 2016, Granger was fired. This is Chris's sixth appearance in *The Best American Sports Writing*, and it will be his last as a writer for *Esquire*. He wants to thank Granger and Griffin for the chance to see his name on the masthead of his dreams, and so, too, in the pages of this book. Fourteen years is a long time to feel lucky. He will always be grateful beyond measure.

SAM KNIGHT is a journalist living in London. His work has appeared in *The New Yorker*, the *Guardian, FT, Grantland, British GQ*, and *Harper's*.

MICHAEL MCKNIGHT has been a reporter and special contributor at *Sports Illustrated* since 2010. He is the author of *Intercepted: The Rise and Fall of NFL Cornerback Darryl Henley* (2012).

MICHAEL J. MOONEY is on staff at *D Magazine* and contributes to *GQ, ESPN: The Magazine, Outside, Success Magazine*, and *Popular Mechanics*. He is codirector of the annual Mayborn Literary Nonfiction Conference. His stories have appeared in multiple editions of *The Best American Sports Writing* and *Best American Crime Reporting*. He lives in Dallas.

ERIC MOSKOWITZ is a reporter and features writer for the *Boston Globe*, where he has worked since 2007. He contributed to the *Globe*'s Pulitzer

Prize–winning coverage of the 2013 Boston Marathon bombings and is a two-time finalist for the Livingston Award for Young Journalists. Previously, he worked for the *Concord Monitor* and the (New Bedford, Massachusetts) *Standard-Times*. A native of Massachusetts, he collected his first paycheck selling souvenirs outside Fenway Park, and his first paycheck in journalism as a *Cape Cod Times* intern covering the Cape Cod Baseball League. He is a graduate of the University of Pennsylvania and lives in Somerville, Massachusetts, with his wife, Hannah Swartz, an arts administrator.

HENLEY O'BRIEN is the pseudonym of a freelance editor who travels widely for work and spends her spare time running, backpacking, and ordering coffees in other languages (often to disappointing effect). She earned her master of philosophy in writing from Trinity College Dublin and currently lives in London.

BRETT POPPLEWELL was a reporter for the *Toronto Star* before joining *Sportsnet*, where he spent four years as a senior writer. A documentary based on "Stopping the Fight" was produced for *Hockey Night in Canada*. His first book, the memoir of a mountain climber, is forthcoming. He teaches at Carleton University and lives with his wife in Toronto.

KEN RODRIGUEZ is a contributing writer for *Sports Illustrated* and *SI.com*. He is a former sports columnist for the *San Antonio Express-News*, a former investigative sports writer for the *Miami Herald*, and a member of the *Herald* team that won the 1999 Pulitzer Prize for investigative reporting.

MICHAEL ROSENBERG joined *Sports Illustrated* as a senior writer in 2012 after working at the *Detroit Free Press* for 13 years, eight of them as a columnist. He is the author of the critically acclaimed book *War as They Knew It: Woody Hayes, Bo Schembechler, and America in a Time of Unrest*. Rosenberg has also worked at the *Washington Post, Chicago Tribune, Philadelphia Inquirer*, and *Sacramento Bee*.

A graduate of Marquette University, STEVE RUSHIN is the author of *Road Swing, The 34-Ton Bat*, and the novel *The Pint Man*.

ELI SASLOW is a reporter at the *Washington Post*, where, after covering the 2008 presidential campaign, he has chronicled the president's life inside the White House. He won the 2014 Pulitzer Prize for explanatory reporting for his yearlong series about food stamps in America. Previously a sportswriter for the *Post*, he has won multiple awards for news and feature writing. Two of his earlier stories have also appeared in *The Best American Sports Writing*.

ALEXANDRA STARR is a magazine writer and radio producer living in New York City. In addition to *Harper's*, she has contributed to the *New York Times*

Magazine, Slate, and *The American Scholar,* among other publications. She frequently reports for National Public Radio. Starr reported "American Hustle" when she was an Emerson fellow at the New American Foundation. She has also been a fellow at the Center on Law and Security at New York University Law School; a Milena Jesenska Fellow in Vienna, Austria; a Japan Society Fellow in Tokyo, Japan; and an Organization of American States Fellow in Caracas, Venezuela. Many years ago, she was an editor at the *Washington Monthly,* and she also did a stint at National Public Radio as Daniel Schorr's research assistant.

WRIGHT THOMPSON is a senior writer for *ESPN: The Magazine.*

CHRIS VAN LEUVEN has been climbing for 24 years and writing professionally for 10. He lives in Colorado's Front Range with his girlfriend and their two dogs. Until recently he served as *Alpinist* magazine's digital editor. He is now working in public relations and writing his first book.

DON VAN NATTA JR. is a senior writer for *ESPN: The Magazine* and *ESPN .com.* He joined ESPN in January 2012 after 16 years as a *New York Times* correspondent based in Washington, London, Miami, and New York. Previously he worked for eight years at the *Miami Herald.* A member of three Pulitzer Prize–winning teams, Van Natta is the author of *First Off the Tee* and the coauthor of *Her Way*—both *New York Times* bestsellers—and *Wonder Girl.* He lives in Miami with his wife, Lizette Alvarez, who is a *Times* correspondent, and their two daughters. This is his third appearance in *The Best American Sports Writing.*

L. JON WERTHEIM is the executive editor of *Sports Illustrated,* as well as a senior writer for the magazine. This is his fifth appearance in *The Best American Sports Writing.*

A native of Anchorage, Alaska, SETH WICKERSHAM is a senior writer at *ESPN: The Magazine,* where he has worked since graduating from the University of Missouri. He is part of a staff that has twice won the National Magazine Award for General Excellence. He lives in Connecticut with his wife, Alison Overholt, and their daughter, Maddie. He is credited as playing himself in the 2014 movie *Draft Day,* though the scene was cut before it was shot.

CHRIS WIEWIORA is from Orlando, Florida, where he used to skateboard drainage ditches before graduating from the University of Central Florida. He earned an MFA in creative writing and environment at Iowa State University. His nonfiction has been published in *Stymie: Journal of Sports & Literature* and *Sports Literate.* Read more at www.chriswiewiora.com.

Notable Sports Writing of 2015

SELECTED BY GLENN STOUT

JEFF KIRSHMAN
  Growing Up as the Fastest
  10-Year-Old Girl in America. *The
  Classical,* September 8
PHIL KLAY
  Over the Edge. *Men's Journal,*
  September

RACHAEL MADDUX
  Fox and Friends. *Longreads,*
  August 15
KUMIKO MAKIHARI
  Go, Speed Racer, Go! *Runner's
  World,* November
BRADY McCULLOUGH
  Baseball Republic. *Pittsburgh
  Post-Gazette,* September 13–17
BUCKY McMAHON
  Will These Robots Save the
  World? *GQ,* November 15
AUSTIN MEEK
  Pre's Lasting Connection on
  the Inside. (Eugene, Oregon)
  Register-Guard, May 29
SAM MELLINGER
  Michael's Pain. *Kansas City Star,*
  November 22
ED MILLER
  Boxer's Death Leaves Family
  with Safety Questions. *Virginian-
  Pilot,* August 9
CHUCK MINDENHALL
  In Search of Strange Brew.
  MMAFighting.com, March 24
KEVIN MITCHELL
  In the Cold Light of Day.
  Saskatoon StarPhoenix, November
  17
J. R. MOEHRINGER
  The Education of Alex
  Rodriguez. *ESPN: The Magazine,*
  January 26
RICHARD MOORE
  Who Punched Eddie Merckx?
  Bicycling, July
LUKE MULLINS
  The Long Snap. *Washingtonian,*
  October

JK NICKELL
  Freedom Riders. *Southwest,*
  September
ALESSANDRA NOLAN
  Channeling Mr. Jordan. *Sport
  Literate,* End of Winter

MIKE OGLE
  On the Fourth Day at Chapel
  Hill. *Charlotte,* February
GWENDOLYN OXENHAM
  Pinie's Biggest Fan. *USSoccer.com,*
  June 14
  The Soccer Moms. *The Atlantic,*
  June 26

CHARLES P. PIERCE
  Tom Brady Died for Our Sins.
  Esquire, August
JOE POSNANSKI
  Pinball Wizards. *Our State,* July
WILLIAM POWELL
  All About the Benjamin. *St.
  Louis,* November
S. L. PRICE
  Serena Williams Is *Sports
  Illustrated*'s 2015 Sportsperson
  of the Year. *Sports Illustrated,*
  December 21

CLAUDIA RANKINE
  The Meaning of Serena
  Williams. *New York Times
  Magazine,* August 25
RON RAPPAPORT
  The Last Years of Ernie Banks.
  Chicago, October
SHAUN RAVIV
  The Lost, True Story of the
  CIA's Greatest Basketball Coach.
  Buzzfeed, September 7
PAUL REIFERSON
  He Wears the Mask. *Southwest
  Review,* vol. 100, no. 3
SAM RICHES
  Leader of the Pack. *Pacific
  Standard,* March 23

THE BEST AMERICAN SERIES®

FIRST, BEST, AND BEST-SELLING

The Best American Comics

The Best American Essays

The Best American Infographics

The Best American Mystery Stories

The Best American Nonrequired Reading

The Best American Science and Nature Writing

The Best American Science Fiction and Fantasy

The Best American Short Stories

The Best American Sports Writing

The Best American Travel Writing

Available in print and e-book wherever books are sold.

Visit our website: *www.hmhco.com/bestamerican*